Between Diplomacy and Non-Diplomacy

"This volume—which coins the term paradiplomacy to examine the foreign relations and activities of Kurdistan-Iraq and Palestine—makes a huge contribution to the study of non-state actors and international relations in general. It also provides the reader with a comparative view of two of the most important de facto states in the Middle East and beyond. The book fills a critical gap in the disciple of IR and area studies."
—Fawaz A. Gerges, *Professor of International Relations, London School of Economics, UK, and author of Making the Arab World (2018)*

"Gürbey, Hofmann and Ibrahim Seyder have assembled a much-needed and timely set of analyses that emphasise the increased importance of the role of two critical non-state actors in international politics. The agency of Kurdistan and Palestine, and the inter-agency they have in regional, and increasingly global, political spaces is presented in a series of insightful essays, making this collection a valuable contribution to our wider understanding of the patterns of processes of international politics."
—Gareth Stansfield, *Professor of Middle East Politics and Pro-Vice-Chancellor of the Faculty of Humanities, Arts and Social Sciences, University of Exeter, UK*

"This is a well-written, informative, and provocative account of the shifting nature of statehood in the Middle East and beyond. A must-read for anyone interested in the future of the region."
—Mehmet Gurses, Professor, *Department of Political Science, Florida Atlantic University, USA*

"World politics has always entailed structured and institutionalized relations among many different kinds of actors. Yet we know little about the dynamics of interactions involving polities other than the territorial states that took shape in western Europe beginning in the sixteenth century. Building on the promising concepts of paradiplomacy and protodiplomacy, this collection offers tightly focused comparisons of the external relations of the Kurdistan Region of Iraq and the Palestinian Authority. Anyone who wishes to expand the scope of theorizing and the range of inquiry concerning contemporary international affairs will derive insight and inspiration from these well-crafted explorations."
—Fred H. Lawson, *Emeritus Professor of Government, Mills College, USA, and author of Constructing International Relations in the Arab World*

"This is an outstanding book that contributes to both the scholarship and practice of international relations and constitutes essential reading for anyone dealing with the Middle East. The theoretical framing is essential in advancing our knowledge of para-diplomacy and the case studies are clear, concise and informative."
—Matteo Legrenzi, *Professor of International Relations, Ca' Foscari University of Venice, Italy*

"For over a century, the Kurdish and Palestinian national movements have struggled for self-determination, sovereignty, and statehood. In this highly recommended volume, editors Gülistan Gürbey, Sabine Hofmann and Ferhad Ibrahim Seyder examine the parallels and intersections of both movements. The editors and contributors explore the contested diplomatic processes that Palestinians and Kurds have embraced as well as the challenges they continue to encounter. This volume will be an essential resource for students and scholars attempting to understand the political and diplomatic obstacles that have prevented Palestinians and Kurds from achieving their goals."
—Osamah F. Khalil, *Associate Professor of History and Chair, International Relations Program, Syracuse University, New York, USA*

Gülistan Gürbey
Sabine Hofmann • Ferhad Ibrahim Seyder
Editors

Between Diplomacy and Non-Diplomacy

Foreign relations of Kurdistan-Iraq and Palestine

palgrave
macmillan

Editors
Gülistan Gürbey
Department of Political and Social Sciences
Freie Universität Berlin
Berlin, Germany

Sabine Hofmann
Department of Political and Social Sciences
Freie Universität Berlin
Berlin, Germany

Ferhad Ibrahim Seyder
University of Erfurt
Erfurt, Germany

ISBN 978-3-031-09755-3   ISBN 978-3-031-09756-0   (eBook)
https://doi.org/10.1007/978-3-031-09756-0

© The Editor(s) (if applicable) and The Author(s), under exclusive licence to Springer Nature Switzerland AG 2023

This work is subject to copyright. All rights are solely and exclusively licensed by the Publisher, whether the whole or part of the material is concerned, specifically the rights of translation, reprinting, reuse of illustrations, recitation, broadcasting, reproduction on microfilms or in any other physical way, and transmission or information storage and retrieval, electronic adaptation, computer software, or by similar or dissimilar methodology now known or hereafter developed.

The use of general descriptive names, registered names, trademarks, service marks, etc. in this publication does not imply, even in the absence of a specific statement, that such names are exempt from the relevant protective laws and regulations and therefore free for general use.

The publisher, the authors, and the editors are safe to assume that the advice and information in this book are believed to be true and accurate at the date of publication. Neither the publisher nor the authors or the editors give a warranty, expressed or implied, with respect to the material contained herein or for any errors or omissions that may have been made. The publisher remains neutral with regard to jurisdictional claims in published maps and institutional affiliations.

This Palgrave Macmillan imprint is published by the registered company Springer Nature Switzerland AG.
The registered company address is: Gewerbestrasse 11, 6330 Cham, Switzerland

Preface

As editors of this book, we are very pleased to present our second anthology on Kurdistan-Iraq and Palestine.

This anthology would not have been possible without the great cooperation and outstanding contribution of our authors, to whom we are deeply grateful. It is a pleasure and an honour for us to have been able to attract such outstanding, internationally recognised authors for our book project.

This book project, with which we look at the international perspectives, connections and interdependencies of Kurdistan-Iraq and Palestine, is the result of a great international cooperation. It was very important for us to include authors from the region, especially to present the view of colleagues from the region and to promote regional scientific cooperation. Therefore, we are very pleased that we were able to attract authors from Kurdistan-Iraq and Palestine. We would like to express our deepest gratitude to all the authors who contributed to this book.

However, the realisation of the anthology would not have been possible without the evaluation by anonymous reviewers. We thank these experts for their positive assessment of our project and their important academic advice on it.

We sincerely thank Palgrave Macmillan for the opportunity to publish this second volume. In particular, we thank Anne Birchley-Brun, Editor, International Studies, for her support throughout the process and Rubina Infanta Rani for her help during the technical process.

Last but not least, we would like to thank Mediha Inan, Larie Mrowka, Lesar Sahin and Annika Ziegler for their great cooperation and support, both in editing and proofreading the chapters and in designing the manuscript.

We hope that our second anthology will provide new impulses, impetus and suggestions for dealing with the topic of paradiplomacy and contribute to a better understanding of Kurdistan-Iraq and Palestine.

Bonn, Berlin, and Erfurt Gülistan Gürbey
January 2, 2023 Sabine Hofmann
Ferhad Ibrahim Seyder

Contents

1 Introduction: Conceptualizing Paradiplomacy of
  Kurdistan-Iraq and Palestine   1
  Gülistan Gürbey, Sabine Hofmann, and Ferhad
  Ibrahim Seyder

Part I   The Rise of Paradiplomacy   27

2 The Evolution of Kurdistan-Iraq's Paradiplomacy: Causes
  and Constraints   29
  Francis Owtram

3 The Evolution of Palestine's Paradiplomacy: Causes and
  Constraints   53
  Mkhaimar Abusada

Part II   The Foundations of Paradiplomacy   73

4 Legal Framework, Institutionalization, Tools, and
  Motives of Kurdistan Iraq's Paradiplomacy   75
  Falah Mustafa Bakir and Sara D. Mustafa

5 Legal Framework, Institutionalization, Tools, and
   Motives of Palestine's Paradiplomacy   93
   Dalal S. M. Iriqat

Part III   Paradiplomacy in Practice (Selected Relations)   111

6 Palestine and USA   113
   Khaled Elgindy

7 Kurdistan-Iraq and EU   135
   Dastan Jasim

8 Palestine and EU   157
   Emile Badarin

9 Palestine and Russia   179
   Raid M. H. Nairat and Ibrahim S. I. Rabaia

10 Kurdistan-Iraq and China   201
   Sardar Aziz and Mohammed Shareef

11 Palestine and China   219
   Guy Burton

12 Kurdistan-Iraq and Turkey   239
   Arzu Yilmaz

13 Kurdistan-Iraq and Iran   263
   Nader Entessar

14 Palestine and Iran   279
   Seyed Ali Alavi

15 Conclusion Gülistan Gürbey, Sabine Hofmann, and Ferhad Ibrahim Seyder	305
Back Matter	321
Index	323

NOTES ON CONTRIBUTORS

Mkhaimar Abusada is Associate Professor of Political Science at Al-Azhar University-Gaza, Palestine, and former chairperson of the Department of Political Science. He holds a PhD from the University of Missouri-Columbia, US. His speciality is Palestinian politics, Arab-Israeli conflict and Middle Eastern political systems.

Seyed Ali Alavi is a senior teaching fellow at Near and Middle East Section, School of Languages, Cultures and Linguistics, SOAS, University of London. He is the author of *Iran and Palestine, Past, Present, Future* (2019).

Sardar Aziz works with a number of European and American think-tanks. His most recent publications include *Debating the State in Iraq After a Century–the Concept of Ladaula. The Iraqi Kurdish Peshmerga: Military Reform and Nation-Building in a Divided Polity.*

Emile Badarin is a research fellow at the College of Europe, Natolin, Warsaw. His research focuses on international relations, Middle East politics, EU-Middle East relations, colonialism and state recognition. He is the author of *Palestinian Political Discourse: Between Exile and Occupation* (2016).

Falah Mustafa Bakir is Senior Foreign Policy Advisor to the President of the KRI, with a ministerial rank. Bakir founded the Department of Foreign Relations and served from 2006 to 2019.

Guy Burton is an adjunct professor at the Brussels School of Governance and a fellow at Lancaster University. He is the author of *China and Middle East Conflicts* (2020) and *Rising Powers and the Arab-Israeli Conflict Since 1947* (2018).

Khaled Elgindy is Director of the Programme on Palestine and Palestinian-Israeli Affairs at the Middle East Institute and author of the book *Blind Spot: America and the Palestinians, from Balfour to Trump* (2019).

Nader Entessar is Professor Emeritus of Political Science at the University of South Alabama. His publications include *Kurdish Politics in the Middle East* (2010) and *Trump and Iran: From Containment to Confrontation* (2020).

Gülistan Gürbey is Adjunct Professor of Political Science at Freie Universität Berlin. She is the author of several books and articles on peace and conflict studies, de facto states, illiberal democracies and foreign policy, with a focus on Turkey, Kurdistan and Cyprus.

Sabine Hofmann is a West Asia scholar with a PhD in Middle East economics. Her research focuses on international political economy and the Middle East conflict. She teaches at Freie Universität Berlin, at Philipps Universität Marburg and at Berlin School of Economics and Law.

Ferhad Ibrahim Seyder is professor emeritus. He was a professor at the University of Erfurt. Previously, he was Professor of International Relations and Area Studies at the Freie Universität Berlin. His recent publications include the research topics Iraq and Syria.

Dalal S. M. Iriqat is Assistant Professor and Vice President of International Relations at the Arab American University Palestine (AAUP). Iriqat is a weekly columnist at *AlQuds* newspaper since 2016 and was identified as a Young Global Leader–World Economic Forum YGL 2021.

Dastan Jasim is a doctoral fellow at the German Institute for Global and Area Studies and a PhD student at the Friedrich-Alexander University Erlangen-Nuremberg. For her dissertation, she researches the political culture of Kurds in Iraq, Iran, Syria and Turkey.

Sara D. Mustafa is a PhD candidate in Political Science at the Universidad Nacional de Educación a Distancia (UNED) in Madrid and is a lecturer at the University of Kurdistan-Hewlêr.

Raid M. H. Nairat is Professor of Political Science at An-Najah National University Nablus and President of the research centre MEDAD. He has published more than 60 scientific studies and is active in the field of public policy analysis training. He is a researcher and a member of many Arab and international research centres.

Francis Owtram holds a PhD in International Relations from the London School of Economics and is honorary research fellow at the University of Exeter. From 2007 to 2012 he taught in the Department of Politics and International Relations, University of Kurdistan-Hewlêr.

Ibrahim S. I. Rabaia is Editor-in-Chief of the periodical *Palestinian Affairs* and part time Assistant Professor of Political Science at Birzeit University. His research interests include political economy and political transitions of the MENA, the politics of Sport, and Palestinian affairs.

Mohammed Shareef is Lecturer in International Relations and Diplomacy at the University of Kurdistan-Hewlêr in the capital of the Kurdistan Region of Iraq. He is the co-editor of *The Kurdish Question Revisited* (2017).

Arzu Yılmaz is an Associate Professor at Politics and International Relations Department of University of Kurdistan Hewlêr. Her study areas are migration and foreign policy. She is the author of the book *Atruş'tan Maxmur'a: Kürt Mülteciler ve Kimliğin Yeniden İnşası*. Istanbul: İletişim Yayınları (2016).

Abbreviations

AANES	Autonomous Administration of North and East Syria
AHK	German Chambers of Commerce Abroad (Iraq: Baghdad and Erbil)
AKP	Justice and Development Party
AMA	Agreement on Movement and Access
ASB	Arbeiter-Samariter-Bund
BDS	Boycott, Divestment and Sanctions
BRI	Belt and Road Initiative
CCP	Chinese Communist Party
CFR	Council on Foreign Relations
CFSP	Common Foreign and Security Policy
CIA	Central Intelligence Agency
CPA	The Coalition Provisional Authority
CSDP	Common Security and Defense Policy
DCCI	Diyarbakır Chamber of Commerce and Industry
DFLP	Democratic Front for the Liberation of Palestine
DFR	Department of Foreign Relations
DOP	Declaration of Principles
DPAL	Delegation for Relations with Palestine
EC	European Community
EEAS	European External Action Service
EMP	Euro Mediterranean Partnership
ENKS	Kurdish National Council in Syria
ENP	European Neighbourhood Policy
EP	European Parliament
ERRIN	European Return and Reintegration Network
EU	European Union

EUBAM Rafah	European Union Border Assistance Mission to Rafah
EUJUST LEX	European Union Integrated Rule of Law Mission for Iraq
EUPOL COPPS	European Union Police Mission for the Palestinian Territories
FDI	Foreign Direct Investment
FRUS	Foreign Relations of the United States
GUPWJ	General Union of Palestinian Writers and Journalists
HDP	People's Democratic Party
HR/VP	High Representative of the Union for Foreign Affairs and Security Policy/Vice-President of the European Commission
ICC	International Criminal Court
ICP	Iraqi Communist Party
IDF	Israel Defense Forces
IDPs	Internally Displaced Persons
IKR	Kurdistan Region of Iraq
IR	International Relations
IRGC	Islamic Revolutionary Guard Corps
IS	Islamic State
ISIS	Islamic State in Iraq and Syria
KDP	Kurdistan Democratic Party
KDP-I	Kurdistan Democratic Party-Iran
KHEC	Kurdistan High Elections and Referendum Commission
Komala	Komala Party of Iranian Kurdistan
KOMKAR	Association of Organizations from Kurdistan in Germany
KRG	Kurdistan Regional Government
KRI	Kurdistan Region of Iraq
MCC	China Metallurgical Group Corporation
MKO	Mujahedin-e Khalq Organization (People's Mojahedin Organization of Iran)
MOA	Memorandum of Agreement
MOFA	Ministry of Foreign Affairs
MRQ	Multiple Response Questionnaire
MSF	Médecins sans Frontières (Doctors without Borders)
NATO	North Atlantic Treaty Organization
NGO	Non-governmental Organization
OECD	Organization for Economic Co-operation and Development
OPT	Occupied Palestinian Territories
ORHA	The Office for the Reconstruction and Humanitarian Assistance
PA	Palestinian Authority
PASSIA	Palestinian Academic Society for the Study of International Affairs

PFLP	Popular Front for the Liberation of Palestine
PICA	Palestinian International Cooperation Agency
PIJ	Palestinian Islamic Jihad
PJAK	Kurdistan Free Life Party
PKK	Kurdistan Workers' Party
PL	Public Law
PLO	Palestine Liberation Organization
PLC	Palestinian Legislative Council
PM	Prime Minister
PMF	Popular Mobilization Forces
PMFAE	Palestinian Ministry of Foreign Affairs and Expatriates
PMOFA	Palestinian Ministry of Foreign Affairs
PNA	Palestinian National Authority
PNC	Palestinian National Council
PUK	Patriotic Union of Kurdistan
PYD	Democratic Union Party
R2P	Responsibility to Protect
REA	Regional Ethnic Autonomy
SDG	Sustainable Development Goals
SMEs	Small and Medium-Sized Enterprises
TOBB	Turkish Union of Chambers and Commodity Exchanges
UAE	United Arab Emirates
UfM	Union for the Mediterranean
UK	United Kingdom (of Great Britain and Northern Ireland)
UN	United Nations
UNAMI	United Nations Assistance Mission to Iraq–Erbil Regional Office
UNESCO	United Nations Educational, Scientific and Cultural Organization
UNGA	United Nations General Assembly
UNLU	Unified National Leadership of the Uprising
UNRWA	United Nations Relief and Works Agency for Palestine Refugees in the Near East
UNSC	United Nations Security Council
US	United States
USA	United States of America
USD	US Dollar
USSR	Union of Soviet Socialist Republics
WTO	World Trade Organization
YPG	People's Defense Units

LIST OF TABLES

Table 7.1   Schematical depiction of EU and KRI diplomatic levels   136
Table 7.2   Representations between KRI and EU   137
Table 7.3   Selection of European NGO's active in KRI after 1996
            (Gautier and Francia 2005, 4)   143
Table 7.4   Selection of European companies present in KRI   146

CHAPTER 1

Introduction: Conceptualizing Paradiplomacy of Kurdistan-Iraq and Palestine

Gülistan Gürbey, Sabine Hofmann, and Ferhad Ibrahim Seyder

There is no doubt that states still shape the international system today; however, they have long ceased to be the only actors. There is also no doubt that states continue to shape the international system today, but they have long ceased to be the only actors. Or, in the words of Joseph Nye: "It is not that governments are not the most important actors on the stage of world politics. It's just that the stage is much more crowded now" (Koch 2011).

States share the international arena with non-state actors and international relations are not the exclusive domain of states. The global shift from state-centrism is reflected in the emergence of other actors in global and national policy processes (Nye and Keohane 1977, 1987). Especially

---

G. Gürbey (✉) • S. Hofmann
Department of Political and Social Sciences, Freie Universität Berlin, Berlin, Germany
e-mail: guerbey@zedat.fu-berlin.de; shofmann@zedat.fu-berlin.de

F. I. Seyder
University of Erfurt, Erfurt, Germany

© The Author(s), under exclusive license to Springer Nature Switzerland AG 2023
G. Gürbey et al. (eds.), *Between Diplomacy and Non-Diplomacy*, https://doi.org/10.1007/978-3-031-09756-0_1

toward the end of the twentieth century, with globalization and regionalization, actors beyond sovereign states have multiplied. New non-state actors such as international organizations, non-governmental organizations (NGOs), transnational corporations, or global cities have entered the international stage. Sub-state and sub-regional actors are also part of the mix. These non-state actors are seeking their ways to promote trade, investment, cooperation, and partnership covering a long list of issues. Thereby they already account for a significant portion of today's cross-border contacts. In fact, it is impossible to imagine international relations without non-state actors. They are politically and economically integrated to some extent in the global system and are serious political actors trying to secure their interests. For these reasons, they have taken an adequate place in research. The term "paradiplomacy," which goes beyond state-centered analytical frameworks, was established to capture and interpret the diverse activities of non-state actors in international relations.

Undoubtedly, the emergence of non-state protagonists puts the conventional state system under pressure and raises many critical questions: What does the involvement of non-state actors in international relations mean for the future of the state system that became the dominant model and basis of the international political order with the Westphalian system in the seventeenth century? What does it mean for diplomacy and foreign policy, which are traditional domains and exclusive practices of states? What are implications for security, stability, and cooperation? Will the international arena have to open up more to non-state actors and the practice of paradiplomacy in the future? What new challenges will this pose for the international community? What impact will this trend have on international structures? With this anthology, we want to put the paradiplomatic activities of Kurdistan-Iraq and Palestine as de facto states into focus and aim to observe both regions in comparative respects. Their common regional location in the Middle East as well as their common historical roots makes an examination of both entities particularly appealing. Both de facto states emerged from violent conflict and established political orders that show similarities and differences. Both are involved in international affairs in different ways and with varying degrees of intensity. In addition, their international relations and foreign policy activities have increased significantly over the past two decades. This anthology is primarily dedicated to these developments.

In this anthology, we are going to focus primarily on foreign activities and relations and the involvement of Kurdistan-Iraq and Palestine in international relations from the viewpoint of practical performance of its foreign activities and relations. The purpose of this study is to familiarize the reader with the character of Kurdistan-Iraq's and Palestine's paradiplomatic activities in international relations:

- It will address the issues of the practical performance and implementation of foreign activities of both de facto states in terms of their capabilities and capacities as well as their respective results to carry out foreign activities and relations and the outcomes of those activities.
- It aims at describing and explaining how, why, and when both non-state actors develop paradiplomacy.
- At the same time, it also aims at comparing the paradiplomatic activities of both de facto states. In doing so, we want to work out the essential similarities and differences between the paradiplomatic activities of both entities without, however, pursuing a systematic, theoretical approach.

As this study focuses primarily on the questions of the practical performance and implementation of both de facto states' paradiplomatic activities, questions related to independence and sovereignty will not be the objects of more detailed examination.

Our book will contribute to the development of studies on paradiplomacy in two ways at least: First, by expanding the geographical scope of the study of paradiplomacy to the non-Western Middle East region, and second, by comparing paradiplomacy of two de facto states in the Middle East. Moreover, it aims to explore and expand our knowledge on how, why, and when de facto states as non-state actors develop paradiplomacy. Thus, it will provide a basis for further research in the field of paradiplomacy of de facto states.

This book will prove most useful for all those interested in both comparative and in-depth studies on de facto states in international affairs. In particular, it is to be welcomed by researchers and students of diplomacy, federalism, multi-level governance, foreign policy, international relations, as well as experts in diplomacy.

Last but not least, this anthology is intended to be the continuation of our first anthology on Kurdistan-Iraq and Palestine, published by Palgrave Macmillan in 2017. While the first volume examined internal political, economic, and social developments, this follow-up volume focuses on the external, paradiplomatic activities of Kurdistan-Iraq and Palestine.

PARADIPLOMACY AS CONCEPTUAL FRAMEWORK

The state-centric world, in which states act as the main protagonists, is challenged by the diverse involvement of various non-state actors. The issue of non-state actors' intervention within the international sphere and conduction relations during the last two decades has rapidly emerged. A growing number of non-state agents have become an inherent element of international relations. They are also setting the contemporary international agenda. Each of them pursues their own foreign policies through paradiplomatic practices. The international activities of regions and non-state actors have gained considerable scholarly attention and have become a subject of the study of international relations. This phenomenon is named as "paradiplomacy" and refers to the involvement of non-state actors in the international arena, their capability and their overall international and foreign policy activities in order to pursue their own specific interests. It describes and explains how and why sub-state entities and non-state actors decide to engage in international and foreign affairs and relations.

Paradiplomacy is tangential to the traditionally dominant role of nation-states in international relations. Diplomacy as the traditional domain of nation-states as well as their unique right and claim to external sovereignty to engage with other actors in the international arena is under pressure to share these sacrosanct privileges. However, diplomacy has traditionally been viewed as a practice exclusively reserved for states: First, diplomacy is done by states, and second, diplomacy is said to be carried out among states. At present states are to share the diplomatic arena as non-state actors emerge. The growing multiplicity of "alternative" diplomatic practices has an impact on the traditional conception of diplomacy, its scope, modes, and the types of actors involved. There has been plentiful discussion about the rise of "new" non-state diplomacies and their practices as well as the role which these "new" actors have in constructing and challenging established modalities of international politics and diplomacy in the academic literature (Hocking 1993, Hocking et al. 2012; Spies 2005; Jönsson and Hall 2005; Kuznetsov 2015). John Robert Kelley, for example, argues that through the increasing influence of non-state actors, a parallel, but different, diplomatic system was emerging in search of other goals such as problem solving, and that the twenty-first century marked an unprecedented moment of change in diplomatic affairs and an institutional upheaval (Kelley 2010, 2014).

But let us first turn to the growing phenomenon of paradiplomacy in international relations. A cursory view at the academic discussion shows that in spite of the increased scientific interest, the theory discussion is still at its beginning whereas a unified theory is still lacking. André Lecours remarked as recently as 2002: "There has been little effort to ground the study of paradiplomacy in a theoretical perspective that could serve as the foundation for a general explanatory framework" (Lecours 2002, 94).

Already in the clarification of the term "paradiplomacy," various suggestions are made in the literature. We find a number of different terms used as equivalents to the term "paradiplomacy" to refer to the cross-border engagement performance of a region and constituent states in the international arena, such as "multilayered diplomacy" (Hocking 1993), "plurinational diplomacy" (Aldecoa 1999), "proto-diplomacy" (Duchacek et al. 1988), "micro diplomacy" (Duchacek 1984), "perforated sovereignty" (Duchacek 1984; Duchacek et al. 1988), "identitary paradiplomacy" (Paquin 2004, 2020), "international activities of region" (Lecours 2000, 2002), "paradiplomacy of stateless nations" (Lecours and Moreno 2001), "substate diplomacy" (Criekemans 2010a, b) or "constituent diplomacy" (Kincaid 1990). Nonetheless, the existence of these multiple terms demonstrates the plurality of paradiplomacy processes and paradiplomacy research trajectories. In Aguirre's (1999) view, we can better conceptualize the multiplicity of actors and relationships as a new "postdiplomatic" world in order to look beyond our limited understanding of diplomacy and the nation-state.

Although there is no single bounded definition of paradiplomacy, the term has become the most widely accepted in contemporary academic literature. It has gained international acceptance as a catch-all term for the phenomenon of non-state involvements in international relations and the multiplicity of "alternative" diplomatic practices, to describe and explain the international activities and foreign policy capacities of subnational entities (Aguirre 1999; Kuznetsov 2015; Tavares 2016; Wolff 2007).[1] Moreover, almost all scholars who have studied this concept agree that

---

[1] The brief overview of the academic discussion about them was written by Alexander Kuznetsov (2015) and the deep semiological analysis by Aguirre (1999).

paradiplomacy has great potential for power (Chan 2016; Curtis 2011; Acuto 2013).

Paradiplomacy takes place on specific profiles in each regional context (Cornago 2013); nevertheless, it has become a truly global practice and can be exercised in many forms. It can be seen not only in federal, democratic Unitarian states, but also in different regions of the world, such as South Africa, China, Japan, India, Brazil, and Russia, to name a few (Cornago 2010, 17; Tavares 2016). Paradiplomacy dynamically evolves from the neutral "parallel," which strictly refers to the centralization and decentralization logic of Duchacek and Soldatos (Aguirre 1999, 196), to the competitive and contentious "diplomacy against the state" or "beyond the state."

The term "paradiplomacy" began to be used in political science terminology in the second half of the 1980s to refer to the activities of sub-state (regional) administrative units in the international political arena (Aguirre 1999, 185; Kuznetsov 2015, 27). Most notably, it was the seminal works of Ivo Duchacek (1984, 1986, 1990) and Panayotis Soldatos (1990) that introduced the concept of "paradiplomacy" to the foreign relations of sub-state governments and laid the foundation for further research. Starting with the study of highly autonomous provinces, such as Canada's Québec[2] (Berniér and Thérien 1994), to federally organized regions, such as Belgium's Flanders (Massart-Piérard 1999), to regions in decentralized states, such as Spain's Catalonia (Vela and Xifra 2015), the objects and dimensions of research continued to expand.

When we look at paradiplomatic action, some typical features can be identified. In general, non-state actors have less room for maneuver in the international system than states. Nevertheless, paradiplomacy offers a variety of opportunities for non-state actors to establish bilateral as well as multilateral relations and to represent their interests externally. These include maintaining contact offices in other countries, establishing missions abroad, traveling abroad, organizing trade fairs, and concluding transregional treaties (Soldatos 1993, 51).

The extent to which paradiplomatic action is developed depends on the financial and personnel capacities and the interests of the regions (Wolff 2007). However, paradiplomacy does not look the same for every actor: "The forms, goals, intensity, frequency, and significance of noncentral

---

[2] The case of Canada's Quebec is perhaps the most explicit example of the rise of paradiplomacy (Lecours 2002, 105).

state appearances on the international stage vary widely" (Duchacek 1986, 240). Paradiplomatic relations are influenced, for example, by the form of the political system, the ideological cohesiveness of the actors, or the self-confidence of the central government (Duchacek 1986, 240). Unlike states, sub-state governments do not pursue one or more clearly defined goals through their diplomatic efforts, but functionally and opportunistically adapt to the political margins (Keating 1999, 11).

But what are the factors that justify strategies of paradiplomacy? Keating (1999) argues that three kinds of motivations underlay paradiplomacy: economic, cultural, and political. Furthermore, Keating argues that nationalistic aspirations could be a major reason for paradiplomacy. For example, regions and constituent states would use it to achieve goals such as sovereignty and independence (Keating 2000). Lecours and Moreno (2001) echo this argument and view paradiplomacy being primarily driven by stateless nationalism or ethnonationalism, especially in the context of nations without states. Thus, paradiplomatic activities are strongest in nationalist regions, such as the Basque Country, Wallonia, Catalonia, Flanders, or Québec. Lecours and Moreno further explored the nationalist dimension of paradiplomacy and constructed a theoretical framework. They distinguish three main processes of nationalism that functionally affect the shaping of paradiplomacy: The construction and consolidation of identity, the definition and articulation of group-specific interests, and political-territorial mobilization (Lecours and Moreno 2001, 3–5). Thus, these processes of nationalism serve as a tool to seek international recognition, promote identity and nation-building internally and externally, or preserve cultural uniqueness.

Furthermore, paradiplomatic relations can also be of a very practical nature, as John Kincaid has shown. Cross-border issues that are of great regional importance but do not affect the host state can be an incentive for paradiplomacy (Kincaid 2003, 82). Examples of these so-called cross-border issues are, for example, infrastructure measures or environmental issues (Happaerts et al. 2010).

Last but not least, national and international structures play an important role in determining paradiplomatic activities and influence the scope of action of paradiplomatic actors. Thus, Lecours emphasizes that a paradiplomatic actor is influenced by the structure surrounding him. Both national and international structures ("opportunity structures") could either inhibit ("constraining") or facilitate ("enabling") the activity of paradiplomatic actors (Lecours 2002, 95–97). As an analytical framework,

Lecours proposes a systematization of structural levels. Since both international and national structures exerted influence, this resulted in four levels of analysis: global, continental, national, and regional (Lecours 2002, 101–104). By examining these four levels of analysis, it would thus be possible to say in what way the paradiplomacy of a regional government is inhibited or favored.

To conclude, the paradiplomatic studies show that academic discourse and research about the involvement of non-state actors in international affairs is very much Western-oriented. However, the research on foreign activities of non-state actors in non-Western regions such as Asia, Middle East, or Africa is not sufficient and should be developed. Moreover, there are still needs for comparative studies that allow comparing and contrasting international activities of non-Western regions. This also applies to paradiplomatic studies on de facto states. De facto states are also among the diverse non-state actors that also operate on the international stage, not only to trade but also to generate international recognition.

With the anthology on hand, we aim to fill the research gaps described above and contribute to research by looking at and comparing the paradiplomacy of two de facto states in the Middle East: Kurdistan-Iraq and Palestine. Our book is the first to compare the paradiplomatic activities of Kurdistan-Iraq and Palestine primarily from the viewpoint of practical performance and in terms of their capabilities, capacities, and practical achievements:

- It describes and explains the emergence and evolution of paradiplomacy of both de facto states.
- It examines the constitutional and the political frameworks, goals, tools, and capabilities of paradiplomacy.
- It explores how and why both de facto states develop paradiplomatic activities and relations.
- It provides an overview over the current paradiplomatic activities and challenges of both de facto states and, further, the foreign relations of both de facto states.
- It shows the similarities and differences between the paradiplomacy of both de facto states and provides explanations for a better understanding of the paradiplomacy of both entities.

With that, we do not claim to have a theoretically based systematic comparison. We will rather set a broad framework in order to ensure the topic's contextual localization. The broader context of paradiplomacy and the academic discourse of paradiplomacy hereby serve as a conceptual starting point.

As far as terminology is concerned, we follow the majority of scholars who use "paradiplomacy" simply as an "umbrella term," which covers many different types of non-state international activities. We use the term "paradiplomacy," as it is the most widely established expression in contemporary academic literature.

In addition, we use the term "de facto states" as regards Scott Pegg's (1998, 2004) understanding of de facto states, completed by Nina Caspersen and Gareth Stansfield (2011). De facto states are non-state actors and are among the many alternatives of political rule beyond internationally recognized statehood. Pegg lists a total of six basic elements that characterize de facto states: An organized political leadership that receives popular support, has achieved sufficient capacity, provides government services to a defined population in a defined spatial area, has effective control of its territory (at least two years), considers itself able to relate to other states, actively seeks but is unable to achieve broad international recognition of its sovereignty, and, regardless of how effective control and governance is, is largely or totally unrecognized by the international community of sovereign states and thus remains illegitimate (Pegg 1998, 2004). Caspersen and Stansfield add the criterion of having to demonstrate the pursuit of independence, for example, through formal declaration or referendum (Caspersen and Stansfield 2011). Following Pegg's definition, completed by Caspersen and Stansfield, Kurdistan-Iraq and Palestine can also be characterized as de facto states.

For ease of reading we—as the anthology's editors—use "Kurdistan-Iraq" as a synonym for the Kurdistan Region of Iraq (KRI), or Kurdistan Regional Government (KRG), and "Palestine" as a synonym for the Palestinian territories in the West Bank and Gaza Strip under the administration of the Palestinian Authority (PA) in 1994 (Gürbey et al. 2017, 262–263). However, our choice of terminology does not oblige the authors of the anthology to take it on. This also applies to the term "de facto state," which we as editors merely use to contextually assign KRG and PA. Naturally, the authors of the anthology are free in their own conceptual-contextual mapping.

The preference for this contextual localization of Kurdistan-Iraq and Palestine as de facto states we account for with two factors:

1. First of all, it is the term itself, because it puts the focus on the connection of the de facto state, and therefore its autonomy and sovereignty, which it achieves with its own actions. Instead of focusing on questions of recognition or non-recognition, the term essentially highlights the actor and his development. It offers clear criteria for the definition of the actor as a de facto state, takes into account the crisis of legitimacy of de facto states and the importance of the permanent striving for legitimation of the understanding of de facto states, and considers the processual causal relationship of interaction and communicative action in a transnational context.
2. Second, the basic elements in Kurdistan-Iraq and Palestine, as mentioned by Pegg, are each to be found in different intensity and shaping. In both areas, political forms of rule or orders beyond national sovereignty have emerged, shaped by external conditions (regional and international politics and economics), by long-lasting historical violent conflicts, and their internal dynamics. In various respects, both areas are undergoing a conflict transformation process, which is not finished and affects internal power structures as well as paradiplomatic performance.

To examine the paradiplomacy of Kurdistan-Iraq and Palestine we use the analytical framework created by Alexander Kuznetsov (2015), which is the main point of reference for our case studies. Paradiplomacy is defined by Kuznetsov (2015) as a form of political communication for reaching economic, cultural, and political or any other types of benefits, the core of which consists in self-sustained actions of regional governments with foreign governmental and non-governmental actors. Kuznetsov constructed a useful analytical framework for other researchers to conduct a study of chosen cases of paradiplomacy. He synthesizes the themes of previous research and literature on paradiplomacy and develops from them an analytical framework based on the multiple response questionnaire (MRQ) technique (Foddy 1993). It consists of a list of questions and a given set of possible responses regarding paradiplomatic activities in the international arena.

Substantially, the framework summarizes the different theoretical dimensions of paradiplomacy in six categories (Kuznetsov 2015, 50–51, 100–116):

(1) Causes of paradiplomacy, (2) The legal grounds for paradiplomacy, (3) Predominant motives, (4) The institutionalization of paradiplomacy, (5) The attitude of the Iraqi and Israeli government towards Kurdish and Palestinian paradiplomacy, and (6) The consequences of paradiplomacy for the development of the whole nation.

For each of the categories Kuznetsov's analytical framework classifies potential answers or supplementary questions that suggest the direction of research briefly as following:

For the first research category it offers eleven potential factors that can determine the growth of paradiplomacy, such as globalization, regionalization, democratization, foreign policy domestication and internationalization of domestic politics, federalization and decentralization, problems with nation building processes, central governments' insufficient effectiveness in foreign relations, influence of external factors, asymmetry of constituent units, personality of leaders and ideology of political parties, and borders.

For the second research category Kuznetsov's explanatory framework contains two dimensions of questions, such as: What is the level of legal permission of treaty-making with foreign actors granted by the constitution/legal acts to the provincial authorities?

For the third research category Kuznetsov's explanatory framework offers four motives that lie behind paradiplomatic activities: Economic, political, cultural, cross-border housekeeping. For the fourth research category Kuznetsov's explanatory framework names at least six ways in which subnational units organize their foreign activities: Establishment of a special Regional Ministry of Foreign Affairs or department which is responsible for the international affairs; opening of permanent subnational offices abroad; official visits of regional authorities to other countries; participation in various international events such as exhibitions or forums that are organized by foreign actors; establishing of and participation in global and trans-border multilateral regional networks and working groups on specific problems, such as agriculture, sustainable development, energy, and transportation; and participation of regional authorities in international events organized by foreign entities within the official delegation of their central government.

For the fifth research category, Kuznetsov's explanatory framework proposes a two-dimensional approach: First, the perception dimension refers to the general perception of paradiplomacy in the eyes of the central government, positioning this attitude between negative (paradiplomacy as a challenge to the nation) and positive (paradiplomacy as an opportunity for the nation), and second, the practical dimension refers to the question how the central government deals in practice with international activities of subnational entities, leading to four different patterns presented by Soldatos (1990).

For the sixth and final research category Kuznetsov's explanatory framework identifies three possible consequences: First, the rationalization of the national foreign policy, that is, the practice of a pro-federalist principle of subsidiarity, based on which the central government should delegate all those tasks that can be performed more effectively by subnational authorities to the latter. Second, the democratization of the decision-making process in national foreign policy, meaning that it brings more plurality and better representation of various interests. Third, the disintegration of the state if paradiplomacy is treated by the region as a step toward disintegration and secessionism.

In summary, Kuznetsov's analytical framework strives to generalize overall paradiplomatic behavior and is a useful methodological guide that can be adopted for further study of paradiplomacy in other cases.

In our volume, we use Kuznetsov's analytical framework mentioned above to analyze the paradiplomacy of Kurdistan-Iraq and Palestine. The focus is on the development of paradiplomacy and the practiced paradiplomatic performance of both de facto states in terms of their capabilities, capacities, and practical achievements, as well as the way paradiplomacy is constructed, conducted, and realized. Based on this, and following Kuznetsov's roadmap, we aim to answer the following guiding research questions:

- What factors determine paradiplomacy of both de facto states?
- What are the legal grounds and instruments of paradiplomacy?
- How has paradiplomacy been institutionalized?
- What are the main motives of paradiplomatic activities?

- How do both de facto states develop paradiplomatic activities and relations?
- How do central governments influence the paradiplomatic activities of both entities?
- What are the outcomes and consequences of paradiplomacy?

Finally, we will answer the questions about the differences and similarities between the two de facto states:

- What are the similarities and differences between the paradiplomacy of the two de facto states?
- What are the specific features of paradiplomatic activities in each of the selected entities?

In this final stage we are going to make a comparative analysis and find answers for the guiding research questions presented above. In doing so, the findings obtained will be compared and summarized on the basis of the formulated guiding research questions presented above. In order to bring together individual contributions with considerable stand-alone value into a simple but comprehensive structure, the comparative analysis will focus on these guiding research questions. The aim is to (a) set out causes, capability, and capacities of Kurdistan-Iraq's and Palestine's paradiplomacy; (b) elaborate how and why Kurdistan-Iraq and Palestine develop and practice paradiplomacy; and (c) provide new insights into paradiplomatic contexts and practices beyond the state.

Anthology Structure

On the basis of the analytical framework of Kuznetsov and the guiding research questions presented above the analysis of Kurdish and Palestinian paradiplomacy occurs in three parts: Part I and Part II provide a basis for a better understanding of the paradiplomacy of Kurdistan-Iraq and Palestine in historical, legal, and institutional terms, as well as the main motives driving paradiplomatic activities.

Part I outlines the historical process of why and how paradiplomacy of both de facto states emerged and developed over time. It will be shown whether there are turning points in this process, in what context, why and how they occurred, and what consequences they had in Kurdistan-Iraq and Palestine.

Part II presents the legal and institutional framework as well as the motives for strengthening paradiplomacy.

Following on from these basics set out in Part I and Part II, Part III then uses examples to show why and how paradiplomatic activities are implemented. In doing so, the practiced paradiplomatic performance of both de facto states in terms of their capabilities, capacities, and practical achievements will be presented, as well as the way in which paradiplomacy is constructed, carried out, and realized.

The theme of Part I is "The Rise of Paradiplomacy" in Kurdistan-Iraq and Palestine with the focus on the guiding research questions: What factors determine paradiplomacy of both de facto states? How do the Iraqi government in Bagdad and Israeli government in Jerusalem influence the paradiplomatic activities of both entities?

The goal of Part I is to examine the emergence and evolution of paradiplomacy of both de facto states. This includes the external and internal determinants (globalization, regionalization, digitalization, regional developments, nation-building, ideology, domestic politics, etc.) that favor and limit paradiplomatic activities, the causal relationship between internal and external factors as well as turning points for growing paradiplomacy of both de facto states. The influence of the Iraqi and Israeli governments on the paradiplomatic room for maneuver of the respective de facto states will also be examined.

Therefore, in Chaps. 2 and 3, Francis Owtram and Mkhaimar Abusada provide an analytical overview on the historical process of emergence and evolution of paradiplomacy of Kurdistan-Iraq and Palestine. Owtram and Abusada elaborate the causes and constraints of paradiplomacy, in which context, why and how paradiplomacy emerged and evolved over time, what internal and external factors have promoted and constrained this process, and how the Iraqi government in Bagdad and the Israeli government in Jerusalem have responded.

Owtram shows in detail the origin and the development of paradiplomacy of KRG. He divides the paradiplomacy or proto-diplomacy of the KRG into different stages. He lays out how the KRG's paradiplomacy and intentions have changed in recent years as a result of events in the region.

So Owtram notes a proto-diplomatic focus in the second phase between 2014 and 2017, which was primarily due to the Kurds' attempts to establish their own economic policy, especially in the oil sector. According to Owtram, the de facto division of the KRI into the Kurdistan Democratic Party (KDP) and the Patriotic Union of Kurdistan (PUK) areas is a structural obstacle to Kurdish state-building projects and the pursuit of unified paradiplomacy. Although Kurdish paradiplomacy is characterized by the pursuit of statehood, this is currently difficult to achieve due to internal political divisions and the geopolitical situation. Mkhaimar Abusada notes that, in contrast to the widespread portrayal of diplomacy by states, there is in principle little research on diplomatic relations by non-state actors, including national liberation movements that developed after World War II. These movements, struggling for independence, faced the task of combining diplomacy and armed struggle, as did the Palestinians. Since the mid-1960s, the Palestinians emancipated themselves from the pan-Arab front led by Egypt, Abusada writes. With the founding of the Palestine Liberation Organization (PLO) in 1964, the Palestinians created an independent actor to represent their rights worldwide. Here Abusada sees the beginnings of Palestinian paradiplomacy. On the basis of five stages, he analyzes its differentiation, changes, and specifics. In doing so, he shows that Palestinian paradiplomacy is always in tension between the PA's goal of forming a state in the West Bank and Gaza Strip and the PLO as a resistance movement against Israeli occupation. According to Abusada, however, the greatest internal obstacle to PLO paradiplomacy was the internal division of the Palestinians.

The theme of Part II is "The Foundations of Paradiplomacy" with the focus on the following guiding research questions: What are the legal grounds and instruments of paradiplomacy? How has paradiplomacy been institutionalized? What are the main motives of paradiplomatic activities?

In detail, in Chaps. 4 and 5, Falah Mustafa Bakir and Sara D. Mustafa and Dalal S. M. Iriqat empirically explore the legal framework, the process of institutionalization, the instruments (tools), motives for paradiplomacy of Kurdistan-Iraq and Palestine, how they evolved and changed over the time, as well as the driving factors for these changes.

Falah Mustafa Bakir and Sara D. Mustafa provide a basis for a better understanding of KRG's paradiplomacy by focusing on the practical and first-hand involvement in the development of the KRG's paradiplomacy. Bakir and Mustafa demonstrate the driving factors and the main tools of the KRG's paradiplomacy, clarify the legal framework under which it practices its international relations as well as illustrate how Kurdistan Region authorities, and its representations abroad, work together to develop the KRG's international outreach. In doing so, the authors emphasize that despite differences with Baghdad over Kurdish paradiplomacy, Erbil exercises it in accordance with the provisions of the Iraqi constitution without violating Iraq's sovereignty or contravening the Iraqi constitution. The KRG would not have secessionist motives in its paradiplomatic efforts; rather, from the KRG's perspective, paradiplomacy is essential to continue to maintain and promote relations with Baghdad in order to protect the Kurdish people's right to autonomy, representation, self-expression, security, identity, and culture without affecting Iraq's integrity. Bakir and Mustafa show how the KRG has made overwhelming progress and success in its international and regional presence following the institutionalization of its practices in the 2005 Iraqi constitution and through its various representations abroad. The authors note an increase particularly from 2014 to the 2017 independence referendum, when the KRG fought militarily on the front lines against the Islamic State (IS) and was able to capitalize on this on the international stage. Above all, the authors emphasize that because of the historical oppression of Kurdish minorities in neighboring states, which have oppressed Kurdish minorities in their own countries and are also opposed to an independent Kurdistan, the KRG, as a landlocked region, continues to be forced to build or maintain trust with its neighbors in order to ensure its own survival and avoid further massacres of Kurds.

The consideration of de facto states from the perspective of paradiplomacy is the logical consequence of the existing mechanism of recognition of states in world politics, Dalal S. M. Iriqat states at the beginning of her chapter. Building on Kuznetsov's conceptual approach to paradiplomacy, she analyzes the institutional design of Palestinian paradiplomacy. For the most important driving force and goal of Palestinian paradiplomatic activities is to achieve state recognition in world politics and to establish Palestine as an international actor. The PLO as a non-state actor has become the most important actor in Palestine's international affairs since 1974. More so, the PLO held the status as the sole legitimate representative of the Palestinian people in the occupied territories and in the diaspora, which was relatively unique. According to Iriqat, the structural turning point in Palestine's paradiplomatic activities was the 1993 Oslo Conference and the PLO's decision to recognize the State of Israel. The agreements officially established the structure of the Palestinian National

Authority (PNA) as a legitimate institution and designated the Ministry of Foreign Affairs (MOFA) as the official body responsible for international relations. The PLO had already opened offices in numerous states under its name. As Iriqat notes, especially with the upgrading of Palestine's status in the United Nations (UN) in 2012, some of these representations changed their names to serve the State of Palestine instead of the PLO. The actual practices of paradiplomacy are indeed stronger than the official diplomacy of the government. Meanwhile, Palestine has a different image from its old official diplomacy, which still relies on the PLO. But the successes of Palestinian paradiplomacy today would not have been achievable without the PLO and charismatic politicians such as Yasser Arafat and Mahmoud Abbas, writes Iriqat.

The theme of Part III is "Paradiplomacy in Practice (Selected Relations)" with the focus on the following guiding research questions: How do both de facto states develop paradiplomatic activities and relations? What are the outcomes and consequences of paradiplomacy?

The practice of paradiplomacy and the paradiplomatic performance of both de facto states are examined in the following Chaps. 6, 7, 8, 9, 10, 11, 12, 13, and 14 on the basis of selected relationships. A selection is necessary for two reasons: First, a claim to completeness would burst the scope of this book.

Second, it is important to ensure a comparison of the paradiplomatic performance of both de facto states. This is possible by analyzing the relations of both de facto states with the same states. For the selection, those states and organizations are identified on the international as well as on the regional level that are of particular importance and play a role for both de facto states in many respects: At the international level, these are primarily the United States (US), the European Union (EU), and Russia as global players and important actors in the Middle East region, and China (China as a new actor in the region with growing global influence). At the regional level, these are Turkey, Iran, and Jordan (Jordan especially for Palestine).

The analysis of paradiplomatic relations with the same states allows comparing the results in terms of paradiplomatic performance of both de facto states.

Based on this selection, in Chaps. 6, 7, 8, 9, 10, 11, 12, 13, and 14, the authors examine the paradiplomatic relations of both de facto states with the US, the EU, Russia, China, Turkey, and Iran.[3] The focus of Chaps. 6, 7, 8, 9, 10, 11, 12, 13, and 14 is on how and why both de facto states establish and develop paradiplomatic relations with each selected state, how paradiplomacy is constructed, carried out and realized, and what the outcomes are. The analysis of the relationship with each state is conducted at four levels: political, economic, cultural, and military. Therefore, the development and transformation of the relationship with each state is analyzed from a historical perspective: How it has changed and become more institutionalized over time, what internal and external factors have contributed, what are the main motives, in what areas collaboration has increased, why and how, where are the differences, how and by what means the paradiplomatic policy was implemented, and what are the results of the paradiplomatic efforts and relations.

Chapter 6 by Khaled Elgindy deals with Palestinian paradiplomatic relations with the US since the founding of the PLO in 1964. In his view, the US have always been, and still are, at the center of Palestinian diplomacy. Elgindy sees the PLO's main motive for this as the basic idea that participation in the US-led peace process is the most effective way to influence Israel and thus the implementation of Palestinian statehood.

Elgindy identifies two transformations in the different phases of this relationship: The first after the Arab-Israeli War in 1973, when the US became the dominant force in Arab-Israeli peacemaking and the PLO sought to gain a seat in the peace process. The second structural change in these paradiplomatic relations, in the author's view, results from the signing of the Oslo Declaration of Principles (DOP) in September 1993. Oslo institutionalized Palestinian dependence on the US and Israel. Thus, paradiplomatic relations evolved from the security level to the socio-economic level, with the US becoming not only the main mediator but also the main donor to the Palestinians. This single-minded focus of the Palestinian leadership on US liberation has not only failed to bring the Palestinians closer to independence or statehood but has actually contributed to the weakening of Palestinian politics, institutions, and leaders, Elgindy assesses. Ultimately, he sees the peace process as well as the Palestinian leadership's "American strategy" as having failed. The asymmetry limits

---

[3] Unfortunately, due to last-minute and unexpected circumstances related to the COVID-19 pandemic, the planned and promised chapters regarding KRG's relations with the US and with Russia, as well as PA's relations with Jordan could not be delivered.

the Palestinians' room for maneuver, Elgindy concludes, but it is also not without options.

Dastan Jasim in Chap. 7 focuses on the relationship between Kurdistan-Iraq and the EU. Jasim describes the KRG's relations with the EU historically by dividing them into temporal stages and conceptualizes the current relations with the EU or some of its member states. She shows how economic relations between Europe and KRI have solidified since 2005, how from the energy industry to mechanical engineering, the automotive industry, construction and retail, many European companies have settled in the Kurdistan Region over the last two decades. The consulates of European states in the KRI also play a role. According to Jasim, the energy sector in particular offered new potential for diversifying Europe's dependence on Russian resources. Kurdish oil and natural gas played an important role in this. Jasim shows also how military cooperation between Europe and the KRI first manifested itself in 2014 in the wake of IS's advance. Jasim emphasizes that the KRI has great potential for the future of relations with the EU. Its increasingly young, resolutely pro-democratic, and innovative population is fertile ground for further progress in relations with the EU.

In Chap. 8, Emile Badarin assumes that Palestinian diplomacy must be seen in the context of decolonization efforts and that the central goal of Palestinian diplomacy is geopolitical in nature. Badarin analyzes the Palestinians' diplomatic relations with the European Community (EC) and later the EU. With state diplomacy, the PLO, in Badarin's view, limited its character as a liberation and anti-colonial movement, but the EU and Palestine grew ever closer. With the 1980 Venice Declaration, the EC recognized the right of the Palestinian people to self-determination and, according to Badarin, thus gave the PLO a new direction to expand its political representation in the EC and in European capitals. Later, the EU transformed the Palestinian representation into the Mission of Palestine to the EU. Badarin shows that while the EU does not recognize Palestine as a state, diplomatic engagement between the two sides has crossed the threshold of liminality and paradiplomacy.

Thus, Palestine is the only non-recognized country to have signed an association agreement with the EU.

In 1993, with the signing of the Oslo Accords, a new phase in PLO/PA-EU relations began, according to Badarin's assessment. The paradiplomatic relationship was gradually institutionalized and consolidated. The economic dimension is central to Palestinian diplomatic activities in order to ensure a continuous flow of economic aid to the PA.

Raid M. H. Nairat and Ibrahim S. I. Rabaia in Chap. 9 elaborate the relationship between Palestine and Russia. As both authors present, the Soviet Union was one of the main supporters of the establishment of the State of Israel in 1948. Thus, paradiplomatic relations between the Soviet Union and the PLO began only through Egypt's mediation in 1968. Initially on an informal level, especially in the cultural, popular, and military spheres, both sides formalized relations very quickly. Both authors go even further and assess that the Palestinian question eventually became a priority for the Soviet Union in terms of foreign policy. Thus, as early as 1974, the Soviet Union officially advocated an independent Palestinian state. The Palestinian revolution benefited from this diplomacy by pushing for military and civil capacity building programs, equipment, and the development of new diplomatic relations with third parties. Consequently, the dissolution of the Soviet Union in 1991 also had a negative impact on Palestinian-Russian paradiplomacy. Both authors assess that it is only since 2002 that a new phase in Russia's relations in the region, and in this case with Palestine, has occurred. Since then, Russia has been active again on the political level, in the economy and in cultural relations. A notable increase in the signing of agreements was in 2016, when six Palestinian-Russian agreements were signed during Russian President Dmitry Medvedev's visit to Palestine.

Sardar Aziz and Mohammed Shareef in Chap. 10 analyze KRG-China relations by dividing them into different phases and showing that economic cooperation is at the forefront of the relationship. The authors note that relations between the KRG and China are primarily reflected in trade and infrastructure projects. In particular, the Chinese New Silk Road plays a role here and could create enormous economic potential for the KRI— especially with regard to the lack of access to the seas. According to Aziz and Shareef, despite rapid development in trade, energy, and construction, the relationship has a number of significant limitations compared to other major powers. Among other things, US influence in the region should not be underestimated, which is why the KRG is concerned about the US response.

Although not at the center of paradiplomatic relations, China is one of the partners with whom the Palestinians have had the longest relationship. Guy Burton in Chap. 11 turns his attention to one of the little-known fields of Palestinian paradiplomacy since its inception in the mid-1960s.

Burton analyzes the stages and systematically presents the most significant changes. While relations were initially characterized primarily by China's military support for the PLO, these ties were nevertheless never decisive for the Palestinians' armed struggle against Israel or the growing confrontation with the Arab host states that had welcomed the Palestinians.

Today, by contrast, China is putting support for the Palestinians in relation to its diplomatic and economic relations with Israel and other Arab partners in the region, as Burton notes. Thus, economic relations with Israel are much more important and profitable than those with the Palestinians. China, as an emerging world power, has economic goals and is interested in the stability of the region. Burton also sees China's support for Palestinian statehood as more of a declarative commitment.

Arzu Yilmaz in Chap. 12 examines the parameters of KRG-Turkey relations, with particular attention to their impact on the intra-Kurdish conflict in the 1990s, the KRG's nation-building efforts after 2003, and their impact on the KRG's relations with Turkey, as well as how relations between the KRG and Turkey have evolved in the context of the Kurdistan independence referendum. Yilmaz shows how KRG has engaged with Turkey not only as a sub-state entity, but as a Kurdish political power in the region that exerts significant influence over the Kurds, including Turkey. In doing so Yilmaz refutes the prevailing view that the KRG is a passive participant in its relations with Turkey, responding mainly to Turkey's concerns and interests. Yilmaz points out that the KRG's foreign policy was ultimately determined by its political interests, even though the survival of the Kurds in the 1990s and economic interests in the 2000s were the main drivers in relations with Turkey. According to Yilmaz the KRG used the new opportunities in its relations with Turkey not only to appease Turkish threat perceptions of separatism, but also to secure its degree of political recognition and status as a Kurdish entity in Iraq, and to increase the political space for the KRG as the leading Kurdish authority in the Middle East.

Chapter 13 by Nader Entessar describes the relations between the KRG and Iran at the political, economic, and military levels. Relations have intensified and continuously expanded since 2005. Iran is the KRG's second-largest trading partner. Despite cooperation, for example, in the energy sector or even in the military field, the KRG is in a political limbo in its relations with Iran, due to the geopolitical (military) situation, consideration for the US, but also the competing roles of Iran and Turkey, both of which are trying to influence events in Iraqi Kurdistan in their favor.

Seyed Ali Alavi in Chap. 14 scrutinizes the paradiplomatic activities of Palestinian factions toward the Islamic Republic of Iran since the 1979 revolution, identifying phases of rapprochement and divergence that he embeds in the contemporary historical context up to the present day. As a basis for relations, Alavi investigates the power aspirations, ideologies, and geopolitical interests of both sides. In particular, he examines how the PLO, Hamas, and the Palestinian Islamic Jihad (PIJ) established and developed paradiplomatic relations with Iran. This side of the Palestinians' foreign relations has been little researched to date. In particular, the author's added value lies in his examination of the roots, reasons, and developments of Palestinian relations with Iran. Seyed documents that the PLO had no alternative source of support after the implosion of the Soviet Union. But even Arafat's recognition of Israel in the wake of the Oslo Accords initially led to a new ice age in the PLO's relations with Iran, Alavi notes. It was not least Israel's policy against Hamas in the Gaza Strip and its continued policy of occupation in the West Bank that then led, as Alavi shows, to Iran becoming the traditional ally of Hamas and PIJ, and the PA also maintaining its diplomatic relations with Iran, despite political and ideological divergences.

Finally, in Conclusions (Chap. 15), we are going to make a comparison: First, the findings will be summarized comparatively, and second, a prospect will be provided without making any claim to a theoretical comprehensive systematic comparison.

In the conclusion, the feedback is offered on the introduction and the key questions (guiding research questions). Based on the key questions, the results are worked out in detail:

> The particular challenges and characteristics of the Palestinian and Iraqi Kurdish paradiplomacy, as well as the outstanding comparative features, similarities and differences of the two cases will be discussed. Finally, a reflection on the future of Kurdistan's and Palestine's paradiplomacy will be provided. Conclusions that go beyond the specific study of the Kurdish and Palestinian paradiplomatic experiences will be drawn from the comparison and contribute to the wider study and better understanding of paradiplomacy of de facto states in the Middle East.

REFERENCES

Acuto, Michele. 2013. *Global Cities, Governance and Diplomacy. The Urban Link.* New York: Routledge.
Aguirre, Inaki. 1999. Making Sense of Paradiplomacy: An Intertextual Enquiry About a Concept in Search of a Definition. *Regional and Federal Studies* 9 (1): 185–209.
Aldecoa, Francisco, and Michael Keating. 1999. *Paradiplomacy in Action. The Foreign Relations of Subnational Governments.* London: Frank Cass Publishers.
Bernier, Ivan, and Jean-Philippe Thérien. 1994. Le comportement international du Québec, de l'Ontario et de l'Alberta dans le domaine économique. *Études internationales* 25 (3): 453–486.
Caspersen, Nina, and Gareth Stansfield. 2011. *Unrecognized States in the International System.* New York: Routledge.
Chan, Dan Koon-hong. 2016. City Diplomacy and "Glocal" Governance: Revitalizing Cosmopolitan Democracy. *Innovation: The European Journal of Social Science Research* 29 (2): 134–160.
Cornago, Noé. 2010. On the Normalization of Sub-State Diplomacy. *The Hague Journal of Diplomacy* 5 (1–2): 11–36.
———. 2013. *Plural Diplomacies: Normative Predicaments and Functional Imperatives.* Leiden: Martinus Nijhoff Publishers.
Criekemans, David. 2010a. *Regional Sub-State Diplomacy Today.* Leiden: Martins Nijhoff Publishers.
———. 2010b. Regional Sub-State Diplomacy from a Comparative Perspective: Quebec, Scotland, Bavaria, Catalonia, Wallonia, Flanders. *The Hague Journal of Diplomacy* 5 (1–2): 37–64.
Curtis, Simon. 2011. Global Cities and the Transformation of the International System. *Review of International Studies* 37 (4): 1923–1947.
Ducachek, Ivo D. 1990. Perforated Sovereignties: Towards a Typology of New Actors in International Relations. In *Federalism and International Relations: The Role of Subnational Units*, ed. Hans J. Michelmann and Panayotis Soldatos, 1–33. Oxford: Oxford University Press.
Duchacek, Ivo D. 1984. The International Dimension of Subnational Self-Government. *Publius: The Journal of Federalism* 14 (4): 5–31.
———. 1986. *The Territorial Dimension of Politics Within, Among and Across Nations.* Boulder: Westview Press.
Duchacek, Ivo D., Daniel Latousche, and Stevenson Garth. 1988. *Perforated Sovereignties and International Relations: Trans-sovereign Contacts of Subnational Governments.* New York: Greenwood Press.
Foddy, William. 1993. *Constructing Questions for Interviews and Questionnaires: Theory and Practice in Social Research.* Cambridge: Cambridge University Press.

Gürbey, Gülistan, Sabine Hofmann, and Ferhad Ibrahim Seyder, eds. 2017. *Between State and Non-State: Politics and Society in Kurdistan-Iraq and Palestine*. New York: Palgrave Macmillan.

Happaerts, Sander, Karoline van der Brande, and Hans Bruyninckx. 2010. Governance for Sustainable Development at the Inter-subnational Level: The Case of the Network of Regional Governments for Sustainable Development. *Regional & Federal Studies* 20 (1): 127–149.

Hocking, Brain. 1993. *Localizing Foreign Policy: Non-Central Governments and Multilayered Diplomacy*. New York: Palgrave Macmillan.

Hocking, Brian, Jan Melissen, Shaun Riordan, and Paul Sharp. 2012. *Futures for Diplomacy: Integrative Diplomacy in the 21st Century*. The Hague: Clingendael The Netherlands Institute of International Relations.

Jönsson, Christer, and Martin Hall. 2005. *Essence of Diplomacy*. New York: Palgrave Macmillan.

Keating, Michael. 1999. Regions and International Affairs: Motives, Opportunities and Strategies. In *Paradiplomacy in Action: The Foreign Relations of Subnational Governments*, ed. Francisco Aldecoa and Michael Keating, 1–16. London: Frank Cass Publishers.

———. 2000. *Paradiplomacy and Regional Networking*. October, Hanover: Forum of Federations; an International Federalism.

Kelley, John R. 2010. The New Diplomacy: Evolution of a Revolution. *Diplomacy & Statecraft* 21 (2): 286–305.

———. 2014. *Agency Change: Diplomatic Action Beyond the State*. Lanham: The Rowman & Littlefield Publishing Group.

Kincaid, John. 1990. Constituent Diplomacy in Federal Polities and the Nation-State: Conflict and Co-Operation. In *Federalism and International Relations: The Role of Subnational Units*, ed. Hans J. Michelmann and Panayotis Soldatos, 54–75. Oxford: Oxford University Press.

———. 2003. Foreign Relations of Subnational Unit. In *Federalism in a Changing World: Learning from Each Other*, ed. Raoul Blindenbacher and Arnold Koller, 74–96. Montreal and Kingston: McGill-Queen's University Press.

Koch, Katie. 2011. Get Smart: Kennedy School's Nye Charts a Course for Continued U.S. Influence. The Harvard Gazette, February 17. Accessed April 11, 2022. https://news.harvard.edu/gazette/story/2011/02/get-smart/.

Kuznetsov, Alexander S. 2015. *Theory and Practice of Paradiplomacy: Subnational Governments in International Affairs*. London, New York: Routledge.

Lecours, André. 2000. Ethnonationalism in the West. A Theoretical Exploration. *Nationalism and Ethnic Politics* 6 (1): 103–124.

———. 2002. Paradiplomacy. Reflections on the Foreign Policy and International Relations of Regions. *International Negotiation* 7: 91–114.

Lecours, André and Louis Moreno. 2001. Paradiplomacy and Stateless Nations: A Reference to the Basque Country. Unidad de Políticas Comparadas (CSIC) Working Paper 01-06.

Massart-Piérard, Françoise. 1999. Politique des relations extérieures et identité politique: la stratégie des entités fédérées de la Belgique. *Études internationales* 30: 701–727.

Nye, Joseph, and Robert Keohane. 1977. *Power and Interdependence: World Politics in Transition.* Boston: Little, Brown and Company.

———. 1987. Power and Interdependence Revisited. *International Organization* 41 (4): 725–753.

Paquin, Stephane. 2004. La paradiplomatie identitaire: Le Québec, la Catalogne et la Flandre en Relations Internationales. *Politiques et Sociétés* 23 (2–3): 204–237.

———. 2020. Paradiplomacy. In *Global Diplomacy. An Introduction to Theory and Practice*, ed. Thierry Balzacq, Frédéric Charillon, and Frédéric Ramel, 49–61. New York: Palgrave Macmillan.

Pegg, Scott. 1998. *International Security and the De Facto State.* Aldershot: Ashgate.

———. 2004. From De Facto States to States-Within-States: Progress, Problems, and Prospects. In *States-Within-States. Incipient Political Entities in the Post-Cold War Era*, ed. Paul Kingston and Ian S. Spears, 35–46. New York: Palgrave Macmillan.

Soldatos, Panayotis. 1990. An Explanatory Framework for the Study of Federated States as Foreign Policy Actor. In *Federalism and International Relations: The Role of Subnational Units*, ed. Hans J. Michelmann and Panayotis Soldatos, 34–53. Oxford: Clarendon Press.

———. 1993. Cascading Subnational Paradiplomacy in an Interdependent and Transnational World. In *States and Provinces in the International Economy*, ed. Douglas M. Brown and Earl H. Fry, 45–64. Berkeley: Institute of Governmental Studies Press.

Spies, Yolanda Kemp. 2005. *Meeting the Challenges of Developing World Diplomacy in the 21st Century: An Assessment of Perspectives on Contemporary Diplomatic Training.* Dissertation. Pretoria: University of Pretoria.

Tavares, Rodrigo. 2016. *Paradiplomacy: Cities and States as Global Players.* Oxford: Oxford University Press.

Vela, Jordi de San Eugenio, and Jordi Xifra. 2015. International Representation Strategies for Stateless Nations: The Case of Catalonia's Cultural Diplomacy. *Place Branding and Public Diplomacy* 11 (1): 83–96.

Wolff, Stefan. 2007. Paradiplomacy: Scope, Opportunities and Challenges. *The Bologna Center Journal of International Affairs* 10 (1): 141–150.

PART I

The Rise of Paradiplomacy

CHAPTER 2

The Evolution of Kurdistan-Iraq's Paradiplomacy: Causes and Constraints

Francis Owtram

INTRODUCTION

On a sunny day in October 2007 just a few days after taking up my post in the Department of Politics and International Relations to teach foreign policy analysis at the University of Kurdistan-Hewlêr, I walked out one morning from our staff residential accommodation in the direction of the campus. I happened to walk by a building on which was a plaque reading: "Department of Foreign Relations, Kurdistan Regional Government." At that time being new to the area both literally and in academic focus, my mind began to mull over what this plaque meant and how could it be analysed and understood within the concepts of the disciplines of comparative politics and international relations. For Kurds, however, such things are no academic matter. Their lived experience of the playing out of European imperial machinations and finding themselves in states which invariably found their identity problematic, determined to impose a dominant ethnic nationalism on them, resulted in displacement and genocidal

F. Owtram (✉)
Institute for Arab and Islamic Studies, University of Exeter, Exeter, UK
e-mail: f.owtram@exeter.ac.uk

© The Author(s), under exclusive license to Springer Nature Switzerland AG 2023
G. Gürbey et al. (eds.), *Between Diplomacy and Non-Diplomacy*,
https://doi.org/10.1007/978-3-031-09756-0_2

attack amongst other atrocities. Indeed, the Kurds notably feature in a recent popular, best-selling book entitled *Prisoners of Geography* (Marshall 2015).

As in many things related to the Kurds and Kurdistan nailing down the political entity that is Kurdistan-Iraq with a conclusive definition is definitely not straightforward and sometimes proves elusive. Thus, as, for example, reviewed by Gürbey et al. (2017), the subject of our analysis—Kurdistan-Iraq—has been referred to variously, as "a de facto state, a federal region, an unrecognised state and a recognised unrecognised state." Unsurprisingly, therefore, we find that scholars have applied a number of apparently relevant terms—foreign relations, foreign policy, international relations, paradiplomacy, protodiplomacy—to the phenomenon which is the focus of this chapter: the paradiplomacy of Kurdistan-Iraq, specifically its evolution, and its causes and constraints.

In the course of this chapter, I will refer to key relevant works in the extant literature on secessionism, Iraqi federalism, paradiplomacy and the paradiplomacy of Kurdistan-Iraq (Danilovich 2014; Danilovich and Owtram 2014; Mohammed and Owtram 2014; Mansour 2017; Zadeh and Kirmanji 2017; Mustafa 2019; Romano 2020). Drawing on, synthesising and complementing this literature, an analysis will be advanced in answer to the following two key questions suggested by this review of selected literature.

1. What is paradiplomacy as defined in the literature and what political entities practice it?
2. How can we explain the aims and practice of Kurdistan-Iraq's paradiplomacy and the distinct periods and shifts that can be identified within its evolution?

The argument advanced by this chapter, drawing on and synthesising the aforementioned selected extant literature relevant to this topic, is stated in summary form here. Interrogating concepts in the neo-realist and neo-liberal approach in the discipline of International Relations before narrowing in on neo-classical realism, Romano outlines an explanation, as to why at crucial points Kurdistan-Iraq moved to a risk-taking policy as regards its position on independence. Of particular note is Romano's use of the terms 'consolidated' and 'unconsolidated' actor. Complementing his interest in sub-state dynamics I apply the basic premise of the 'bureaucratic politics' model[1] in foreign policy analysis, which contends that (in contrast to the assertion of neo-realism) the 'black box' of the state needs to be unpacked in order to understand the operation of the actor in the international system. Here I find Stansfield's (2017) review of the political structures of Kurdistan-Iraq and the role of the Kurdistan Democratic Party (KDP), the Patriotic Union of Kurdistan (PUK) and their foreign relations offices instructive. In explaining these cleavages, I find it useful to refer to Nigel Greaves' (2019) meticulous analysis of the material basis of power in Kurdistan-Iraq to account for the structures identified by Stansfield. This also augments Romano's analysis as to why the KRG seemingly shifted between being a 'consolidated actor,' exhibiting behaviour characterised by risk avoidance, to an 'unconsolidated' actor pursuing policies that could be deemed more risky, in connection to the issue of secession and independence. I further argue that Greaves' analysis of the dynamics behind Kurdistan-Iraq can be usefully supplemented by the allocation of appropriate analytical weight to the key role in the outcome of secessionist dynamics of a superpower as an enabler/spoiler of the secessionist entity. In this part of my argument, I refer to my chapter (Owtram 2019b) which draws on Riegl et al.'s (2017) analysis of the significance of an external power to secessionist outcomes.

This shift of Kurdistan-Iraq from paradiplomacy to protodiplomacy and back to paradiplomacy since 2005 as part of the inclusion of the Kurdistan Region in federal Iraq is thus the key focus of the chapter. These phenomena can be identified as an aspect of politics and policy that can be placed in the overall context of the 'syndrome of post-colonial sequestration' which saw the lands occupied by Kurdish people sequestered (i.e., legally owned) into the states created at the end of the First World War. This concept, originally sketched out in a short essay by the late Professor Fred Halliday (2011), is one I have applied and am advancing as an analytical category.[2]

Before we proceed further, it remains to note that a key observation of, in my estimation, the foremost authorities on secessionism, Aleksandar Pavković and Peter Radan (2012), is that secessionist movements oscillate between the aims of achieving autonomy and state independence. A key connection made in this chapter is to link this oscillation with the

---

[1] See Christopher Hill's outline (2003, 85–92) of this theory from its inception with Graham Allison's pioneering work Essence of Decision.
[2] For further details see Owtram (2011, 2019b, c, 2023).

distinction between paradiplomacy and protodiplomacy, most succinctly outlined by Cornago (2018).

The brief given by the chapter title suggested, with reference to the existing literature, a necessary emphasis on the explication of definitions and underlying dynamics of the character and periodisations of Kurdish Regional Government (KRG) paradiplomacy, rather than an in-depth case study of the paradiplomatic activities of Kurdistan-Iraq with any one particular country.[3] The main focus of the chapter is on the period since 2005 when Kurdistan-Iraq decided, encouraged by Washington, to remain in, or as some see it re-join, federal Iraq, created with a constitution hammered out through negotiation. This link with federalism is a point to which we will return: suffice it to say that, whilst there is no doubt the activity of political parties might come under the term 'paradiplomacy,' the greater part of literature on paradiplomacy has indeed been in relation to the activities of sub-state governments in federal states.

Necessarily, there will be more mention of Turkey, Iran, Syria, the United States (US), Russia, the United Kingdom of Great Britain and Northern Ireland (UK), and the United Nations (UN), the European Union (EU) and individual EU states. A further point to keep in mind is that, as in all social science research and its attendant process of classification and comparison, concepts seek to place social phenomena in broad categories to aid the purpose of comparative research; thus no one category will fully cover or define individual cases but in building the number of case studies underlying similarities, differences may be elucidated. The structure of the chapter is as follows. Firstly, a section reviewing key literature on paradiplomacy as a concept, paradiplomacy of Kurdistan-Iraq and protodiplomacy and secessionism. Following this, and drawing on relevant sources, I sketch out a chronological narrative of this evolution paying particular attention to the tilt from paradiplomacy to protodiplomacy in the period 2014–2017. Then follows a discussion section highlighting

---

[3] For a book-length, in-depth analysis of the foreign relations of Kurdistan-Iraq within the conceptual framework of de facto state literature, see Hajar Sadoon (2020—based on PhD completed in July 2017). This is undoubtedly an important contribution to the literature, although to my mind, in the period of federal Iraq (2005 to date) it assigns insufficient analytical weight to the enduring reality of the Barzani-KDP/Talabani-PUK cleavage and concomitantly arguably overstates the depth and of actual unification of KRG policy-making including in the realm of foreign relations. Thus, the contention and argument that "after 2007 … the KRI transformed into an independent foreign policy actor" (2020, 467) is possibly difficult to sustain, particularly in the light of the events of October 2017.

the causes and constraints and drawing together the argument and analysis, before concluding with a summary of the chapter and final thoughts. We first turn to consider the relevant extant literature.

Definitions and Theoretical Deliberations

This chapter, in tackling its task, must first lay down some definitional context in considering the phenomenon of the paradiplomacy of Kurdistan-Iraq. Firstly, we have to be aware that it is no simple matter to conceptually label Kurdistan-Iraq. As Harvey and Stansfield (2011, 19) note in their review of terminology assigned by political scientists: "between 1961 and the present, a wide array of Kurdish political systems have theoretically operated in the northernmost provinces of the Iraqi state." Prior to 1991 terms such as 'insurgent state' or 'state proxy' could be applied; the period 1991–2003 was a period of autonomy under the umbrella given by the demarcation under UN Resolutions of no-fly zones and the exclusion of the airborne units of Saddam Hussein's regime in which the terms 'de facto state' or 'de facto states, unrecognized state' were terms ascribed; and since 2005 even a 'recognized unrecognized state' which is constitutionally a regional state of federal Iraq.

Further, in terms of analytical precision, while they are sometimes treated as synonymous terms, foreign policy is not the same as diplomacy and I find it enlightening to consider a definition rendered by Christopher Hill of the London School of Economics:

> A brief definition of foreign policy can be given as a starting point: foreign policy is the sum of official external relations conducted by an independent actor (usually but not exclusively a state) in international relations. The phrase 'an independent actor' enables the inclusion of phenomena such as the European Union or Hezbullah; external relations are 'official' to allow the inclusion of outputs from all parts of the governing mechanisms of the state or enterprise (that is, not just the foreign ministry) while also maintaining parsimony with respect to the vast number of international transactions now being conducted; policy (as opposed to decisions) is the 'sum' of these official relations because actors usually seek some degree of coherence towards the outside world—and are assumed by others to be following a reasonably coherent and predictable line. Lastly, the policy is 'foreign' because the world is still more separated into distinctive communities than it is a single, homogenizing entity. These communities therefore need strategies for coping with foreigners (that is, those who are not part of their own

polity). This is in itself an alternative definition of foreign policy if one wishes to emphasize its purposive and cohesive dimensions. (Hill 2015, 5)

An important point to which we will later return is to note that in including an entity such as Hezbullah, Hill's definition allows the consideration of a political party controlling a piece of territory. This allows us in turn to include, as part of this conceptualisation, the dominant political parties of Kurdistan-Iraq: the KDP and the PUK, whose role in international affairs of Kurdistan-Iraq has already been flagged. It is also interesting to note Hill's (2003, 3) comment that the word "foreign" derives from the Latin 'foris' meaning 'outside.'

In connection to this, if we consider Kurdistan-Iraq any kind of political entity then it can meaningfully speak of a communication process with institutions outside of itself which could include other institutions in and geographic parts of federal Iraq. Also, we need, with reference to federalism, to be aware of the possible shared nature of sovereignty in federal states in which the executive, legislative and judiciary and indeed the federal sub-units can be legally co-equal constitutionally, although the powers, including reserved powers, accorded to the different parts of the polity, will differ according to individual federal constitutions of, for example, the US, Canada, Germany, India and Iraq.

PARADIPLOMACY: MAPPING THE LITERATURE

In his aim of analysing Mediterranean paradiplomacies Duran (2015) delved into "the archaeology" of the term and indeed we certainly need to conduct the necessary terminological investigations in an attempt to avoid analytical confusion. Further, in considering the word 'paradiplomacy' we should be cognizant that the word is made by attaching the prefix 'para' to the word 'diplomacy' so it may be helpful to remind ourselves of the meaning of these terms and how they may differ from foreign policy.

Diplomacy is a practice going back to ancient times which originated before the emergence of the Westphalian state system (Stern 2000, 177–192). It can be characterised as the communication process between different political actors and the skills such as tact and patience necessary for successful negotiation. Germane to our discussions is Hill's (2003, 139) assessment: "As a means of implementing policy, diplomacy is particularly important to weak states. With few resources they have little choice but to play a poor hand as skilfully as possible. Yet these are also the states with the smallest and least experienced diplomatic services." Paradiplomacy originated in the term 'parallel diplomacy' and thus conveys the notion of it being alongside. In the last few years, a number of books (Duran 2015; Schiavon 2019, Kuznetsov 2015) have been published which have sought to address the issues of what constitutes paradiplomacy as they seek to develop an analytical framework.

They all build on *Paradiplomacy in Action: The Foreign Relations of Subnational Governments* (Aldecoa and Keating 1999) which stands as one of key texts in the study of paradiplomacy. It included, as Kuznetsov notes (2015, 34), one of the first attempts—Aguirre's (1999) contribution 'Making Sense of Paradiplomacy'—to collate the development of the literature.

A key point to note from these book-length investigations is that paradiplomacy as a concept was initially mainly applied as a concept in analysis to regions of federal states in the 'developed world' and can be considered as a form of diplomacy undertaken by sub-state units in parallel or besides the diplomacy of the sovereign state. In so doing they become actors in the international system. Wolff (2007) observes that this may feel disconcerting to central governments used to diplomacy being an exclusive domain of central governments, but it should be embraced, he argues, as a way of managing what otherwise might potentially become protracted self-determination conflicts. It is often associated with the activities of regional governments in federal states but equally it has been applied to those by regions or countries with devolved administrations in unitary states, for example, in Scotland and South Africa. In considering the activity of Kurdistan-Iraq since 2005, since it has been a constitutionally recognised part of the nascent federal state of Iraq, I personally find the term 'sub-state' more appropriate than 'sub-national' as sub-national would seem to ignore the possibility of multi-national states. However, it is without doubt unwise to become overly focussed on pursuing all-encompassing definitions. As Kuznetsov puts it:

> There is no final consensus in academia on which term is more convenient for defining sub-national governments' external activities, and researchers usually prefer not to waste their time on terminological debates and prefer to use those concepts that look more convenient for them. Hence, beside the concept of 'paradiplomacy,' we can find a number of different terms that label the region's performance in the international arena. (Kuznetsov 2015, 25)

In secessionism studies a prefix can be extremely important in making a significant definitional distinction. In this regard for the purposes of this chapter I find the definition and explication offered by Noé Cornago (2018) extremely useful as it expertly and succinctly defines paradiplomacy and a closely related term 'protodiplomacy.'

> The ability to conduct diplomatic relations is generally considered an exclusive attribute of sovereign states, but the participation of local and regional governments in international relations is becoming increasingly important worldwide. This phenomenon, also known as 'paradiplomacy' has important historical antecedents but has acquired in recent decades a new prominence, as a result of the transnationalization of the global economy and the rise of global connectivity. Despite the initial reluctance of central/federal governments to accept this new reality, paradiplomacy is rapidly gaining institutional and legal recognition by states and international organizations in the most diverse geopolitical contexts. Beyond its instrumental value, paradiplomacy is always a form of political agency that facilitates the representation of collective identities at a global scale, expressing generally a will of greater political autonomy and sometimes even the aspiration to create a new independent state. In those cases, in which this latter ambition prevails over any other possible political design, 'paradiplomacy' mutates in to 'protodiplomacy.' But protodiplomacy rarely produces the results expected by its proponents, namely to secure significant international support for a secessionist process, being more frequently conducive to international isolation and ethnopolitical conflict with the consequent economic, social, and political costs. (Cornago 2018)

Thus, protodiplomacy can be defined as the variant of paradiplomacy utilised by sub-state units active in the international arena as they more explicitly seek independence. However, this distinction is not as neat and tidy as we might like. Firstly, the delineation between phases of para- and protodiplomacy is more of a 'continuum than totally distinct time periods' (Romano 2020: 349). Secondly, we should remember that seemingly well-established federal states, or indeed unitary states with devolved powers, have had constituent parts of the state come very close to seceding via referenda agreed with the home state—Quebec/Canada and Scotland/UK as illustrations.

The literature on secessionism and secessionist movements is voluminous and I do not intend to venture into this in great deal as I have considered it more fully elsewhere (Owtram 2019a). I would just like to pick out a key point made by Pakovic here:

The concept of secession is highly contested; scholars still disagree on what should count as a secession. As the concept of secessionism appears to be less contested, we start by expanding J. R. Wood's original definition as follows: secessionism is a political program based on the demand for a formal withdrawal of a bounded territory from an internationally recognized state with the aim of creating a new state on that territory, which is expected to gain formal recognition by other states (and the UN). Secessionism clearly differs from separatism which aims only at a reduction of the central authority's control over the targeted territory and its population; as Wood pointed out, political movements can and often do 'oscillate' between separatist and secessionist programs, initially starting with the former and ending up with the latter and vice versa. Irredentism, in contrast, aims at the withdrawal of territory but not at the creation of a new state. According to the 1960 UN Declaration on the Granting of Independence to Colonial Peoples, granting independence to colonies does not breach the 'territorial integrity' of UN member states; since a colony, accordingly, is not part of the territory of an existing state, decolonization is not a secessionist project. (Pakovic 2015)

STUDIES ON THE PARADIPLOMACY OF THE KURDISTAN REGION OF IRAQ (KRI)

During the research of the extant literature for the purpose of writing this chapter I have identified the following chapters and articles as literature of high quality and analytical utility (Natali 2010; Mohammed and Owtram 2014; Danilovich 2014; Mansour 2017; Mustafa 2019; Romano 2020; Sadoon 2020).

Not surprisingly this literature reflects the passage of time and unfolding of political dynamics in the Kurdistan-Iraq, surrounding states (Arab Spring) and indeed global political economy (oil price fluctuations). In a co-authored article based on research undertaken in the period 2008–2013, we argued that paradiplomacy did not indicate an intention to secede from Iraq and that the involvement of the KRG international, once inhabiting the area of de facto autonomous zone, was "more firmly consolidated into the activity of foreign relations of federal states" (Mohammed and Owtram 2014, 65). However, we did put the necessary qualifier that "the Middle East is currently a fast-changing environment, and the implications and effects of the Arab spring, the US withdrawal from Iraq, and the war in Syria are unlikely yet to be fully played out" (Mohammed and Owtram 2014, 66).

David Romano's article (2020) in Kurdish Studies has set out some phases into which the paradiplomacy of Kurdistan-Iraq can be placed and reflects the aforementioned fast-changing environment. In his analysis of foreign policy risk taking and levels of consolidation of sub-state governments, Romano identifies three key periods as crucial to understanding 'Iraqi Kurdish foreign policies': "The 1991 to 2002 period (a period of unrecognised and unconsolidated autonomy); the 2003–2014 period (a period of a more consolidated KRI and strategic Kurdish foreign policy); and the post-2014 (a period of flux, with a weakened KRI at risk of sliding back into less strategic foreign policy behaviour)" (2020, 348).

Considering overall strategy, in an insightful analysis Mansour (2017) posits that Kurdistan-Iraq's diplomacy is used by the KRG as a method to develop alternative options to the central government and to attract investment. Fascinatingly, he specifies the way in which the cadre of officials in the Department of Foreign Relations under Falah Mustafa were instructed on the accepted etiquette and professionalism of diplomacy in order to indicate their socialisation into diplomatic norms, and that they have an expectation that they should be treated as equivalent to diplomatic staff and ambassadors.

Commenting on the presence of a cadre of KRG staff outside of Kurdistan-Iraq, Danilovich (2014, 95–97) details the provisions of the federal constitution and the stipulation that foreign policy and international relations are a role reserved to the exclusive authority of the federal government. However, the constitution also allows any federal regions to set up offices in Iraqi embassies in order to follow cultural, social and developmental affairs. This has allowed the development of a network of KRG offices in selected states all over the world. On a number of occasions KRG officials have pointed out to the author of this chapter that any KRG offices opened are always in states where there is an Iraqi embassy and also, sometimes with a wry smile, that nowhere in the constitution does it specify that the region's offices have to be co-located within the Iraqi embassy. Furthermore, in connection with this, Danilovich and Abdulrahman (2017) highlight the offices which make up the KRG Department of Foreign Relations (DFR), which gives us an insight into its operations and activity:

> The DFR has seven offices, each in charge of one specific task: (1) The Office of International Relations facilitates activities of foreign diplomatic representations in the IKR [Kurdistan Region Iraq], organizes visits of foreign delegations, as well as promotes the KRG's relations with their respective countries. (2) An office that deals with the KRG representations abroad.

(3) The third is the Protocol Office. It also liaises with the federal Ministry of Foreign Affairs in Baghdad and federal bureaus in the region. (4) The fourth is the Office of International Organizations, such as United Nations agencies and international NGOs operating in the Region. (5) The fifth is the Legal Office, which certifies and validates documents relating to foreign consulates in the IKR. (6) The sixth is the Media and Communication Office, responsible for dissemination of the KRG's messages; it works closely with the foreign press in the region and maintains the DFR official website. (7) The last unit is the Office of Human Resources and Finances. (KRG-DFR Official Website, 2017)

Since 2019 Safeen Dizayee has been the Head of the DFR as it has sought to rebuild relationships with Baghdad and its regional neighbours after the 2017 independence referendum. Although at first glance the DFR might be thought to be of key significance in this process Mustafa (2019) contends that the KRG's foreign policy is formulated mainly by the President, Prime Minister and their associated diplomatic cadres. The DFR, established in 2008, plays, according to Mustafa, a secondary role of organising minor diplomatic activities inside and outside of Kurdistan-Iraq.

This section has considered key insights from important contributions in the literature to the study of the paradiplomacy of Kurdistan-Iraq. It is, however, impossible to understand Kurdistan-Iraq's paradiplomacy without setting it in its necessary historical context in the modern state-formation process of the Middle East, and it is to this we now turn.

Evolution of the Paradiplomacy of Kurdistan-Iraq

It is important therefore to embed the consideration of the paradiplomacy of the Kurdistan Region in federal Iraq in the historical trajectory of Kurdistan-Iraq from the end of First World War which "encompassed uprisings in 1923, 1932, and 1943, the signing of an autonomy agreement in 1970 subsequently reneged on by Baghdad, the de facto autonomous area created within the no-fly zone 1991–2003, and since 2005 its current federal incarnation as a constitutionally recognized region of federal Iraq" (Owtram 2017b, 522).

At the end of the First World War the Kurds were incorporated into states in which—following the example of Russification of other ethnicities in Tsarist Russia—a dominant Turkish or Arab nationalist identity was imposed (Gunter 2019). During this time in Kurdistan-Iraq resistance to this process was led by Shaikh Mahmud Barzanji. On May 22, 1919,

Barzanji rebelled against British state-building efforts but his rebellion was crushed with aerial bombings and he was imprisoned (Sharif 2018). In their occupation and veiled colonial rule the British encountered major resistance during the Second World War, when forces led by Mustafa Barzanji gained control of large parts of Erbil (Seyder 2017).[4] Royal Air Force bombers were deployed to repress this outbreak of resistance, causing the rebels to flee over the border into Iran. In 1946 the sunshine of the flag of Kurdistan briefly flew over the Republic of Kurdistan in Mahabad, Iran, until it was crushed ruthlessly by the Shah of Iran and Barzanji departed the Middle East for exile in the Soviet Union.

The brutal overthrow of the Iraqi monarchy in the revolution of 1958 marked the end of the British-organised Baghdad Pact designed to contain the Soviet Union and ushered in a new phase of nation and identity building (Owtram 2017a, 2019b). The development of Iraq as a regional power under the Baath party controlled by Saddam Hussein (with his inner circle from Tikrit) and using nationalised oil resources proceeded apace in the 1970s. The 1970 Iraqi-Kurdish Autonomy Agreement on paper offered meaningful autonomy but on the ground an Arabisation programme of Kurdish areas was implemented and the Kurds and their Peshmerga under Masoud Barzani took up armed rebellion again. In this they received support from the Shah of Iran who played the Kurdish card against Saddam Hussein—providing safe areas in Iran for them to launch attacks against the Iraqi army. In order to cut off this Iranian support for the Kurds of Iraq, Saddam made concessions to the Shah on the border line between Iraq and Iran on the Shatt al Arab waterway codified in the 1975 Algiers agreements. Saddam then proceed to easily crush his Kurdish rebellion. During this time and for various reasons, Jalal Talabani split off from the Kurdistan Democratic Party to form the PUK. Thus, an intense and sometimes blood rivalry was inaugurated within the Kurds of Iraq, with rival Peshmerga forces and networks of patronage (Natali 2005; Stansfield 2019; Aydoğan 2020).

1991–2004 (Formative Years)

This period remains a critical time as, fundamentally, the dynamics which were laid down here, based on the split in the 1970s, remain in place to this day. Tellingly, Gareth Stansfield (2003) refers to "Kurdistan Regional

---

[4] This section is drawn from Seyder (2017) and Owtram (2017a, 2019b, c).

Government(s)"—there were, in reality, separate administrations in Erbil and Sulaimaniyah who fought each other in disputes over cross-border revenues which flared hot in a bitter intra-Kurdish war from 1994 to 1996. The basis of power was the control of territory achieved and enforced by the Kurdish militias (Peshmerga—those who face death) loyal to either Barzani or Talabani. Although initially based on some ideological difference or rural/urban sociological factors essentially, these territories were held together by tribal and personal loyalties, cemented and maintained by a network of patronage oiled by material interests (money). Physical and military control of a block of territory was key. Control of territory (land/estate) meant the rulers of that territory can take control of revenues from international aid (Natali 2010) and informal tax on smuggled goods such as oil. The civil war of 1994–1996 in Kurdistan-Iraq saw these personal and economic rivalries come to a head. It is shocking but perhaps not surprising that faced with the loss of their power base in Erbil to the PUK, Masoud Barzani and the KDP called in the military forces of Saddam Hussein regime in order to tilt the balance of armed force to their favour and eject the PUK militia from Erbil in 1996. Where the informal ceasefire lines were drawn became, and have remained to this day, the de facto borders with associated checkpoints between the KDP- and PUK-controlled areas (indeed, as we will see, as evidenced in the events of October 2017, it is at times of heightened tensions that the underlying dynamics are made clear). The US were eager for the Kurdish parties to unite under American auspices and the rival parties convened in Washington in 1998 to sign a formal ceasefire and concluded an agreement to work together (Makovsky 1998). In 2002 the Kurdish Parliament convened for the first time in six years and agreed to discuss a new KRG constitution with eyes on a new federal Iraq as part of American-backed regime change (Romano 2020, 353).

2005–2013 (Paradiplomacy)

Following the removal of Saddam Hussein and the inception of federal Iraq in 2005, this period has been termed the 'Golden Decade' when a united Kurdish front in Baghdad and high oil prices allowed the Kurdistan Region to prosper and even present itself in a public relations campaign as 'the other Iraq.' As part of this in 2008 the leadership established the DFR in a bid to institutionalise the sub-state's foreign relations and move away from party politics. However, as Stansfield (2021, 367) notes, "the KRI remains very much a tale of the interaction, competition, alliances and rivalries between the two constituent regions." The political actors in Kurdistan-Iraq understood they had to give the image to the Western democratic powers what they wanted: a democratic, secular government in the process of transition to institutionalisation of power and authority. However, the reality was enormous corruption and patronage politics, in reaction to which the Goran movement split from the PUK in 2009. Whilst the KDP had more centralised control leading to completion of projects, the PUK was increasingly fissiparous particularly after the incapacitation in 2012 and then death in 2017 of its founder Jalal Talabani. The PUK's vote declined and with it the 50:50 deal with the KDP began to unravel.

2014–September 2017 (Protodiplomacy)

With the rise of the Islamic State (IS) and capture of Mosul in June 2014, a 'security imperative' compelled the Kurds to meet this existential threat. At this point Kurdistan-Iraq tilted to a more explicit secessionist aim which culminated in the independence referendum held on September 25, 2017.[5] As Stansfield (2021) outlines, it was felt by the KRG President, Masoud Barzani, that the federal government in Baghdad had not kept its part of the bargain: the constitutional articles that stipulated a referendum on Kirkuk and the disputed territories based on a census before Arabisation took place had not taken place. Barzani also perceived that support for the KRG was conditional upon the threat to western interests from the IS, which was now beginning, seemingly, to diminish. Furthermore, due to the economic crisis, the KRI was almost bankrupt, and it was perceived that independence would allow access to international funding restricted to sovereign states. For all these reasons, Barzani decided to start plans for an independence referendum in 2017.

Crucially, however, the sovereign authority (the federal government in Baghdad) had opposed the holding of the independence referendum, from the start: Iraqi Prime Minister, Haider al-Abadi, declared it

---

[5] There have been considerable discussions and academic debates as to the circumstances and motives of Masoud Barzani in pushing the referendum at this point in time. See, for example, Palani et al. (2019); and O'Driscoll and Baser (2019).

unconstitutional and the Iraqi Supreme Court ordered the suspension of the referendum.

In the absence of support for the referendum from the sovereign state, major international and regional powers as well as intergovernmental organisations were unanimous in opposing the unilateral holding of the referendum and actively sought to dissuade the KRG from proceeding with it (Park et al. 2017). Statements were issued by the US and the UK opposing the vote and suggesting the focus should remain on defeating the IS. Germany and France also opposed the referendum, as did Russia. The Security Council of the UN issued a statement "expressing concern over the potentially destabilizing impact of the Kurdistan Regional Government's plans to unilaterally hold a referendum" (United Nations Organisation 2017) and supporting the territorial integrity of Iraq. The day after the referendum the Secretary-General issued a similar statement noting the opposition of Iraq's constitutional authorities and regional neighbours, and that holding the referendum in the disputed areas, notably Kirkuk, could be particularly destabilising. The foreign ministers of the European Union counselled against unilateral actions. Not surprisingly, Turkey and Iran promised there would be a 'price to pay' and a reaction if the vote went against ahead. Just two days before the referendum Rex Tillerson, US Secretary of State, made a last-ditch request to President Barzani to postpone the referendum in a letter to President Barzani but to no avail. Only Israel supported the poll taking place. A few days after the independence vote Baghdad first closed the airspace over Kurdistan-Iraq. Then on October 16, facilitated by the withdrawal of the militia loyal to the Bafel Talabani faction of the PUK, Iraqi troops, supported by Iranian-backed militias, retook Kirkuk and other disputed areas. This was orchestrated by Qasem Soleimani, Commander of the Quds force of the Islamic Revolutionary Guards Corp, using divide-and-rule tactics offering inducements or threats to the Talabani family. The events of October 2017 have been framed by some as a Talabani revenge for 1996. As a result, the KRG lost 50 per cent of the disputed territories and half its oil revenues. After the referendum, international diplomats unequivocally expressed disbelief over the call of KDP politicians to the international committee to play a mediating role between Erbil and Bagdad. Mediation and support had been offered in return for not organising a referendum, but now that the referendum had been held, the KDP found itself alone.

October 2017 to Date (Return to Paradiplomacy)

Kawa Hassan (2018) outlines the main features of Kurdistan-Iraq's paradiplomacy since the independence referendum which he characterises as a 'colossal miscalculation.' He notes that since then Kurdistan-Iraq has recovered politically and has implemented a pragmatic strategy to revitalise the economy and internal affairs. The KRG also launched diplomatic initiatives to restore relations with Iran and Turkey and has pursued a policy of neutrality to manage the Region's myriad of crises (Shamsi 2020). Of huge importance initially was the building of bridges with Baghdad in order to open the airports of Erbil and Sulaimaniyah and also to come to an agreement where the federal government partially paid the salaries of public employees in Kurdistan-Iraq due to the KRG being virtually bankrupt. Indeed, this reflects the assessment of the Barzanis as told to Gareth Stansfield: for the time being, Kurdistan-Iraq is 'obliged' to be part of Iraq (Stansfield 2021).

Unpacking the 'Black Box' of Kurdistan-Iraq's Paradiplomacy

Looking back on this narrative we can usefully refer to the insights of the bureaucratic politics approach to foreign policy analysis which enjoined researchers to look inside the 'black box' of the state, something regarded as contaminating the parsimony of realism. Stansfield (2017, 62) unpacks the structures of the Kurdish political system in Kurdistan-Iraq which have developed sometimes by design and sometimes by accident since the 1960s. He notes the "shadow role" played by the KDP and PUK: "Until recently, it was almost impossible to identify who had authority to represent, for example, the KRG in an international setting—whether it was the KDP or PUK foreign relations offices, for example, or the KRG's department of foreign relations" (2015, 69). This duality of Kurdistan-Iraq between an area largely under the influence of the KDP/Barzani and a PUK/Talabani area is a significant structural constraint on Kurdish state-building projects and pursuit of a unified paradiplomacy. From this perspective it undoubtedly would be better if they were able to peacefully unite, but the underlying structures of wealth and patronage make such a united front much more difficult. Control of territory equals control of resources such as border crossing revenues, hydrocarbons and all significant large companies and sectors such as construction and telecoms are ultimately controlled by Barzanis or Talabanis or their associated networks.[6] Nigel Greaves (2019, 58–59) meticulously articulates the dynamic underlying this and notes that "the parties were initially forced into cooperative dialogue largely out of concern for internal security. A power-sharing system, aptly named the 50:50 split was established which facilitated interparty cooperation in this task. If this necessity for cooperation had not been present at the time, and did not remain so, it would be difficult to conceive of any further voluntary basis for cooperation between the main political parties." Greaves posits persuasively that the social, political and economic power articulated by Kurdistan's dominant political parties has become effectively "two parallel aristocratic estates … a political class unable to transcend national sectarian division by political means, because to do so would require that it voluntarily abolish itself–a highly unlikely scenario" (Greaves 2019, 65). For this reason a de facto dual administration in Erbil and Sulaimaniyah continues. We should therefore not be surprised that moves to unite and institutionalise the Kurdistan Regional Government—particularly in the sensitive ministries of Peshmerga, interior and finance—remain more on paper than in reality (Aydoğan 2020).

Causes and Constraints of Kurdistan-Iraq's Paradiplomacy

We can summarise, then, that the main cause of the paradiplomacy of Kurdistan-Iraq is the motivation and opportunity to build the capacities of statehood. This correlates to the opportunities identified by Wolff (2007) of federal systems to allow paradiplomacy as an assistance to manage conflicts of self-determination. The constitution of Iraq, whilst seemingly reserving diplomacy to the central government, is sufficiently ambiguous to allow Kurdistan-Iraq to pursue its paradiplomacy. This partially reflects the inherent paradox of federalism—that it can on the one hand act to maintain the territorial integrity of the existing state and on the other be a stepping stone to secession (Danilovich and Owtram 2014; Danilovich and Abdulrahman 2017; Owtram 2017b; Akreyi 2019).

The main constraint on the paradiplomacy of the Kurdistan Regional Government, as with the putative state-building project, has been the division of Kurdistan-Iraq into the KDP/Barzani block centred in Dohuk and

[6] For further details and an excellent elaboration on this, see Aziz (2017).

Erbil provinces and the PUK/Talabani block centred around Sulaimaniyah, along with the difficult geopolitical position due to the landlocked nature of Kurdistan-Iraq. As Riegl et al. (2017, 153) put it, Kurdistan-Iraq has been "trapped in internal and geopolitical rivalries."

Paradiplomacy, Protodiplomacy and Secession—The Role of Luck and Leadership

Finally, given the focus of this chapter it is not unreasonable to ponder the extent to which the 2017 independence referendum and associated protodiplomacy was a window of opportunity for Kurdistan-Iraq in its quest for an independent state. If Charles Tilly was right and "war made the state, and the state made war" (Tilly 1975, 42) then arguably the war against the IS was a golden opportunity for Kurdistan-Iraq to escape the confines of post-colonial sequestration. Referring to state-building efforts in a different era Michael Gunter (1997) notes that Kurdistan has had no Bismarck or Garibaldi[7]—conceivably a Barzani might have played that role—but was too equally matched militarily with the Talabani/PUK in terms of resources and external support. Further, it might be speculated that had the Kurdish Peshmerga held a united line in 2017 against the Iraqi forces for some days then possibly in the end the US would have been compelled to intervene to institute a ceasefire. In this way, the Kurds would have maintained their control of the disputed territories and could have further edged towards independence. As Halliday (2011, 242) notes, much can turn on luck and leadership. However, he also views that "only if there is a major political shift in the hegemonic state that has committed the sequestration, and which has secured some international indulgence for it, is there a realistic prospect of post-colonial annexation being reversed." He therefore enjoins the peoples subject to post-colonial sequestration to focus on their efforts on securing democratic (including federal) freedoms. Denise Natali, based on her analysis (2010) of the dependence of the Kurdistan Region on the central government of Iraq, is unequivocal in her judgement: "Iraqi-Kurdistan was never ready for statehood" (2017). We will never know the outcome of such a possible alternative history but it seems likely that as well as refocused attention on their obligations in the Iraqi federal project some Kurdish political actors in Kurdistan-Iraq will take a firm note of this assessment by Griffiths (2019, 123) that "Admission

---

[7] This point is made by Gunter (1997) cited by Romano (2020, 352).

to the sovereignty club is a fuzzy process, shaded by luck, and the right constellation of events could suddenly persuade Baghdad to open the gate and/or bring the right actors over to the Kurdish cause."

CONCLUSION

This chapter has, following a review of the relevant literature, outlined how Kurdistan-Iraq's paradiplomacy has evolved to respond to opportunities and constraints. The ultimate prisoners of geography, their paradiplomacy-cum-protodiplomacy is one tool they have used to try to pick the lock on their prison door to escape from the constraints imposed on them by Britain, Turkey, Iraq and Iran and their own internal division. In the end the state system proved durable and was reimposed, ending, seemingly for the foreseeable future, the Kurdish dream of an independent sovereign state. Protodiplomacy returned to paradiplomacy and the necessary activities to maintain themselves in their obligation, for the time being, to remain part of the dysfunctional Iraqi federal state.

On an observer mission to the 2017 independence referendum, I visited the University of Kurdistan-Hewlêr. My old office looked out on Erbil railway station, built during the time of the British-installed monarchy era. No trains connected there anymore and now it was being used as a prison. A few days after the independence vote the Iraqi government declared that it was closing the airspace of Kurdistan-Iraq and the international airports of Erbil and Sulaimaniyah. On the last plane out of Erbil airport I looked below, aware that the door was being firmly slammed shut by Baghdad on the structures which had constrained the Kurds in the state-building of the British in the days after the First World War. One thing you can be sure of, however, is that many Kurds will never let go of their dream of freedom in an independent state. To this end they will continue to practice paradiplomacy, and possibly shift to protodiplomacy when the pendulum of events swings their way again.

REFERENCES

Aguirre, Inaki. 1999. Making Sense of Paradiplomacy? An Intertextual Inquiry about a Concept in Search of a Definition. In *Paradiplomacy in Action: The Foreign Relations of Subnational Governments*, ed. Francisco Aldecoa and Michael Keating, 185–209. London: Frank Cass & Co.

Akreyi, Hemin. 2019. The Paradox of Federalism and the Iraqi Federation. In *Federalism, Secession, and International Recognition Regime: Iraqi Kurdistan*, ed. Alex Danilovich, 15–34. Abingdon: Routledge.

Aldecoa, Francisco, and Michael Keating, eds. 1999. *Paradiplomacy in Action: The Foreign Relations of Subnational Governments*. London: Frank Cass.

Aydoğan, Bekir. 2020. The Iraqi Kurds' Destructive Infighting: Causes and Consequences. *LSE Middle East Centre blog*, April 15. Accessed January 30, 2020. https://blogs.lse.ac.uk/mec/2020/04/15/the-iraqi-kurds-destructive-infighting-causes-and-consequences/.

Aziz, Sardar. 2017. The Economic System(s) of the Kurdistan Regional Government, Iraq. In *Between State and Non-State: Politics and Society in Kurdistan-Iraq and Palestine*, ed. Gülistan Gürbey, Sabine Hofmann, and Ferhad I. Seyder, 103–122. New York: Palgrave Macmillan.

Cornago, Noé. 2018. Paradiplomacy and Protodiplomacy. In *Encyclopedia of Diplomacy*, ed. Gordon Martel, 1–8. Oxford: Wiley-Blackwell.

Danilovich, Alex. 2014. *Iraqi Federalism and the Kurds: Learning to Live Together*. Farnham: Ashgate.

Danilovich, A., and H.S. Abdulrahman. 2017. Aiming at Secession: The KRG's Activism in the International Arena. *UKH Journal of Social Sciences* 1 (1): 24–35. https://doi.org/10.25079/ukhjss.v1n1y2017.pp48-59.

Danilovich, Alex, and Francis Owtram. 2014. Federalism as a Tool to Manage Conflicts and Associated Risks. In *Iraqi Federalism and the Kurds: Learning to Live Together*, ed. Alex Danilovich, 25–59. Farnham: Ashgate.

Duran, Manuel. 2015. *Mediterranean Diplomacies: The Dynamics of Diplomatic Reterritorialization*. Leiden: Brill.

Greaves, Nigel. 2019. United We Stand, Divided We Fall: Transcending the Obstacles to Internal Sovereignty in Iraqi Kurdistan. In *Federalism, Secession, and International Recognition Regime: Iraqi Kurdistan*, ed. Alex Danilovich, 53–71. Abingdon: Routledge.

Griffiths, Ryan D. 2019. Kurdistan, the International Recognition Regime and the Strategy of Secession. In *Federalism, Secession, and International Recognition Regime: Iraqi Kurdistan*, ed. Alex Danilovich, 111–126. Abingdon: Routledge.

Gunter, Michael. 1997. The Foreign Policy of the Iraqi Kurds. *Journal of South Asian and Middle Eastern Studies* 20 (3): 1–19.

———. 2019. *The Kurds: A Divided Nation in Search of a State*. Princeton: Markus Wiener Publishers.

Gürbey, Gülistan, Sabine Hofmann, and Ferhad I. Seyder, eds. 2017. *Between State and Non-State: Politics and Society in Kurdistan-Iraq and Palestine*. New York: Palgrave Macmillan.

Halliday, Fred. 2011. Post-Colonial Sequestration: Tibet, Palestine and the Politics of Failure. In *Political Journeys: The Open Democracy Essays*, ed. David Hayes, 238–243. London: Saqi Books.

Harvey, James, and Gareth Stansfield. 2011. Theorizing Unrecognized States: Sovereignty, Secessionism, and Political Economy. In *Unrecognized States in the International System*, ed. Nina Caspersen and Gareth Stansfield, 11–26. Abingdon: Routledge.
Hassan, Kawa. 2018. The KRG's Para-Diplomacy Post-Referendum: From de Facto 'Independence' to Regional Dependence, *LSE Middle East Centre*, April 18. Accessed January 13, 2022. https://blogs.lse.ac.uk/mec/2018/04/18/the-krgs-para-diplomacy-post-referendum-from-de-facto-independence-to-regional-dependence/.
Hill, Christopher. 2003. *The Changing Politics of Foreign Policy*. Basingstoke: Palgrave.
———. 2015. *Foreign Policy in the Twenty-First Century*. Basingstoke: Palgrave.
Kuznetsov, Alexander S. 2015. *Theory and Practice of Paradiplomacy: Subnational Governments in International Affairs*. Abingdon: Routledge.
Makovsky, Adam. 1998. Kurdish Agreement Signals New U.S. Commitment. The Washington Institute for Near East Policy. Accessed January 30, 2020. https://www.washingtoninstitute.org/policy-analysis/kurdish-agreement-signals-new-us-commitment.
Mansour, Renad. 2017. In Pursuit of Friends: The Kurdistan Region of Iraq's Foreign Affairs and Diplomacy. In *The Kurdish Question Revisited*, ed. Gareth Stansfield and Mohammed Shareef, 449–462. London: Hurst and Company.
Marshall, Tim. 2015. *Prisoners of Geography: Ten Maps that Tell You Everything You Need to Know about Global Politics*. London: Elliot and Thompson.
Mohammed, Herish K., and Francis Owtram. 2014. Paradiplomacy of Regional Governments in International Relations: The Foreign Relations of the Kurdistan Regional Government (2003–2010). *Iran and the Caucasus* 18: 65–84.
Mustafa, Sara S. 2019. KRG Survival in Iraq and in the Middle East: Nonalignment and Sectarian Neutrality. In *Federalism, Secession, and International Recognition Regime: Iraqi Kurdistan*, ed. Alex Danilovich, 90–109. Abingdon: Routledge.
Natali, Denise. 2005. *The Kurds and the State: Evolving National Identity in Iraq, Turkey and Iran*. Syracuse: Syracuse University Press.
———. 2010. *The Kurdish Quasi-State: Development and Dependency in Post-Gulf War Iraq*. Syracuse: Syracuse University Press.
———. 2017. Iraqi-Kurdistan Was Never Ready for Statehood. *Foreign Affairs*, October 31. Accessed February 10, 2022. https://foreignpolicy.com/2017/10/31/iraqi-kurdistan-was-never-ready-for-statehood/.
O'Driscoll, Dylan, and Bahar Baser. 2019. Independence Referendums and Nationalist Rhetoric: The Kurdistan Region of Iraq. *Third World Quarterly* 40 (11): 2016–2034.
Owtram, Francis. 2011. The Foreign Policies of Unrecognized States. In *Unrecognized States in the International System*, ed. Nina Caspersen and Gareth Stansfield, 128–144. Abingdon: Routledge.

———. 2017a. Oil. In *the Kurds, and the Drive for Independence: An Ace in the Hole or Joker in the Pack? In Iraqi Kurdistan in Middle Eastern Politics*, ed. Alex Danilovich, 99–120. Abingdon: Routledge.

———. 2017b. The Kurdistan Region of Iraq and the Federal Constitution: A Perimeter Plinth of State Territorial Integrity or a Stepping Stone to Secession? In *The Kurdish Question Revisited*, ed. Gareth Stansfield and Mohammed Shareef, 521–532. London: Hurst.

———. 2019a. From Shotgun Marriage to Amicable Divorce? The Kurdistan Region of Iraq: Self-Determination, Secession and Recognition in Comparative Perspective. In *Federalism, Secession, and International Recognition Regime: Iraqi Kurdistan*, ed. Alex Danilovich, 72–90. Abingdon: Routledge.

———. 2019b. The State We're in: Postcolonial Sequestration and the Kurdish Quest for Independence since the First World War. In *Routledge Handbook on the Kurds*, ed. Michael Gunter, 299–317. Abingdon: Routledge.

———. 2019c. 'No Friends But the Mountains': The Toxic Legacy of British Officialdom for the Kurds After the First World War. *LSE Middle East Centre blog*, March 5. Accessed January 30, 2022. https://blogs.lse.ac.uk/mec/2019/10/15/no-friends-but-the-mountains-the-toxic-legacy-of-british-officialdom-for-the-kurds-after-the-first-world-war/.

———. Forthcoming, 2023. *The Kurdish Quest for Independence since the First World War: The Struggle for Identity, Autonomy, and State Sovereignty*. London: IB Tauris.

Palani, Kamaran, Jaafar Khidir, Mark Dechesne, and Edwin Bakker. 2019. The Development of Kurdistan's de Facto Statehood: Kurdistan's September 2017 Referendum for Independence. *Third World Quarterly* 40 (12): 2270–2288.

Park, William, Joost Jongerden, Francis Owtram, and Akiko Yoshioka. 2017. Field Notes: On the Independence Referendum in the Kurdistan Region of Iraq and Disputed Territories in 2017. *Kurdish Studies* 5 (20): 199–214.

Pavković, Aleksandar. 2015. Secession and Secessionism. *H-Net Monthly Series*, October 20. Accessed January 30, 2022. https://networks.h-net.org/node/3911/discussions/90459/secessionism-and-separatism-monthly-series-secession-and.

Pavković, Alexandar, and Peter Radan. 2012. *Creating New States: Theory and Practice of Secession*. Farnham: Ashgate.

Riegl, Martin, Bohumil Doboš, Jakub Landovský, and Shmuel Bar. 2017. Kurdistan Region's Quest for Independent Statehood: Trapped in Internal and Geopolitical Rivalries. In *Unrecognized States and Secession in the 21st Century*, ed. Martin Riegl and Bohumil Doboš, 153–168. Cham: Springer International Publishing.

Romano, David. 2020. Sub-state Actors and Foreign Policy Risk-Taking. The Kurdistan Regional Government of Iraq. *Kurdish Studies* 8 (2): 339–369.

Sadoon, Hajar. 2020. *The Kurdish De Facto State: Foreign Policy Transitions and Trends*. Erbil: Salahaddin University Press.

Schiavon, Jorge. 2019. *Comparative Paradiplomacy*. Abingdon: Routledge.
Seyder, Ferhad I. 2017. The Iraqi Kurds: Historical Backgrounds of a Nonstate Nation. In *Between State and Non-State: Politics and Society in Kurdistan-Iraq and Palestine*, ed. Gülistan Gürbey, Sabine Hofmann, and Ferhad I. Seyder, 25–41. New York: Palgrave Macmillan.
Shamsi, Pishko. 2020. The Kurdistan Region of Iraq After the Failure of the 2017 Independence Referendum. Foreign Policy Research Institute. Accessed January 30, 2022. https://www.fpri.org/wp-content/uploads/2020/04/iraq-vol-2.pdf.
Sharif, Shkow. 2018. The Hero's Rock: When the Kurds Rebelled. *Asian and African Studies blog*, January 19. Accessed January 30, 2022. https://blogs.bl.uk/asian-and-african/2018/01/the-heros-rock-when-the-kurds-rebelled.html.
Stansfield, Gareth. 2003. *Iraqi Kurdistan: Political Development and Emergent Democracy*. Abingdon: Routledge.
———. 2017. The Evolution of the Political System of the Kurdistan Region of Iraq. In *Between State and Non-State: Politics and Society in Kurdistan-Iraq and Palestine*, ed. Gülistan Gürbey, Sabine Hofmann, and Ferhad I. Seyder, 61–76. New York: Palgrave Macmillan.
———. 2019. Segmentation of Political Parties in Underdeveloped Contexts—The Case of the Kurds. In *The Kurds in a Changing Middle East: History, Politics and Representation*, ed. Faleh A. Jabar and Renad Mansour, 68–85. London: I.B. Tauris & Co. Ltd.
———. 2021. The Kurdistan Region of Iraq, 1991–2018. In *The Cambridge History of the Kurds*, ed. Hamit Bozarslan, Cengiz Gunes, and Veli Yadirgi, 362–381. Cambridge: Cambridge University Press.
Stern, Geoffrey. 2000. *The Structure of International Society: An Introduction to the Study of International Relations*. London: Continuum International Publishing Group.
Tilly, Charles. 1975. Reflections on the History of European State-Making. In *The Formation of National States in Western Europe*, ed. Charles Tilly, 42. Princeton: Princeton University Press.
United Nations Organisation. 2017. Security Council Press Statement on Iraq. Accessed April 1, 2022. https://www.un.org/press/en/2017/sc13002.doc.htm.
Wolff, Stefan. 2007. Paradiplomacy: Scope, Opportunities and Challenges. *The Bologna Center of International Affairs* 10 (1): 141–150.
Zadeh, Yoosef Abbas, and Sherko Kirmanji. 2017. The Para-Diplomacy of the Kurdistan Region in Iraq and the Kurdish Statehood Enterprise. *Middle East Journal* 71 (4): 587–606.

CHAPTER 3

The Evolution of Palestine's Paradiplomacy: Causes and Constraints

Mkhaimar Abusada

THE EMERGENCE OF ARMED STRUGGLE AND PARADIPLOMACY IN PALESTINE

The most important step by the Palestinians after the Nakba (Catastrophe) in 1948 was the establishment of the Palestine Liberation Organization (PLO) in May 1964. The PLO was originally dedicated to the destruction of Israel and the establishment of an independent Palestinian state on all of historic Palestine through armed struggle. However, the PLO found itself in a more complicated political situation after Israel seized control of the West Bank and Gaza in the June 1967 war. Israel gained total control over all the territory that was designed by the United Nations General Assembly (UNGA) for the Palestine State. The UNGA Resolution No. 181, passed on November 29, 1947, called for the partition of Palestine into two states: a Jewish state and an Arab state.

The Zionist movement accepted the UNGA partition plan; however, the Palestinians rejected it. The partition resolution was in favor of the

---

M. Abusada (✉)
Department of Political Science, Al-Azhar University-Gaza, Gaza City, Palestine
e-mail: m.abusada@alazhar.edu.ps

© The Author(s), under exclusive license to Springer Nature
Switzerland AG 2023
G. Gürbey et al. (eds.), *Between Diplomacy and Non-Diplomacy*,
https://doi.org/10.1007/978-3-031-09756-0_3

Jews who were a minority in Palestine at that time. According to many historians and United Nations (UN) agencies, they estimated that "at the beginning of 1947 Palestinians numbered 1.3 million, compared with a Jewish population of 600.000. The latter [Jews] owned only 6–7 percent of the total land area. Nevertheless, the partition plan awarded the Jewish state the larger portion" (Bill and Springborg 1990, 308). The partition plan meant that a significant percentage (approximately 40 percent) of the Palestinians were to live under Jewish rule or to be evacuated from their homes and villages. The partition plan also awarded the most fertile coastal plains to the Jewish state (Khalidi 1992, 61–62). The United States (US) under direct Jewish lobbying urged several UN members to vote for the partition (Smith 1988, 139).

The Establishment of the Palestine Liberation Organization

The early days of Palestinian armed struggle were inspired by national liberation movements in the 1960s and 1970s, for example, the Algerian and the Vietnamese revolutions. It was also inspired by Pan-Arabism led by Egyptian President Gamal Abdel Nasser. The PLO was established in 1964 and has been the embodiment of the Palestinian national movement. It is a broad national front, or an umbrella organization, comprised of numerous organizations of the resistance movement, political parties, popular organizations, and independent personalities and figures from all sectors of life (Abusada 2017, 198–199).

The establishment of the PLO was sponsored by the Arab League at its summit meeting in January 1964. In May 1964, a Palestinian conference was convened in Jerusalem with many prominent Palestinian political activists led by Ahmad Shuqairi,[1] and at the end of their meeting, they declared the establishment of the PLO. Ahmad Shuqairi was the first chairman of the PLO Executive Committee from 1964 to 1967 (Abunahel and Abusada 2009, 23–25). In 1967, he was replaced by Yahia Hammuda. Yasser Arafat occupied the position from 1969 until his death in 2004, when he was succeeded by Mahmoud Abbas.

---

[1] Ahmad Shuqairi convened the Palestinian Conference in Jerusalem with support from President Gamal Abdel Nasser of Egypt. Shuqairi became the first chairman of the PLO until his resignation in December 1967.

Many Arab countries supported the creation of the PLO to speak on behalf of the Palestinian people after the Nakba. Egyptian support for the creation of the PLO was detrimental for its political survival amid Arab rivalries. Walid Khalidi asserts that "the very creation of the PLO reflected the Palestinian shift in orientation from pan-Arab to a more particularistic self-image" (Khalidi 1992, 8). However, Mark Tessler argues that the Arab primary purpose in creating the PLO "was not to give expression to Palestinian desires for self-determination. It was rather to co-opt and restrain the Palestinian resistance Movement" (Tessler 1994, 374). Michael Hudson asserts that "From the Spring of 1968 until the Fall of 1970, the guerrillas [PLO factions] developed the capacity to carry out serious protracted violence against Israel. The guerrilla organizations themselves became more elaborate structurally and began to develop important political functions of a nation-building character" (Hudson 1972, 64).

The PLO consisted of three main political institutions, the most important among them is the Palestine National Council (PNC) established in 1964. The PNC is the highest decision-making body of the PLO, and is considered to be the parliament of all Palestinians inside and outside of the Palestinian territories, including East Jerusalem. The PNC normally sets PLO policies, elects members of the Executive Committee, and makes the necessary changes in its own membership, as well as changes to the Palestine National Charter. The composition of the PNC represents all sectors of the Palestinian community worldwide and includes numerous organizations of the resistance movement, political parties, popular organizations, and independent personalities and figures from all sectors of life, including intellectuals, religious leaders, and businessmen (Permanent Observer Mission of the State of Palestine to the United Nations, New York 2021).

The Central Council, which was established by the PNC in 1973, is the second leading body of the PLO. The council functions as an intermediary body between the PNC and the Executive Committee. The Central Council serves as a mini parliament, when the PNC cannot convene. The PNC in its meeting in September 2018 assigned and mandated all of its responsibilities to the Central Council. At present, the number of members of the Central Council stands at 124.

The Executive Committee, the third most important body within the PLO, was also established in 1964. The Executive Committee is the daily leading body of the PLO (therefore the de facto government) and it represents the organization at the international level. Members of the Executive Committee are elected by the PNC, and it is also responsible to the PNC. Its main function is to execute the policies and decisions set out by the PNC and the Central Council. The committee is also responsible for adopting a budget and for overseeing the functioning of the departments of the PLO, the responsibilities of the Executive Committee are distributed among its members. Decisions of the committee are taken by a simple majority. The number of its members stands at 18, including its chairman.

The Executive Committee established a number of departments to oversee day-to-day business and politics of the Palestinians. The PLO established the Political Department to run foreign relations regionally and internationally. The Political Department succeeded in forming foreign relations with almost all Arab countries after the Arab League recognized the PLO as the sole legitimate representative of the Palestinians in 1974. It has also succeeded in establishing relations with foreign countries, mainly China, former the Soviet Union, and East European countries in the 1970s and 1980s (Twam 2013, 35–38).

Following the defeat of the Arab armies in 1967 and the Israeli occupation of the West Bank and Gaza Strip, and other Arab land, the UN and the international community sought to solve the Arab-Israeli conflict peacefully. Six months after the June 1967 War and after intense diplomacy and consultations among members of the UN Security Council (UNSC), the UNSC Resolution 242, which was introduced by the British ambassador to the UNSC, was passed.

The UNSC Resolution 242 has since become the focus of any peaceful solution to the Arab-Israeli conflict, including the Palestinians'. One of the most disputed provisions of the resolution is the "withdrawal of Israel armed forces from territories occupied in the recent conflict" (UNSC 1967). The Arab countries and the Palestinians have insisted that Israel must withdraw completely from all the territories occupied in the 1967 war, a position still held by the Arab League in the Arab Peace Initiative adopted by all Arab states in the Arab Summit in Beirut in 2002. However, Israel, supported by the US, has insisted that the UNSC resolution calls for Israel to withdraw, but not from all the territories. The vagueness of the UNSC resolution was intended to persuade all parties in the conflict to support it.

The consequences of the 1967 War led to the resignation of the first chairman of the PLO, Ahmad Shuqairi, in December 1967. The post-1967

War era saw an intense Palestinian activity to restructure the PLO and their struggle against Israel. In February 1969, during the Fifth Palestinian National Council (PNC) which served as a parliament for the PLO, Yasser Arafat was elected the new chairman of the PLO. Under Arafat's leadership, the PLO was restructured and included many Palestinian factions, namely Fatah, the Popular Front for the Liberation of Palestine (PFLP), the Democratic Front for the Liberation of Palestine (DFLP), and other factions who empowered and solidified the legitimacy and effectiveness of the PLO among the Palestinians and regionally. Palestinian factions "amended the PLO charter to specifically include armed struggle as the only means of total liberation" (Khalidi 1992, 8). It is hard to speak about Palestinian paradiplomacy before the creation of the PLO in 1964. Rashad Twam states that the most important achievement of the Palestinians before 1964 was Palestinian public diplomacy which led to the creation of the PLO. Nasser Al-Qidwa believes that the roots of Palestinian official diplomacy were seen in the late 1960s, and what took place before that were revolutionary activities in external relations, but cannot be described diplomacy (Twam 2013, 33).

Ahmad Shuqairi, the first chairman of the PLO, did not believe much in diplomacy, and dedicated his political activity to armed struggle. It was Fatah movement, who sent a letter to the UN Secretary General in June 1965, requesting to be part of any UN deliberations concerning the Palestinian issue (Cobban 1984, 216). China was the first non-Arab country to recognize the PLO in the mid-1960s. In addition, Yasser Arafat made his first visit to the Soviet Union in 1968, which led to financial Soviet support to the PLO and the establishment of a Palestinian diplomatic mission in the mid-1970s (Cobban 1984, 221–222).

PLO Paradiplomacy Between 1974 and 1987

The PLO under Yasser Arafat adopted the first diplomatic move from its viewpoint toward the Palestinian-Israeli conflict in 1969: the establishment of a secular and democratic Palestine for all Palestinians and Israeli Jews (Abunahel, Abusada, and Abdul-Wahed 2012, 43–48), but that initiative was not even considered by the international community who adopted the two-state solution since 1947, the partition plan. But a breakthrough in the Arab-Israeli conflict came after the October 1973 (Yom Kippur) War.

On October 6, 1973, Egypt and Syria launched coordinated attacks on Israeli military units in the Sinai Peninsula and the Golan Heights.[2] Although the war did not achieve significant military victories for either side, it created an atmosphere for a political solution to the Arab-Israeli conflict. After the war, US Secretary of State, Henry Kissinger, was engaged in a very active diplomacy to bring both Egypt and Israel to the negotiating table. After intensive and hard bargaining by Kissinger, Egypt and Israel signed the first disengagement agreement in January 1974, and the first Arab-Israeli peace treaty between Egypt and Israel (Camp David Accords) were signed in September 1978.

Following the failure of the armies of Egypt and Syria to defeat Israel in October 1973 War, which broke the status quo existing since June 1967, the PLO began formulating a strategic diplomatic alternative that is based on a political solution to the Palestinian-Israeli conflict—an alternative which is compatible with the two-state solution and based on the partition plan of 1947. The partition plan was the backbone of PLO's paradiplomacy in the 1970s. The PLO intended to establish a "national authority" over any Palestinian territory that can be liberated from the Israeli occupation. The PNC held its 12th meeting in Cairo and on June 8, 1974, the Ten Point Program was adopted. The Program stated:

> The Palestine Liberation Organization will employ all means, and first and foremost armed struggle, to liberate Palestinian territory and to establish the independent combatant national authority for the people over every part of Palestinian territory that is liberated. This will require further changes being affected in the balance of power in favor of our people and their struggle. (The PNC Program 1974)

By "every part of Palestinian territory that is liberated" was implicitly meant the West Bank and Gaza Strip. While clinging to armed struggle as the prime means, the PLO no longer excluded peaceful and diplomatic means. Therefore, the Ten Point Program was considered the first serious attempt by the PLO at a peaceful resolution. In response to the adoption of the Ten Point Program, the Arab League recognized the PLO as "the sole legitimate representative of the Palestinian people" in October 1974, and also the UN recognized the PLO and Yasser Arafat, chairman of the

---

[2] The Egyptian Sinai Peninsula and the Syrian Golan Heights were occupied by Israel in the 1967 War.

PLO, was invited to deliver a speech at the UNGA (Abunahel, Abusada, and Abdul-Wahed 2012, 129–131). In the same year, the PLO also received full membership at the Islamic Conference Organization on February 22, and recognition by the Arab League on October 28 (Abusada 2017, 200). It is safe to say that a diplomatic gate was opened to the PLO regionally and internationally. On the other hand, the program was rejected by the more radical Palestinian factions, mainly the PFLP, and eventually caused a split in the PLO.

The single most important diplomatic move by the PLO in the 1970s was its adoption of the Ten Point Program, which paved the road toward regional and international recognition of the PLO. The Ten Point Plan contained clauses which were widely interpreted by the Arab states and the UN that the PLO would settle for the creation of a Palestinian state in the West Bank and Gaza Strip, the territory which was occupied by Israel in 1967 (Abusada 2017, 200). But that was not enough to Israel who considered the PLO a terrorist organization and embarked on building illegal Jewish settlements in these occupied territories. On the other hand, the PLO, at this point, refused to enter peace negotiations on the precondition of recognizing Israel and UNSC Resolution 242. The PLO explicitly rejected Resolution 242 at its PNC meeting in June 1974:

> The PNC reaffirm the Palestine Liberation Organization's previous attitude to Resolution 242, which obliterates the national right of our people and deals with the cause of our people as a problem of refugees. The Council therefore refuses to have anything to do with this resolution at any level, Arab or international, including the Geneva Conference. (The PNC Program 1974)

Although the Palestinians and the PLO made considerable concessions in the Ten Point Program, they were not part of the Camp David Accords. The US conditioned the PLO's participation in the Camp David peace negotiations on its recognition of Israel and acceptance of UNSC Resolution 242. The PLO had for long rejected it, because it deals with the Palestinians only as a refugee problem that needs to be solved on humanitarian basis and not as a political issue. The resolution did not mention the right of Palestinians to self-determination, or their right to establish their own independent state.

There are many Palestinians and others who classify this period as the golden era of Palestinian paradiplomacy. During this period, the PLO scored a number of achievements politically and militarily. The PLO succeeded in extracting regional and international recognition as the sole legitimate representative of the Palestinians, but also strengthened its strategic relationship with China and the Soviet Union (Twam 2013, 42). The Soviet Union invited the PLO to inaugurate the opening of its mission in Moscow in September 1974 (Sayigh 2003, 494–496). Rashad Twam indicates that Yasser Arafat instructed PLO diplomats to initiate contacts with American personalities indicating the PLO's readiness for negotiations (Twam 2013, 43).

However, Israel was and has been determined to retain the West Bank which is considered part of the biblical land of Israel and was not prepared to acknowledge the right of the Palestinians to self-determination. The Camp David Accords proposed self-autonomy to the Palestinians in the West Bank and Gaza, but under Israeli control and sovereignty. Contrary to Israeli ambitions, the autonomy plan failed due to Palestinian opposition. Furthermore, the co-architect of the autonomy plan, Egyptian president Anwar Sadat, was assassinated in October 1981. But the signing of the first Arab-Israeli peace treaty which neutralized the most powerful Arab country left no doubts among leading elements within the PLO to envision a diplomatic road to self-determination.

PLO Paradiplomacy Between 1987 and 1993

Even though Palestinian paradiplomacy in the 1970s and early 1980s could not break the stalemate because of Israeli and American refusal to engage the PLO, however, a breakthrough in Palestinian diplomacy was made after the eruption of the first Palestinian uprising (Intifada) in the West Bank and Gaza and paved the road for the PLO in November 1988 to declare the establishment of the state of Palestine in the 1967 territory and recognize UNSC Resolution 242, which calls for the right of all states in the region to live in peace and security.

In 1987, the Palestinian First Intifada broke out in the West Bank and Gaza Strip. The Intifada's massive protests caught both Israel and the PLO by surprise, and the leadership of the PLO abroad could only indirectly influence the events. On December 8, 1987, spontaneous and widespread protests erupted against the Israeli Army in Gaza following a car accident between an Israeli truck and a Palestinian vehicle full of laborers, which took their lives, and the Palestinians accused the truck driver of intentionally killing them. The protests spread out to the West Bank in the following days. In the following weeks and months, what started as spontaneous protests took the form of organized and coordinated resistance.

A new Palestinian local leadership emerged, the Unified National Leadership of the Uprising (UNLU), comprising many leading PLO factions, but not Hamas who was not part of the UNLU. The eruption of the Intifada led King Hussein of Jordan to declare the cessation of administrative and legal relations with the West Bank from Jordan in 1988.[3] The outbreak of the Intifada and the decision by Jordan to legally cease its relationship to the West Bank pushed the PLO to consider a more serious and acceptable diplomatic solution to the Palestinian-Israeli conflict. The Palestinian nationalist leadership in the West Bank and Gaza sent the PLO in Tunis and its leader Yasser Arafat a clear message that the uprising [Intifada] must be translated into a political program grounded in reality (Benvenisti 1995, 97).

The PNC convened in Algiers, Algeria, in mid-November 1988 and adopted a bold diplomatic decision which was backed and supported by the Palestinians in the Occupied Territories. The PNC declared the PLO's readiness to negotiate with Israel on the bases of all UN resolutions and proclaimed the Declaration of Independence, declaring an independent State of Palestine. Arafat announced the PLO's acceptance of UN Resolutions 242 and 338, which granted Israel a window to secure and recognized boundaries. A month later, Arafat declared in Geneva that the PLO would support a solution to the conflict based on these resolutions. Effectively, the PLO recognized Israel's right to exist within pre-1967 borders, with the understanding that the Palestinians would be allowed to set up their own state in the West Bank and Gaza. The US accepted this clarification by Arafat and began diplomatic contacts with PLO officials.

Although the Declaration of Independence did not lead to statehood, over 120 states recognized the State of Palestine, and above all the US opened dialogue with the PLO in late 1988 (Abusada 2017, 204). The US which sponsored the Camp David Accords between Egypt and Israel was a key to any future negotiations between the PLO and Israel. The Soviet Union at that time was suffering from internal problems and the

---

[3] Jordan annexed the West Bank in 1950 in the aftermath of the Palestinian Nakba in 1948. The West Bank which includes East Jerusalem is the home of the third holiest shrine in Islam, Al-Aqsa Mosque, and the home of many Christian (Church of Resurrection) and Jewish holy places. Jordan had competed with the PLO on the political representation of the Palestinians until 1988.

backlash of its invasion of Afghanistan in 1979. The Soviet Union and East European countries helped and supported the PLO politically and militarily, but they were not capable of mediating between Israel and the PLO.

The eruption of the First Intifada and the scenes of Israeli brutality against Palestinian civilian protesters brought international condemnation against Israel. There was growing pressure from the international community to push for peace talks with the Palestinians. But the Iraqi invasion of Kuwait on August 2, 1990, shifted world attention from the Intifada to the Persian Gulf. Iraqi leader Saddam Hussein refused to withdraw from Kuwait until Israel withdraws from occupied Palestinian land. Although the US and the international community refused to equate the two cases of occupation, the US promised to put more efforts to solve the Palestinian-Israeli conflict.

In the aftermath of the liberation of Kuwait and following intense bargaining and diplomacy by US Secretary of State James Baker III, the US sent invitations to all parties of the conflict in the Middle East to attend and participate in the international peace conference in Madrid, Spain, in late October 1991. The PLO was not invited by the US, but a Palestinian delegation from the West Bank and Gaza approved by the PLO represented the Palestinians as part of a joint Jordanian delegation (Abusada 2017, 204). However, there was no major breakthrough between the Palestinians and Israelis. Peace negotiations moved very slowly until the opening of the secret channel in Oslo in 1992.

The turning point in the Palestinian-Israeli conflict and Palestinian paradiplomacy was achieved in 1993 when the Israeli government led by the Labor Party negotiated secretly with the PLO in Oslo, Norway. Israel decided it was time for negotiations and a deal with the PLO. Israel and the PLO signed the Declaration of Principles, which aimed to peacefully resolve the Palestinian-Israeli conflict. The Oslo Accords marked the first time Israel and the PLO formally recognized one another. The Oslo Accords were signed in the White House, but named after Norway's capital city, where the secret negotiations took place. The Oslo Declaration of Principles was not a peace treaty; rather, its aim was to establish interim governance arrangements and a framework to facilitate further negotiations for a final agreement, which would be concluded by the end of 1999. The Oslo Agreement aimed at achieving a peace treaty based on UNSC Resolutions 242 and 338, and at fulfilling the right of the Palestinian people to self-determination.

The Oslo Agreement was also based on exchanged letters between Israeli Prime Minister Yitzhak Rabin and Yasser Arafat, chairman of the PLO. Arafat renounced violence and terrorism and committed the PLO to diplomatic options to reach a permanent peace agreement with Israel and recognized the right of the state of Israel to live in peace and security. Rabin responded by recognizing the PLO as the sole legitimate representative of the Palestinians. Israel, however, did not recognize the right of the Palestinians to independence and statehood. During these secret negotiations, Israel capitalized on Arafat's weakness in the wake of the Gulf War. The PLO had supported Iraq, angering many Arab and Western countries; thus, Saddam Hussein's defeat in 1991 left the PLO weakened. Arafat entered the negotiations with Israel with few options and even less clout (Palestine Remix 2015).

The Oslo Agreement was rejected by significant elements in both the Palestinian and Israeli side. Many Palestinians viewed the Oslo Agreement as a sellout to Israel. Their justification at that time was that Israel did not commit to put an end to its occupation of Palestinian land and continued to construct more settlement units for Jews on Palestinian occupied land. Mustafa Barghouti asserted that "Oslo was the greatest idea Israel ever had. It let them continue the occupation without paying any of the costs" (Palestine Remix 2015). The Israeli rejection to Oslo came from the right wing and the settlers movement who vowed to fight against it. They view the West Bank as part of the biblical land of Israel. This rejection transformed itself in the assassination of Israel's Prime Minister Rabin by a Jewish extremist opposed to the Oslo Agreement in November 1995.

Palestinian Paradiplomacy Between 1994 and 2004

The signing of the Oslo Agreement led to the establishment of the Palestinian Authority (PA). The PA is only responsible for the Palestinians in the West Bank, Gaza, and East Jerusalem, but the PLO represents the Palestinians inside and outside Palestine. Yasser Arafat and the PLO moved from Tunisia to Gaza and then to Jericho in the West Bank in July 1994, and the PA started to assume its security and civilian responsibilities toward the Palestinians, and the first Palestinian legislative and presidential elections were held in January 1996. Positive relations between the PLO and Israel were moving forward and confidence building measures were replacing decades of tension and conflict.

Yasser Arafat was elected the President of the PA in addition to his chairmanship of the PLO, and a government was sworn in and was held accountable to the parliament, the Palestinian Legislative Council (PLC). In the past, the PLO's Political Department was responsible for paradiplomacy, but now the PA established the Ministry of International Cooperation and later became the Ministry of Foreign Affairs, responsible for international relations with other countries. However, Yasser Arafat kept his grip on foreign relations and negotiations with Israel personally.

The PLO and the newly established PA continued its foreign contacts and paradiplomacy with regional countries and the international community. But disputes between the PLO's Political Department and the PA's Ministry of Foreign Affairs erupted from the beginning. Yasser Arafat decided that the Political Department will be responsible for relations with Arab and Islamic countries, and the PA's Ministry of Foreign Affairs will be responsible for international countries, mainly the US and European countries (Hammed 2010, 14). Palestinian-Israeli negotiations continued to take place with the help and support of the US and Arab countries, mainly Egypt and Jordan. Between May 1994 and 1999, five other Agreements were signed between the PLO and Israel: The Paris Economic Protocol signed in April 1994, the Gaza-Jericho Agreement signed in May 1994, Oslo II Agreement signed in September 1995, Wye River Agreement signed in October 1998, and other security arrangements to combat terror and violence in the PA-led territory.

According to the Oslo Agreement, final status issues, Jerusalem, refugees, Israeli settlements, final borders, and other issues were supposed to be finalized before May 1999. However, the assassination of Israeli Prime Minister Rabin, and the election of Benyamin Netanyahu, leader of the Likud Party who incited against Rabin and the Oslo Agreement, delayed the final status issues until Camp David talks in the summer of 2000. US President Bill Clinton and Israeli Prime Minister Ehud Barak, elected in May 1999, pushed for final status talks, but without enough preparation. After three weeks of secluded negotiations in Camp David, the US and Israel blamed Yasser Arafat for the failure of talks and accused him of rejecting a generous peace offer by Israel. The failure of the Camp David talks led later to the eruption of the violent Palestinian Second Intifada that ended with the death of Yasser Arafat, isolated and besieged in his headquarter in the city of Ramallah in the West Bank.

The ten-year period between 1994 and 2004 witnessed a very intense and bold diplomacy from the Palestinians who were eager to put an end to

Israeli occupation and move one step forward, toward the establishment of an independent and sovereign Palestinian state. Although the Oslo Agreement did not grant the Palestinians their political goals of statehood and independence, it was a monumental moment to the PLO and the Palestinians. The Oslo Agreement allowed tens of thousands of PLO fighters and their families to return to the West Bank and Gaza.

The Oslo peace process carried with it a generation of hope—of young Palestinians who were dedicated to building new hope and a new state. The Palestinians, for the first time in their modern history, were in charge of internal affairs, security, education, health, and other services. Regional and international governments inaugurated their diplomatic missions in Gaza and Ramallah, and PLO offices were upgraded to diplomatic missions in the US and European countries. Yasser Arafat was a frequent visitor at the US White House, the UK Prime Minister's Office at Downing Street 10, the Élysée Palace in France, and other European capitals.

Palestinian Paradiplomacy Between 2005 and Present

The death of Yasser Arafat and the election of a new leader, President Mahmoud Abbas in January 2005, opened new opportunities for Palestinian diplomacy. President Abbas was the architect of the Oslo Agreement in 1993; therefore, he was no stranger to Israel and Western countries. From the beginning, he vowed to restore internal security and to push for statehood for the Palestinians after years of chaos in the West Bank and Gaza resulted from the outbreak of the Second Intifada. He succeeded in convincing Hamas and other Palestinian factions to prepare the ground work for the second Palestinian legislative elections, held in January 2006, which Hamas won overwhelmingly. However, his diplomatic task just became almost impossible with the formation of a Hamas led-government, isolated and boycotted by Israel and the international community.

The internal Palestinian crisis opened the door for new diplomatic opportunities for Abbas. Friction between the PA and Hamas erupted from the early days of the establishment of the PA in mid-1994. But a dramatic shift in Palestinian politics happened after Hamas won the majority of seats in the Palestinian parliament in 2006 and PLO factions boycotted Hamas' government, which later led to internal clashes between PA security forces and al-Qassam brigades, the military wing of Hamas, and resulted in Hamas' total control of Gaza in June 2007. This has marked the beginning of Palestinian political division, which till now has been almost impossible to resolve.

The Palestinian political split encouraged the US government to convene the Annapolis peace conference in November 2007. Palestinian-Israeli negotiations moved forward and tackled the most contentious issues like Jerusalem, refugees, Israeli settlements, and final borders. Israeli Prime Minister Ehud Olmert presented a map of proposed swapped territory between the Palestinians and Israel. Olmert proposed that "Israel was prepared to withdraw to borders very similar to the pre-1967 lines and swap areas of northern and southern Israel in return for maintaining the larger settlement blocs" (Winer 2013). However, before the completion of these negotiations, Israel waged a war against Gaza at the end of December 2008 that resulted in death and destructions, and corruption allegations against Ehud Olmert, which led to his resignation, and the election of Binyamin Netanyahu who opposed any negotiations that will lead to the two-state solution.

The election of Netanyahu who turned his back to progress made between Abbas and Olmert by insisting on expanding Israeli settlement in the West Bank and East Jerusalem, which kills the possibility of a Palestinian viable and contiguous state, left the Palestinians with limited options. President Abbas and Palestinian diplomats shifted gears and focused on waging a legal and diplomatic battle against Israel at the UN. Palestinian diplomacy under Abbas scored effectively at the UNGA by voting overwhelmingly for Palestine as an observer non-member state at the UNGA. On November 29, 2012, 138 countries voted for Palestine, more than two-third of the UN member states (Abusada 2017, 208).

The UNGA Resolution 67/19 is a resolution upgrading Palestine to non-member observer state status in the UNGA. It was adopted in the 67th session of the UNGA on the International Day of Solidarity with the Palestinian People and the 65th anniversary of the adoption of Resolution 181, the partition of Palestine into two states, by the General Assembly. The UNGA resolution came a year after Palestine obtained membership of United Nations Educational, Scientific and Cultural Organization (UNESCO). The decision was hailed as a big victory for Palestinian diplomacy internationally.

The objective of the resolution is to accord an upgraded status to the Palestinian delegation and recognizes Palestine's boundaries as they were prior to 1967. It stresses the need for the withdrawal of Israel from the Palestinian territory occupied since 1967, including East Jerusalem, and the complete cessation of all Israeli settlement activities in the Occupied Palestinian Territory, including East Jerusalem. The decision also reaffirms the right of the Palestinian people to self-determination and to independence in the State of Palestine on the Palestinian territory occupied since 1967 (UNGA 2012).

The UN recognition of Palestine was later followed by accepting Palestine's membership in many UN agencies and organs, including the International Criminal Court (ICC) in 2015 (Abusada 2017, 209). Palestine became a member of the ICC on April 1, 2015. By joining the ICC, Palestinian leaders hoped to increase their political leverage by threatening to bring charges against Israeli officials for war crimes committed in the Occupied Territories. The decision to join the ICC has been greeted with delight by many in the region but was rejected by Israel and the US. A total of 69 Members of the European Parliament have hailed Palestine's accession to the ICC, describing it as a "historic moment in the Palestinian people's struggle for justice, freedom and peace" (Middle East Policy Council 2015).

Palestine's membership in the ICC has opened the door for the PA and Palestinian human rights groups to initiate legal cases against Israeli war crimes and crimes against humanity. The ex-ICC prosecutor Fatou Bensouda had already opened preliminary investigation of these crimes. On February 5, 2021, the chamber decided, by a majority, that the ICC may exercise its criminal jurisdiction in the situation in Palestine, and that the territorial scope of this jurisdiction extends to Gaza and the West Bank, including East Jerusalem. On March 3, 2021, she announced that the investigation will cover crimes within the jurisdiction of the court that are alleged to have been committed since June 13, 2014, the date to which reference is made in the Referral of the Situation to her Office (International Criminal Court 2021).

Palestine's legal and diplomatic battle against Israel's occupation of Palestinian land and illegal settlement activities has just begun. It is expected that many Israeli leaders and army generals will not be able to travel outside Israel. Israel has expressed its anger toward this move by suspending sporadically the transfer of PA money (customs and taxes collected by Israel on behalf of the PA). Additionally, Israeli Prime Minister Naftali Bennett announced on September 4, 2021, that he would not meet with PA President Mahmoud Abbas because he took Israel to the ICC on charges of war crimes (Middle East Monitor 2021).

CONSTRAINTS AND IMPEDIMENTS FACED BY PALESTINIAN PARADIPLOMACY

The most important hurdle affecting PLO paradiplomacy was internal Palestinian divisions. The PLO contained many Palestinian factions, some of the factions adhered to Marxist-Leninist ideology (e.g., PFLP, DFLP), other factions subscribed to Pan-Arabism, and other factions (Hamas and the Islamic Jihad who are not members of the PLO) subscribe to Islamic ideology. They do not differ on the goal of liberating Palestine, but they have disagreed on the tools and means to reach that goal (Abunahel, Abusada, and Abdul-Wahed 2012, 34). The diverging political ideologies of Palestinian factions made it difficult for the PLO to pursue consistent and stable foreign relations. What made things worse was that some of the Palestinian factions were satellites of Arab regimes in Syria, Iraq, and Libya, and there was also an Arab Cold War parallel to the global Cold War (Kerr 1971). By the way, regional Arab rivalries have continued to this date. The region has been divided lately between the so-called resistance camp led by Iran and its allies, and the moderate camp led by Egypt and Saudi Arabia.

Internal Palestinian divisions have paralyzed the PLO and crippled its ability to pursue serious diplomatic initiatives. For example, after the PLO adopted the Ten Point Program, a number of Palestinian factions, mainly PFLP, suspended their membership in the PLO, protesting the new road of the PLO exemplified in the Ten Point Program which accepted the establishment of a Palestinian Authority on any liberated part of Palestine. Some of the Palestinian factions (Abu Nidal) sponsored by Iraq and Libya assassinated prominent and senior members of the PLO accused of meeting with the Israeli left in the 1970s and 1980s (Seale 1992).

However, internal divisions among the Palestinians went to a higher level after the founding of Hamas in the late 1980s. Divisions between nationalism and Islam highly escalated after the signing of the Oslo Agreement in September 1993 between the PLO and Israel and the establishment of the PA in 1994. Hamas' opposition to the Oslo Agreement stems from the fact that it views PA's self-rule as more dangerous than the Israeli occupation; for Hamas, PA's self-rule is a reorganization of the occupation in a way that is more comfortable to the Israelis. Hamas has continuously described the PA as subcontractor of the Israeli occupation to deliver security to Israel and municipal services to the Palestinians. The Oslo Agreement does not give the Palestinians the right to establish an independent sovereign state. The agreement also fell short of full recognition of the political rights of the Palestinians. Moreover, Israel has not abandoned its territorial claims over the West Bank and East Jerusalem.

Hamas has rejected the Oslo Accords and vowed from the beginning to fight against it. Hamas decided to sabotage the Oslo Agreement and the PA through suicide bombings and military resistance against Israel. Hamas exploited the Second Palestinian Intifada for its own interests. When the second Palestinian legislative elections were held in the West Bank and Gaza in January 2006, Hamas swept the legislative elections and won a landslide victory against the ruling party Fatah. Palestinian internal relations went from bad to worse after deadly clashes between Hamas and Fatah loyalists in the Gaza Strip in the summer of 2007, which led to Hamas' total control of Gaza and expelled the PA and its institutions to the West Bank. From 2006 until the present time, Hamas has been competing with the PLO and the PA on Palestinian political representation. Israel has exploited the internal Palestinian divide to discredit the PLO and the PA and claim that there is no Palestinian partner to pursue peace with.

The Arab rivalries also constrained the ability of the PLO to construct a coherent diplomacy. Jordan, which annexed the Palestinian West Bank between 1950 and 1967, competed with the PLO to represent the Palestinians and was suspicious of Palestinian leaders, particularly Yasser Arafat, who battled the Jordanian Army in a bloody civil war in Jordan in 1970. Arafat's relationship with the Syrian regime was also antagonistic after the PLO's departure from Beirut in 1982. It is worth noting that the PLO political institutions and fighters were hosted on Arab land, first in Jordan, then Lebanon and Syria, and after 1982, the PLO moved its headquarter to Tunisia. Therefore, the PLO lacked the sovereignty they experienced in Lebanon to implement its policies and strategies. The PLO came under direct Arab pressure, and Arab interference in PLO's decisions and policies became more apparent in the 1980s. The Arab sponsorship of some Palestinian factions was also to discredit the PLO and its ability to represent the Palestinians. Jordan resisted PLO representation until 1974, when the Arab League recognized the PLO as the sole legitimate representative of the Palestinians. Part of the Arab sponsorship of Palestinian factions was also to deprive the PLO from reaching a separate peace deal with Israel without Arab acknowledgment. Iraq, Syria, and Libya sabotaged the PLO's moderation in the 1980s, by sponsoring the Abu Nidal group who was responsible for assassinating key Palestinian moderate figures. These assassinations crippled the PLO capacities to engage with the Israeli left.

Another constraint to Palestinian paradiplomacy was American and Israeli reaction to PLO's moderation which came very late. The American administration decided to engage with the Palestinians only after the PLO recognized UNSC Resolutions 242 and 338 in December 1988. The US engagement with the PLO was characterized by reluctance and fear from the Israeli right. The US assumed the role of mediator between the Palestinians and Israeli after the Madrid Peace Conference of 1991. The Americans opened direct contacts with the PLO only after Israel negotiated secretly with the PLO in Oslo and signed the Declaration of Principles in September 1993.

European countries played a more positive role toward the political aspirations of the Palestinians. The European Community (EC) issued the Venice Declaration in June 1980 which presented a framework for a comprehensive solution to the Arab-Israeli conflict. Fifteen months earlier, Egypt and Israel had signed their bilateral peace treaty. The EC promoted a broader agreement between the parties to the conflict and specifically elevated Palestinian rights, above what they were defined in the 1978 Camp David Accords. The EC called for "recognition of the legitimate rights of the Palestinian people, a just solution to the Palestinian problem, their right to self-determination and for the PLO to be associated with the negotiations" (European Community 1980). The Venice Declaration helped the PLO to open political contacts with many European governments.

Conclusion

Palestinian paradiplomacy has faced many successes and failures. The most important success was the recognition of the PLO as the sole legitimate representative of the Palestinians in 1974. This recognition opened the door for the PLO to formally establish relations with many regional and international countries. In addition, the Palestinians succeeded in keeping their cause on the regional and international agenda. The UN recognition of Palestine as an observer state at the UNGA is an urgent reminder to the international community that the Palestinian cause needs to be resolved.

But the sad part of the Palestinian struggle is that they have paid a very heavy price since 1948. They have utilized armed resistance and paradiplomacy, but they have not succeeded so far to put an end to the Israeli occupation of their land and to establish an independent state. Palestinian divisions and Arab meddling have obstructed Palestinian paradiplomacy; however, the international community is to be blamed for its dysfunctional resolutions and double-standards policies.

REFERENCES

Abunahel, Osama, and Mkhaimar Abusada. 2009. The Creation of the Palestine Liberation Organization between Arab Interests and Palestinian Ambition: A New Reading. *Journal of Al-Azhar University* 11: 1–136. (In Arabic).

Abunahel, Osama, Mkhaimar Abusada, and Maher Abdul-Wahed. 2012. The Impact of Political Changes on the Belief Structure and Policies of the P.L.O from 1968–1974. Annals of the Arts and Social Sciences 33: 1–180. (In Arabic).

Abusada, Mkhaimar. 2017. Palestinian Diplomacy: Past and Present. In *Between State and Non-State: politics and society in Kurdistan-Iraq and Palestine*, ed. Gülistan Gürbey, Sabine Hofmann, and Ferhat I. Seyder, 197–212. New York: Palgrave Macmillan.

Benvenisti, Meron. 1995. *Intimate Enemies: Jews and Arabs in a Shared Land*. Berkeley: University of California Press.

Bill, James A., and Robert Springborg. 1990. *Politics in the Middle East*. New York: HarperCollins.

Cobban, Helena. 1984. *The Palestinian Liberation Organization: People, Power, and Politics*. Cambridge: Cambridge University Press.

European Community (EC). 1980. Venice Declaration on the ME Concerning Inclusion of PLO in Negotiations. Accessed 29 March 2022. https://israeled.org/resources/documents/venice-declaration-concerning-inclusion-plo-negotiations/.

Hammed, Dalal B. 2010. *Palestinian Public Diplomacy After Second Legislative Elections*. Unpublished Master Thesis, Birzeit University. (In Arabic).

Hudson, Michael. 1972. Developments and Setbacks in the Palestinian Resistance Movement 1967–1971. *Journal of Palestine Studies* 1 (3): 64–84. https://doi.org/10.2307/2535867.

International Criminal Court (ICC). 2021. Statement of ICC Prosecutor, Fatou Bensouda, respecting an investigation of the Situation in Palestine. Accessed 11 March 2022. https://www.icc-cpi.int/Pages/item.aspx?name=210303-prosecutor-statement-investigation-palestine.

Kerr, Malcolm H. 1971. *The Arab Cold War: Gamal 'Abd al-Nasir and His Rivals, 1958–1970*. London: Oxford University Press.

Khalidi, Walid. 1992. *Palestine Reborn*. London: I. B. Tauris & Co.

Middle East Monitor. 2021. Bennett Won't Meet Abbas Because He Took Israel to ICC. September 4. Accessed 11 March 2022. https://www.middleeastmonitor.com/20210904-bennett-wont-meet-abbas-because-he-took-israel-to-icc/.

Middle East Policy Council. 2015. Accessed 12 March 2022. https://mepc.org/commentary/palestine-joins-international-criminal-court.
Palestine Remix. 2015. The Price of Oslo. Accessed 3 March 2022. https://interactive.aljazeera.com/aje/palestineremix/the-price-of-oslo.html#/14.
Permanent Observer Mission of the State of Palestine to the United Nations: New York. 2021. Palestine Liberation Organization. Accessed 3 March 2022. https://palestineun.org/about-palestine/palestine-liberation-organization.
Sayigh, Yezid. 2003. *Armed Struggle and the Search for State: The Palestinian National Movement, 1949–1993*. Beirut: Institute for Palestine Studies.
Seale, Patrick. 1992. *Abu Nidal: A Gun for Hire*. New York: Random House.
Smith, Charles D. 1988. *Palestine and the Arab-Israeli Conflict*. New York: St. Martin's Press.
Tessler, Mark. 1994. *A History of the Israeli-Palestinian Conflict*. Bloomington: Indiana University Press.
The PNC Program. 1974. Accessed 20 February 2022. http://www.mideastweb.org/plo1974.htm.
Twam, Rashad. 2013. *Diplomacy of National Liberation: The Palestinian Experience*. Ramallah: Ibrahim Abu-Lughod Institute of International Studies. (In Arabic).
United Nations General Assembly (UNGA). 2012. Resolution 67/19. Status of Palestine in the United Nations. Accessed 27 March 2021. https://www.un.org/ga/search/view_doc.asp?symbol=A/RES/67/19.
United Nations Security Council (UNSC). 1967. Resolution S/RES/242. Accessed 21 April 2022. https://undocs.org/Home/Mobile?FinalSymbol=S%2FRES%2F242(1967)&Language=E&DeviceType=Desktop&LangRequested=False.
Winer, Stuart. 2013. Hand-Drawn Map Shows What Olmert Offered for Peace. *Times of Israel*, May 23. Accessed 27 March 2022. https://www.timesofisrael.com/hand-drawn-map-shows-what-olmert-offered-for-peace/.

PART II

The Foundations of Paradiplomacy

CHAPTER 4

Legal Framework, Institutionalization, Tools, and Motives of Kurdistan Iraq's Paradiplomacy

Falah Mustafa Bakir and Sara D. Mustafa

INTRODUCTION

In recent decades, the practice of paradiplomacy has witnessed an increase around the globe. Though paradiplomacy has increasingly normalized, there remain clear differences in the international relations practiced by sovereign states and that of substate actors. Whereas sovereign states have the goal of total national interest and broad state-wide objectives, regional governments have a narrower focus in comparison and operate in considerably restricted parameters. Compared to other substate actors in the Middle East, the KRG has experienced an overwhelming amount of

F. M. Bakir (✉)
The Kurdistan Region Presidency, Erbil, Kurdistan Region, Iraq

University of Kurdistan Hewlêr, Erbil, Kurdistan Region, Iraq
e-mail: falah.mustafa@presidency.krd; falah.mustafa@ukh.edu.krd

S. D. Mustafa
University of Kurdistan Hewlêr, Erbil, Kurdistan Region, Iraq
e-mail: sara.dilzar@ukh.edu.krd

© The Author(s), under exclusive license to Springer Nature Switzerland AG 2023
G. Gürbey et al. (eds.), *Between Diplomacy and Non-Diplomacy*,
https://doi.org/10.1007/978-3-031-09756-0_4

75

progress, and success, in its international and regional outreach since its establishment in 1992. This is of course owed to the Region's unique history. Attaining these international ties was no simple undertaking, especially considering the internal and external obstacles the KRG had to withstand, some of which continue.[1] It is crucial to the marginalized literature on paradiplomacy of regions in the Middle East, to present the unique developmental history of the KRG's paradiplomacy with emphasis on the objectives, obstacles, and influences behind it.

This chapter aims to demonstrate the exact driving factors behind the institutionalization of the Kurdistan Region's paradiplomacy as well as to clarify the legal framework under which it practices its international relations. By focusing on practical, and first-hand, involvement, this research will illustrate how Kurdistan Region authorities in Iraq, and its representations abroad, work together to develop the KRG's international outreach.

The Process of Institutionalization and Its Driving Factors

The facilitation of the Kurdistan Region's autonomy and de facto government was born from a status of renunciation. In the aftermath of the First Gulf War in 1991, and in the wake of failed negotiations between the Ba'ath government and the Kurdish liberation movement concerning Kurdish autonomy, the then Iraqi President Saddam Hussein withdrew administrative support from, and imposed internal sanctions on, the Kurdish areas in northern Iraq; these actions came in addition to the sanctions imposed on Iraq by the United Nations (UN) (McDowall 2007). Faced with a double embargo, no budgetary support, a humanitarian crisis, and a security and administrative vacuum, the leaders of the Kurdish liberation movement were unintentionally afforded a unique opportunity

---

[1] The first cabinet of the KRG, established on July 4, 1992, had established a Ministry of Humanitarian Aid and Cooperation. The understanding at the time had been that through this Ministry the KRG would have access to the international community. The region had been left nearly destroyed after years of violence and conflict and plundering of villages and towns and the KRG sought to approach the international community through humanitarian aid. Through incoming humanitarian aid, the KRG managed to create ties with other states and establish representations abroad.

to establish de facto autonomy over Kurdish areas[2] and actualize a formalized government structure (McDowall 2007). Thirteen years later, these designated Kurdish areas and the Kurdistan Regional Government, along with its existing powers, would be formally recognized and protected in the 2005 Iraqi Constitution.

From 1992 to 2003, the KRG's primary methods of paradiplomacy involved humanitarian, economic, and commercial relations. Following the Kurdistan Region's first parliamentary elections and the creation of the Kurdistan Regional Government in 1992, the Ministry of Humanitarian Aid and Cooperation was established to allow the KRG to lobby international organizations and states for humanitarian aid. This was an essential first step in the KRG's paradiplomacy as it was through this Ministry the KRG's first extraterritorial offices were established. KRG Representation offices[3] were set up in the United States of America (US), the United Kingdom (UK), Sweden, and Belgium to lobby for aid, protection, and support.

In a region where instability, hostility, and violence are everyday themes, the KRG has recognized diplomacy as a means of development, stability, and survival. However, diplomatic ties and economic prosperity are only feasible in a peaceful and stable environment.[4] The KRG was practicing de facto autonomy surrounded by neighbors who have historically oppressed their Kurdish communities and been against Kurdish independence. Landlocked, the KRG needed to build trust with its hostile neighbors to survive. Navigating this precarious predicament required patience, pragmatic leadership, and a long-term vision focusing on securing the Kurdistan Region and the safety of all its occupants. This vision was shaped by fears of past atrocities, such as the 1980s Anfal genocide campaign where up to 182,000 people perished, the chemical attacks on Halabja and other

---

[2] The boundaries of the Kurdish designated autonomous areas were first outlined during World War I and shifted throughout the century to reflect areas historically inhabited by Kurds.

[3] In 1994 a civil war broke out between the two main leading parties of the Kurdistan Region of Iraq, thus creating two separate administrations in the Region: KDP and PUK. This also led to a split in the KRG Representations abroad that lasted until the official unification of the KRG in 2005.

[4] The KRI reached out to its neighbors and to the Arab states to communicate the KRI's values, aims, and expectations for the new Iraqi state. We encouraged them to be diplomatically present in Baghdad first before showing diplomatic presence in Erbil, as it would be the only way Baghdad would allow it.

Kurdish areas, the mass murder of 8000 Barzanis, the destruction of almost 5000 villages, forced displacement of 1.5 million people, and the mass poisoning of Kurdish refugees in displacement camps (Human Rights Watch 1993; McDowall 2007). For the KRG, establishing good international relations and securing international support would safeguard the next generations in the KRI from these atrocities (Rogg and Rimscha 2007).

Although Kurdish leaders negotiated and interacted with the international world well before the 1990s,[5] the creation of the Kurdistan Regional Government and its foreign institutions offered the KRG legitimate momentum to cultivate its relations; this served crucial in the creation of the new Iraq and the KRG's transformation from a de facto entity into a de jure government. In the months prior to the US-led intervention in Iraq, Kurdish authorities worked together with Iraqi opposition parties and international leaders to agree on an action plan for the new Iraq. Once Saddam Hussein and his regime were overthrown in March 2003, caretaker governments consisting of various ethnic and religious groups of Iraq, including the Kurds, was set up to manage the country's internal and foreign affairs and draft a new constitution. During 2003–2005, KRG authorities heavily negotiated with other Iraqi parties and the US-led coalition to ensure the new constitution would guarantee a federal, democratic, pluralistic country that safeguards the KRG's status and existing institutions. The KRG's reliability as an ally assisted it in cementing these rights, strengthening existing relationships, and procuring new ones.

The KRG has seen an overwhelming amount of progress and success in its international and regional outreach since the institutionalization of its practices into the 2005 Iraqi constitution. In 2006, the KRG established the Department of Foreign Relations[6] (DFR) with the main aim of cultivating relations with the international community; promoting trade,

---

[5] The Kurds have an extensive history of engaging with international actors regarding Kurdish issues, one that predates the twentieth century. However, it was the policies of Mullah Mustafa Barzani, the leader of the Kurdish liberation movement during the 1940s to the late 1970s, that afforded the Kurds of Iraq sustained international attention.

[6] Before this, I had been the Minister of State at the Office of the then Prime Minister, Nechirvan Barzani, in charge of international relations. PM Barzani had the idea to establish a DFR and place me as its Minister, which I wholeheartedly accepted. In September 2006, a decree was signed to appoint me as the Head of the Department of Foreign Relations, with a ministerial rank. All I had to work was the PM's vision for the DFR to coordinate the KRG's paradiplomacy. When we started this endeavor, there was no office, no instructional manual, and no foreign diplomatic presence in the KRI. I along with my small team built the DFR from scratch. Today we have 40 diplomatic offices in the KRI and 14 KRG offices abroad.

investment, and tourism; overseeing KRG's offices abroad; organizing visits of political and economic delegations to the KRI; coordinating with the Iraqi Ministry of Foreign Affairs; promoting political, economic, cultural, and social ties with foreign states; as well as providing legal and authentication services to the people of the region and its citizens abroad (Danilovich and Abdulrahman 2017). The KRG's Department of Foreign Relations has nine directorates: Office of the Head of DFR, Offices Abroad, Protocol and Delegations, Media and Communication, Administration and Finance, Quality Assurance, Legal Affairs, International Organizations, and International Relations in the Region (Salih and Najmalddin 2016, 51).

The extensiveness of the KRI's paradiplomacy can be seen through its various representations abroad, the number of diplomatic missions present in the Region, the frequent travels of international political actors to the KRI, as well as the KRG's official visits abroad. The KRG has managed to establish fourteen foreign offices.[7] Similar to other regions, the KRG Representations act as embassies and provide almost all services, except for those that are exclusive to the power of the federal government, in which case the Representations coordinate with Iraqi embassies. KRG Representations have become the main actors of Kurdish lobbying in host countries, working to represent the KRI's interests abroad and serve its diasporic community (Baser 2018). As the main diplomatic wing of the KRG, the DFR and its Representations have grown substantially in their ability to facilitate communication between the KRG and the international community; invite direct foreign investment (FDI); promote Kurdistani art, language, and culture; lobby for humanitarian aid; and highlight the Kurdistan Region's reputation as a place of peace, co-existence, stability, and security in Iraq and the greater middle east.

There are 40 diplomatic missions in the KRI, which include the Embassy Offices of Canada, Sweden, and Japan; the Consulates of Italy, South Korea, and Egypt; the Consulate Generals of the US, Russia, Germany, France, the UK, Czech Republic, Hungary, Netherlands, Armenia, the Hellenic Republic, Poland, Turkey, India, China, Iran, Jordan, Sudan, Palestine, the United Arab Emirates (UAE), Kuwait, and Saudi Arabia; the Consular Office of Romania; the Commercial Offices of the Republic of Austria and the Republic of Bulgaria; the EU

---

[7] KRG Representations are present in the US, the UK, Belgium, France, Austria, Sweden, Switzerland, Germany, Italy, Spain, Iran, Australia, Poland, and Russia.

Delegation-Erbil Liaison Office; and the Honorary Consuls of Spain, Denmark, Belarus, Slovakia, Ukraine, Cyprus, and Sri Lanka. There is also the UN Assistance Mission to Iraq—Erbil Regional Office (UNAMI) and the Regional Office of the International Committee for the Red Cross.[8] The KRG has Representations in Australia, Austria, Belgium-EU, France, Germany, Iran, Italy, Poland, Russia, Spain, Sweden, Switzerland, the UK, and the US (Department of Foreign Relations 2021). The number of offices present in the KRI and abroad is testament to the strength of the KRG's paradiplomacy and the willingness of the international community to participate in the KRI.

Official international visits made by the Region's political actors also demonstrate the success of the KRG's paradiplomacy efforts. The year 2010 saw a peak in the paradiplomatic relations between the KRG and the international community.[9] Then President Masoud Barzani, ministers, and other senior officials participated in more than 28 visits abroad; these included official visits to the US, Germany, France, Italy, Austria, Turkey, Saudi Arabia, Jordan, Lebanon, Egypt, and so on. The significance of these visits is projected in the diplomatic, economic, and cultural ties that developed between the KRI and these states. In many of these visits, then President Barzani had been received as a head of state (Salih and Najmalddin 2016). The visit to the Kingdom of Saudi Arabia in 2010 had been a particularly successful development for the KRI as King Salman bin Abdulaziz al-Saud had adorned President Barzani with the King Abdul Aziz Medal of the First Degree. This medal has previously been presented to heads of state only.

The year 2014 was monumental in enhancing KRG's international relations due to the KRI's position as frontline fighters in the war against the Islamic State of Iraq and Syria (ISIS). From 2014 until the independence referendum in 2017, the KRG had welcomed almost 200 high-level

---

[8] Sudan's Consulate has since 2018 been temporarily discontinued, first due to financial reasons provided by the state which then and now due to political turmoil in Sudan. Belarus' honorary consulate has also been shut down in November 2021 due to their role in the Poland-Belarusian migration crisis.

[9] The building of the Erbil International Airport had been a joint venture between a Turkish company, Makyol-Cengiz, and a British company, Scott Wilson. The then Prime Minister, Recep Tayyip Erdogan, had come to the 2010 opening ceremony of the airport, delivering a speech under the Iraqi and Kurdistan flag. It became clear to the KRI the power of commerce and commercial diplomacy in forging a new era of relations with neighbors who have traditionally been against Kurdish national aspirations.

foreign visitors, which included ministers, ambassadors, and political officials from states and organizations in North America, Europe, Australia, Asia, and the Middle East. Among these visits had been the US Vice-President; Polish Prime Minister; Canadian Prime Minister; Foreign and Defense Ministers from the US, Britain, France, Germany, Canada, Belgium, and Turkey; the Special Representative of the UN Secretary General as well as Secretary General, Ban Ki-Moon; Secretary General of the Arab League; and representatives of the EU (El-Dessouki 2012). In 2017, then President Masoud Barzani was received in Ankara under the Kurdish flag (Barzani 2020). This significant move demonstrated the progress and strength of the KRG's paradiplomacy.

While the KRG enjoys many liberties in its international affairs, there are constitutional limitations to the types of activities it can engage in. For this reason, it is important to highlight the tools the KRG uses to facilitate its paradiplomacy, which are communications, economic strategies, and the promotion and protection of the KRI's secure and stable environment. Strong public relations and public affairs strategies that highlight the values of the Region, its opportunities, and promote the safety and security of the KRI, have been critical in generating interest in the Kurdistan Region and establishing relations with the KRG. At the forefront of the tools used by the KRG, economic strategies have been the most pragmatic and successful. These have resulted in direct foreign investment, and economic partnerships between the KRG and foreign corporations, organizations, and other governments. These partnerships have been critical in developing the infrastructure of the Region and in turn supporting its foreign relations objectives (Soderberg and Phillips 2015). By focusing heavily on investment opportunities in the public sector, private sector, education, as well as tourism, a broad range of partnerships have been formed with different states.[10] To illustrate, many Turkish, American, British, German, and Swedish partnerships are present in the

---

[10] Speaking as a former Minister of State, a current Minister, and the previous Head of the DFR, we can consider a third sector, just as crucial as the private and public sector, which is the civil society. The Kurdistan Region has focused on supporting democratic values such as the freedom of speech and the rule of law. The region has a history of its people being deprived of such rights, being persecuted for their beliefs, and fighting for freedom. Therefore, we chose the path of democracy to right these wrongs. We are committed to democracy and democratic values, which enable the region to further develop relations with the rest of the free and democratic world. Policies have been implemented targeting women and engaging the youth as well as developing institutions.

KRI's agriculture, tourism, and infrastructure sectors. The KRG's diplomatic strategy to secure economic stability has been largely aided by the KRI's oil and gas industry. By developing an economically appealing investment law,[11] the oil industry has allowed the development of diplomatic ties with multiple countries interested in investing in KRI (Jalal 2021). Thus far, companies from several states have reaped the opportunities the KRI has to offer; these include the US, Russia, China, Turkey, Norway, Canada, Australia, the UAE, France, the UK, India, South Korea, Hungary, Spain, Austria, and plenty others (ibid.). To facilitate these partnerships, and to attract foreign offices to the Region, the KRG ensures the Kurdistan Region remains a stable, secure, and peaceful environment. Stability and security have been a crucial component of the message the KRG has echoed over the years, that is, the Kurdistan Region is a place of stability and tolerance for all religions, ethnicities, cultures, and peoples.[12] Preserving the Kurdistan Region's security is the key to the success of all other paradiplomatic instruments.

Exploring the Legal Framework

One of the leading obstacles facing the KRG's paradiplomacy efforts had been the constitutional argument and the very definition of diplomacy itself. The common argument has been that diplomacy is practiced by central governments of sovereign states (Vienna Convention on Diplomatic Relations 1961; Schwietzke 2011; Danilovich and Abdulrahman 2017; Zadeh and Kirmanj 2017; Nanyonga 2019). However, recent decades have seen a shift and a new paradigm of diplomacy practiced by non-state

[11] Then PM Nechirvan Barzani's goal was to create a lucrative investment law to attract Foreign Direct Investment and build the energy industry to develop KRI's infrastructure and ensure internal security and stability.

[12] The KRI is presented as an international partner that stands for the core values of peace and stability, welcomes and supports Internally Displaced Persons (IDPs) and refugees, protects religious minorities, and fights terrorism and extremism. After 2014, representing the KRI had become easier as I had much to communicate to the outside world and they wanted to listen. The fight with ISIS had been ongoing and the KRI was proud to be the frontline fighters against this brutal terrorist organization. The frontline had been 1050 km in length and the war had been very costly and deadly to the KRI and to its Peshmerga fighters. Despite this, we proudly hosted up to 2 million refugees and IDPs from Syria and the rest of Iraq. Therefore, representing the KRI began to include presenting ourselves as a partner to the international community in furthering peace and stability and a partner in protecting refugees, IDPs, religious and ethnic minorities.

actors, international organizations, and non-governmental organizations. Paradiplomacy is the involvement of substates or regions in international relations with an agenda that serves the substate or regional agenda (Wolff 2007). Paradiplomacy is commonly practiced in federal states, but not all constituents of a federal state develop the capability to practice extensive paradiplomacy and develop an "international personality" (Lecours and Moreno 2001, 6). There are three prerequisites to this level of paradiplomacy: the level of autonomy of a region, the constitutional framework and institutional arrangements, and the national foreign policy and international affairs (ibid., 6–7). The Kurdistan Region enjoys a significant amount of autonomy from the federal government which it preserved from its inception in 1992. In fact, from 1991 until 2003, the KRI was almost independent. It had its own government, parliament, judicial system, foreign representation, and security force, and economically supported itself. It was attached to Iraq by name only. Rather than pushing for independence following the fall of the Baath Regime, Kurdish authorities agreed to a federal compromise that would preserve the autonomy of the Kurdistan Region, its government institutions, and its legislations. Given the geographic difficulties and history of the neighboring areas, Kurdish political actors recognized the benefits of cooperating with Baghdad under a federal state versus complete independence.[13]

The 2005 constitution, written together with representatives of Iraq's various ethnic and religious groups, and under the guidance of the US, institutionalized the KRG and its practices (Gailan 2017). The Iraqi constitution recognized the existing structure of the KRG including the Kurdistan Region's presidency, parliament, and judicial systems as well as upheld all decisions and legislation passed since 1992 (Article 117,[14]

---

[13] In fact, the Kurdish political actors were heavily engaged in the political process in Baghdad and were interested in making Iraq work. The KRG was devoted to achieving a democratic, federal Iraq to safeguard its rights, protect its people, and ensure stability for Iraq and the greater region. The Kurds had experienced too much oppression and war. The KRI could and can only benefit from a stable, secure, and prosperous Iraq, strong in its institutions rather than in its militarization.

[14] Article 117 First, this Constitution, upon coming into force, shall recognize the region of Kurdistan, along with its existing authorities, as a federal region.

121,[15] 141[16]); it granted the KRI the right to adopt its own constitution as a federal region (Article 120[17]); it protected the status of the KRI's armed forces, the Peshmerga (Article 121[18]); Kurdish became the second language of Iraq to be used in all official federal government communications, both verbal and written (Article 4[19]); it protected the Kurds to exploit their own natural resources (Article 111,[20] 141[21]); and manage its customs as well as regulate electric and water resources for the Region (Article 114[22]).

[15] Article 121 First, the regional powers shall have the right to exercise executive, legislative, and judicial powers in accordance with this Constitution, except for those authorities stipulated in the exclusive authorities of the federal government.

[16] Article 141 Legislation enacted in the region of Kurdistan since 1992 shall remain in force, and decisions issued by the government of the region of Kurdistan, including court decisions and contracts, shall be considered valid unless they are amended or annulled pursuant to the laws of the region of Kurdistan by the competent entity in the region, provided that they do not contradict with the Constitution.

[17] Article 120 Each region shall adopt a constitution of its own that defines the structure of powers of the region, its authorities, and the mechanisms for exercising such authorities, provided that it does not contradict this Constitution.

[18] Article 121 Fifth, the regional government shall be responsible for all the administrative requirements of the region, particularly the establishment and organization of the internal security forces for the region such as police, security forces, and guards of the region.

[19] Article 4 The Arabic language and the Kurdish language are the two official languages of Iraq. Second, the scope of the term "official language" and the means of applying the provisions of this article shall be defined by a law and shall include: a. Publication of the Official Gazette, in the two languages; b. Speech, conversation, and expression in official domains, such as the Council of Representatives, the Council of Ministers, courts, and official conferences, in either of the two languages; c. Recognition and publication of official documents and correspondence in the two languages; d. Opening schools that teach the two languages, in accordance with the educational guidelines; e. Use of both languages in any matter enjoined by the principle of equality such as bank notes, passports, and stamps.

[20] Article 111 Oil and gas are owned by all the people of Iraq in all the regions and governorates.

[21] Legislation enacted in the region of Kurdistan since 1992 shall remain in force, and decisions issued by the government of the region of Kurdistan, including court decisions and contracts, shall be considered valid unless they are amended or annulled pursuant to the laws of the region of Kurdistan by the competent entity in the region, provided that they do not contradict with the Constitution.

[22] Article 114 First, to manage customs, in coordination with the governments of the regions and governorates that are not organized in a region, and this shall be regulated by a law. Second, to regulate the main sources of electric energy and its distribution. Seventh, to formulate and regulate the internal water resources policy in a way that guarantees their just distribution, and this shall be regulated by a law.

According to the provisions of Iraqi constitution, the KRG practices both foreign relations and paradiplomacy without violating the sovereignty of Iraq or violating any of the constitution's premises (Mohammed and Owtram 2014; Salih and Najmalddin 2016). As mentioned, article 117 of the Iraqi constitution recognizes the jurisdiction of the KRG while article 141 preserves the decisions, contracts, and legislation of the KRG that existed prior to 2005. What is more, in situations where some of these practices may conflict with aspects of the federal government's exclusive powers, through Article 115,[23] the Kurdistan Region has the right to nullify or modify any federal legislation (O'Leary 2008; El-Dessouki 2012; Ababakr 2020). Given that the Iraqi constitution preserves KRG practices, contracts, and legislation from 1992 to 2005, the Iraqi constitution itself protects the KRG's ability, through its own legal framework, to conduct foreign relations and develop its paradiplomacy (Wolff 2007; Ababakr 2020). It is important to note that the KRG respects the federal government's exclusive power to set and formulate foreign policy and follows Iraqi foreign policy to the best of its ability, except in those cases where a policy violates the constitution or contradicts or threatens the interests of the KRI and its population.

The Evolution of Kurdistan Region's Paradiplomacy

There are arguments that paradiplomacy places state sovereignty at risk (Lecours 2002; Forrest 2003) and that the KRI's paradiplomacy and foreign missions abroad are secessionist in their practice; this is not the case.[24] Paradiplomacy helps mediate self-determination conflicts, as a denial of such practice can be detrimental to the state itself (Wolff 2007). The Kurds have experienced a history of oppression by governments whose duty was

[23] Article 115 All powers not stipulated in the exclusive powers of the federal government belong to the authorities of the regions and governorates that are not organized in a region. With regard to other powers shared between the federal government and the regional government, priority shall be given to the law of the regions and governorates not organized in a region in case of dispute.

[24] In 2005, the Kurdish leadership at the time, President Masoud Barzani and the late President Jalal Talabani, played a major role in convincing the people that we would be better off as part of a federal, democratic, pluralist Iraq, in which we would have legitimate, constitutional recognition. Iraq was recognized as a state by the international community, the United Nations, and the Security Council. By joining Iraq as a constitutionally recognized federal region, it would allow the Kurdistan region to become a de jure entity, instead of the de facto entity it was recognized by until 2003.

to protect them. It was this history that fueled calls for self-determination. Paradiplomacy has been fundamental in maintaining a working relationship between Baghdad and Erbil. It ensures the Kurdistani people's right to autonomy, representation, self-expression, security, identity, and culture are protected while also preserving the sovereignty of Iraq.

Erbil's evolving relationship with Baghdad and the changing realties of the greater region and Iraq have influences on the direction of the KRG's paradiplomacy. There is a staggering difference between the paradiplomacy activities of the KRG in the present day compared to a decade ago and especially during the 2017 referendum preparations and post-referendum phase. The main goal of the DFR during its establishment had been to provide a formal institution to organize the missions of the KRG Representations abroad, organize official visits to the KRI, promote the new status of the KRI as a federal autonomous region with protected rights, gain international support to push the federal government to implement the mandatory referendum of the disputed territories as per article 140.2 of the Iraqi constitution,[25] and promote commercial activity to build basic infrastructure in the Region (Department of Foreign Relations 2021). As it became apparent that the resolution of the disputed territories would not be addressed, the recognition of the Peshmerga[26] as a component of the Iraqi national force would not be honored, there was

---

[25] Article 140 First, the executive authority shall undertake the necessary steps to complete the implementation of the requirements of all subparagraphs of Article 58 of the Transitional Administrative Law. Second, the responsibility placed upon the executive branch of the Iraqi Transitional Government stipulated in Article 58 of the Transitional Administrative Law shall extend and continue to the executive authority elected in accordance with this Constitution, provided that it accomplishes completely (normalization and census and concludes with a referendum in Kirkuk and other disputed territories to determine the will of their citizens), by a date not to exceed the 31st of December 2007.

[26] Article 9 First, the Iraqi armed forces and security services will be composed of the components of the Iraqi people with due consideration given to their balance and representation without discrimination or exclusion. They shall be subject to the control of the civilian authority, shall defend Iraq, shall not be used as an instrument to oppress the Iraqi people, shall not interfere in the political affairs, and shall have no role in the transfer of authority. Article 121 five, the regional government shall be responsible for all the administrative requirements of the region, particularly the establishment and organization of the internal security forces for the region such as police, security forces, and guards of the region. It is interesting to note that the Popular Mobilization forces (Hashd ash'Sha'bi), formed in 2014 in response to ISIS, was ordained in 2018 by then Prime Minister Haidar al-Abadi as a component of Iraq's national guard, receiving financial salary from the federal government, yet the Kurdistan Region's Peshmerga have not.

4 LEGAL FRAMEWORK, INSTITUTIONALIZATION, TOOLS, AND MOTIVES... 87

no will in the federal government to update the national census[27] so as to avoid the fair allocation of the national budget in proportion to the population distribution across Iraq,[28] Baghdad's disagreements with the KRG's oil and gas policies grew,[29] the federal government cut the constitutionally mandated budget to the KRI,[30] and the war with ISIS had begun, the KRG's paradiplomacy from 2014 shifted from nation-building toward crisis management.

Up until this time, the KRG had been committed to the Iraqi constitution and in making a federal Iraqi system work. However, after the numerous constitutional violations by the federal government, the KRG could not see a partnership with Baghdad working in the future unless they could gain some amount of leverage. The sacrifices of the Peshmerga in the battle against ISIS, though costly, had unintentionally afforded the

[27] Article 140.
[28] Article 112 First, the federal government, with the producing governorates and regional governments, shall undertake the management of oil and gas extracted from present fields, provided that it distributes its revenues in a fair manner in proportion to the population distribution in all parts of the country, specifying an allotment for a specified period for the damaged regions which were unjustly deprived of them by the former regime, and the regions that were damaged afterwards in a way that ensures balanced development in different areas of the country, and this shall be regulated by a law.
[29] The federal government of Baghdad was not honoring the KRG's oil practices prior to the adoption of the Iraqi constitution of 2005 as per article 141 of the Iraqi constitution, nor were they interested in abiding by article 112 of the constitution which stipulated the federal government of Iraq must together with the federal regions draft a hydrocarbon law, and can together with the federal regions manage the oil & gas industry if, and only if, it is distributed in a fair manner that is in proportion to the true population distribution of Iraq. Per article 112 the federal government of Iraq together with the federal regions must draft a hydrocarbon law that is reflective of the population distribution; The KRG drafted its own Oil & Gas Law due to delays in the drafting of the Hydrocarbon Law (Rogg and Rimscha 2007) which has yet to be drafted. Given that the federal government has shown no political will to update the national census nor pass a national hydrocarbon law, the KRG manages its own oil and gas industry.
[30] Article 121 Second, Regions and governorates shall be allocated an equitable share of the national revenues sufficient to discharge their responsibilities and duties, but having regard to their resources, needs, and the percentage of their population. While the Peshmerga were battling ISIS, the KRG was at the same time in a dispute with the federal government over these multiple constitutional violations. Then Iraqi Prime Minister Nuri Al-Maliki placed a halt on the KRI's portion of the federal budget in retaliation for the KRG Ministry of Oil wanting to independently sell the oil of the Region. This action together with the war and humanitarian crisis caused a socioeconomic crisis in the KRI.

KRI international visibility[31] (Palani et al. 2019). Kurdish political actors used this momentum to pressure the international community into mediating all outstanding issues between the KRI and Baghdad. To gain leverage in its negotiation with Baghdad over the outstanding constitutional issues, then President Masoud Barzani, in 2015, made the bold decision to hold an independence referendum (Barzani 2020). President Barzani explicitly stated that he had no plans for immediate declarations of statehood after the referendum; the goal was to use the results of the referendum as a negotiation tool in resolving disputes between Baghdad and Erbil (ibid.). Since becoming a constitutionally recognized region, the KRI has established deep rooted political, economic, and commercial ties with Turkey[32] and Iran, which have also benefited the KRI in its leverage with Baghdad (Tezcur 2019). The Region's continued livelihood depends on good diplomatic ties with the states surrounding it (Sumer and Joseph 2018). The referendum had brought about harsh reactions from those neighboring states which the KRI has worked hard to mend using all the diplomatic instruments at its disposal.

Despite the setbacks from the independence referendum, the Kurdistan Region continues to grow its paradiplomacy toolkit and the institutions it has built in order to push forward its agenda. There now exist many government positions under the auspices of Foreign Relations in the region including the Foreign Policy Advisor to the President, Head of Foreign Relations Department, Deputy Head of Foreign Relations Department, Head of Foreign Relations of the President's Office, as well as an entire Department of Foreign Relations. Technology has also been a new tool that has been useful for the advancement of KRG's paradiplomacy. It is evident that through the use of social media and public diplomacy, diplomatic ties between states and non-state actors have increased (Omar Bali et al. 2018). Compared to a decade ago when we could rely on the traditional methods of communication, developing ties with foreign officials of different states has been made easier and quicker thanks to social media. The KRG is positive in its own future for further paradiplomacy and

---

[31] The KRI also saw a dramatic increase in diplomatic activity in the Region; humanitarian aid increased to address the needs of the nearly 2 million displaced persons and refugees in the Region. Furthermore, international forces partnered with the Peshmerga forces and provided them with military training.

[32] In 2012, 70% of US $11 billion trade between Turkey and Iraq was accredited to trade with the Kurdistan Region (Kurdistan Democratic Party 2012).

extending its outreach through the aid of its representations abroad, KRG officials, related offices, and officials of other states.

Concluding Remarks

It is crucial to recognize, first and foremost, the main motives driving paradiplomacy in the Kurdistan Region, and how these motives have evolved over time under different circumstances. One of the key objectives has been to explore the legal framework under which the KRI practices paradiplomacy, the process of institutionalization, as well as the tools used by KRG officials. An overwhelming amount of success in international and regional activity has been observed since the establishment of the DFR in 2006. By focusing on the practical and first-hand involvement in the development of paradiplomacy in the region, it has been clarified how Kurdistan Region authorities in Iraq and its representations abroad work together to develop the regions international outreach. The Iraqi constitution has paved the way for Kurdistan's paradiplomacy and there are no constitutional violation concerns in the way the Region has developed and maintained its paradiplomacy. The KRI's commitment to democratic values is unwavering; connecting with the rest of the democratic world has been a tool in order to achieve this. By connecting to other states who value democracy, freedom, and equality, the KRI has focused on building a foundation for the Region based on these principles.

References

Ababakr, Y.M., 2020. Iraqi Kurdistan Region: From Paradiplomacy to Protodiplomacy. *Review of Economics and Political Science.* https://doi.org/10.1108/REPS-01-2020-0002

Barzani, Masoud. 2020. *Staking Our Claim.* Erbil: Roksana Printing House.

Baser, B. 2018. Homeland Calling: Kurdish Diaspora and State-building in the Kurdistan Region of Iraq in the Post-Saddam Era. *Middle East Critique* 27 (1): 77–94.

Constitution of the Republic of Iraq [Iraq]. 2005. October 15. Accessed February 4, 2022. https://www.constituteproject.org/constitution/Iraq_2005.pdf?lang=en.

Danilovich, A., and Abdulrahman, H. S., 2017. Aiming at Secession. *UKH Journal of Social Sciences, 1*(1): 48–59. Accessed December 12, 2021. https://doi.org/10.25079/ukhjse.v1n1y2017.1-3%0D.

Department of Foreign Relations. 2021. Accessed December 12, 2021. http://dfr.gov.krd.

El-Dessouki, A.I. 2012. Structural Contexts and Paradiplomacy of Iraqi Kurdistan. *Al-Nahda* 13 (2): 1–38.

Forrest, J. 2003. Networks in the Policy Process: An International Perspective. *International Journal of Public Administration* 26 (6): 591–607.

Gailan, M., 2017. *National Security Concerns and The Kurdistan Region In A New Middle East: From Rebellion To Statehood: The Influences Of Power, Threat Environment And Opportunity Structures On The Choice Of Becoming An Independent State.* Master Thesis., Swedish Defence University.

Human Rights Watch. 1993. *Iraq's Crime of Genocide: The Anfal Campaign Against the Kurds.*

Jalal, H.D. 2021. Hydrocarbon Fuels as a Basis of the Kurdistan Region's Global Diplomacy. Мировая политика 1: 39–56.

Kurdistan Democratic Party. 2012. Prime Minister: Kurdistan's Energy Relations with Turkey to Enter a New Phase. May 21. Accessed November 13, 2021. https://www.kdp.info/a/d.aspx?s=040000&l=12&a=36832

Lecours, A. 2002. Paradiplomacy: Reflections on the Foreign Policy and International Relations of Regions. *International Negotiation* 7 (1): 91–114.

Lecours, A., and L. Moreno. 2001. *Paradiplomacy and Stateless Nations: A Reference to the Basque Country.* Working paper 01–06. Unidad de políticas Comparadas (CSCI).

McDowall, D. 2007. *Modern History of the Kurds. Kurds.* London: IB Tauris.

Mohammed, H.K., and F. Owtram. 2014. Paradiplomacy of Regional Governments in International Relations: The Foreign Relations of the Kurdistan Regional Government (2003–2010). *Iran and the Caucasus* 18 (1): 65–84.

Nanyonga, S., 2019. How Globalization has Changed Diplomacy. In *Proceedings of the 14th International RAIS Conference on Social Sciences and Humanities* (pp. 146–152). Scientia Moralitas Research Institute.

O'Leary, B. 2008. *The Kurdistan Region: Invest in the Future.* An Official Publication of the Kurdistan Regional Government.

Omar Bali, A., M.S. Karim, and K. Rached. 2018. Public Diplomacy Effort across Facebook: A Comparative Analysis of the US Consulate in Erbil and the Kurdistan Representation in Washington. *Sage Open* 8 (1). https://doi.org/10.1177/2158244018758835.

Palani, K., J. Khidir, M. Dechesne, and E. Bakker. 2019. The Development of Kurdistan's de facto Statehood: Kurdistan's September 2017 Referendum for Independence. *Third World Quarterly* 40 (12): 2270–2288.

Rogg, I., and H. Rimscha. 2007. The Kurds as Parties to and Victims of Conflicts in Iraq. *International Review of the Red Cross* 89 (868): 823–842.

Salih, D.A., and B.A. Najmalddin. 2016. Paradiplomacy of the Kurdistan Region After 2003: Present and Future. *JL Pol'y & Globalization* 53: 44.

Schwietzke, J. 2011. Ernest Satow's Guides to Diplomatic Practice. From the First Edition in 1917 to the Sixth Edition (2009). *Journal of the History of International Law/Revue d'histoire du droit international 13* (1): 235–245.

Soderberg, N. and Phillips, D., 2015. *State-Building in Iraqi Kurdistan.* Institute for the Study of Human Rights.

Sumer, F., and J. Joseph. 2018. The Paradox of the Iraqi Kurdish Referendum on Independence: Contradictions and Hopes for Economic Prosperity. *British Journal of Middle Eastern Studies* 45 (4): 574–588.

Tezcür, G.M. 2019. A Century of the Kurdish Question: Organizational Rivalries, Diplomacy, and Cross-ethnic Coalitions. *Ethnopolitics, 18*(1), 1–12.

Vienna Convention on Diplomatic Relations and Optional Protocol on Disputes, Done at Vienna, April 18, 1961. [Washington]; [For Sale by the Supt. of Docs., U.S. Govt. Print. Off.], 1973.

Wolff, S. 2007. Paradiplomacy: Scope, Opportunities and Challenges. *The Bologna Center Journal of International Affairs* 10 (1): 141–150.

Zadeh, Abbas Y., and S. Kirmanj. 2017. The Para-diplomacy of the Kurdistan Region in Iraq and the Kurdish Statehood Enterprise. *The Middle East Journal* 71 (4): 587–606.

CHAPTER 5

Legal Framework, Institutionalization, Tools, and Motives of Palestine's Paradiplomacy

Dalal S. M. Iriqat

INTRODUCTION: DIPLOMACY BEYOND INTERNATIONAL RELATIONS—PARADIPLOMACY

If we look at diplomacy beyond the theory of international relations (IR), paradiplomacy comes under the scope of diplomatic practice with regard to a multiplicity of actors beyond states but also with regard to conflict resolution or transformation, reconciliation and peace-building, dialogue of civilizations, place-branding/public diplomacy, or strategic communication. The rise of those critical approaches has helped to bring the field of diplomatic studies into conversation with other fields of IR and underscored the significance of opening up diplomacy to scholarly developments beyond the discipline.

One of the first essential functions of diplomacy as envisioned in Westphalia 1648 and later in the Vienna convention of diplomatic relations 1961 (United Nations 2005b) and Vienna convention of consular

D. S. M. Iriqat (✉)
Social Sciences Department, Arab American University Palestine AAUP, Ramallah, Palestine
e-mail: dalal.S.Iriqat@aaup.edu

© The Author(s), under exclusive license to Springer Nature Switzerland AG 2023
G. Gürbey et al. (eds.), *Between Diplomacy and Non-Diplomacy*,
https://doi.org/10.1007/978-3-031-09756-0_5

relations 1963 (United Nations 2005a) is *representation*. Diplomatic presence is also interpreted as a direct or indirect way of according or denying political standing of any state, nation, people, or in some cases organizations.

It is common that states use diplomatic missions to recognize other states. Once diplomats are sent to a host country, that means this country is de facto and de jure recognized and is accorded political standing. This is what the Vienna convention referred to as *mutual consent*.[1]

The Palestinian diplomatic history indicates a relatively unique experience under the Israeli military occupation; for example the PLO, which is not a country or state, was accorded political standing since its representatives were officially recognized after the Seventh Arab League Summit Conference in Rabat, Morocco, on October 28, 1974, where the resolution on Palestine designated the PLO as the sole and legitimate representative of the Palestinian people in the occupied territories and in the diaspora (United Nations 1974). The resolution affirmed the right of the Palestinian people to establish an independent national authority under the command of the PLO, the sole legitimate representative of the Palestinian people in any Palestinian territory that is liberated. This authority, once it is established, shall enjoy the support of the Arab states in all fields and at all levels; therefore, although the PLO is not recognized officially as a state, it has been accorded state privileges. It is a political agent treated as a state; consequently, it legally represents the Palestinian people in international organizations. This observation illustrates that a state or a state-like political agent, in our case, the PLO, needs to be recognized by the international system of states in order to gain political standing.

The PLO case study applies smoothly to the theory of paradiplomacy when it came to practice, unlike the Kurdish experience, where on the contrary, the Kurdish movement tried to gain political standing in order to be recognized and treated as a legal political actor. However, the Kurdish case can be framed under Butler's definition of paradiplomacy of covert, unofficial, or secret negotiations (1961, 12–25).

---

[1] Article 2 of the Vienna Convention on Diplomatic Relations 1961, Article 2.

The establishment of diplomatic relations between States, and of permanent diplomatic missions, takes place by mutual consent.

These aforementioned cases reflect the relationality of international relations. Diplomacy is, inter alia, a way of denying or according political standing and thus proves to be an important parameter of international relations. It implicates the constitution and acknowledgment of political actors. Paradiplomatic activities represent the force of low politics from its bottom level, which plays a significant role in shaping the foreign and domestic policies of the central governments. Some argue there is a lack of theoretical perspective that can explain how regional governments have acquired international agency. As a result, Alexander S. Kuznetsov's book came in 2015 to cover the existing research gap and provide a study on paradiplomacy which came in the format of a theory proposing project of paradiplomacy and examining the role of subnational governments in IR.

To examine paradiplomacy in Palestine, this chapter relied on available literature in addition to accumulative research and publishing on the field, moreover, interviews with key people in Palestinian Ministry of Foreign Affairs (PMOFA) and online accessible documents including some media sources and debates related to diplomacy and IR of Palestine. Furthermore, the proposed theoretical pattern in Kuznetsov's book will be considered to be a research tool for exploring paradiplomacy in Palestine through an attempt of providing potential answers to the following key questions: What are the legal grounds of paradiplomacy in Palestine? What is the predominant motive of Palestinian subnational groups to be involved in international affairs? How has paradiplomacy been institutionalized in Palestine? What are the consequences of paradiplomacy for the development of the whole nation?

As we write, the focus of the world's diplomacy is shifting onto contemporary areas dealing with global challenges and interests starting with climate change, nuclear powers, democratization, and sustainability. However, the struggle for statehood and nationalism continues to be the challenge of the Palestinian people despite the effect of globalization and technological revolution that resulted in bridging gaps between nations and introducing the global challenges as shared interests of all nations. As a result of increased focus on low politics, diplomatic actors are not any longer restricted to states but also heavily include non-state actors.

Palestinian Paradiplomacy: Legal Framework and Institutionalization

In examining possible angles of interpretation of the phenomenon, Kuznetsov introduced 11 major dimensions/approaches which are used in social sciences to examine paradiplomacy as follows: constitutional, federalist, nationalist, IR, border, globalized, geopolitical, global economic, environmental, diplomatic, and separatist dimensions (2015). To examine the Palestinian experience in paradiplomacy, the *separatist dimension* was found the most appropriate. The problem of so-called non-recognized states that was especially actualized after the collapse of the communist federations (Yugoslavia and the Union of Soviet Socialist Republics [USSR]) brought to paradiplomacy studies a new important separatist dimension. The struggle for statehood and search for international recognition by subnational governments (de facto states) like Kosovo, Abkhazia, or South Ossetia fueled further research on the opportunities and limits of the phenomenon of paradiplomacy (Bartmann 2006, 169–178). André Lecours and Luis Moreno state that "nationalism logically leads regional governments to seek international agency" and therefore paradiplomacy "needs to be re-conceptualized through a theoretical linkage with substate or stateless nationalism" (Lecours and Moreno 2001, 2). The correlation of paradiplomacy and identity construction was expressed by Lecours and Moreno: cultural defense and promotion tend to be the most important issues of paradiplomacy because they are central to its underlying force, nationalism. A nation's identity or reputation is about the country as a whole, individuals, and groups and not restricted on its government's actions and personalities.

The Palestinian case of paradiplomacy, among other dimensions, can be examined from a nationalist/cultural perspective that considers the involvement in international affairs of those subnational entities that wish to affirm their identity, cultural and linguistic differences, and transform them into greater political and economic autonomy. In Palestine, the phenomenon of struggling for freedom and statehood was the challenge that the PLO found itself acting on behalf of the central government of the aspired future state, as the PLO held the official status of representing the Palestinian people. The problem of non-recognized states has definitely a tight linkage with paradiplomacy influenced by the urgent political right of self-determination of the people of Palestine.

The examination of de facto states through the paradiplomacy angle is the logical consequence of the existent nature of state recognition mechanism in world politics. As generally known, there are two main doctrines of statehood and its recognition—"constitutive" and "declarative" doctrines. The first constitutive approach defines a state as a person of international law through the recognition of other sovereign states that are recognized members of the international community. The second declarative theory is reflected in the Montevideo Convention of 1933, where four criteria for statehood were proposed: (1) a clearly defined territory; (2) a permanent population; (3) an effective government; and (4) a capacity to enter into international relations with other states (Grant 1999). Both approaches are widely used in international affairs to determine the basic precondition: to determine whether the claims of particular entities to obtain international recognition of their statehood are well founded or not. However, the theories of state sovereignty recognition and international law are usually countered by power of politics where the leading powers in the international arena serve their own interests which obstruct the implementation of international legal norms. That it is why in practice the process of self-determination and transformation from de facto to de jure status usually has no real solution through the channels of international law but depends more on deals and agreements between key players in the global scene. For example, Palestine without doubt matches all criteria to be named a sovereign state, but it currently still lacks official recognition as a full state. In their struggle for statehood, the Palestinians employed both ways: in 1988 the Palestine National Council (PNC), the legislative body of the PLO, announced the declaration of independence of the Palestinian people. The Arab League countries recognized the PLO as the sole representative of the Palestinian people at their 1973 summit in Algiers, and again at their 1974 summit in Rabat. In 1982, Arab League countries went further by recognizing the right of the Palestinian people to an independent state, with Jerusalem as its capital, guaranteed by international legitimacy embedded in United Nations (UN) resolutions. Less than six years later, Jordan officially surrendered claims on the West Bank when King Hussein declared in a televised speech that legal and administrative links with that territory would be dismantled. Most importantly, the PNC declared in Algiers on November 15, 1988, the state of Palestine with Jerusalem as its capital, and at the same time recognized the UN resolutions 181, 194, 242, and 338, and renounced terrorism.

Later in 2011, the Board of the United Nations Educational, Scientific and Cultural Organization (UNESCO) approved Palestine's application for membership of this UN special agency. On November 29, 2012, and through several Arab and other friendly states, Palestine submitted a draft resolution to the United Nations General Assembly (UNGA) in a bid to upgrade its status at the UN. On that day, the General Assembly accorded Palestine non-member observer state status with 138 in favor, 9 against, and 41 abstentions.

In 2011 and as part of its internationalization strategy, the PLO submitted a request to the United Nations Security Council (UNSC) for statehood, which was not passed. Instead in 2012, the Palestinians resorted to the UNGA and obtained a non-state observer status at the UN and Palestine accessed this international platform as state number 194 by majority vote of 138 of the 193 member states. Consequently, the Palestinian flag was officially raised at the UN headquarters in New York on September 10, 2015.

This accession seems symbolic to many critics; however, from a diplomatic perspective, this accession gave way to the Palestinians to access and be member in more than 500 international treaties and organizations.[2] On April 1, 2014, Palestine joined 15 multilateral treaties and conventions.

[2] 15 conventions and treaties as follows:
1. The Four Geneva Conventions of 12 August 1949 and the First Additional Protocol
2. The Vienna Convention on Diplomatic Relations
3. The Vienna Convention on Consular Relations
4. The Convention on the Rights of the Child and the Optional Protocol to the Convention on the Rights of the Child on the Involvement of Children in armed conflict
5. The Convention on the Elimination of All Forms of Discrimination against Women
6. The Hague Convention (IV) respecting the Laws and Customs of War on Land and its annex: Regulations Concerning the Laws and Customs of War on Land
7. The Convention on the Rights of Persons with Disabilities
8. The Vienna Convention on the Law of Treaties
9. The International Convention on the Elimination of All Forms of Racial Discrimination
10. The Convention against Torture and Other Cruel, Inhuman or Degrading Treatment or Punishment
11. The United Nations Convention against Corruption
12. The Convention on the Prevention and Punishment of the Crime of Genocide
13. The International Convention on the Suppression and Punishment of the Crime of Apartheid
14. The International Covenant on Civil and Political Rights
15. The International Covenant on Economic, Social and Cultural Rights

Later in January 2015, the Palestinians requested to join the International Criminal Court (ICC). The non-fully recognized state, Palestine is extremely active in the international scene via its paradiplomacy, which is actually somewhat similar to the traditional understanding of sovereign nation diplomacy. Palestine enjoys resident diplomats in total approximately 114 missions around the world and more than 60 non-resident representations. Those paradiplomatic offices were functioning in world leading states like the USA—shut down during Trump's administration in 2017—Canada, Japan, and Russia where the official position toward Palestine is not official recognition; therefore, paradiplomatic channels can be considered as appropriate. At the same time the occupied Palestinian territories host a great number of foreign nation missions that frequently carry on the traditional diplomatic duties, under the names of embassies, consulates, but also representation offices. More than 45 countries have official representation offices in Ramallah and it is worth mentioning that major consulates are actually based in East Jerusalem (UK, France, Turkey, Italy, Spain, USA until 2017, Sweden, and Belgium).

The case of Palestine is one of the most illustrative, but not unique, for understanding the essence of paradiplomacy in the dimension of non-recognized nations; the examination of other cases of de facto states like Taiwan, Abkhazia, Nagorno-Karabakh, or Kosovo inevitably brings up the research agenda of the issue of constituent diplomacy.

Non-recognized or partly recognized entities go abroad and actively try to perform their paradiplomacy in order to search for maximum foreign support and acknowledgment of their sovereign existence among members of the international community. Barry Bartmann adds that paradiplomacy for unrecognized states plays an important "state-building" function (2006, 547). In other words, we can assume that for those subnational governments which belong to the group of separatist/non-recognized entities paradiplomacy is a vital activity because it is considered as an essential supplementary tool for completing their crucial mission of obtaining full international recognition of their statehood.

The strong application of the separatist approach on the Palestinian case should not exclude the other dimensions. From an IR perspective, paradiplomacy is no doubt a valuable phenomenon in Palestinian global affairs, as the PLO, as a non-state actor, has become the major player in Palestine's international affairs since 1974; despite the fact that the PLO is not officially recognized as a state, it has been accorded state privileges. It is a political agent treated as a state; therefore, it legally represents the Palestinian people in international organizations. From an environmental perspective, we must acknowledge that the PLO as a subnational entity became a member of many paradiplomacy projects which proclaim global principal goals, such as climate change and nature conservation, but in reality the PLO participation in this paradiplomacy activity can be driven by underlying reasons in the pledge for statehood and exposure of the Israeli environmental crimes against the Palestinian people; nationalistic goals which fall within the official goal.

Talking about soft power and *celebrity diplomacy* for Palestine, it is crucial to speak about individual heroes on political or cultural angles. Yasser Arafat is a good example for how identity is not only about the nation's image but about the political image of its leaders. Some nations have seen major change in national identity under radical leadership, both for good and for ill. From a cultural angle, historical old cities in Palestine or listed cities in the UNESCO world heritage record can be a good focus. Jerusalem, Hebron, Jericho, Batir, and Bethlehem, for example, have great significance in tourism, culture, history, and religion, for Palestine to consider branding itself with focus on those cities and what makes them unique is much needed to promote.

Palestine engaged in strong *city diplomacy* practices as demonstrated in a huge number of city twining agreements; it is unfortunate that the ministry of local governance lacks a compiled data or file of those city twinning agreements. City diplomacy correlates with the definition of the region as a coherent territorial entity situated between the local and national levels with a capacity for authoritative decision making (Hooghe et al. 2012, 4). There is a principal dissemblance between "regional" and "local" levels of governance. The idea to separate them from each other correlates with Noé Cornago's argument on the ambiguity of the term "region", that makes distinction between "region" and "city", government bodies with relevant competences and significant administrative resources. Therefore, Cornago argues that the internationalization of cities is not a challenge to the integrity of the state's sovereignty (2012).

Palestinian paradiplomacy proves that paradiplomacy is not exclusive to federal countries and established democracies. By contrast, paradiplomacy is a process that has a universal character that applies for all types of nations; moreover, the boundaries between paradiplomacy and diplomacy are very blurred today.

MOTIVES FOR PARADIPLOMACY IN PALESTINE

In accordance with Kuznetsov's framework, there are four sets of motives for regions to be active internationally: political, economic, cultural, and cross-border housekeeping. A number of causes had been identified and classified as external or internal. Reflecting on the causes that accelerate Palestinian paradiplomacy to go abroad, one must mention 11 potential variables that can determine the growth of paradiplomacy (globalization; regionalization; democratization; foreign policy domestication and internalization of domestic politics; federalization and decentralization; problems with the nation-building process; central government insufficient effectiveness in foreign relations; asymmetry of constituent units; outside stimulus; regional leader/political party; borders).

If we consider that external causes of paradiplomacy include globalization, democratization and foreign policy domestication and internalization of domestic politics, in the case of Palestine, most external factors apply strongly as globalization is an international phenomenon that influences mostly all processes that take place in the international arena and domestic affairs of almost all countries; hence, Palestine cannot remain indifferent. Globalization eroded economic and cultural boundaries between states and granted subnational entities more opportunities to pursue their economic goals not only within their home state but across the national frontiers as well. As a result we see trade agreements conducted by the chambers of commerce in Palestine on city level with chambers of cities around the world to promote economic and trade relations between the people.

Democratization had allowed many societies around the world to start the political transformation from authoritarian or totalitarian systems to free regimes. We can observe the same correlation between the strength of democracy and the development of regional involvement in international relations. Palestine was heavily involved in international projects on nongovernmental organization (NGO) level which focused on state building, democracy, and the empowerment of public opinion and power sharing along with focus on elections on local and national levels. However, one might argue that despite the volume, those projects did not achieve the aspired effect in advancing the process of democratization and practice of human rights locally and Palestinians did not exercise their right of voting on national level since 2015. The fact that introduced another global tendency that had a direct impact on the renaissance of paradiplomacy is the emergence of overlap between "domestic policy" and "foreign policy" and between "low politics" and "high politics"; this is evident in Palestine's public diplomacy.

The remaining six variables are considered the "internal"/"domestic" causes of paradiplomacy which include federalization and decentralization, nation-building process, insufficient effectiveness of the central government in foreign relations, outside stimulus, role of regional leader/political party, and role of borders. The role of the regional leader/political party is surely a strong cause for Palestinian paradiplomacy. As illustrated previously under celebrity diplomacy, Arafat as a ruling political party leader is considered a significant factor for the rise of subnational Palestinian aspirations to go abroad. The problem of some countries in their nation-building process also actualizes paradiplomacy. This statement was demonstrated with the analysis of the cases of the so-called non-recognized states like Palestine. Paradiplomacy is closely related to the struggle of the constituent entities to gain statehood and international recognition. We conclude that paradiplomacy is strongly linked to the national aspirations of the regions. In Palestine, the inefficiency of the central government in managing an effective foreign policy in general or in particular spheres provoked paradiplomacy on city and individual levels under the scope of public diplomacy.

Paradiplomacy can be caused and fueled by the influence of external factors. Trends in IR, conferences, and treaties influenced the rise of paradiplomacy in Palestine. The analytical outlook on the Palestinian case of constituent diplomacy shows that the personality of the regional leader as well as the political ideology of the particular regional party can determine the intensity and the course of subnational involvement in international affairs, the impact of the subnational ruling elite on regions' aspirations and self-identification in international relations domain. Yasser Arafat role as a political leader and freedom fighter had a huge effect on the rise of the PLO diplomacy on behalf of the Palestinian people.

The analysis of the data on Palestine's paradiplomacy shows that the predominant motive of the PLO interest in international affairs has a political nature. This political motivation mainly shapes the whole content of the Palestine's paradiplomacy since its emergence in the early 1970s until the present moment. The aspiration to go abroad consists in the desire to promote Palestinian political rights in the international arena; the call for liberation and state building through the internationalization strategy are considered significant motives behind Palestinian paradiplomacy.

The objective "to build Palestine's reputation as a global citizen" (Iriqat 2019) is an attempt by Palestinians to create a system of efficient public and government relations in international affairs that will improve the current negative image of Palestine in the perception of an international audience. The main challenge for Palestine's reputation is linked to the circumstance that Palestine's international profile is primarily associated with the Israeli occupation, Palestinians being the poor, beggars, and terrorist in the eyes of the international audience.

Obviously, besides political motivations, there are cultural, economic, and cross-border housekeeping motives in Palestine's paradiplomacy. Palestine develops relations with neighboring Jordan, Egypt, and Israel and those relations are determined by cross-border housekeeping motivation: both interact on the issues of transfrontier transport system development, nature conservation, water, and emergency. Palestine pioneers twining relationships on city level; the motive of the involvement on city level is based on cultural rather than political reasons. However, political goals with the intention to gain its own statehood or at least a high autonomous status are considered the most applicable in the case of Palestinian paradiplomacy. Certainly, these international activities can be called a soft power project with strong political meaning. Non-state actors pursue a few aims in their international activities simultaneously, but evidently one motive might be more dominant than others: the political motive remains the most predominant motive applicable in the case of Palestine paradiplomacy.

Palestinian Paradiplomacy Beyond the PLO

To understand how paradiplomacy was institutionalized in Palestine, this chapter explained how the PLO emerged as a non-state actor with legal standing to represent the Palestinian people in fulfilling its aspirations for self-determination. The legal grounds of Palestine paradiplomacy emerged from the PNC which is the legislative body of the PLO when it was recognized as representative of the Palestinian people in the 1970s and later when it issued the declaration of independence on November 15, 1988.

The engagement of the PLO in the Oslo peace process resulted in the establishment of a government for the PNA in 1994 and elections were carried out for the first time in 1996. The peace accords stipulated the structure of the PNA and identified the MOFA as the official body responsible for IR. However, the overlap continued to exist between the PLO and the PNA as official bodies in representation of the Palestinian interests on the international level especially after the Palestinian Basic Law saw light in 2002. Closer acquaintance with the Palestinian Basic Law does not show any article or statement that clarifies the relationship between the PLO and the MOFA; on the contrary, the Palestinian diplomatic law 2005 actually specifies that the creation of MOFA should not contradict the fact of the superiority of the PLO being the sole and legitimate representative of the Palestinian people.

A decade later, Palestinians started to go abroad through new means. For example, a department which is responsible for the international affairs at MOFA seems a very convenient choice to not create a separate bureaucratic body that will professionally conduct subnational policy making in international affairs, but to harmonize and complete efforts on national and subnational levels by employing public diplomacy side by side with official diplomacy. In Palestine, the PICA was established in 2015.

In addition to the other types of diplomacy, Palestinian diplomacy in the age of globalization includes economic diplomacy, cultural diplomacy, parliamentary diplomacy, military diplomacy, or defense diplomacy. All these types enhance the concept of international development, which was led by the UN representatives in the 2030 agenda to come up with the Sustainable Development Goals (SDGs). This initiative resulted in creating SDG departments in the ministries of foreign affairs in the related countries to serve those goals. In the case of Palestine, this resulted in the creation of the aforementioned PICA, as the main public diplomacy tool of the State of Palestine, and worked as a national coordinator for South-South and North-South Cooperation. It is essential to highlight that development is a tool for paradiplomacy, which is also soft power that can together create a solid base for countries to interact and establish relations. It is important to emphasize that PICA does not possess complete control of regional IR but is functioning semi-independently under the umbrella of the PMOFA, so in other words, PICA is considered a branch of PMOFA that operates as a division which carries out international projects.

The title of the ministry in Palestine was changed a few times and currently it is titled the Ministry of International Affairs and Expatriates. The main goal of the PMOFA started with Palestine's IR and then moved to advocate the political right of return for refugees promoting national interests. People hired in PICA have experience of working internationally, have significant language skills and significant cultural understanding.

It is relatively new that Palestine is branded differently than it was branded in its old official diplomacy that still relies on the guard of the PLO.

It is necessary to mention that besides the MOFA and PICA, who provide the overarching support for all of Palestine's international activities, there are other stakeholders within the government of Palestine who are involved in bilateral relations through their specific professional angles. For example, the ministries of Agriculture, Economy, Energy, Environment, Education, Culture, and some other government agencies play an important role.

The presence of multiple stakeholders within the government brings a challenge to the government of Palestine on how to manage international activities in an efficient and well-coordinated manner in the existing complex administrative realities. Palestine's international strategy does not officially recognize this internal administrative challenge that expertise across government must be better coordinated.

Diplomacy, traditionally, was viewed as the product of states, and, therefore, is rendered as a sovereign function that is neither divisible nor transferable. Stefan Wolff describes paradiplomacy as the "foreign policy capacity of sub-state entities, their participation, independent of their metropolitan state, in the international arena in pursuit of their own specific international interests" (Tewari 2017, 3). As opposed to conventional diplomatic relations by sovereign nation states exercised by central governments, paradiplomacy came to make space for external relations of subnational, federal units or non-state actors. In many ways, globalization has contributed to the growth of paradiplomacy. With the world economy becoming increasingly global and, thus, more integrated in a variety of ways, subnational units (regions, states, provinces, and even cities) find their functions and activities circumscribed by the global system. Paradiplomacy can, therefore, be used for purposes ranging from making space for a "decentralised dimension to international debates", to "internationalisation of domestic issues by bringing regional issues on the global stage, promoting trade, tourism, cultural ties and even post-conflict reconciliation, and to local political activism being sought for international support" (Tewari and Pant 2016).

More recently, *city diplomacy* has also gained increased usage and acceptance, particularly as a strand, if not as a variant, of paradiplomacy and public diplomacy. *Town twinning*, as it is more commonly called, is a concept where cities develop their own foreign relations based on cooperative agreements. These pairings can be conducted for cultural or economic exchanges, which, in turn, are beneficial to both cities/towns. While such city-to-city relationships or twinning model is not entirely new to Palestine, there is a need for Palestine to substantially increase its engagements with other nations at the subnational level.

As illustrated above, one can wrap that Palestinian paradiplomacy employed different channels and organizational formats in its paradiplomatic activities, Palestinians establishing a special public diplomacy department for IR, opening permanent overseas offices, conducted official visits to foreign countries, participated in various international exhibitions and forums, and worked within global and transborder networks. However, actions of those channels lack proper coordination from the center; this is not to say that they are not in harmony with national foreign policy. Some actions focus on trade, economy, commerce, or cultural relations; nevertheless, the presence of harmony is guaranteed by the principle that was nationally and diplomatically formulated in the Palestinian aspirations of self-determination and statehood.

Paradiplomacy and COVID-19 in Palestine

COVID-19 like other pandemics and natural disasters impacts the adaptation of development cooperation schemes. The twenty-first-century pandemic has introduced different methods to ensure cooperation. Governments and institutions alike found themselves provoked to come about with creative solutions to respond to the consequences of COVID-19 with the least negative impact on development and cooperation. Paradiplomacy of non-state actors was largely witnessed between South-North (support from Latin America to Europe) and South-South (Jordan to Palestine) countries where we found central states and non-states cooperating on different levels though the "old" strategy of "twinning" between cities and other international networks. Revisiting paradiplomacy in light of the pandemic, the pandemic energized the actions of cities in search of quick responses. This, in turn, repromoted international articulation through networks (Alvarez and Oddone 2020). Therefore, the pandemic reinforced the need for a change in the approaches to paradiplomacy. Traditionally, paradiplomacy has been analyzed from the dimensions of transnationalism, interdependence, and globalization, examining how these phenomena opened the doors for cities to interact internationally.

While countries were busy dealing with the need for an international presence and participation focused on budgets, institutional capacities, internet connectivity leading to more focus on economic paradiplomacy, Palestine was busy facing a double lockdown imposed by the policies of the Israeli occupation (Iriqat 2020, 40–50). It could be argued that Israel did cooperate with Palestine by allowing the entry of testing kits to the West Bank and Gaza, or by allowing thousands of workers to stay in Israel for a two-week quarantine period if they wished to. Israel also allowed Palestinians returning to the West Bank to enter via Ben Gurion Airport and released some of the Palestinian tax revenues withheld by Israel. Despite these cooperative measures, Israel continued to violate international law even during the pandemic. Several actions by Israel confirm its violation of international law and failure to meet its obligations as an occupying state. For example, Israel did not institute health measures to Palestinian workers before their return to Palestine. Israel forced Palestinian workers, including those who were sick, to return to the occupied Palestinian areas without coordinating with the Palestinian government, and without testing them or giving them medical attention concerning the coronavirus. Furthermore, Israel did not release any Palestinian prisoners from its jails, nor did it provide hygiene or protective measures, despite repeated calls by Palestinian officials to the international community to oblige Israel to respect the Fourth Geneva Conventions, specifically Article 91 under Chapter IV on hygiene and medical attention. This includes the provision of adequate healthcare under the direction of a qualified doctor, with treatment and an appropriate diet (United Nations 1949). Israel also froze visits to prisoners without offering at least virtual meetings.

Conclusion

Inspired by the work of Alexander S. Kuznetsov, this chapter tried to explore the Palestinian paradiplomacy. One of the key tasks of this chapter was to look at Palestinian paradiplomacy through the lenses of its historical development and to define motives behind the rise of the phenomenon in Palestine. It is necessary to emphasize that in this chapter Palestinian paradiplomacy was examined not only in its current status but in the attempt to provide a comprehensive snapshot on paradiplomacy from the moment of its appearance in the early 1970s until 2021.

The Palestinian Basic Law failed to clarify the level of authority that the PNA in general and MOFA in particular possess in treaty-making with foreign actors; also, there is no reference on how relations should be in the case when foreign affairs issues overlap areas of PLO competence. There is nothing in the Palestinian Basic Law that prohibits Palestinian paradiplomacy of non-state actors. Actually, the overlap of mandate produced an ambiguity of authorities and limitations which made it easier for MOFA to justify any poor performance by lack of competence in comparison with the PLO or to the executive authority. Paradiplomacy of Palestine as well as the international activities of the PLO is embedded in the Palestinian Basic Law. Hence, if we wish to grasp the essence of PLO's paradiplomacy, it is very crucial to realize that the constitution gave superiority to the PLO. The real practices of paradiplomacy are in fact stronger than official diplomacy practiced by the MOFA.

It seems significant to pay attention to the uniqueness of the PLO case in paradiplomatic channels. In other words, leader of the PLO, Arafat, and others at very senior levels of PLO representation used to conduct official visits abroad. Members and leaders of the organization also participate in international events like exhibitions and forums organized by foreign actors. This again is yet another activity that the PLO carried out in participation in global and transborder multilateral regional networks and working groups on specific problems like different international symposiums and fora on agriculture, sustainable development, energy, and transportation. Paradiplomacy in some countries worked through permanent subnational offices labeled as "paraconsulates", because they often provide consultations for regional communities in developing international contacts in business, culture, and other spheres. This is not the case for Palestine. The PLO managed to open offices under its name up until the creation of the PNA, and more specifically with the upgrade of status of Palestine in the UN in 2012, some of those representation offices changed name to serve the state of Palestine instead of the PLO. Palestinians in PICA act in foreign affairs responsibly primarily and foremost as Palestinians and that is why the case study concludes that Palestinian PICA paradiplomacy contributes positively to the development of the whole nation.

Considering the correlation between paradiplomacy, democracy, and federalism, it is quite interesting to also mention the case of Palestine, where, for the last three decades, we can examine the opposite tendencies in political development: democratization and decentralization in the 1990s under the presidency of Yasser Arafat and then Mahmoud Abbas.

The active involvement of Palestine in international affairs started in the late 1960s. There is various evidence that vividly shows a significant increase of Palestinian interest in IR since the establishment of the PLO. Thus, later in early 1990s, Palestine after the Oslo Peace process had its first government and the PNA started to open its first offices abroad; however, it should be noted that there exist overlaps between the mandates of the PLO and the PNA as the Oslo accords placed IR in the hands of the PLO rather than the MOFA.

Paradiplomacy is not an end in itself. It is an uncontested tool. The rise of paradiplomatic activity should not be seen as a displacement of the state but as its complement. Paradiplomacy can be a challenge for the central governments, either because they perceive it as a threat to their sovereignty, or because the multiplicity of voices makes it difficult to present a coherent national foreign policy. The question is no longer if noncentral governments should get involved in foreign affairs, but how paradiplomacy can feed into the national foreign policy.

Digital diplomacy and strategic communication are the gold standard for designing persuasive messages and media strategies for enhancing national images, advocating policies, and influencing publics. Strategic communication is instrumental in the competitive pursuit among countries to enhance their soft power. Digital media have empowered non-state political actors capable of rivaling state communication efforts. Digital media have brought state and non-state actors into reciprocal contact with the very same publics that they are trying to influence. The new diplomatic space is not defined by its actors—whether state, non-state, or publics—so much as by its communication dynamics. To end the Israeli occupation and fulfill the dream of freedom, dignity, and liberation, Palestinians must employ all kinds of diplomatic actors to capitalize on their strategic communication such as owning their narrative and branding their national story. In the twenty-first century, stories rather than armed force impact international relations.

REFERENCES

Alvarez, Mariano, and Nahuel Oddone. 2020. Revisiting Paradiplomacy in the Context of COVID-19. E-International Relations, August 5. Accessed March 15, 2022. https://www.e-ir.info/2020/08/05/opinion-revisiting-paradiplomacy-in-the-context-of-covid-19.
Bartmann, Barry. 2006. In or Out: Subnational Island Jurisdictions and the Antechamber of Paradiplomacy. *The Round Table* 96 (386): 541–599.
Butler, Rohan. 1961. Paradiplomacy. In *Studies in Diplomatic History and Historiography*, ed. Arshag O. Sarkissian, 12–25. London: Longman.

Cornago, Noé. 2012. On the Normalization of Sub-State Diplomacy. *The Hague Journal of Diplomacy* 5 (1–2): 11–36. Accessed March 15, 2022. https://www.researchgate.net/publication/233521043_On_the_Normalization_of_Sub-State_Diplomacy.

Grant, Thomas D. 1999. *The Recognition of States: Law and Practice in Debate and Evolution*. Westport: Greenwood Publishing Group.

Hooghe, Liesbet, Gary Marks, and Arjan Schakel. 2012. *The Rise of Regional Authorities: A Comparative Study of 42 Democracies*. Oxford, New York: Routledge.

Iriqat, Dalal. 2019. Palestinian Nation Branding via Public Diplomacy. *International Relations and Diplomacy* 7(5): 202–216. Accessed May 2, 2022. http://www.davidpublisher.org/Public/uploads/Contribute/5d005eec16e36.pdf.

———. 2020. Israeli Politics During COVID-19 and the Impact on Palestine. In *The Double Lockdown: Palestine Under Occupation and Covid 19*, ed. Saeb Erakat and Mitri Raheb, 40–49. Bethlehem: Diyar Publisher.

Kuznetsov, Alexander S. 2015. *Theory and Practice of Paradiplomacy. Subnational Governments in International Affairs*. London, New York: Routledge.

Lecours, André, and Luis Moreno. 2001. Paradiplomacy and Stateless Nations: a Reference to the Basque Country. Accessed February 27, 2022. https://digital.csic.es/bitstream/10261/1472/1/paradiplomacy_statelesspdf.

Tewari, Falguni. 2017. Paradiplomacy in India: Evolution and Operationalization. *ORF Occasional Paper* 117: 1–27. Accessed March 15, 2022. https://www.orfonline.org/research/paradiplomacy-india-evolution-operationalisation/.

Tewari, Falguni, and Harsh V. Pant. 2016. Paradiplomacy and India: Growing Role of States in Foreign Policy. *Observer Research Foundation*, December 6. Accessed May 2, 2022. https://www.orfonline.org/expert-speak/paradiplomacy-and-india/.

United Nations. 1949. The Geneva Convention Relative to the Protection of Civilian Persons in Time of War of August 12 1949. Accessed March 15, 2022. https://www.un.org/en/genocideprevention/documents/atrocity-crimes/Doc.33_GC-IV-EN.pdf.

———. 1974. PLO sole legitimate representative of the Palestinian people—LAS Rabat Summit—resolution. Seventh Arab League Summit Conference. Resolution on Palestine. Accessed March 15, 2022. https://www.un.org/unispal/document/auto-insert-194621/.

———. 2005a. Vienna Convention on Consular Relations 1963. Accessed March 15, 2022. https://legal.un.org/ilc/texts/instruments/english/conventions/9_2_1963.pdf.

———. 2005b. Vienna Convention on Diplomatic Relations 1961. Accessed March 15, 2022. https://legal.un.org/ilc/texts/instruments/english/conventions/9_1_1961.pdf.

PART III

Paradiplomacy in Practice (Selected Relations)

CHAPTER 6

Palestine and USA

Khaled Elgindy

The U.S. has long been at the center of Palestinian diplomacy and remains so to this day. This is so despite the failures of the U.S.-led peace process and the many ups and downs in Palestinian-American relations. While the relationship with Washington has produced a number of distinct benefits, most notably the PLO's entry into the peace process, the Palestinian leadership's "American strategy" has come at considerable cost, particularly in terms of its domestic legitimacy and internal Palestinian political and institutional cohesion. Since the PLO's founding in 1964, Palestinian diplomacy toward the U.S. has undergone two major transformations. The first occurred following the 1973 Arab-Israeli war, which established the U.S. as the dominant force in Arab-Israeli peacemaking. At that time, PLO diplomacy was focused mainly on wooing the U.S. in order to secure a seat in the U.S.-led peace process, which Palestinian leaders viewed as the most effective path to influencing Israel and, hence, to Palestinian statehood. The second major transformation occurred when the PLO achieved that objective with the signing of the 1993 Oslo Accords, after which the U.S. was no longer simply the chief mediator but also the

K. Elgindy (✉)
Middle East Institute, Washington, DC, USA
e-mail: kelgindy@mei.edu

© The Author(s), under exclusive license to Springer Nature Switzerland AG 2023
G. Gürbey et al. (eds.), *Between Diplomacy and Non-Diplomacy*, https://doi.org/10.1007/978-3-031-09756-0_6

113

Palestinians' most important chief benefactor. In return for the U.S. "delivering" Israel, the PLO was prepared to give up a degree of autonomy over its internal political and institutional affairs.

Palestinian expectations did not pan out, however. Not only did the U.S.-sponsored peace process fail to end Israel's occupation or lead to Palestinian statehood, it actually helped weaken Palestinian political leaders and governing institutions. Thus, while the PLO's diplomatic strategy was on the surface highly successful, the Palestinian leadership's growing weakness and dependence on the U.S. have severely hampered its ability to serve as an effective peace partner or to address the myriad challenges facing the Palestinian people.

BACKGROUND (1948–1973)

Israel's creation in 1948 led simultaneously to the displacement of some 800,000 Palestinians, roughly two-thirds of the country's Arab population, an event known as the Nakba, or "calamity." Thus, for the first two decades of the Arab-Israeli conflict, there was no Palestinian-American relationship to speak of, in large part because the U.S., like much of the international community, continued to view Palestinians as refugees, and hence as a humanitarian, rather than a political, problem.

In the wake of the Nakba, Palestinian political representation fell to the Arab states, many of which began organizing Palestinian guerilla units, known as *fedayeen*, to carry out periodic attacks on Israel, as well as rival Palestinian political entities as a means of controlling the nascent Palestinian movement while burnishing their own nationalist credentials (Sayigh 2011, 73–78). Even after the emergence of autonomous Palestinian political activism in the 1950s and 1960s, groups like Fateh and the more Marxist-leaning Popular Front for the Liberation of Palestine (PFLP), while remaining broadly pan-Arabist and anti-colonialist, continued to operate within the framework of Arab states and intra-Arab rivalries.

Such groups hardly registered in Washington, however, which viewed any Palestinian political activity as a ruse aimed at undermining two U.S. allies: Israel and Jordan (CIA 1958). The creation of the PLO under Arab League auspices in 1964 did little to alter this perception. Though the PLO was still subject to Arab, especially Egyptian, tutelage and did not yet include Fateh and other *fedayeen* groups, the State Department dismissed it as yet another ploy in the intra-Arab "struggle for power," even as it banned official contacts with the PLO (FRUS 1965, Document 199).

Moreover, by late 1966, U.S. officials had begun describing it as a "terrorist" organization—although it had not engaged in armed operations against Israel at the time (FRUS 1966; CIA 1967).

Ironically, it was only after Fateh and other guerilla groups took control of the PLO that U.S. officials began to look seriously at the Palestinians in political terms. Israel's decisive defeat of Egyptian, Syrian, and Jordanian forces in June 1967 convinced Palestinian factions and *fedayeen* groups of the need to take matters into their own hands. The March 1968 Battle of Karameh, in which armed Palestinian groups helped stave off invading Israeli troops, put Fateh and the *fedayeen* "on the global map of Third World revolutionaries," paving the way for the former's takeover of the PLO under the charismatic leadership of Fateh's Yasir Arafat (Sayigh 2011, 147). The meteoric rise of the *fedayeen* also put the PLO, which had by then established a virtual "state within a state" in Jordan, on a collision course with its Jordanian hosts, leading to a bloody civil war in September 1970 and the PLO's subsequent expulsion. Despite its defeat in Jordan, the PLO, now based in Beirut, succeeded in establishing Palestinian nationalism as a force to be reckoned with in the region and beyond, and, more importantly, affirmed its role as the central address for Palestinian decision-making. In addition to consolidating Arab state support for Palestinian resistance and political objectives, PLO diplomacy focused on building alliances with other liberation and "revolutionary" movements, as well as with the global non-aligned movement (Chamberlin 2012, 22).

With regard to the superpower rivalry, the PLO remained ambivalent. Although officially nonaligned, most PLO factions took a more favorable view of the Soviet Union than the U.S., which they viewed with suspicion, both for its role in Israel's creation and for its reputation among "third world" liberation movements as a neocolonial power. Yet, Arafat also had a pragmatic side; as early as late 1969 the PLO leader authorized secret contacts with the Central Intelligence Agency (CIA) in the hopes of establishing a political dialogue (Bird 2015, 105). The CIA track would later blossom, particularly in the realm of intelligence and security cooperation, which would become the most prominent aspect of PLO-U.S. relations over the next several decades.

Meanwhile, the U.S. remained deeply conflicted about the Palestinians throughout this period. While some U.S. officials were beginning to push for some kind of accommodation with Palestinian nationalism (FRUS 1970), most remained highly distrustful of Palestinian political leaders.

Washington's aversion to the PLO was partly due to its involvement in terrorism, such as the September 1972 Munich Olympics massacre, but was primarily political.

Despite the PLO's nuanced approach to the Union of Soviet Socialist Republics (USSR), in the Cold War mindset of U.S. policymakers, the PLO fell squarely in the "radical" camp, alongside Syria, Algeria, North Yemen, and other Soviet "clients." This was especially true for Henry Kissinger, the powerful U.S. secretary of state under Presidents Richard Nixon and Henry Ford and a dyed-in-the-wool Cold Warrior. For Kissinger, the architect of the Arab-Israeli peace process and U.S. Palestinian policy, the PLO was not only a tool of the Soviet Union, and hence irrelevant to the diplomatic process, but an "overtly anti-American" force that needed to be marginalized and weakened for Arab-Israeli diplomacy to succeed (Kissinger 1982, 503, 625, 628, 1139; FRUS 1972).

Genesis: Origins of the PLO's "American Strategy" (1973–1982)

The October 1973 Arab-Israeli War marked a decisive shift in the PLO's diplomatic strategy and its approach to the U.S., as well as in U.S. attitudes toward the Palestinians. The surprise attack by Egypt and Syria shattered the aura of Israeli invincibility, giving new impetus for a diplomatic settlement and creating new opportunities for PLO-U.S. engagement. United Nations Security Council Resolution 338 reaffirmed the "land for peace" formula enshrined in Resolution 242 and paved the way for a new peace conference in Geneva in December 1973. Although officially sponsored by both superpowers, the Arab-Israeli peace process was now under the purview of the U.S.

Like Egypt's Anwar Sadat, Arafat had concluded that Washington "held all the cards." Hoping to earn the PLO a seat at the table in the new Geneva process, Arafat intensified his outreach to Washington after the war. Having previously rebuffed Arafat's gestures, Kissinger was now more responsive, authorizing CIA Deputy Director Vernon Walters to engage in the first-ever high-level U.S. contacts with the PLO in late 1973 and early 1974 (FRUS 1973a; Kissinger 1982, 626). Through the secret CIA track, the PLO agreed to refrain from targeting U.S. interests as well as to provide security for American diplomats stationed in Lebanon and valuable intelligence on various anti-American threats (Bird 2015, 353–354).

Despite the PLO's expanding ties to the Soviet Union, the relationship remained a marriage of convenience. Though the official Soviet position, which called for a unified Arab stance toward Israel and upheld "the just struggle of the Palestinian Arab people for their legitimate national rights" (Qtd. in Reppert 1989, 115), was closer to that of the PLO, there was little doubt which superpower the PLO leadership preferred. As Arafat's envoy confessed to the CIA's Walters during their first meeting, the PLO regarded the dialogue with Washington as "historic," adding "that everything the Palestinians had done had been to get the attention of the U.S. because only it could give them territory" (FRUS 1973b).

Meanwhile, Arafat went to some lengths to demonstrate the PLO's flexibility. In the run-up to Geneva—to which the PLO was not invited—Arafat privately assured U.S. officials that the PLO "in no way seeks the destruction of Israel, but accepts its existence as a sovereign state; the PLO's main aim at the Geneva conference will be the creation of a Palestinian state out of the 'Palestinian part of Jordan' plus Gaza" (CIA 1973). This was the first—albeit unofficial—endorsement by the PLO leadership of a two-state solution, a quarter century before either the Israelis or the Americans warmed to the idea. Although PLO factions remained deeply divided over the Geneva process and the idea of a Palestinian mini-state in the West Bank and Gaza Strip, Arafat continued to push his pragmatic agenda both internally and externally.

To buttress its outreach to Washington, the PLO embarked on an aggressive diplomatic campaign, securing official recognition by the Arab League as "the sole legitimate representative of the Palestinian people" (League of Arab States 1974) and culminating in the November 1974 United Nations General Assembly vote—over strong U.S. objection—to grant observer status to the PLO (UN General Assembly 1974a, 1974b).

It was all for naught, however. Kissinger's limited engagement with the PLO was strictly utilitarian. In addition to formalizing PLO-U.S. security and intelligence cooperation and placating Arab leaders, it was also a way to limit the PLO's ability to create problems for his diplomatic strategy (Bird 2015, 174; Kissinger 1982, 625). Indeed, just as the PLO leadership had come to see the U.S. as the key to its political strategy, Kissinger was equally committed to keeping the PLO out of the diplomatic process (Kissinger 1999, 1053; Ryan 1982, 34).

Under Kissinger's "step by step" diplomacy, Israel would deal with the Egyptian, Syrian, and Jordanian tracks separately. The Palestinians could be brought into the process at the end, preferably after the PLO had been weakened (Kissinger 1982, 758). The PLO's diplomatic exclusion was formalized in September 1975; the U.S. signed a secret memorandum of agreement (MOA) with Israel pledging not to "recognize or negotiate with" the PLO until it recognized Israel's right to exist and accepted Security Council Resolution 242. The agreement, the first of many anti-PLO measures to be enacted in Washington, would tie the hands of future U.S. administrations for decades to come.

The arrival of Jimmy Carter to the White House in 1977 presented a new opening in Palestinian-American diplomacy and the peace process. Both Carter and his Secretary of State, Cyrus Vance, were more attuned to Palestinian grievances and hoped to bring the PLO into the peace process. Hoping to capitalize on the change, Arafat renewed his call for a dialogue with Washington. Communicating through various third parties, Arafat reiterated his willingness to live in peace with Israel in return for a state in the West Bank and Gaza Strip. For its part, the Carter administration focused on securing PLO acceptance of Resolution 242, paving the way for a dialogue with the U.S. and ultimately for the PLO's participation in the peace process.

Attempts to find a mutual accommodation faced several significant challenges, including Israel's hardline Prime Minister Menachem Begin. Begin, a former militia leader and a champion of Israeli settlements in the occupied territories, bitterly opposed any Israeli withdrawal from the West Bank and Gaza as well as any accommodation with the PLO. Instead, Begin proposed a form of limited autonomy for Palestinians in the occupied territories. For the Carter administration, the primary challenge remained finding a way to bring the Palestinians into the process while working within the narrow constraints imposed by Kissinger's 1975 pledge and the pro-Israel lobby. Arafat was also constrained by Palestinian rejectionists and by the Syrians, who were now the main power brokers in Lebanon.

Attempts to bring the PLO into the peace process came to an abrupt end, however, following Egyptian President Anwar Sadat's surprise visit to Israel in November 1977, preempting the planned peace conference in Geneva and paving the way for a separate peace treaty between Egypt and Israel. In the wake of Sadat's visit, the focus shifted from bringing in the Palestinians into the peace process to what Egyptian and American negotiators might secure on their behalf. With neither Sadat nor Carter prepared to risk the potential breakthrough on the Palestinians, the two sides settled an American-backed Israeli proposal for limited Palestinian autonomy in the West Bank and Gaza as part of a separate framework for Middle East Peace.

CRISIS: FROM THE LEBANON INVASION TO THE INTIFADA (1982–1993)

Israel's invasion of Lebanon in June 1982 put the PLO's U.S. strategy directly to the test. Despite Israeli claims that the operation would be limited and focused on ending PLO rocket attacks on northern Israel, Israeli defense minister Ariel Sharon's real aims were to eradicate the PLO presence in Lebanon and to install a friendly government in Lebanon dominated by Israel's right-wing Christian allies, the Phalange (Brynen 1990, 39). As Israeli forces made their way to Beirut, besieging the capital and subjecting it to a massive air and mortar assault, U.S. President Ronald Reagan dispatched his special envoy, Philip Habib, to broker a ceasefire. With U.S. officials still barred from talking to the PLO directly Habib was forced to communicate through third parties.

After two months of fierce fighting, numerous truce failures, and tens of thousands of Lebanese and Palestinians killed, Habib finally secured a comprehensive ceasefire; Palestinian fighters and PLO personnel would be allowed to leave Beirut in exchange for an Israeli pledge not to invade West Beirut and American guarantees to protect the tens of thousands of Palestinian civilians left behind. Meanwhile, Reagan announced a new peace plan calling for Palestinian autonomy in the West Bank and Gaza in association with Jordan while ruling out the possibility of a Palestinian state and precluding a role for the PLO.

The ceasefire quickly collapsed, however. Following the PLO's departure from Beirut in mid-September 1982, Israeli-allied Phalangist militiamen entered the Palestinian refugee camps of Sabra and Shatila, which had been surrounded and illuminated by the Israeli army, and massacred 1000–2500 women, children, and elderly men (Sayigh 2011, 551). In response, President Reagan expressed "outrage and revulsion over the murders" and ordered U.S. Marines back to Lebanon under a new multinational force. But as Reagan's Secretary of State, George Shultz, later confessed, "The brutal fact is we are partially responsible" (Shultz 1993, 48).

That the first instance of American mediation between the PLO and Israel had ended in disaster did little to dampen Arafat's enthusiasm for U.S. mediation, however. Indeed, in the aftermath of the Lebanon war the PLO leadership doubled down on its U.S.-focused diplomatic strategy.

The Lebanon debacle left the PLO badly weakened and internally divided. But instead of radicalizing the leadership, PLO weakness reinforced Arafat's pragmatism and his desire to win over Washington. Whereas the Israelis had flatly dismissed the Reagan Plan, Arafat was keen not to reject it outright. Moreover, to compensate for his weakness, Arafat sought an alliance with the PLO's former nemesis, Jordan's King Hussein, solidified in the February 1985 Amman Accord, all of which antagonized hardline Palestinian factions and fueled intra-Palestinian fighting in Lebanon.

The Amman Accords softened the U.S. stance as well. However, as the State Department began to look at the possibility of allowing the PLO an indirect role in the peace process, pro-Israel forces in Washington worked to keep it out. In August 1985, Congress enacted Kissinger's 1975 MOA into law, to which it added a third condition requiring the PLO to "renounce the use of terrorism" (PL 1985, 99–83), in addition to recognizing Israel and accepting Resolution 242. Two years later, shortly after the outbreak of the Palestinian uprising in the occupied territories, Congress passed a new law, which for the first time defined the PLO as a "terrorist organization" and barred it from operating in the U.S.

The outbreak of the Palestinian uprising, or Intifada, in late 1987 presented both an opportunity and a challenge for the PLO's diplomatic strategy. Despite putting the Palestinian question and Israel's occupation squarely on the international agenda, the popular uprising shifted the center of gravity of Palestinian politics away from the PLO leadership in Tunis to a new generation of Palestinian leaders inside occupied territories. The rise of a new opposition force, Hamas, only heightened Arafat's political insecurities. The Intifada also forced a change in U.S. political calculations. King Hussein's decision to officially sever legal and administrative ties to the West Bank put an end to the "Jordan option," a key pillar of U.S. Middle East policy since 1948, along with Washington's futile search for alternatives to the PLO.

Buoyed by these developments, the PLO's parliament in exile, the Palestinian National Council (PNC), voted in November 1988 to declare an independent Palestinian state in the West Bank and Gaza Strip. Though it implicitly recognized Israel, the declaration failed to satisfy U.S. officials. It took three weeks and two more attempts before Arafat finally "read the script which we had crafted for him" (ADST 1998, 413) allowing the Reagan administration to open an official dialogue with the PLO. The short-lived dialogue marked a major turning point in Palestinian-American relations and in the Palestinians' integration into the peace process, but thanks to the many restrictions imposed by the administration Congress ultimately went nowhere. "In effect," U.S. Secretary of State James Baker later explained, "we were asking Arafat to disenfranchise himself on the grounds of political expedience" (1995, 118).

Iraq's invasion and occupation of Kuwait in August 1990 created both opportunities and setbacks for the PLO. Arafat's apparent siding with Saddam Hussein alienated the PLO's onetime Arab allies in the Gulf and ended any hope of resuming a dialogue with Washington.

At the same time, Iraq's defeat by American-led coalition forces created the conditions that led to the historic Madrid peace conference, convened in late 1991, bringing the Palestinians into the diplomatic process for the first time, albeit under the auspices of a joint Palestinian-Jordanian delegation. Although Arafat and the PLO were officially excluded from the conference, it was clear to both the U.S. and Israel that Arafat was calling the shots, both in Madrid and in subsequent negotiations in Washington (Ashrawi 1994, 81–83, 95–101, 109–110, 115–120, 124, 129).

Metamorphosis: Oslo and the Remaking of Palestinian Politics (1993–2011)

The signing of the Oslo Declaration of Principles (DOP) in September 1993 marked a new phase in Palestinian-American relations as well as in Palestinian politics. Having secured its place in a U.S.-led peace process, the PLO leadership now set out to build the foundations of a future Palestinian state while demonstrating it could be a responsible peace partner—in the expectation that the U.S. would eventually compel Israel to end its occupation. The vast power asymmetry between the Palestinians and both the U.S. and Israel and the special relationship between the U.S. and Israel, however, created a very different dynamic. Instead of "delivering" Israel, the Oslo process effectively flipped this formula by institutionalizing Palestinian dependence on both the U.S. and Israel.

Faced with PLO political isolation and a dire financial crisis following the 1990–1991 Gulf Crisis and the collapse of the Soviet Union, Oslo offered Arafat a lifeline by which to rescue the PLO while ensuring his and

Fateh's continued dominance of Palestinian politics. In doing so, however, Oslo fundamentally reorganized Palestinian politics and governing institutions. Indeed, Oslo was not one process but two—combining traditional conflict-resolution between two parties with a process of "state-building" for the Palestinians. Among other things, this meant that outside actors, including the U.S., foreign donors, and even Israel, now had a direct say in key aspects of Palestinian political life (Elgindy 2019, 135–152; Hilal 1993, 46).

As the PLO's human and institutional resources were hollowed out and transferred to the newly created Palestinian Authority (PA), the presumed embryo of a future Palestinian state, the latter effectively replaced the former as the de facto locus of Palestinian politics. Moreover, as the Palestinian struggle was transformed from a national liberation movement to a state-building project so too were the Palestinians' external benefactors. Unlike the PLO, which had relied mainly on the largesse of Arab states, the PA's new donor base was made up mostly of western nations along with Israel, which collected taxes from Palestinians on behalf of the PA, all of which profoundly influenced Palestinian priorities and freedom of action. Unlike Arab aid, the massive influx of western—especially U.S.—donor aid, which totaled more than $2.7 billion from 1993 to 1999, came with a host of political, economic and administrative strings (Wake 2008, 109).

The relationship with the U.S.—which was no longer just the chief mediator but also the PA's main political sponsor and its largest single donor—became more central than ever. The U.S. poured hundreds of millions of dollars into PA coffers, particularly the security sector, a central pillar of the Oslo process (Lasensky 2005, 47). International security assistance was used to strengthen the PA and its ability to implement agreements, fight terrorists, and neutralize Oslo's opponents (Lia 2007, 289; Wake 2008, 113). The basic theory was that enhanced security for Israelis would increase the willingness of Israeli leaders to make concessions like turning over territory to the Palestinians, though there was little evidence for this.

For a time anyway the arrangement appeared to be working, particularly after the election of Benjamin Netanyahu as Israel's Prime Minister in 1997, whom U.S. President Bill Clinton saw as failing to live up to Israel's obligations. The high-water mark in U.S.-Palestinian relations occurred in late 1998, when as a reward for the PA's security performance Clinton made an unprecedented visit to Bethlehem and Gaza in December 1998. After overseeing the inauguration of the newly built Gaza International

Airport, Clinton delivered a historic speech before a session of the PNC, declaring that "[f]or the first time in the history of the Palestinian movement, the Palestinian people, and their elected representatives now have a chance to determine their own destiny on their own land." It was the closest any sitting U.S. president had come to supporting a Palestinian state (Qurie 2008, 72).

Despite the appearance of a budding bilateral relationship, however, relations with the U.S. remained highly precarious and conditional, as the collapse of the Camp David negotiations in July 2000 and the outbreak of the Al-Aqsa Intifada two months later demonstrated. All sides, including the U.S.-Americans, had contributed to the failure of negotiations before and after the summit as well as to the escalating violence, as various Palestinian, American, and even Israeli negotiators have since clarified (Agha and Malley 2001; Miller 2008, 288–289; Sontag 2001). Nevertheless, Clinton joined Barak in laying the blame solely at the feet of Arafat and the Palestinians, which contributed to the escalation in violence and narrowed the political space for an agreement during Clinton's remaining time in office.

The outbreak of the Al-Aqsa Intifada reflected widespread Palestinian frustration with the Oslo process, which had failed to bring about improvements in Palestinian life while providing cover for Israeli settlement expansion. Economically Palestinians were worse off than they were before the Oslo process, including a 20 percent decline in living standards and a tripling of the unemployment rate between 1992 and 2001 (Sontag 2001; AHLC 2000, 13).

Meanwhile, the Israeli settler population grew from roughly 270,000 to more than 370,000 from 1993 to 2000 (FMEP 2012). Moreover, the PA's growing dependency on international aid along with its inordinate spending on security, which comprises more than a fifth of its overall budget, raised questions about whether Palestinian leaders should be more responsive to the needs of its donors and benefactors or those of its constituents (Jamal 2012, 16). Israel's heavy-handed response to the uprising and the mounting death toll continued to the rise of armed Palestinian groups and the militarization of the Intifada. Though still committed to a diplomatic resolution and his U.S. strategy, Arafat—not unlike Israeli leaders—was not above using violence to enhance his negotiating. The costs of this approach were considerably higher for the Palestinians, however, particularly following the 9/11 terror attacks on the U.S.

After a string of deadly suicide bombings in Israel in March 2002, Israel launched a massive military offensive in the West Bank, its largest since 1967 and from which the PA would never fully recover. In addition to reoccupying Palestinian cities and besieging Arafat inside his Ramallah headquarters, Israeli forces targeted a wide range of Palestinian institutions and national symbols, including Gaza's international airport, numerous PA ministries, and several municipalities (Palestinian NGOs 2002; Rubenberg 2003, 350–353; Hass 2002). As the Intifada was subsumed under the global "war on terror," President George W. Bush demanded that Palestinians "elect new leaders … not compromised by terror" before progress could be made toward Palestinian statehood (White House 2002), while abandoning multilateralism and diplomacy.

Ironically, the PA's growing weakness only intensified its dependence on the U.S., as became clear under Arafat's successor, Mahmoud Abbas. As a critic of Arafat's handling of the Intifada, Abbas was even more committed to the PLO's U.S.-American strategy than his predecessor. After concluding a ceasefire agreement with Sharon in February 2005, Abbas brought Palestinian factions together to solidify the truce with Israel, quietly ending four years of violence (Harel 2006). The election of a new Palestinian leadership and dramatic decline in violence, however, did not lead to a revival of the diplomatic process, as U.S. officials had promised. Instead, the Bush administration abandoned its own peace plan, the 2003 Road Map, and backed Israel's plans to unilaterally "disengage" from the Gaza Strip while providing Sharon with assurances regarding the fate of Israeli settlements, Palestinian refugees, and other issues ostensibly up for negotiation (White House 2004).

Although highly skeptical of its planned unilateral disengagement from Gaza, Abbas agreed to coordinate the process with Israel. The U.S.-brokered Agreement on Movement and Access (AMA), aimed at ensuring the flow of people and goods in and out of Gaza, was never implemented, however, leading to the closure of Gaza's borders (Kurtzer et al. 2013, 195; Elgindy 2019, 184–185). The result was a "sudden economic free fall" in Gaza as well as an upsurge in rocket attacks into Israel, which in turn triggered Israeli military reprisals and even tighter border restrictions (Samhouri 2006, 4). Hamas quickly capitalized on the situation, crediting the "resistance" with driving the Israelis out of Gaza and pointing to the AMA's collapse as further evidence that Abbas's negotiations were futile, thus paving the way for Hamas's surprise election victory in January 2006.

The election was a major blow to Abbas and the most serious challenge yet to the leadership's longstanding American strategy. The election of a designated "foreign terrorist organization" to head the PA posed serious legal and political challenges for Israel, U.S., and international donors. But it also presented an opportunity for a course correction in what many viewed as a highly lopsided peace process as well as a chance to encourage Hamas's political evolution and moderation. The Bush administration adopted a zero-sum approach, however, urging the European Union (EU), Russia, and the United Nations (UN) to suspend diplomatic and financial ties to the PA until the new Hamas-led government agreed to lay down its arms, recognize Israel, and abide by previous agreements. While Israel withheld tax revenues essential to the PA's budget, the U.S.-led international boycott all but paralyzed the PA and sent the Palestinian economy into a tailspin (IMF and The World Bank 2007, 9).

Desperate for a way out of the crisis, in February 2007 Abbas struck a unity deal with Hamas, which agreed to relinquish most ministries and share power with Fateh. However, American officials rejected any arrangement that allowed Hamas to remain in government and continued to press Abbas to take the extraordinary—and unconstitutional—step of dissolving the government and call new elections. Predictably, fighting broke out between PA forces and Hamas, ending in the latter's forcible takeover of Gaza and the ouster of the PA in June 2007 (Rose 2008).

While ordinary Palestinians saw the division as a blow to their national project, the Bush administration embraced it as an opportunity to advance the peace process with Abbas without the negative influences of Hamas, now presumably contained in Gaza by an international boycott and an Israeli blockade. Once again, however, events played out differently. In the wake of the Palestinian civil war, the Bush administration launched new peace negotiations with Israel in late 2007 while increasing aid to the West Bank. The talks collapsed a year later when fighting broke out between Israel and Hamas in late December 2008, the first of several deadly Gaza wars in the decade that followed.

The arrival of Barack Obama to the White House in 2009 brought Abbas little reprieve. With Gaza still smoldering, the PA hopelessly divided, Israeli settlements expansion continuing unabated, and the return of a right-wing, pro-settlement government under Benjamin Netanyahu in Israel, prospects for a negotiated two-state solution looked bleaker than ever. Despite hinting at a new approach to the conflict, Obama did little to challenge these negative trends—especially in Gaza, which remained isolated both politically and physically. Abbas was also comfortable with the status quo, which assured continued U.S. support while relieving him of the burdens of governing the war-ravaged and impoverished Gaza Strip.

From Stagnation to Triangulation (2011–Today)

It would take another major regional upheaval to shake Abbas out of his complacency. The popular uprisings that swept the region in 2010–2011 dealt another major blow to Abbas, forcing him to rethink his domestic priorities as well as his diplomatic strategy. The overthrow of Egypt's Hosni Mubarak, Abbas's most important Arab ally, and the rise of the Egyptian Muslim Brotherhood put Abbas and Fateh on the defensive while emboldening his Hamas rivals. The uprisings also exposed the vulnerability of Abbas's leadership, which, given the ongoing internal division, institutional stagnation, and mounting corruption and repression, had its own legitimacy problems to contend with.

As the wave of popular unrest made its way to the West Bank and Gaza, Abbas signed a new reconciliation agreement with Hamas calling for the formation of a new government of "national consensus" along with new PA presidential and legislative elections and reforming the long-dormant PLO. At the same time, Abbas began to pull away—albeit reluctantly—from a U.S.-led peace process by doubling down on internationalization and reiterating plans to seek formal recognition in the UN. In November 2012 the UN General Assembly, despite active opposition by the Obama administration, voted overwhelmingly to recognize Palestine as a "non-member state," allowing the Palestinians to join a host of other international bodies, including the International Criminal Court (ICC), and giving Abbas a much-needed domestic boost (JMCC 2012).

Both the reconciliation deal with Hamas and the UN statehood bid drew fierce Israeli and American opposition, underscoring the underlying tension between the leadership's domestic legitimacy and its dependence on the U.S. Moreover, in the wake of the 2012 UN vote and the 2015 accession to the ICC, the U.S. Congress enacted new laws conditioning the PLO's ability to operate in the U.S. on the Palestinians refraining from joining any other UN agencies or taking steps against Israel at the ICC—the latter of which was invoked by the Trump administration to close down the PLO mission in Washington in 2018 (PL 2011, 112–74, 2015, 114–113).

Despite his defiant posture, Abbas was too weak and dependent on the U.S. to pull away completely. At the same time, continuing to adhere to what most Palestinians viewed as a highly skewed U.S.-led peace process had become a serious liability for him domestically. In an attempt to balance these conflicting interests, as well as ensure his own political survival, Abbas adopted a strategy of triangulation, alternating between all three tracks—internal reconciliation, internationalization, and negotiations— without fully committing to any of them. Abbas's triangulation strategy would continue to guide his behavior right up to this day—albeit with diminishing success.

When U.S. Secretary of State John Kerry pushed the parties to resume peace talks in 2013, Abbas was alone within his inner circle to favor a return to negotiations (Abu Aker and Rudoren 2013). While most of the Fateh and PLO leaderships doubted Netanyahu's commitment to a two-state solution and Kerry's ability to hold the Israeli leader to his word, Abbas saw an opportunity to buy time while extracting some tangible benefits. In return for refraining from joining any international bodies for the nine-month duration of the talks, Abbas would receive a "slow-down" in Israeli settlement construction, the release of more than a hundred Palestinian political prisoners, and some $4 billion in aid and investments (U.S. Department of State 2014). When the talks collapsed in late March 2014, Abbas immediately pivoted back to the international and domestic tracks, signing letters of accession to 15 international treaties and initialing a new reconciliation deal with Hamas.

The outbreak of yet another devastating war in Gaza in the summer of 2014, which left some 2200 Palestinians, mostly civilians, and 72 Israelis, including 66 soldiers, dead (UNHRC 2015), again put the Palestinian leader on the defensive. In the face of mounting public anger that fueled the perception that the PA had sided with Israel and the U.S. against Hamas, Abbas pivoted back to the internationalization track, culminating in the long-delayed decision to join the ICC in late 2014 and triggering fresh sanctions by Israel and the U.S. Congress.

Despite getting a momentary boost from the ICC, Abbas's leadership continued to flounder. By late 2015, Abbas's popularity hit an all-time low, with nearly two-thirds of Palestinians saying they wanted him to resign (PCPSR 2015). With his political options rapidly dwindling, Abbas hinted at the possibility of cancelling the PA's security cooperation with Israel, which, while highly unpopular among Palestinians, remained central to continued U.S. and Israeli support as well as to the PA's survival, and ultimately never carried through on the threat. Abbas's frustration with the Obama administration would pale in comparison to what came next. After initially trying to ingratiate himself to the new U.S. president, Donald Trump, Abbas's pretense quickly evaporated following Trump's decision to recognize Jerusalem as Israel's capital, overturning 70 years of U.S. policy and international consensus, and taking Jerusalem "off the table" (Beaumont, January 3, 2018). An infuriated Abbas responded by officially boycotting the U.S. while girding himself for the inevitable U.S. backlash. "If Jerusalem is off the table, then America is off the table as well," declared a spokesperson for Abbas (Fabian 2018). Trump retaliated by cutting U.S. assistance to United Nations Relief and Works Agency for Palestine Refugees in the Near East (UNRWA), the UN agency responsible for Palestinian refugees, before eventually eliminating all U.S. aid to Palestinians. Meanwhile, the Trump administration focused on dismantling the basic principles undergirding the peace process, including Resolution 242 and the "land for peace" formula, and the two-state solution itself. Trump's ostensible peace plan of January 2020, which called for a Palestinian entity made up of disconnected patches of territory surrounded and controlled by Israel, was more reminiscent of the Bantustans of apartheid South Africa than a sovereign state. Meanwhile, the Trump administration worked to further marginalize the Palestinians by pushing for normalization between Israel and several key Arab states, many of which also scaled back their financial support for the PA.

Ironically, despite marking a historic low in Palestinian-American relations, the Trump era may have inadvertently helped Abbas's leadership. Although faced with a severe financial and political crisis, Abbas's defiance of the U.S. gave the beleaguered Palestinian leader a much-need boost to his popularity (PCPSR 2018) while compelling him to focus inward. In response to the Trump plan and growing talk in Israel of formal annexation of parts of the West Bank, Abbas finally carried through on his threat to cut security ties with Israel in May 2020. Moreover, the September 2020 normalization deals between Israel and the United Arab Emirates (UAE) and Bahrain, in addition to shattering the Arab consensus on Israel, forced Palestinians to close ranks and breathed new life into Palestine's otherwise stagnant internal politics. Faced with what most Palestinians regarded as an existential threat to the national struggle, Fateh and Hamas signed their most far-reaching reconciliation deal yet, including a timetable for legislative and presidential elections.

Yet once again Abbas's domestic maneuvers proved to be largely tactical as well as highly deferential to Washington, as Joe Biden's election as the new U.S. president demonstrated. Even before Biden had been sworn in, Abbas announced the resumption of PA security coordination with Israel along with other gestures to the incoming administration. But whereas Abbas was eager to get back in Washington's good graces, the new administration was less enthusiastic about the Palestinian issue. Despite reaffirming the two-state solution, restoring aid to the Palestinians, and promising to reopen the U.S. Consulate in Jerusalem, the Biden administration made clear the issue was not a priority and that it saw little hope in reviving a diplomatic process (Crowley 2021; Toosi 2021). The administration's lethargic response to the May 2021 Gaza war—offering blanket statements of support for Israel's right to defend itself while quietly pushing for a truce, even as it blocked the Security Council from calling an immediate ceasefire—further highlighted its reluctance to challenge the status quo. Meanwhile, Abbas's decision to cancel planned elections along with the murder of Nizar Banat, a popular political activist and outspoken critic of Abbas, at the hands of PA security forces underscored the increasingly erratic and repressive nature of PA rule as well as Abbas's dwindling choices. Thus far, Abbas has been able to use his dependence on the U.S. or the prospect of a U.S.-led diplomatic process to avoid dealing with domestic problems like Gaza, the split with Hamas, and the growing internal political dysfunction. However, the Biden administration's conspicuous disinterest in the Palestinian issue has all but rendered Abbas's triangulation strategy obsolete.

Conclusion

Whether Abbas has the ability—or even the inclination—to put the internal Palestinian house in order or whether that task will fall to his successor is not yet clear. What is clear, however, is that the Palestinian leadership's single-minded focus on American deliverance has not only failed to bring Palestinians closer to independence or statehood but has actually helped weaken Palestinian politics, institutions, and leaders. The PA's inordinate dependence on the U.S., along with other international donors and Israel itself, has simultaneously limited its freedom of action while eroding its domestic legitimacy. Moreover, the existing incentive structure of a U.S.-dominated peace process helps to ensure that Palestinian leadership is ultimately more responsive to the U.S. and Israel than to its own citizens or constituents. Thus, while the PA is rewarded for maintaining the status quo, attempts to reform or revive Palestinian political institutions—such as through elections or national reconciliation—are met with indifference, resistance, or, in the case of the latter, outright sanctions. Despite the asymmetry, however, the Palestinians are not without options. Just as the PA cannot exist without U.S. support, there can be no two-state solution without a viable, legitimate, and minimally cohesive Palestinian polity.

REFERENCES

Abu Aker, Khaled, and Jodi Rudoren. 2013. Palestinians Call Kerry's Formula for Talks Insufficient. *New York Times*, July 18.

Ad Hoc Liaison Committee Secretariat (AHLC). 2000. Aid Effectiveness in the West Bank and Gaza. https://prrn.mcgill.ca/research/documents/WB_AEreport2000/WorldBank_AidEffectiveness_1.pdf. Accessed 18 Mar 2022.

Agha, Hussein, and Robert Malley. 2001. Camp David: The Tragedy of Errors, *New York Review of Books*, August 9.

Ashrawi, Hanan. 1994. *This Side of Peace*. New York: Simon & Schuster.

Association for Diplomatic Studies and Training (ADST). 1998. *Foreign Affairs Oral History Project*. Ambassador William Andreas Brown. https://adst.org/OH%20TOCs/Brown,%20William%20Andreas.toc.pdf. Accessed 18 March 2022.

Baker, James A. 1995. *The Politics of Diplomacy: Revolution, War and Peace; 1989–1992*. New York: Putnam.

Beaumont, Peter. 2018. Trump threatens to cut US aid to Palestinians. *The Guardian*, January 3.

Bird, Kai. 2015. *The Good Spy: The Life and Death of Robert Ames*. New York: Broadway Books.

Brynen, Rex. 1990. *Sanctuary and Survival: The PLO in Lebanon*. Boulder: Westview Press.

Central Intelligence Agency (CIA). 1958. *Central Intelligence Bulletin*, February 15. http://www.foia.cia.gov/sites/default/files/document_conversions/5829/CIA-RDP79T00975A003500130001-8.pdf. Accessed 18 Mar 2022.

———. 1967. *Central Intelligence Bulletin*, January 20. http://www.foia.cia.gov/sites/default/files/document_conversions/5829/CIA-RDP79T00975A009600030001-2.pdf. Accessed 18 March 2022.

———. 1973. Central Intelligence Bulletin, December 14. http://www.foia.cia.gov/sites/default/files/document_conversions/5829/CIA-RDP79T00975A025800090001-6.pdf. Accessed 18 Mar 2022.

Chamberlin, Paul Thomas. 2012. *The Global Offensive: The United States, the Palestine Liberation Organization, and the Making of the Post-Cold War Order*. Oxford: Oxford University Press.

Crowley, Michael. 2021. Violence in Israel Challenges Biden's 'Stand Back' Approach. *New York Times*, May 11 (Updated May 19).

Elgindy, Khaled. 2019. *Blind Spot: America and the Palestinians from Balfour to Trump*. Washington, DC: Brookings Institution Press.

Fabian, Jordan. 2018. Trump Threatens to Cut More Aid to Palestinians. *The Hill*, January 25.

Foreign Relations of the United States (FRUS). 1965. *Volume XVIII, Circular Airgram From the Department of State to Certain Posts*. March 30, Document 199. https://history.state.gov/historicaldocuments/frus1964-68v18/d199. Accessed 18 Mar 2022.

———. 1966. *Volume XVIII, Intelligence Memorandum, No. 2205/66*, December 2, Document 356. https://history.state.gov/historicaldocuments/frus1964-68v18/d356. Accessed 18 Mar 2022.

———. 1970. *Volume XXIII, Paper Prepared by the National Security Council Staff*, November 13, Document 182. https://history.state.gov/historicaldocuments/frus1969-76v23/d182. Accessed 18 Mar 2022.

———. 1972. *Volume XXIV, Paper Prepared by Harold Saunders of the National Security Council Staff*, July 11, Document 118. http://history.state.gov/historicaldocuments/frus1969-76v24/d118. Accessed 18 Mar 2022.

———. 1973a. *Volume XXV, Paper for Response to Palestinian Approach, Memorandum of Conversation*, August 3, Document 81. http://history.state.gov/historicaldocuments/frus1969-76v25/d81. Accessed 18 Mar 2022.

———. 1973b. *Volume XXV, Backchannel Message From the Deputy Director of Central Intelligence (Walters) to Secretary of State Kissinger*, November 4, Document 318. https://history.state.gov/historicaldocuments/frus1969-76v25/d318. Accessed 18 Mar 2022.

Foundation for Middle East Peace (FMEP). 2012. *Comprehensive Settlement Population, 1972–2011*. http://fmep.org/resource/comprehensive-settlement-population-1972-2010/. Accessed 2 Feb 2022.

Harel, Amos. 2006. Shin Bet: Palestinian Truce Main Cause for Reduced Terror. *Haaretz*, January 2.

Hass, Amira. 2002. Operation Destroy the Data. *Haaretz*, April 24.

Hilal, Jamil. 1993. PLO Institutions: The Challenge Ahead. *Journal of Palestine Studies* 23 (1): 46–60.

International Monetary Fund (IMF) and The World Bank. 2007. *West Bank and Gaza Economic Developments in 2006—A First Assessment*. https://www.imf.org/~/media/external/np/wbg/2007/eng/032607ed.ashx. Accessed 29 Mar 2022.

Jamal, Manal. 2012. Democracy Promotion, Civil Society Building, and the Primacy of Politics. *Comparative Political Studies* 45 (1): 3–31.

Jerusalem Media and Communication Centre (JMCC). 2012. *Poll No. 78, Dec. 2012—Gaza, Resistance and the UN Bid.* http://www.jmcc.org/Documentsandmaps.aspx?id=858. Accessed 18 Mar 2022.

Kissinger, Henry. 1982. *Years of Upheaval.* Boston: Little Brown & Co.

———. 1999. *Years of Renewal.* New York: Simon & Schuster.

Kurtzer, Daniel C., Scott B. Lasensky, William B. Quandt, Steven L. Spiegel, and Shibley Z. Telhami. 2013. *The Peace Puzzle: America's Quest for Arab-Israeli Peace, 1989–2011.* Ithaca: Cornell University Press.

Lasensky, Scott. 2005. Chequebook diplomacy: the US, the Oslo process and the role of foreign aid. In *Aid, Diplomacy and Facts on the Ground; the Case of Palestine,* ed. Michael Keating, Anne Le More, and Robert Lowe, 41–58. London: Royal Institute for International Affairs/Chatham House.

League of Arab States. 1974. *PLO Sole Legitimate Representative of the Palestinian People, Seventh Arab League Summit Conference.* http://unispal.un.org/UNISPAL.NSF/0/63D9A930E2B428DF852572C0006D06B8#sthash.Ru9Ifqrl.dpuf. Accessed 18 Mar 2022.

Lia, Brynjar. 2007. *Building Arafat's Police: The Politics of International Police Assistance in the Palestinian Territories after the Oslo Agreement.* London: Ithaca Press.

Miller, Aaron David. 2008. *The Much Too Promised Land.* New York: Bantam Dell.

Palestinian Center for Policy and Survey Research (PCPSR). 2015. *Palestinian Public Opinion Poll No—57,* September 17-19. https://www.pcpsr.org/en/node/621. Accessed 18 Mar 2022.

———. 2018. *Palestinian Public Opinion Poll No—70,* December 27. https://pcpsr.org/sites/default/files/Poll%2070%20English%20press%20release%20Dec%202018.pdf. Accessed 18 Mar 2022.

Palestinian NGO Emergency Initiative in Jerusalem. 2002. *Report on the Destruction to Palestinian Governmental Institutions in Ramallah Caused by IDF Forces Between March 29 and April 21.* https://web.archive.org/web/20030323112115/http:/www.pna.gov.ps/new/repintrod02.pdf. Accessed 18 Mar 2022.

Public Law (PL) 112–74: 125 Stat. 1184. December 23, 2011.

Public Law (PL) 114–113: 129 Stat. 2769. December 18, 2015.

Public Law (PL) 99-83: 99 Stat. 1302. August 8, 1985.

Qurie, Ahmed. 2008. *Beyond Oslo, the Struggle for Palestine: Inside the Middle East Peace Process, from Rabin's Death to Camp David.* New York: I. B. Tauris.

Reppert, John C. 1989. In *The Soviets and the PLO: The Convenience of Politics.* In *The International Relations of the Palestine Liberation Organization,* ed. Augustus R. Norton and Martin H. Greenberg, 109–137. Carbondale & Edwardsville, IL: Southern Illinois University Press.

Rose, David. 2008. Gaza Bombshell, *Vanity Fair*, March 3. https://www.vanityfair.com/news/2008/04/gaza200804. Accessed 18 Mar 2022.

Rubenberg, Cheryl A. 2003. *The Palestinians: In Search of a Just Peace*. Boulder: Lynne Rienner.

Ryan, Sheila. 1982. Israel's Invasion of Lebanon: Background to the Crisis. *Journal of Palestine Studies* 12 (1): 23–37.

Samhouri, Mohammed. 2006. *Gaza Economic Predicament One Year After Disengagement: What Went Wrong?* Middle East Brief, Brandeis University, Crown Center for Middle East Studies.

Sayigh, Yezid. 2011. *Armed Struggle and the Search for State the Palestinian National Movement 1949–1993*. Oxford: Oxford University Press.

Shultz, George P. 1993. *Turmoil and Triumph: Diplomacy, Power, and the Victory of the American Deal*. New York: Charles Scribner's Sons.

Sontag, Deborah. 2001. And Yet So Far: A Special Report; Quest for Mideast Peace: How and Why It Failed. New York Times, July 26.

Toosi, Nahal. 2021. Joe Biden is not planning to solve the Israeli-Palestinian conflict. *Politico*, April 6.

U.S. Department of State. 2014. *Initiative for the Palestinian Economy, Remarks by Anne W. Patterson, Assistant Secretary for Near Eastern and North African Affairs*.

UN General Assembly. 1974a. *Resolution 3236, Question of Palestine, A/RES/3236(XXIX)*. https://www.un.org/en/ga/search/view_doc.asp?symbol=A/RES/3236(XXIX). Accessed 18 Mar 2022.

———. 1974b. *Resolution 3237, Observer Status for the Palestine Liberation Organization, A/RES/3237(XXIX)*. https://www.un.org/en/ga/search/view_doc.asp?symbol=A/RES/3237(XXIX). Accessed 18 Mar 2022.

UN Human Rights Council (UNHRC). 2015. *Report of the Independent Commission of Inquiry Established Pursuant to Human Rights Council Resolution S-21/1*. https://digitallibrary.un.org/record/800872. Accessed 18 Mar 2022.

Wake, Chris. 2008. An Unaided Peace? The (Unintended) Consequences of International Aid on the Oslo Peace Process. *Conflict, Security & Development* 8 (1): 109–131.

White House. 2002. President Bush Calls for New Palestinian Leadership. https://georgewbush-whitehouse.archives.gov/news/releases/2002/06/20020624-3.html. Accessed 18 Mar 2022.

———. 2004. *Letter From President Bush to Prime Minister Sharon*. https://georgewbush-whitehouse.archives.gov/news/releases/2004/04/20040414-3.html. Accessed 18 Mar 2022.

CHAPTER 7

Kurdistan-Iraq and EU

Dastan Jasim

INTRODUCTION TO KRG-EU RELATIONS

The study of the relations between a supranational regime like the European Union and a subnational regime like the Kurdistan Region of Iraq must first consider the many layers and avenues of paradiplomatic action at hand. Table 7.1 shows the different diplomatic levels at play in KRI-EU paradiplomacy from highest to lowest.

On the EU diplomatic level, the High Representative acts as a de facto foreign representer, while the European External Action Service (EEAS) is equivalent to the foreign ministry. The Common Security and Defense Policy (CSDP) structure manages all issues regarding EU defense (Lehne 2012, 19). On the lower national level, although all 27 EU member states are equal in principle, the reality is that until Brexit EU foreign policy was mostly influenced by the Big Three: Germany, United Kingdom (UK), and France (Lehne 2012). Furthermore, on the higher-level transnational regimes that the EU is embedded in are also important specifically in the context of member states that are in the North Atlantic Treaty Organization (NATO). Especially after France re-joined NATO fully in 2009 under

D. Jasim (✉)
German Institute for Global and Area Studies (GIGA), Hamburg, Germany
e-mail: Dastan.Jasim@giga-hamburg.de

© The Author(s), under exclusive license to Springer Nature Switzerland AG 2023
G. Gürbey et al. (eds.), *Between Diplomacy and Non-Diplomacy*,
https://doi.org/10.1007/978-3-031-09756-0_7

Table 7.1 Schematical depiction of EU and KRI diplomatic levels

Transnational regimes with EU involvement (NATO, World Trade Organization [WTO], Organisation for Economic Co-operation and Development [OECD], etc.)	Iraqi federal government level
EU diplomatic level (EEAS + CSDP)	KRG level
EU member state level	Party level (PUK Bureau for International Relations, KDP Foreign Relations Office)

then-president Nicolas Sarkozy, NATO considerations were of increasing importance and the initial project of expanding the CSDP, which was urged by France, was rather neglected and only seen as "a complement to rather than a substitute for NATO" (Belkin 2009, 14). Therefore, very different, intersecting, and sometimes competing levels of diplomacy are at play, when talking about diplomatic dealings of the EU.

As Table 7.1 shows, this is also the case of KRI levels of diplomacy. On the top we have the Iraqi federal government level, where the KRI, as well as different politicians from the KRI, has a significant say, as the President is traditionally a Kurd and even the current Foreign Minister is a Kurd. Below the Iraqi federal level, we have the official Kurdistan Regional Government (KRG) level with the foreign representative and the mentioned department of foreign policy. Finally, there is the party level of Kurdish paradiplomacy, mostly impacted by the ruling Kurdistan Democratic Party (KDP) and Patriotic Union of Kurdistan (PUK) who have foreign affairs bureaus on their own. Whether it is allowed for KRG to conduct own foreign relations is disputed. Article 110 of the Iraqi constitution of 2005 clearly states that only the federal government has the authority to engage in international relations and represent the country, as well as decide upon any legally binding foreign policy decisions foreign policy. However, Article 121 specifies that regions, therefore the constitutionally enshrined entity that the KRI is, can engage in foreign relations with regard to cultural, social, and developmental affairs. Based on this, Executive Order No. 143 of the Kurdistan Region's Council of Ministers was issued in 2009, creating the KRI Department of Foreign relations (Doherty 2011, 103). While the KRI is very careful with its wording, calling it a department and not a ministry, and specifically stating on every website of their foreign representations that they only "promote the interests of the Kurdistan Region [...] in accordance with the Region's legislation and the Constitution of the Republic of Iraq" (KRG Department of Foreign Relations 2021), the KRI is on many levels engaging in international diplomacy.

Nevertheless, now we see that never have as many EU-member state representations existed in the KRI as now. Table 7.2 gives an overview of the different EU representations in the Kurdistan Region and vice versa including consulates general, consulates as well as representative offices along with their years of foundation. It is evident that from as early as 2005 to 2018 various representations opened while unofficially many EU diplomats and diplomats from EU member states have entered the Kurdistan Region as early as 1991. This was the case especially in the context of the Second Gulf War that lasted from August 1990 to March 1991, and Operation Provide Comfort that was conducted from March 1991 to December 1996 where many EU states engaged militarily and on a humanitarian level to defend and provide for the newly created safe zone in Northern Iraq out of which today's KRI evolved (Rudd 2004).

Table 7.2 Representations between KRI and EU[a]

EU Representations in KRI	Established	KRI representations in EU	Established
EU Liaison office	2015	EU office	2015
Austria	2006	Austria	2012
France	2009	France	2009
Germany	2009	Germany	2009
Italy	2015	Italy	2015
Poland	2005	Poland	2004
Sweden	2010	Sweden	2010
(United Kingdom)	2011 (before embassy office)	(United Kingdom)	2005
		Spain	2011
Czech Republic	2006		
Greece	2018 (before representative office)		
Hungary	2014		
Netherlands	2013		
Romania	2012		

Consulates General, Consulates, Representative offices

[a]Although the UK has left the EU by January 31, 2020, it was part of it when the named offices were established and therefore was included

Over the last 16 years, the scope of paradiplomatic presence for both the Kurdistan Region and the European Union has developed immensely and what used to be a humanitarian or security case is now a political entity that has reciprocal relations to the EU. It is evident that behind these many mutual representations lie various avenues of economic, defense, and diplomatic cooperation that have developed over many decades of unofficial and official politics of the Kurdish administration in Iraq. This chapter sheds light on these avenues and gives a historical-chronological analysis of EU-KRI relations, their development, common interests, successes, and failures.

The Pre-autonomy Quest for Visibility (Pre-1991)

Long before the de facto establishment of the KRI in 1992 have Iraqi Kurdish parties engaged politically in Europe and the fact that throughout the twentieth century the repeated fleeing of Kurds has led to their diaspora communities growing in Europe has also added another layer to the Kurdish-European relationship of this time. Much of the groundwork of today's institutional setting of Iraq was laid in the then-largest city of the European Union, London (Rogg and Rimscha 2007, 830), where the political Kurdish diaspora has been growing stronger since the 1970s and proved to become a material and diplomatic lifeline to the isolated and impoverished Kurds (Paasche 2020; Bakir, November 2021). This phase of paradiplomatic action can be separated between the diaspora and the party level, where overlaps of these levels have been frequent, though.

On the diaspora level, we see that in various European countries the number of Kurdish people fleeing the war in the Kurdish areas of Iraq, Iran, Syria, and Turkey peaked toward the 1980s and 1990s which also had great effects on how political activism was institutionalized. In Germany where a large population of Kurdish migrants lived, organizations like the Association of Organizations from Kurdistan in Germany (KOMKAR) were founded in 1979, in Paris, which has always been a hub of Kurdish cultural diaspora the Kurdish Institute was founded in 1983, and in 1992 the Kurdish Human Rights Project was founded in London. These groups enabled diaspora Kurds to get in touch with European policymakers and to raise awareness for the Kurdish cause far ahead of the formal acknowledgment of the KRI. An example of the fruitfulness of these endeavors was the Kurdish Conference of 1989 which was organized in collaboration with the late French president's wife Danielle Mitterrand, who was to become one of the most known European supporters of Kurdish self-rule (Zubaida 1990). Authors like Eccarius-Kelly (2000) and van Bruinessen (1999) have therefore suggested that this phase has led to a significant "Europeanization," "Internationalization," and "Deterritorialization" of the Kurdish question. This has, of course, not happened in a party-political vacuum, but often different political parties had an increasing play in these processes of institutionalization. Both the KDP, founded in 1946, and the PUK, founded in 1975, have established their own bureaus for international relations, that they still run to this day, and have built diplomatic connections to Europe throughout their struggle against the Iraqi regime and each other before the KRI was established as a polity. One of the first larger Europe visits of any Kurdish party leader was of that of the late PUK leader Jalal Talabani in Eastern Europe in 1955 (van Bruinessen 1986) and especially the city of London quickly became a PUK hub, as more and more leading PUK figures had to flee Saddam Hussein's repression and established connections to UK politicians. Likewise, other cities like Vienna, where the Gorran party (Kurdish: Change, 2009 founded) founder and former PUK figure Nawshirwan Mustafa studied and lived for a long time, became important centers of Kurdish and Iraqi-oppositional political presence. Not coincidentally the city was the place of the foundation and first meeting of the Iraqi National Congress in 1992, a coalition of Iraqi oppositional groups including KDP and PUK working toward the end of Ba'ath rule in Iraq (Katzman 2003).

Both on a civil society and a party-political level Europe has been an important space of political mobilization and still is. Many of the official diplomatic relations that now exist have been informally established and influenced in this time and many leading Kurdish figures of federal Iraqi and KRI diplomacy and paradiplomacy have had a background in party-level or even pre-2003 paradiplomacy. Iraqi Foreign Minister and KDP member Fuad Hussein spent years in European diaspora before, where he headed the Kurdish Students Union and became deputy head of the Paris Kurdish Institute afterwards. Ahmad Tahsin Berwari, who is an undersecretary in the Iraqi foreign ministry, used to be PUK's representative to Germany (Iraqi Ministry of Foreign Affairs 2022b), and likewise Bakir Fatah Hussein, who is now Iraq's ambassador to Austria, was chief PUK's representative to Spain (Iraqi Ministry of Foreign Affairs 2022a). Another important example is Dilshad Barzani, who is the KRG representative to Germany in Berlin and used to be KDP representative to Germany in Bonn throughout the 1990s. Links between civil society, party, KRG, and federal paradiplomacy have therefore always existed and developed out of each other and were fundamental to establishing the foundation to today's paradiplomatic relations.

NASCENT AUTONOMY AND HUMANITARIAN CRISIS (1991–2003)

After Ba'athist Iraq was isolated from the international community for years under the rule of Saddam Hussein, the Second Gulf War and the creation of the no-fly zone in the context of the Iraqi no-fly zones[1] conflict in Kurdish-inhabited Northern Iraq in 1991 ended this isolation. Journalists and non-governmental organizations (NGOs) suddenly had access to the country through the military protection of the no-fly zone and could see for themselves what has been done to the population there (Bakir, November 2021; Malanczuk 1991). People that had suffered for years under the genocidal Anfal operations[2] were fleeing and scattered in camps all over the region and the incoming humanitarian help was greatly needed as thousands of Kurds died fleeing to Turkey and thousands of others were stranded without even a camp to head to (Miller 1991). The humanitarian sector that quickly established itself in consequence to this can therefore be regarded as the first big European engagement in the KRI, especially through those European countries that were part of Operation Provide Comfort I and II[3] and the Iraqi no-fly zones conflict, namely the UK, Germany, France, the Netherlands, Italy, Spain,

---

[1] After Saddam Hussein invaded Kuwait on August 2, 1990, the United States together with its allies started Operation Desert Shield in August 1990 to push back Saddam. Saddam retaliating against his population was feared and the United Nations (UN) Security Council decided in their Resolution 688 on April 5, 1991, that a no-fly zone should be established in the northern and southern Iraqi areas. Kurdish areas were covered by this no-fly zone and gave Kurds the leverage to declare their autonomy.

[2] The Anfal operations were a series of eight genocidal operations conducted by Saddam's Ba'ath regime from 1986 to 1989, with the biggest operation being the Halabja chemical attack that killed 5000 civilians on the spot. The operations all in all are estimated to have killed 50,000–100,000 Kurdish civilians.

[3] Operations Provide Comfort I and II were military and humanitarian operations that commenced after the establishment of the no-fly zones and were running from March 1991 to December 1996. They aimed at helping the Kurdish population in Northern Iraq and containing their mass fleeing. The operations were headed by the United States, with the UK, Germany, France, Australia, the Netherlands, Turkey, Italy, Spain, and Portugal being allies.

and Portugal (Rudd 2004). A great number of European groups like Christian Aid, Handicap International, Doctors without Borders (MSF), or the Norwegian Refugee Council all set foot on Iraqi ground in the KRI for the first time in 1991 and established their networks from then on (Participant 2, February 2022).

Although European states were involved in these operations, on a political and economic level many of them still kept up economic relations with Saddam Hussein that were very lucrative (Krüger 2003; Styan 2004) which became most evident during the Oil for Food scandal where existing sanctions on Iraq were circumvented on a large scale (Raphael 2004). This led many European countries to stay reluctant when it came to direct political support for the Kurdish cause in Iraq that went beyond humanitarian help and made a coherent EU approach to the Kurds impossible. In a European comparison, while the UK was traditionally much more on the US side of defense politics throughout the 1990s and 2000s, and therefore pro-regime change in Iraq, France switched to a less pro-Kurdish position under President Jacques Chirac, successor to pro-Kurdish François Mitterrand, while Germany feared Turkey and its Turkish population so much it avoided the Kurdish issue overall—and often still does so for the same reasons.

To "avoid the K-word" during this military and humanitarian intervention was not only because of the Turkish population in Europe though but mainly because of the EU and NATO-ally Turkey itself, as the humanitarian operations that started in 1991 largely relied on the Turkish route to Kurdistan and Turkish air support (Rudd 2004, 42). Then-President Turgut Özal was afraid of the Kurdish "mountain men" that would be "difficult to integrate" (Montalbano and Pope 1991) fleeing from Saddam and crossing the border to Turkey, where Ankara was dealing violently with its own "Kurdish problem." In this context the creation of the safe zone in Northern Iraq was following Özal's wish to keep the Kurds away, that often fled crossing the border to Turkey or Iran, and the EU became an ally helping Turkey breach the non-refoulement principle by pushing them back into this zone. The establishment of this humanitarian EU-Turkey corridor to KRI and ultimately the Middle East impacts EU-KRI dealings to this day and greatly shaped how this humanitarian corridor developed economically and politically. The role of Turkey acting as a bridge in this regard can therefore not be underestimated. Europe never needed a direct presence in the KRI simply because Turkey and its vital Incirlik Base were always at disposal for military and humanitarian access and the seeming natural enmity between Turkey and the KRI was to dissolve in 1992 the latest when the KDP became a vital partner in the fight against the Kurdistan Workers' Party (PKK) (Gunter 1996).

Therefore, the de facto establishment of the KRI did not change much about the fact that whoever wanted to deal with Iraqi Kurds had to do so firstly through Turkey and secondly through one of the leading parties which largely influenced the course of paradiplomatic avenues for the years to come (Participant 2, February 2022; Participant 3, February 2022).[4] This worsened in the following years since both KDP and PUK found themselves in a deadlock after the first elections of the Kurdistan Region on May 19, 1992. This political dispute culminated in a bloody four-year war starting in 1994. The KRI was divided into two zones and humanitarian access often had to happen via party channels of those that controlled the respective zone (Participant 1, February 2022; Participant 2, February 2022; Participant 3, February 2022). Organizations like Caritas and the Arbeiter-Samariter-Bund (ASB), for example, often dealt with KDP officials (Participant 2, February 2022; Participant 3, February 2022), and organizations like Medico International or MSF established connections to PUK officials to access the Northeast, which was harder to access in the early 1990s as the no-fly zone did not cover many of those areas (Participant 2, February 2022). Another problem to humanitarian access was that Baghdad was not allowing the presence of many organizations in the self-administered Kurdish areas, and many American organizations retreated after the beginning of the Oil for Food program in 1996 (Gautier and Francia 2005; Participant 1, February 2022). Nevertheless, many European organizations persisted with the national and international pressure and continued cooperating with the local administration, as Table 7.3 shows.

The presence of these organizations and the material support they provided were nevertheless a lifeline for the nascent Kurdish autonomy and these links are important to this day. Many organizations are still active and NGOs are such an integral part of the KRI that it has a specific Department of Non-Governmental Organization that oversees the multitude of organizations working in the region. However, on a political level

---

[4] Three interviews with people from the humanitarian sector were conducted, that started working in KRI from 1991 on. Participant 1 is an expat manager of an NGO. Participant 2 is an expat senior logistics officer of MSF. Participant 3 is a local project co-coordinator of an independent NGO in KRI.

Table 7.3 Selection of European NGO's active in KRI after 1996 (Gautier and Francia 2005, 4)

Name	Country	Still active
Qandil	Sweden	Yes
MAG	UK	Yes
Norwegian People Aid	Norway	Yes
Emergency	Italy	Yes
Handicap International	Belgium	Yes
Help Age	UK	No
CDN	Netherlands	No
France Libertés	France	Yes
Wadi	Germany	Yes
Diakonia	Sweden	No

party-infighting and reliance on Turkey for access have led to these avenues not unifying and institutionalizing on a higher level for this time.

BUILDING ECONOMIC BRIDGES IN A NEW IRAQ (2003–2014)

In the following years, the humanitarian network of European organizations, as well as Kurdish diaspora and Kurdish party diplomacy with the EU, would be the only links between the Kurds and the EU. EU hesitancy toward official engagement in the KRI did not change with the US invasion of Iraq in 2003 since the war was supported by only one of the EU "big three": the UK (Lehne 2012). While the US private sector quickly flooded the country and a sophisticated network of local warlords, party leaders, and businessmen tried to get a piece of the pie (Muttitt 2012), European countries were disinclined to economically engage in a region, where the US invasion was quick to be followed by a bloody civil war. It was only until the late 2000s and the opening of the Erbil airport on July 7 and Sulaimaniyah airport on July 20, 2005, that EU countries became more and more willing to invest in Iraq and especially the Kurdistan Region and even open representations in the place that was advertised as "The Other Iraq" (Schorn 2007; Bakir, November 2021).

Although the unification agreement between KDP and PUK was signed in 2006 and both ran for the 2005 elections as a unified list, in terms of economic and military development nothing changed much about the duopoly established in the 1990s and therefore increasing political officiality and legality did not develop. Since the Kurdish parties proved to be helpful allies to the west and the Kurdish market boomed quickly at that time while the rest of Iraq was drowning in sectarian conflict (Barkey and Laipson 2005), it was not a strategic aim of the military powers of the Iraq war to intervene in this duopoly system. Much rather established party channels between Europe and the KRI switched from a humanitarian-only mode to market-liberal channels of a never-before-seen influx of goods and currencies.

Kurdish so-called small and medium-sized enterprises (SMEs) have professionalized greatly after the end of the double-embargo on KRI in the 1990s[5] and became lucrative business partners for many Turkish and European companies from 2007 on but many of these SMEs had to have party affiliations in the first place and trade relations developed on an unofficial level. Therefore, talking about privatization is only a part of the truth of this period, as the needed institutional backing of these SMEs has in most cases been partisan.

With the foundation of the KRG Ministry of Trade and Industry in 2010 this slowly changed and trade relations between Europe and KRI became more official since now a central, however still party-influenced, institution existed. Before only the Board of Investment existed since 2006 which, however, only helped investors in attaining licenses and establishing contacts to relevant authorities. European business ventures in the KRI expanded and the number of businesses creating branches in the Kurdistan Region has developed greatly. From the energy to engineering, automotive, construction, or retail sector many European companies have set foot in the Kurdistan region over the last two decades as the local market is characterized as high risk but also high revenue. The establishment of the Ministry of Trade and Industry was followed by more formal visits of economic delegations from Europe, for example, in 2010 when at this time largest British business delegation visited Erbil. Every year the Erbil International Fair is hosting a multitude of national and international companies from different sectors such as agriculture, construction, and automotive. Most European consulates in Erbil also have a special office offering their services to companies willing to invest in KRI; for

---

[5] From August 6, 1991, following Saddam's invasion of Kuwait to May 22, 2003, Iraq was under sanctions under the UN Security Council resolution 1956. The 1996 Oil for Food program allowed Iraq to export oil under the sanctions regime while receiving humanitarian goods in return. Saddam, however, effectively stopped any re-distribution of humanitarian aid to the Kurdish north of the country which leads many scholars to call this a double embargo (Prados 1994; Natali 2007; Mohammed and Alrebh 2020).

example France has an Economic department, Italy has an "Italy Desk" for Italian entrepreneurs established in 2012, and the Czech Republic has an Economic and Commercial Section since 2018. Germany has its own Erbil branch of the Liaison Office for Industry and Commerce in Iraq (AHK) which was established in 2010. Most consulates also list the Erbil, Sulaimaniyah, Duhok, and Halabja Chambers of Commerce as contacts to reach out to, as well as the relevant ministries which are in most cases the Ministries of Trade and Industry and Natural Resources. As Table 7.4 shows, over the past years, European companies of different sectors diversified their involvements in the KRI while sectors like energy or engineering still are the dominating ones.

Especially in the energy sector there has been increasing European interest in diversifying its energy sources as tensions between the EU and Russia grew more and more in the 2010s which also made Turkey an EU partner and as an important actor in KRI's energy sector come to the forefront. The KRI was repeatedly mentioned as one of the potential providers for the Southern Gas Corridor project led by Turkey who already established various deals with the KRI (Tagliapietra 2016; Zulal 2012) while paradoxically Russian companies like Rosneft already had their foot in the KRI game (Pirani 2018). Oil and Gas deals with European and Turkish companies have been used as a foreign policy tool and as a lifeline for the KRG repeatedly that had increasing political conflicts with the federal government in Baghdad under then-prime minister Nuri al Maliki, who was in office from May 20, 2006, until September 8, 2014 (Hiltermann 2012). Therefore, economic deals and especially deals with companies for the energy sector have not followed a coherent strategy (Zulal 2012) but rather tried to create as much interdependence and therefore leverage for Erbil against Baghdad as possible.

MILITARY COOPERATION AND THE WAR AGAINST THE SO-CALLED ISLAMIC STATE (2014–2017)

As Tezcür puts it: "The US invasion of Iraq in 2003 was the first time when geopolitical interests of a superpower were completely aligned with the interest of a Kurdish minority" (Tezcür 2019, 7) and this was certainly true for KRG-US cooperation on the economic and military level but it was not until 2014 when the European Union and EU member states became active military allies of the KRI as well.

Table 7.4 Selection of European companies present in KRI

Country	Company	Sector
Germany	Grohe	Sanitation
	ILF Consulting Engineers	Engineering
	Knauf	Construction
	MAN Trucks	Automotive
	Würth	Fasteners, chemicals, safety products, tools, inventory management
	PricewaterhouseCoopers	Consulting
France	Carrefour	Retail trade
	France Télécom	Telecommunications
	Lafarge	Construction
	Perenco (French & British)	Energy
	Renault Trucks	Automotive
	Schneider Electric	Engineering
	SCP	Sanitation
	Total	Energy
	Veolia	Environmental services
Italy	Ansaldo Energia	Energy
	Eni	Energy
	Studio Galli	Consultancy
	Webuild (Salini Impregilo)	Construction
Hungary	Mol	Energy
Norway	DNO International	Energy
United Kingdom	Aspect Energy	Energy
	Chevron	Energy
	Costain	Construction, Civil engineering
	Hess	Energy
	HSBC	Financial Services
	Hunt Petroleum	Energy
	JCB	Heavy equipment, Agricultural machinery
	Murphy Oil Corporation	Energy
	Parsons Brinckerhoff	Engineering
	Scott Wilson Group	Support Services Consultancy
	Shell	Energy

On August 30, 2014, the EU foreign ministers agreed on arming the Iraqi forces including the Kurds in the fight against the so-called Islamic State in Iraq and Syria (ISIS)[6] that rose to power in the same year officially, this time taking a clear stand in an Iraqi conflict (Andersson and Gaub

[6] The so-called Islamic State is a Jihadist group that controlled a large territory from Northern and Western Iraq to Central and Eastern Syria from 2014 to 2019.

2015). As the Kurdistan Region and specifically the KDP became a viable and long-term military partner of Turkey by then, Germany was also not afraid this time to give the biggest military contribution to the Peshmerga forces in consequence to the EU decision and put a parliamentary mandate for the military mission in place (Andersson and Gaub 2015). Similarly, the Hungarian Deputy State General for Global Affairs Péter Wintermantel visited Erbil in 2014 as well and 116 Hungarian troops were sent immediately to train Peshmerga forces. Italian prime minister Matteo Renzi also headed to Erbil for a high-level visit in 2015, sending 450 Italian troops to support the forces, and a year later Dutch Prime Minister Mark Rutte also deployed more soldiers for the mission against ISIS.

In the course of the massacres and genocides conducted by ISIS, especially those against the Yezidi people of Shengal throughout the summer of 2014, humanitarian cooperation between the EU and the Kurdistan region also saw a peak again and the humanitarian channels that were built as early as 1991 during the Kurdish mass exodus proved to be central avenues of paradiplomatic cooperation again (Participant 2, February 2022).

The engagement of international powers and especially European ones in the fight against ISIS has quickly proven to be effective, as the territorial decline of the caliphate continued and many areas in the so-called disputed territories[7] between Erbil and Baghdad were taken over by Kurdish Peshmerga forces. The territorial gains of the Peshmerga forces of PUK and KDP were unprecedented and left the KRG controlling the biggest de facto territory since 1991, including cities like Kirkuk. The frequent official visits of European heads of state and government, the military support, and the territorial stretch that KRG achieved by then led the region to become not only an economic but a military partner and an acknowledged political ally until 2016 and elevated KRG paradiplomacy to a much more sophisticated level (Abbas Zadeh and Kirmanj 2017). The international fight against ISIS was not only a military fight but a humanitarian, cultural, and political one and therefore KRG's involvement in this

---

[7] The disputed territories of Iraq that span from the Shengal mountains to the city of Khanaqin are territories with mixed ethnic and religious. They are disputed in the sense that both KRI and the Iraqi federal government claim the areas. Article 140 of the 2005 Iraqi constitution calls for a referendum to resolve whether the regions want to be part of KRI or the federal government, but this has not been implemented so far.

fight as one of the main actors on the ground has diversified the channels of paradiplomacy that were at the disposal of the region.

The other side of this rise in power and relevance is that although in the years before the ISIS resurgence protests amassed in the KRI with people calling for an end to corruption, a true unification of political powers, and democratization (Gunter 1998; Bali 2018), these calls were ignored when the fight against ISIS was much more urgent than any call for a western engagement in the democratization of KRI. The government and the armed forces that still were run in the party-duopoly system that ruled the region since its establishment were now in a position of ultimate power thanks to the establishment of economic interdependencies and military allyships. Then-KRG president Masoud Barzani prolonged his term unconstitutionally during this time (Salih 2015), and both KDP and PUK were repeatedly accused of stockpiling the weapons they received for the fight against ISIS for their means (Helfont 2017). Overall, the often-cited securitization (Hama 2020) of the Kurdish question trumped any other focus of EU foreign policy in the region and the existing fragile institutional setting; this had major repercussions for not only the way paradiplomacy was conducted but how democratization, rule of law, and institutional responsiveness developed in KRI.

EU-KRG Post-Referendum: The Current Phase (Post-2017)

The built economic and military interdependency has helped the KRI in many cases and has shaped EU-KRI relations. The 2017 independence referendum in which KRI citizens as well as citizens of the disputed territories were asked whether they want the Kurdish areas of Iraq to become an independent state, however, was one of the biggest setbacks of established Kurdish paradiplomacy. The referendum to which 92.73 percent of the population that voted said yes was answered by not only the shutting down of all border crossings on the overland route but also to the shutdown of the airports, which were once the most crucial opening of the region to the world, by the Iraqi federal government and the bordering Iranian and Turkish government. These governments, among others, reacted furiously to the referendum calling it a "foreign sectarian plot," as then-president Hassan Rouhani did in remarks with Turkish President Recep Tayyip Erdogan (Regencia 2017) who previously threatened military action in case of KRG executing the referendum (Al Jazeera 2017). Troops of the Iranian-backed Popular Mobilization Forces (PMF) took over most of the territories that Peshmerga regained in bloody years of war against ISIS, and committed heavy human rights abuses (Human Rights Watch 2017). This takeover was even made easier for PMF because of internal PUK divisions concerning the question of the referendum and whether to engage in a military operation to fight against PMF in Kirkuk. The political and territorial repercussions of the referendum were fatal and the Kurdistan Region of Iraq was arguably in its most isolated stage since the double embargo it had to go through in the 1990s. However, in the aftermath of the diplomatic crisis between the Baghdad and Erbil referendum, former KRG Foreign Minister Falah Mustafa Bakir recalls the invitation of then-prime minister Nechirvan Barzani to the World Economic Forum in Davos in January 2018 as having been the turning point. After both French President Emmanuel Macron and former German Chancellor Angela Merkel had talks with Barzani and brokered the much-needed talk between Barzani and then-premier minister (PM) Haider al-Abadi, Davos was the place where the first Erbil-Baghdad meeting happened after the referendum (Bakir, November 2021). Therefore, paradiplomatic relations with EU member states have been vital in helping KRG out of this crisis. After all, much needed diplomatic reconciliation between Erbil and Baghdad that was long overdue during the Maliki administration from 2006 to 2014 already had to be navigated through an international economic conference after the damage was already done and the Kurdistan referendum was only the peak of a long-running diplomatic crisis between the two centers of power. While EU-KRI paradiplomacy, therefore, developed over time, it did not do so in a way that would forward the needed institutionalization and the clarification of constitutional flaws that were not taken care of (Anderson 2015).

Therefore, as much as the EU has developed a strong hand in the region and has proven to be able to navigate military, economic, and political crises, the official programs that the EU provided for federal Iraq have never had pendants for the Kurdish side, as Falah Mustafa Bakir recalls: "therefore, this was not easy for us to deal with, even when the EU and Iraq signed a partnership agreement. There was a pact, a contract or cooperation, and whatever partnership with Iraq. We tried hard to be part of it. It took so long until the EU invited me as a minister from the Kurdistan Region when former High Representative Federica Mogherini and I went to Brussels to sit next to foreign minister Ja'fari" (Bakir, November 2021).

Programs like the European Union Integrated Rule of Law Mission for Iraq (EUJUST LEX),[8] which has been the first integrated rule of law mission conducted under the CSDP (EEAS 2014), were exclusively addressed to the needs of federal Iraq, while, clearly, the judicial system in the Kurdistan Region is facing other challenges that need customized approaches (Falah Mustafa Bakir, November 2021).

The dealings of the EU with Baghdad and Erbil represent these many institutional gaps that were elaborated in this chapter. Instead of help filling, the EU learned to simply circumvent them. Adding to that is the reality that not only this schism between Erbil and Baghdad exists, but that between KDP and PUK as well. These schisms are not addressed as well and the EU approach of circumvention is probably the most evident when even during a normal diplomatic visit of EU representatives, to this day, all relevant sides of the political parties and the figures inside the parties have to be visited one by one, which for the KDP alone means visiting PM Masrour Barzani, President Nechirvan Barzani, and KDP president Masoud Barzani (European Council 2021).

Nevertheless, KRG's paradiplomacy which clearly includes the paradiplomacy of the ruling parties is expanding. Interestingly, a slight tendency can be seen that in the last years more and more countries of central, eastern, and southern Europe have opened representations in the Kurdistan Region, which likely has economic and migration policy–related reasons. Countries like Poland have developed strong economic ties with the Kurdistan Region in the course of their presence in Iraq and in general we see an increasing activity of the Viségrad group consisting of the Czech Republic, Poland, Hungary, and Slovakia there (O'Driscoll and Sasnal 2015). However, specifically with the refugee crises that repeatedly came up since 2015 and that often include a multitude of refugees from KRI, the Viségrad countries have repeatedly urged that they assist whatever country holds back refugee flows (Maurice 2015). This is not only true for this EU group, though, but for the EU, in general, that is in cooperation with the EU member states' foreign ministries running the European Return and Reintegration Network (ERRIN) which has offices not only in Erbil but also in Duhok in Sulaimaniyah and that facilitates the return of migrants from Iraq and the KRI. The 2021 escalation of the refugee crisis on the border between Belarus and Poland and the quick cooperation

---

[8] EUJUST LEX was launched in Iraq in 2013. The mission was engaged in capacity building on the Iraqi judicial, legal, and civil society levels.

between Polish, Belarusian, and KRI officials to fly back as many refugees as possible to Erbil have shown how efficient the cooperation on this level is by now (KRG Department of Foreign Relations 2021; Sherwani 2021). Therefore, the war against terror might not be the only dominating topic in the future, but the measures the EU is taking against refugees that often cross the KRI are of increasing importance.

Conclusion

The Kurdistan Region started out as a de facto autonomy fighting against Iraqi occupation and has over the course of the last 30 years taken on more and more state-like tasks, with paradiplomatic relations being one of those (Gürbey et al. 2017). On the societal level, Kurdish diaspora in Europe has quickly built a bridge between then-isolated KRI and Europe. The leading political parties, KDP and PUK also established their own foreign relation bureaus at that time. After the establishment of KRI, relations to the EU were greatly impacted on the humanitarian level, as many European organizations entered KRI after 1991 and stay until now. After the fall of Saddam, economic relations became increasingly important and shaped the expansion of European presence in KRI. The war against ISIS, finally, added the military level of cooperation. Overall, official venues of KRI-EU paradiplomacy have developed but have seen a little stagnation in the post-Referendum years.

For the future of these relations the KRI has great potential, and its increasingly young, decidedly pro-democratic (Jasim 2021), and innovative population is fertile soil for further progress in that regard. Investing not only in large businesses and established political elites but in civil society will be of increasing importance. The big question of the future will be about how these relations will not only be relations of the elites but relations that society can profit from and for society to profit from these relations, they must happen in a much more official and strategically coherent level. This is a general issue for both EU and KRI, as we have a general debate on the future of the EU foreign and defense structure and the problem that KRI is in limbo in its relation to federal Iraq. As long as these issues are not resolved, there cannot be societal ownership to paradiplomacy or any policy.

For a non-state actor, the Kurdistan Region therefore has comparatively sophisticated paradiplomatic relations that go into both directions. The challenge lies in the level of officiality and consequently longevity and stability that these KRI-EU relations can take on. This is in the end depending on the institutional development of these actors domestically. For the EU it is the question whether it is going to accentuate its supranational character more or whether individual member state's diplomatic approaches will have more importance. For the KRG it is about fundamental issues of legality. These are linked to many questions of general unresolved institutional problems of the KRG. Among them is the constitutional clarification vis-à-vis Baghdad of what foreign policies the KRG is entitled to as per the constitution, as well as how autonomously the KRG can get into foreign relations including economic long-term cooperation, as the recent Iraqi Supreme Court rejection of the KRG oil and gas law on February 15, 2022, made clear. On a KRG level, legality can be achieved only if the general issue of unification and hence democratization is achieved. As long as armed forces, large economic conglomerates, and political pathways to participation are exclusively running through the KDP and PUK systems, there is no way a coherent diplomatic approach can be achieved, as there is no one legitimized institutional actor that could engage in these relations. Whether it is about economic cooperation or defense, an ununified KRG will always be approached by the EU or other foreign partners through different partisan actors and not through one actor which ultimately leads to this type of backdoor negotiation we currently see that will not lead to formality and liability. This one actor would in the ideal case be a department of foreign relations that is both legitimized to conduct a clear set of political tasks by the Iraqi constitution and led by ministers that are legitimized by election and election only. That in turn is only possible in a KRG where a democratic monopoly of power and therefore rule of law exists.

These points set the preconditions for a type of paradiplomacy that can foster democratization through international interdependence—this interdependence must, however, exceed the backdoor negotiation nature of past and present economic and security dealings with the KRI but enter a true space of legality.

References

Abbas Zadeh, Yoosef, and Sherko Kirmanj. 2017. The Para-Diplomacy of the Kurdistan Region in Iraq and the Kurdish Statehood Enterprise. *The Middle East Journal* 71 (4): 587–606.

Al Jazeera. 2017. Erdogan Warns of Armed Action over Kurdish Referendum: Saying That the Turkish Military Stands Ready, President Threatens to Cut the Kurds' Oil Exports Through His Country. September 25. Accessed February 14, 2022. https://www.aljazeera.com/news/2017/9/25/erdogan-warns-of-armed-action-over-kurdish-referendum.

Anderson, Liam. 2015. The Dangerous Legacy of a Flawed Constitution: Resolving Iraq's Kurdish 'Problem'. In *The Legacy of Iraq: From the 2003 War to the 'Islamic State'*, ed. Benjamin Isakhan, 82–96. Edinburgh University Press.

Andersson, Jan J., and Florence Gaub. 2015. *Adding Fuel to the Fire? Arming the Kurds.* European Union Institute for Security Studies. Accessed March 6, 2022. https://www.iss.europa.eu/sites/default/files/EUISSFiles/Alert_37_Kurds.pdf.

Bakir, Falah Mustafa. 2021. Interviewed on 9 November.

Bali, Ahmed O. 2018. The Roots of Clientelism in Iraqi Kurdistan and the Efforts to Fight it. *Open Political Science* 1 (1): 98–104.

Barkey, Henri J., and Ellen Laipson. 2005. Iraqi Kurds and Iraq's Future. *Middle East Policy* 12 (4): 66–76.

Belkin, Paul. 2009. *France: Factors Shaping Foreign Policy and Issues in U.S.-French Relations.* Washington: The Library of Congress.

Doherty, Patrick. 2011. Revere and Adhere: Examining the Legality of Kurdistani Diplomatic Engagement. *NIMEP Insights* 6: 96–113.

Eccarius-Kelly, Vera. 2000. Radical Consequences of Benign Neglect: The Rise of the PKK in Germany. *The Fletcher Forum of World Affairs* 24 (1): 161–174.

EEAS. 2014. Factsheet: EU Integrated Rule of Law Mission for Iraq (EUJUST LEX-Iraq). European Union External Action. Accessed November 11, 2021. https://eeas.europa.eu/archives/csdp/missions-and-operations/eujust-lex-iraq/pdf/facsheet_eujust-lex_iraq_en.pdf.

European Council. 2021. EU HR Borrell Visits Iraq. Council of the European Union Newsroom. Accessed November 29, 2021. https://newsroom.consilium.europa.eu/videos/shotlist/131471-eu-hr-borrell-meets-president-of-kurdistan-region-20210907.

Gautier, Gérard, and Giorgio Francia. 2005. A Recent Story of NGOs in Northern Iraqi Kurdistan. *Humanitaire, enjeux, pratiques, débats* 12: 40–49.

Gunter, Michael M. 1996. The KDP-PUK Conflict in Northern Iraq. *The Middle East Journal* 50: 224–241.

———. 1998. Turkey and Iran Face Off in Kurdistan. *Middle East Quarterly* 5 (1): 33–40.

Gürbey, Gülistan, Sabine Hofmann, and Ferhad I. Seyder. 2017. *Between State and Non-State. Politics and Society in Kurdistan-Iraq and Palestine.* New York: Palgrave Macmillan.

Hama, Hawre H. 2020. The Securitization and De-Securitization of Kurdish Societal Security in Turkey, Iraq, Iran, and Syria. *World Affairs* 183 (4): 291–314.

Helfont, Samuel. 2017. Getting Peshmerga Reform Right: Helping the Iraqi Kurds to Help Themselves in Post-ISIS Iraq. Foreign Policy Research Institute and Institute of Regional and International Studies. Accessed March 6, 2022. http://xiaoyewudao.com/content/dam/ethz/special-interest/gess/cis/center-for-securities-studies/resources/docs/FPRI-Getting%20Peshmerga%20Reform%20Right.pdf.

Hiltermann, Joost R. 2012. Revenge of the Kurds: Breaking Away from Baghdad. *Foreign Affairs* 91: 16.

Human Rights Watch. 2017. Iraq: Fighting in Disputed Territories Kills Civilians: Iraqi Forces Slow to Prevent Looting. October 20. Accessed February 9, 2022. https://www.hrw.org/news/2017/10/20/iraq-fighting-disputed-territories-kills-civilians.

Iraqi Ministry of Foreign Affairs. 2022a. Iraqi Ambassadors. Accessed February 7, 2022. http://www.mofa.gov.iq/iraqi-ambassadors.

———. 2022b. Undersecretaries. Accessed February 7, 2022. https://www.mofa.gov.iq/undersecretaries.

Jasim, Dastan. 2021. Kurdish Youth and Civic Culture: Support for Democracy Among Kurdish and Non-Kurdish Youth in Iraq. In *Youth Identity, Politics and Change in Contemporary Kurdistan*, ed. Shivan Fazil and Bahar Başer, 97–123. London: Transnational Press.

Katzman, Kenneth. 2003. *Iraq: US Regime Change Efforts, the Iraqi Opposition, and Post-War Iraq*. Washington: The Library of Congress.

KRG Department of Foreign Relations. 2021. KRG Representation in the European Union. Accessed February 7, 2022. https://gov.krd/dfr-en/krg-representations/krg-representation-in-the-european-union/.

Krüger, Jens. 2003. In Deutschland Fand Saddam Immer Eine Helfende Hand. *Welt am Sonntag*, April 4. Accessed November 27, 2021. https://www.welt.de/print-wams/article131115/In-Deutschland-fand-Saddam-immer-eine-helfende-Hand.html.

Lehne, Stefan. 2012. *The Big Three in EU Foreign Policy*. Washington: Carnegie Endowment for International Peace.

Malanczuk, Peter. 1991. The Kurdish Crisis and Allied Intervention in the Aftermath of the Second Gulf War. *European Journal of International Law* 2: 114.

Maurice, Eric. 2015. Refugee Quotas 'Unacceptable' for Visegrad States. *EU Observer*, September 4. Accessed November 17, 2021. https://euobserver.com/migration/130122.

Miller, Judith. 1991. The World; Displaced in the Gulf War: 5 Million Refugees. *The New York Times*, June 16.

Mohammed, Jihan A., and Abdullah F. Alrebh. 2020. Iraqi Kurds: The Dream of Nation State. *Digest of Middle East Studies* 29 (2): 215–229.
Montalbano, William D., and Hugh Pope. 1991. Turgut Ozal: The Kurds Must Go to Their Own Places. *Los Angeles Times*, May 6. Accessed November 25, 2021. https://www.latimes.com/archives/la-xpm-1991-05-06-me-815-story.html.
Muttitt, Greg. 2012. *Fuel on the Fire: Oil and Politics in Occupied Iraq*. London: Vintage Books.
Natali, Denise. 2007. The Spoils of Peace in Iraqi Kurdistan. *Third World Quarterly* 28 (6): 1111–1129.
O'Driscoll, Dylan, and Patrycja Sasnal. 2015. Is Three a Crowd? The Kurds, Baghdad and Poland. *The Polish Institute of International Affairs* 30 (132): 1–6.
Paasche, Erlend. 2020. Elites and Emulators: The Evolution of Iraqi Kurdish Asylum Migration to Europe. *Migration Studies* 8 (2): 189–208.
Participant 1. 2022. Interviewed on 16 February.
Participant 2. 2022. Interviewed on 19 February.
Participant 3. 2022. Interviewed on 20 February.
Pirani, Simon. 2018. *Let's Not Exaggerate–Southern Gas Corridor Prospects to 2030*. Oxford Institute for Energy Studies.
Prados, Alfred B. 1994. *The Kurds in Iraq: Status, Protection, and Prospects*. Washington: The Library of Congress.
Raphael, Therese. 2004. The Oil-for-Food Scandal. *Wall Street Journal*, March 11. Accessed February 8, 2022. https://www.wsj.com/articles/SB107896733191552156.
Regencia, Ted. 2017. Erdogan, Rouhani United in Opposition to Kurdish State. *Al Jazeera*, October 4. Accessed February 14, 2022. https://www.aljazeera.com/news/2017/10/4/erdogan-rouhani-united-in-opposition-to-kurdish-state.
Rogg, Inga, and Hans Rimscha. 2007. The Kurds as Parties to and Victims of Conflicts in Iraq. *International Review of the Red Cross* 89 (868): 823–842.
Rudd, Gordon W. 2004. *Humanitarian Intervention: Assisting the Iraqi Kurds in Operation Provide Comfort, 1991*. Washington: U.S. Government Printing Office.
Salih, Mohammed A. 2015. KRG Parliament Speaker: Barzani's Term Extension 'Against the Law'. *Al-Monitor*, August 2018. Accessed February 7, 2022. https://www.al-monitor.com/originals/2015/08/kurdish-parliament-speaker-challenge-barzani-legitimacy.html.
Schorn, Daniel. 2007. Kurdistan: The Other Iraq. *CBS News*, February 16. Accessed November 26, 2021. https://www.cbsnews.com/news/kurdistan-the-other-iraq/.
Sherwani, Halgurd. 2021. KRG Facilitates the 'Voluntary Return' of Migrants Stranded on Poland-Belarus Border: Spokesperson. *Kurdistan24*, November

11. Accessed February 8, 2022. https://www.kurdistan24.net/en/story/26277-KRG-facilitates-the-%E2%80%98voluntary-return%E2%80%99-of-migrants-stranded-on-Poland-Belarus-border:-Spokesperson.
Styan, David. 2004. Jacques Chirac's 'Non': France, Iraq and the United Nations, 1991–2003. *Modern & Contemporary France* 12 (3): 371–385.
Tagliapietra, Simone. 2016. *Energy Relations in the Euro-Mediterranean*. New York: Palgrave Macmillan.
Tezcür, Güneş Murat. 2019. A Century of the Kurdish Question: Organizational Rivalries, Diplomacy, and Cross-Ethnic Coalitions. *Ethnopolitics* 18 (1): 1–12.
Van Bruinessen, Martin. 1986. Major Kurdish Organizations in Iraq. *Middle East Report* 141: 14–27.
———. 1999. *The Kurds in Movement: Migrations, Mobilisations, Communications and the Globalization of the Kurdish Question*. Tokyo: Islamic Area Studies Project.
Zubaida, Sami. 1990. Report from Paris: The Kurdish Conference. *Middle East Report* 163: 40–41.
Zulal, Shwan. 2012. Survival Strategies and Diplomatic Tools: The Kurdistan Region's Foreign Policy Outlook. *Insight Turkey* 14 (3): 141–158.

CHAPTER 8

Palestine and EU

Emile Badarin

INTRODUCTION

Diplomacy involves a set of practices that govern formal dialogue between sovereign states. This state-based conception fails to capture the complex and networked international politics that involve a multiplicity of actors (Kuus 2014). Diplomacy is a product of the Westphalian geopolitical ordering. Political struggles against the binary divide of the world into sovereign centres of power and unsovereign peripheries of unrecognised and subaltern subjects are constantly challenging this ordering. From this perspective, self-determination and anti-colonial movements are always involved in various forms of diplomatic practices in an attempt to resist their exclusion from the world's map and relegation to unsovereign or 'liminal' spaces (McConnell 2017).

As critical scholarship suggests, geopolitics is an imperialist discipline that imbricates knowledge and power to impose an imagined spatial order (Dalby 2008; Tuathail 1996). The universalisation of state-based division of the earth is premised on denying many nations their right to exercise

E. Badarin (✉)
European Neighbourhood Policy Chair, College of Europe, Natolin, Warsaw, Poland
e-mail: emile.badarin@coleurope.eu

© The Author(s), under exclusive license to Springer Nature Switzerland AG 2023
G. Gürbey et al. (eds.), *Between Diplomacy and Non-Diplomacy*,
https://doi.org/10.1007/978-3-031-09756-0_8

self-determination and self-representation over their territories. Subjugated nations retaliate against this exclusionary geopolitical and diplomatic structuring. To that end, these 'liminal' actors engage in diplomacy in an attempt to "carve out subject positions, repertoires of practice and alternative spaces of diplomacy which embrace inbetweenness, processuality and ambivalence" (McConnell 2017, 2). To interpret non-state actors' conduct of diplomacy, relevant literature qualifies the term 'diplomacy' by adding prefixes (e.g., para-or protodiplomacy) or adjectives (e.g., constituent, multi-layered, plurinational or transnational diplomacy). According to Alexander Kuznetsov (2015), these concepts refer to the same phenomenon and may be used interchangeably.

This chapter demonstrates the explanatory limitations of these frameworks and concepts with respect to liberation and resistance movements against alien rule. It does so by examining Palestinian diplomatic interactions with the EU. This chapter seeks to answer the following questions: How and why does Palestine engage in diplomacy with the EU? What are the concrete achievements of this diplomatic effort? The Palestine Liberation Organization (PLO) is the official representative of the Palestinians and has been leading its diplomatic struggle since its creation in 1964. Hamas is another significant Palestinian political and resistance movement that conducts diplomacy outside the PLO. Hamas's (para-) diplomatic interactions with the EU are limited because of ideological and political reasons (Charrett 2019; Pace and Pallister-Wilkins 2018). For reasons of space, this chapter focuses only on the representative Palestinian diplomatic activities.

I argue that Palestinian diplomacy is inextricable from their pursuit of independence and must therefore be situated in the context of decolonisation struggles. The central aim of Palestinian diplomacy is geopolitical. Through diplomatic action, Palestinian actors seek to achieve self-determination and reposition 'Palestine' on the world's map as a sovereign state. The precise shape of this desired statehood varied over time. The PLO initially defined independence as the creation of a democratic Palestinian state for all in the entire historical space of Palestine (Palestinian National Charter 1968). In 1974, however, the PLO settled for a Palestinian state in 22 percent of this space, i.e., the West Bank (including East Jerusalem) and the Gaza Strip—known as Occupied Palestinian Territories (OPT).

Considering the colonial context and extensive Palestinian diplomatic representation worldwide, and in the EU in particular, there is a need to critically appraise the debate on paradiplomatic practices. This chapter contributes to this effort by focusing on liberation movements and colonised authorities' use of diplomacy in their struggle for decolonisation and independence. The chapter makes two contributions. Theoretically, it questions the applicability of the paradiplomacy framework to colonial situations. First, actual colonial or occupation authorities lack the normative and legal dimensions of sovereignty, and, by implication, liberation movements are not sub-units of the colonial state. Second, it demonstrates that the nature of their diplomatic conduct is contingent on the degree of institutionalisation of diplomatic presence within the international society and how the majority of other states and international institutions diplomatically interact with liberation movements.

The other contribution concerns the Palestinian diplomatic interactions with the EU and shows that although the EU does not recognise Palestine, the level of diplomatic engagement between them has crossed the threshold of liminality and paradiplomacy. A related argument I make posits that PLO-EU advanced diplomatic structures are founded on the EU's terms. The PLO is entrapped in state-level diplomacy that affords it a semblance of statehood that restricted its authentic character as liberation and anti-colonial movement.

Palestine (represented by the PLO) and the EU are atypical diplomatic actors. As Merje Kuus (2014, 75) suggests, "EU diplomacy is transnational rather than international" and runs through multiple networked institutions. This multiplicity provides unrecognised diplomatic figures, various opportunities and access points to convey their political interests. For instance, Palestinian and Sahrawi 'diplomats' found the European Parliament (EP) a convenient political environment to practice diplomacy and lobbying techniques, and began to seek new avenues to communicate with other EU institutions such as the Commission and European External Action Service (EEAS) (Bouris and Fernández-Molina 2018; Voltolini 2016).

Since 2012, Palestine has achieved extensive international diplomatic presence. This presence and action fit neither the classical grammar of diplomacy nor paradiplomacy or protodiplomacy. The last two frameworks seek to explain diplomatic practices of sub-units of states such as provinces, regions and secessionist areas. Although the Palestinians have no sovereign control over any part of Palestine between River Jordan and the Mediterranean, their supposed 'statehood' in the OPT has wide international recognition. The EU-Palestine interactions are multifaceted and deeply institutionalised in ways that transcend the limitation of paradiplomacy, as the following sections demonstrate. Against this backdrop, the diplomatic activities of political entity that has an extensive level of diplomatic relations, international recognition and a priori right for independence and sovereign self-representation transcend the exegesis of paradiplomacy.

Irrespective of exact terms, all forms of diplomacy are political practices that originate from how diplomats see the world, judge and act. What matters here is diplomatic practices and their outcomes, which the following four sections seek to illustrate. The first section provides a brief overview of the concepts that attempt to theorise non-sovereign diplomacy. The second section situates the Palestinian conduct of diplomacy within the broader struggle for self-determination and independence against Israeli settler-colonial practices. The third section examines the Palestine-EU diplomatic relationship and illustrates its evolution, consolidation and institutionalisation. The fourth section explores proactive Palestinian diplomatic conduct involved in the so-called internationalisation of the Palestinian cause. This chapter concludes by underlining the need for broadening the scholarly debate on diplomacy in order to account for diplomatic practices of colonised and unrecognised authorities or states.

Diplomacy, Politics and Non-sovereign Actors

In the aftermath of World War II, nation-states further institutionalised diplomatic conduct as an exclusive sovereign competence. Almost all United Nations (UN) member states, including the 'non-member observer state' of Palestine, ratified the 1961 Vienna Convention on Diplomatic Relations, which defines diplomatic privileges (UN 1961). Although this structural exclusion has pushed non-sovereign players (e.g., de facto states, native peoples, national movements, supranational institutions, multinational corporates, cities and regions) to the margins of the international society, it failed to prevent them from developing innovative and parallel diplomatic practices in order to transcend the relatively closed state-based geopolitical order. Non-sovereign diplomats tend to actively replicate "UN structures and mimicking the protocols of formal state diplomacy" (McConnell 2017, 2). Moreover, diplomatic privileges are no longer restricted to state representatives but may also be extended to non-sovereign diplomats. For example, Norway (in 2011) and Sweden (in 2012) granted the Palestinian Missions in Oslo and Stockholm and their diplomatic personnel and families diplomatic privileges equivalent to the Vienna Convention (Riksdag 2012; Norweagian Government 2011).

International Relations (IR) scholars who embrace a non-state-based research agenda emphasised role non-sovereign diplomatic practices play in international politics. To capture this phenomenon, diplomacy literature developed different concepts that, for example, include: "paradiplomacy", "protodiplomacy" (Duckacek 1990), "constituent diplomacy" (Kincaid 2001), "multilayer diplomacy" (Hocking 1993), "plurinational diplomacy" (Aldecoa 1999) and "liminal" diplomacy (McConnell 2017) to account for non-sovereign diplomacy.

Paradiplomacy and protodiplomacy are relevant for the purpose of this chapter and therefore must be clarified here. The former refers to the international political activities of sub-state governments such as local authorities of cantons, cities, provinces, regions, sub-states or federates. These sub-state actors engage in paradiplomatic practice to advance a variety of low politics objectives (e.g., promotion of local development, resolving transborder issues, cultural exchange) without challenging the central state's sovereignty. Protodiplomacy, however, is enacted with the intention of contesting the parent state's authority, and therefore has a secessionist dimension (Duckacek 2019; Cornago 2018; Kuznetsov 2015). Alexander Kuznetsov (2015, 88) distinguishes separatist and non-recognised states' diplomacy from "nationalist/cultural" paradiplomacy. Separatist diplomacy stands in direct opposition to the parent state and uses diplomacy to break away from its authority.

Protodiplomacy is strongly linked to struggles for state recognition, and thus it presents an opportunity to cross the threshold and leave the 'liminal' space and join the sovereignty club (Coggins 2014; McConnell 2017). Furthermore, a central aspect of unrecognised or de facto states' diplomatic practices is ideational. Actions of representatives of unrecognised states or secessionist entities are premised on their firm self-perceived sovereign agency and legitimacy to represent their people in international forums. For that purpose, they usually emulate orthodox diplomatic protocols as a means to satisfy their identity (as sovereign agents) and accrue symbolic power and demonstrate their state-like capabilities to the international community.

It is worth mentioning that Kuznetsov (2015) excluded diplomatic actions of Palestine and Western Sahara, and did not refer to them as cases of para- or protodiplomacy. As far as Palestine is concerned, the following remarks must be clarified before applying either framework. First, Palestine and the Palestinians (this also applies to Western Sahara and East Timor until 1999) is a colonised space and nation rather than a sub-national group (or sub-unit) of Israel. Israel is an external settler-colonial power from which the Palestinians seek freedom and independence (Veracini 2006; Pappé 2017; Badarin 2015). Second, this is also a struggle for decolonisation rather than secession/separation (Badarin 2021d). Third, Palestine is not a de facto state but rather meticulously colonised spaces, some of which are partially administered by the Palestinian Authority (PA) in populated Palestinian towns in the West Bank or by Hamas in the Gaza Strip. Although Israel is the only sovereign power in the historical land of Palestine, its control of the OPT—and the Occupied Syrian Golan—is illegal under international law, and therefore the international community and the EU do not recognise Israel's sovereignty over these territories (European Commission 2013).

Fionna McConnell (2017) uses the notion of 'liminal space' to account for the diplomatic activates that stand outside the state/non-state binary division. According to her, these actors are situated on the threshold and occupy the in-between space. It is vital, however, to emphasise that the threshold position and marginality are the outcome of contingent and heterogeneous conditions of international politics. Unrecognised diplomats' degree of 'liminality' and marginalisation in the international system is experienced differently, depending on their capabilities, legal and moral legitimacy and resources. Thus, their diplomatic conduct must be carefully differentiated.

Although colonised nations, as in the case of Palestine, remain within this liminal geopolitical space, international law grants them a priori right for independence and self-representation. Post–World War II, normative architecture articulated self-determination of colonised nation as a positive right (Fabry 2010), which enabled anti-colonial movements to establish diplomatic contacts with different states and international institutions. The Palestinian right for self-determination and the illegality of the Israeli occupation provide the legal and moral scaffolding for the Palestinian political and diplomatic interaction with the international society. This effort culminated in an international consensus affirming the need to establish a Palestinian state and wide international recognition of Palestine (Badarin 2021d). This widespread international consensus not just enabled the broadening of Palestinian diplomatic presence globally, but also prompted numerous countries and international organisations like the EU to set up representative diplomatic missions and offices in the OPT.

Diplomacy Versus Settler-colonial Elimination

In 1799, Napoleon sought to establish a foothold in Palestine and offered to transform it into a Jewish homeland under French protection (Merkley 1998). In 1882, this vision became a concrete project and European Jewish settlers began to arrive at and establish their first settlements in Palestine. In the late nineteenth century, the Zionist movement was founded as a response to hostility towards Jews and rampant anti-Semitism in Europe. Zionism is driven by theological and irredentist impulses calling for 'redemption' and 'return' of Jewry to 'the Land of Israel' and establishing Jewish sovereignty there. European imperial expansions and Zionism coincided and overlapped (Badarin 2021d).

The conquest and occupation of Palestine in 1917 are direct results of European imperialist and geopolitical designs. Unlike former colonial spaces, European powers, Britain in particular, denied the Palestinian people the right to independence after the collapse of the Ottoman Empire. In 1917, Britain's support for the Zionist project was unequivocally articulated in the so-called Balfour Declaration, a pledge to turn Palestine into a Jewish homeland regardless of the native population's interests and desires (Schneer 2011). Many scholars interpret this structuring from the paradigm of settler-colonialism (Veracini 2006; Khalidi 2020; Pappé 2012). As Patrick Wolfe (2006) forcefully argues, the desire to establish a settler state in the conquered territory, which usually requires the elimination of the natives and replacing them with settlers, is the essence of settler-colonialism. European colonialism and Zionist settler-colonialism of Palestine are premised on the problematisation of the relationship between the Palestinians and their land (Masalha 1992). Breaking this bond and eliminating the Palestinian presence on the land is the core of the Palestine-Israel conflict (Badarin 2021c).

In 1948, the combined effects of British imperialism and Zionism resulted in two indivisible outcomes: the foundation of Israel and the displacement of the majority of the Palestinian population (about 800,000) and the destruction of over 500 of their villages and towns (Pappé 2007; Morris 2004). From the Palestinian perspective, this process put in place an-Nakba (the Catastrophe), a phenomenon that represents the continued spatial and social fragmentation of Palestine.

Since 1948, this struggle can be characterised not just as a one for decolonisation, liberation and independence but also as a struggle for *sumud* (steadfastness) on the land of Palestine and resistance to settler-colonial elimination (Badarin 2021a). An-Nakba and the breakdown of the Palestinian political elite and system inflected a diplomatic void. The Palestinian people were subsequently left without self-representation. In 1964, the PLO was founded to officially embody the Palestinian political agency in the international arena (Heikal 1996; Al-Shuqayri 1964). Further, the centre of their political and diplomatic system was repeatedly displaced. It was initially displaced from Palestine in 1948 and 1967, from Jordan in 1971, from Lebanon in 1982 and from Tunisia in 1993 to Gaza, and now it is located in Ramallah in the West Bank. The Palestinian diplomatic centre has been built either in exile and on borrowed or on colonised land and premises, and has therefore been chronically unstable and deeply vulnerable to external pressure.

In 1967, the PLO prioritised the armed struggle over diplomatic and political action as a strategy for liberation and the establishment of a democratic state in Palestine's historical space. In 1974, however, the Palestinian National Council (PNC) reversed this order. It adopted the so-called Ten-Point Program (PNC 1974), and officially prioritised diplomacy as a tool for creating a Palestinian state in the OPT, on only 22 percent of its original position (Badarin 2016). Since the mid-1970s, diplomacy dominated the PLO's activities abroad. The PLO's 1974 concession was a stepping stone into its normalisation and socialisation within the UN and European diplomatic and political realms. The UN recognised the Palestinian people's right to self-determination and the PLO as their legitimate representative. It also invited the PLO to set up an observer mission in the UN headquarter. In 1988, the PLO declared the independence of the State of Palestine, and over 80 states recognised it within a few months. In 1988, while being part of the Warsaw Pact, Bulgaria, Czech Republic, Hungary, Poland, Romania, and Slovakia (currently EU member states) recognised Palestine thanks to the PLO's close relations with the Soviet Union. In addition to these Eastern European countries, Palestine has full diplomatic representation with Cyprus, Malta and Sweden.

In hindsight, the PLO's major territorial concession and clutch to diplomacy engendered an array of events that gave rise to the 1993 Oslo Accords. As stipulated in these accords, the PA was established as the executive body of the PLO in populated Palestinian urban centres in the West Bank and the Gaza Strip. Although the PLO remains the official representative of the Palestinian people, its actual capacity to represent is deficient for two main reasons. First, it has failed to adapt to the Palestinian political environment, and thus major Palestinian political movements are still unrepresented in the PLO. Second, the overlap between the PLO and PA (and, since 2012, the 'State of Palestine') relegated the PLO's role in practice. The PA adopted a state-like structure and discourse and began to act as a state and employ diplomatic protocols. It founded various ministries and ministers. The PLO/PA developed extensive diplomatic corps. In the early 2000s, the PA officially established the Ministry and Minister (subject positions) of Foreign Affairs and Expatriates (PMFAE). The PMFAE and the 'President of Palestine' are responsible for the diplomatic relations. However, it is hard to assess their degree of influence over Palestinian diplomacy because of the institutional overlap and authoritarian structure of the PA.

Palestine-EU Relations Beyond Paradiplomacy

Palestine and Europe both have prefigured in each other's geopolitics, history and narratives. As noted earlier, the roots of the ongoing conflict in Palestine is inextricable from the European imperialist legacy and its colonial and neo-colonial geopolitical designs and interventions in non-European spaces (Badarin and Wildeman 2021; Pace and Roccu 2020). Palestinian and EU diplomatic and political relations are always already performed against this background and the path-dependence it produced.

Human imaginations, judgements and narratives about the world shape their political actions. During the 1950s and 1960s, many European actors perceived Israel and Zionism (the ideological movement) as embodiments of progressive social ideals (Lidén 2017). At the same time, the Palestinian narrative was generally dismissed, and started to gain traction only in the 1980s (Pappé 2017). The acceptance of the Zionist narrative and denial of its Palestinian counterpart constrained the latter's diplomatic interactions with official Europe for a long time.

In the early 1970s, the PLO arrived at the European diplomatic stage through the Euro-Arab Dialogue between the European Community (EC) and Arab states. The EC opposed initially any Palestinian representation alongside the Arab delegations, at a time when the PLO already embraced the EC's position and implicitly recognised the UN Security Council (UNSC) resolution 242. The European rejection coincided with the UN invitation to Yasser Arafat, then head of the PLO, to deliver a speech and participate in the General Assembly's debates.

To outmanoeuvre the Palestinian diplomatic representation, the EC proposed that only cooperation and technical issues may be discussed in the meetings of the Euro-Arab Dialogue. It also downgraded the political stature of these meeting by sending delegations of experts. This arrangement, dubbed the 'Dublin formula', permitted a form of PLO's representation within the Arab delegations. The PLO accepted a technocratic representation and sent a representative from the Palestine National Fund who conveyed its desire to establish a cultural, economic and political dialogue with EC. Despite their reduced stature, the PLO considered its participation in these meetings as an opportunity to engage in future diplomatic communication with Europe (Al-Dajani 1980).

The discussion of the political issues proved to be unavoidable. Despite its diluted political representation, the PLO played a significant role in the background (Al-Dajani 1980). In 1977, the EC issued a statement supporting the "legitimate right of the Palestinian people" and their "need for a homeland"; it also reaffirmed its support of the UNSC resolution 242 and non-recognition of Israel's occupation of the OPT (European Council 1977, 2). Meanwhile, the EC adopted a restrictive policy towards diplomatic contacts with the PLO; its constituents (Belgium, Britain, France, Germany, Italy) permitted the PLO to set up information offices in their capitals. The PLO's presence in Belgium, in particular, facilitated its communication with the EC's institutions in Brussels.

The Euro-Arab Dialogue created a platform for indirect diplomatic interactions between the PLO and EC. The PLO's growing political socialisation in the European and international arena further consolidated its shift from the liberation of historical Palestine to independence and statehood in the OPT (Badarin 2016). In 1980, the EC issued the Venice Declaration, which outlined a common European position recognising the need to enable the Palestinian people to "exercise fully its right to self-determination" (EC 1980). The Venice Declaration created a new direction for the PLO to widen its political representation in the EC and other European capitals. Later, the EU promoted the Palestinian representation into the Mission of Palestine to the EU, and the "Mission of Palestine to the Kingdom of Belgium, the EU and Luxemburg" in 2012.

Since the early 1990s, the PA/PLO-EU relations have experienced a significant evolution. In 1993, this relationship entered a new phase following the signing of the Oslo Accords. This created a new political impetus and a gradual institutionalisation of the PLO-EU diplomatic communications and economic and security relations. In particular, the EU used its economic and diplomatic weight to manage the conflict and to govern from a distance (Badarin 2021b). Furthermore, the EU undertook the Oslo peace process and its relationship with the PLO/PA as a central feature of its foreign policy in the Middle East (EUGS 2016), and presented its interventions as state-building and development aid (Bouris 2014; Wildeman 2018). The EU considered its active diplomatic and economic engagement with the PA as central to its geopolitical and security strategy in the Middle East. It accordingly established a network of cultural, economic, political and security institutions and programmes and stepped up its influence over Palestinian civil society and non-governmental organisations.

In November 1993, the European Parliament formed a temporary delegation for Palestine, which became permanent (in 1996) before it was renamed as the "Delegation for relations with Palestine" (DPAL) in 2015 (European Parliament n.d.). Its main mission is to provide information on Palestine to the European Parliament and its committees. It also organises visits to the OPT and holds meetings with various Palestinian political actors and non-governmental organisations. In doing so, the DPAL combines both traditional diplomatic and activist actions. In the following year, the EU founded the Office of the European Union Representative for the West Bank, Gaza Strip and United Nations Relief and Work Agency (UNRWA) (previously known as the European Commission Technical Assistance Office) to facilitate the EU-funded projects and interventions in the OPT. In particular, the European Commission appoints its own representative within the office's diplomatic personnel who provides it with a direct access to the "diplomatic community along with the Member States represented locally" in Palestine. The EU uses the office to conduct diplomatic communications with the Palestinians (EEAS n.d.).

In 1996, the EU founded the subject position of the EU Special Representative (or Envoy) to the Middle East Peace Process. The representative performs specific diplomatic tasks in coordination with the High Representative of the European Union for Foreign Affairs and Security Policy (HR/VP) and the Common Foreign Security Policy (CFSP) missions operating in the OPT (e.g., EUBAM, EUPOL COPPS). The following year, the EU-PA/PLO relationship acquired legal force after they had signed the Association Agreement in 1997 (EEC 1997).

The PA-EU economic and political relations are tightly focused on the security field. The EU approaches the Palestinian-Israeli conflict through the prism of the CFSP, and thus it places a particular emphasis on geopolitics and security (Müller 2017). In 2005, and within the framework of the 2003 Roadmap, drafted by the Quartet on the Middle East (the EU, the

United States [US], Russia and the UN), the EU deployed the European Union Border Assistance Mission for the Rafah Crossing Point (EUBAM Rafah) and the European Union Police Mission for the Palestinian Territories (EUPOL COPPS). The EU security mission focused on disciplining and training the Palestinian police forces, developing criminal justice and the judiciary system based on EU (foreign) codes. These missions provide a medium for direct interaction between the EU and its sub-commissions and multiple Palestinian political institutions and actors (e.g., Ministry of Interior, Prime Minister) (Council of the EU 2005). Official EU discourse presents these missions in the guise of technical assistance. However, critical research demonstrates how they serve the EU's efforts to impose its geopolitics through social and economic reforms, which are premised on securitisation, governmentality and disciplinary rationalities (Badarin 2021b; Tartir and Ejdus 2018).

The Palestine-EU diplomatic interactions are further consolidated by incorporating the PA into various EU geopolitical projects. For example, Palestine has full membership in the 1995 Euro-Mediterranean Partnership (EMP), the 2004 European Neighbourhood Policy (ENP) and the 2008 Union for the Mitterrandian (UfM). Moreover, the EU considers "political dialogue" with the Palestinians a central piece of their relationship (EEAS n.d.). These frameworks provide an institutional and legal umbrella for a wide-ranging PLO/PA-EU relationship and direct diplomatic communication at different levels and fields (cultural, economic and political), including bilateral agreements (e.g., Action Plan 2013, Special Support Framework 2014–2016, European Joint Strategy in Support of Palestine 2017–2020).

Diplomacy and recognition are intimately interlinked (Bull 1977). In the post-1945 international order, external recognition is constitutive of statehood and sovereignty (Coggins 2014). The PLO appreciates the constitutive value of external recognition, especially from global actors, and uses diplomacy to accomplish this goal. Despite the EU's non-recognition, the institutionalised diplomatic relations with the EU constitute a critical external economic and political scaffolding that sustains the PA's authority. More importantly, these diplomatic structures are the only vestiges left from the two-state solution, which both the PA and EU (at least rhetorically) aspire to achieve.

Palestinian Diplomacy, Internationalisation and the EU

Having discussed the general decolonial premise of Palestinian diplomatic practices and the institutionalisation of the PLO/PA-EU diplomatic interactions, the analysis now proceeds to examine a recent Palestinian diplomatic campaign, which was referred to as the 'internationalisation of the Palestinian cause' (*tadwil al-qadiyya al-falastinia*).

In 2009, the PA anticipated that the Obama Administration would be more responsive to the Palestinian needs. The leaked negotiation record reveals that the maximum this administration offered was "a mutually agreed outcome" (i.e., not a two-state solution on the 1967 borders) that would tolerate "subsequent developments" in the West Bank (i.e., Israeli settlements) and the annexation of East Jerusalem (Document 4899 2009). The PA's optimism vanished rapidly. It began to seek avenues to break away from the US-Israel-dominated political process. In this context, the PA invoked the so-called 'international legitimacy' and recognition as a way forward. This diplomatic strategy, dubbed 'internationalisation', focused on the recognition of Palestine as an independent state in the OPT. It aimed to "re-put the state of Palestine on June 1967 with East Jerusalem as its capital on the geographic map" and to keep the Palestinian cause at the centre of Arab and international politics (Erekat 2012, 4).

The internationalisation campaign involved active diplomatic actions at the international stage to promote the recognition of Palestine. Accordingly, the PLO/PA released the 'State 194' campaign (the number 194 signifies both the Palestinian right of return and the total number of the UN's member states if Palestine were to be recognised) in an attempt to influence the international opinion and to lobby other states, in particular the EU and its member states, to support its application for a UN membership, which was submitted in September 2011(PA 2011). The US vowed to veto this bid, and therefore the PA approached the UN General Assembly in 2012, which accorded Palestine an observer non-member state status (UN 2012).

The EU and its member states were primary sites for the Palestinian diplomatic campaign. For example, the PA lobbied in the European Parliament, held official meetings with EU representatives, sent official letters, constructed online campaigns and mobilised Palestinian embassies and missions in European capitals to convince the EU and its member states to support the Palestinian UN membership. Several European parliaments (e.g., France, Greece, Ireland, Italy, Portugal, Spain and the United Kingdom [UK]) adopted non-binding motions urging their governments to recognise Palestine.

The EU did not develop a common position on recognition, and by implication, it was up to each member state to vote according to its foreign policy (Euractive 2012). On November 29, 2012, the same day the UN General Assembly granted Palestine a non-member observer state status, the EU issued a statement pledging to recognise a Palestinian state when "appropriate" (EU 2012). In 2014, the EU Parliament echoed the EU's statement and expressed its readiness to recognise Palestine "in principle"; it also acknowledged the PA's state-like functions and capacities (European Parliament 2014). This was a pragmatic way to balance the EU's so-called state building interventions and the refusal to support the recognition of Palestine when it was required.

Palestine's new non-member observer state status enabled it to gain membership in several international organisations and to become a party to international agreements and conventions. Some western European states upgraded the Palestinian representative missions and granted them diplomatic immunity, while Iceland and Sweden recognised Palestine in 2011 and 2014, respectively (Badarin 2020).

As the official EU recognition seemed unforthcoming, the PA focused on urging the EU to take concrete measures to corroborate and consolidate its non-recognition of Israel's control over the OPT. Official Palestinian representatives and advocacy groups resorted to diplomacy to extract an unambiguous exclusion of the OPT from EU-Israel cooperation projects and trade arrangements (Voltolini 2016). The Palestinians concentrated intensely on EU rules of origin and preferential treatment of products made in Israeli settlements. Since 2012, the EU has adopted positions that require an unequivocal "differentiation" between pre-1967 Israel and the OPT; these positions also affirmed the inapplicability of the EU-Israel agreements beyond the 1967 borders (Azarova 2017).

In 2013, the European Commission issued "guidelines" outlawing EU support in the form of financial instruments, grants and prizes for Israeli entities and activities in territories occupied by Israel in 1967 (European Commission 2013). In 2015, the EU required that Israeli goods produced in the territories occupied in 1967 must be labelled clearly as originating from the settlements (European Commission 2015). The issue of settlements' products has significant legal and symbolic impacts for both the Palestinians and the EU. Non-preferential treatment of settlement products has broader legal, normative and symbolic significance as a concrete manifestation of the EU's commitment to the illegality of Israel's control over these areas.

The 2012 UN recognition of Palestine bolstered the Palestinian diplomatic practices. Since then, the PA started to identify itself as the State of Palestine. It has been officially using state semantics in its discourse, emblems, titles and structures, and acts like a state (even if only symbolically). The PMFAE (2019) continues to situate its diplomatic activities within the context of 'internationalisation'.

It is worth noting that the Palestinians understand their diplomatic action as a component of their "political struggle" to attain their national rights. Politically, PLO/PA-led diplomacy aspires to (1) affirm the legal character of the state of Palestine, (2) represent Palestinian interests in the UN and its organisations, (3) promote the popular support for the Palestinian cause, (4) hold Israeli leaders to account, (5) impel Israel to implement international law and resolutions, (6) expand the international recognition of Palestine and pursuing full membership in the UN (PMFAE 2019; n.d.-a, n.d.-b). The economic dimension is central to Palestinian diplomatic activities. The PA relies on diplomacy to safeguard the Palestinian representation at donor nations and organisations to ensure a consistent flow of economic aid to the PA (PMFAE n.d.-b).

For Israel, Palestinian diplomatic activities that seek to hold it to account are "political terrorism" (Jerusalem Post 2014; Ynet 2019). Israel counteracts Palestinian diplomacy in several ways. Israel practices assassination as a strategy to silence Palestinian political leaders both in Palestine and abroad (Bergman 2018). Israel's spatial control of the Palestinian centre of diplomacy is another powerful tool. In 2002, for example, Israel raided and destroyed the PA's headquarter (*al-muquata'a*) in Ramallah and imposed a siege on it as a means to isolate and restrict Arafat's communication with the outside world. Furthermore, Israel controls the spatial movement of Palestinian diplomats through a permit system and VIP Cards. In May 2021, for instance, Israel revoked the Palestinian foreign minister's VIP permit after his return from a mission at the International Criminal Court (ICC) in The Hague to follow on the Court's investigation of potential Israeli war crimes in the OPT (Aljazeera 2021). Another method Israel (along with the US and certain European states) uses to inhibit Palestinian diplomacy and recognition is the application of counter diplomatic and economic pressure on states and international organisations to forestall further recognition of Palestine. For example, Israel and the US withdrew from the United Nations Educational, Scientific and Cultural Organisation (UNESCO) and withheld funds as punitive measures against it after its 2011 decision to grant Palestine full membership (Aljazeera 2019). A similar pattern of threats was witnessed after Palestine joined the Rome Statute in 2015 and requested the ICC to investigate potential Israeli war crimes.

Conclusion

This chapter makes two contributions. Theoretically, it questions the applicability of the paradiplomacy framework to colonial situations on two grounds. First, actual colonial or occupation authorities lack the normative and legal dimensions of sovereignty, and, by implication, liberation movements are not sub-units of the colonial state but have a priori right to self-determination and self-representation. The second considers liberation movements' diplomatic practices and demonstrates that the nature of their diplomatic conduct is contingent on the degree of institutionalisation of their diplomatic presence within the international society. How the majority of others states and international institutions diplomatically interact with these actors are essential factors that determine the attributes of the diplomatic conduct in practice. The case of Palestine illustrates these points well. The widespread international recognition of Palestine has normalised its diplomatic activities and presence in the international society. Palestinian politicians are treated as accomplished diplomats by 139 states and multiple international organisations, including the UN, that recognise Palestine. The concept of paradiplomacy reaches its explanatory limits when considering the post-1993 diplomatic context and conditions of the PLO/PA. Thus, there is a need for a conclusive theoretical and empirical engagement with the diplomatic practices of recognised liberation and anti-colonial movements.

The second contribution concerns the Palestinian diplomatic interactions with the EU. Since 1993, diplomatic relations between PA/PLO have been steadily extending and consolidating. Although the EU does not recognise Palestine, their level of diplomatic engagement has crossed the threshold of liminality and paradiplomacy. Palestine is the only non-recognised polity that has signed an Association Agreement and is a member 'state' in various EU geopolitical regional formations alongside other states.

This intricate network of diplomatic structures is founded on the EU's initiatives and terms. They co-opt the PLO in state-level diplomatic practices that afford it a semblance of statehood and restrict its authentic character as liberation and anti-colonial movement. The PLO has become bound to the trappings of diplomacy as a result of its absorption into the EU's double process of full diplomatic relations and denial of external recognition (which is necessary to achieve sovereignty). This exhausted the PLO's identity as a liberation movement and restricted its ability to lead the struggle for self-determination. In the Palestinian context, diplomatic and economic trappings are extensive and used to curb local agency. In 2006, for example, the EU broke its economic and political relationship with the Palestinian government after Hamas's electoral victory. The EU refused to deal with the results of the democratic process and decided to reorient this relationship away from the legitimate government. Against this backdrop, one can start to see how the PLO's state-level diplomatic relations with the EU are, in reality, part of the EU's geopolitical schemes of governmentality rather than recognition and statehood.

REFERENCES

Al-Dajani, Ahmad Sidiqi. 1980. The PLO and the Euro-Arab Dialogue. *Journal of Palestine Studies* 9 (3): 81–98.

Aldecoa, Francisco. 1999. Towards Plurinational Diplomacy in the Deeper and Wider European Union (1985–2005). In *Paradiplomacy in Action: The Foreign Relations of Subnational Governments*, ed. Francisco Aldecoa and Michael Keating, 82–94. London: Frank Cass Publishers.

Aljazeera. 2019. US and Israel Formally Quit UNESCO. January 1. Accessed November 10, 2021. https://www.aljazeera.com/news/2019/1/1/us-and-israel-formally-quit-unesco.

———. 2021. Israel Revokes Permit of Palestinian Foreign Minister. March 22. Accessed January 5, 2022. https://www.aljazeera.com/news/2021/3/22/israel-revokes-permit-of-palestinian-foreign-minister.

Al-Shuqayri, Ahmad. 1964. Al-Shuqayri Speech at the Opening the first PNC session in Jerusalem, May 28. In *Al-Shuqayri Speeches: the Leader of the PLO*, 37–46. Beirut: Centre for Arab Unity Studies.

Azarova, Valentina. 2017. *Israel's Unlawfully Prolonged Occupation: Consequences under an Integrated Legal Framework*. European Council on Foreign Relations: 1–20.

Badarin, Emile. 2015. Settler-Colonialist Management of Entrances to the Native Urban Space in Palestine. *Settler Colonial Studies* 5 (3): 226–235.

———. 2016. *Palestinian Political Discourse: Between Exile and Occupation.* Abingdon: Routledge.

———. 2020. States Recognition in Foreign Policy: The Case of Sweden's Recognition of Palestine. *Foreign Policy Analysis* 16 (1): 78–97.

———. 2021a. Localising Resilience: Discursive Projections, Entrapments, and Domination. *British Journal of Middle Eastern Studies*, 1–16. https://doi.org/10.1080/13530194.2021.1981234

———. 2021b. Politics and Economy of Resilience: EU Resilience-Building in Palestine and Jordan and Its Disciplinary Governance. *European Security* 30 (1): 65–84.

———. 2021c. Politics of Recognition, Elimination and Settler-Colonialism. *Critical Sociology*, 1–20. https://doi.org/10.1080/13530194.2021.1981234

———. 2021d. Recognition of States and Colonialism in the Twenty-First Century: Western Sahara and Palestine in Sweden's Recognition Practice. *Third World Quarterly* 42 (6): 1276–1294.

Badarin, Emile, and Jeremy Wildeman. 2021. Aid, Security and Fortress Europe: EU Development Aid in the Middle East and North Africa. In *Routledge Handbook of EU–Middle East Relations*, ed. Dimitris Bouris, Daniela Huber, and Michelle Pace, 401–410. London: Routledge.

Bergman, Ronen. 2018. *Rise and Kill First: The Secret History of Israel's Targeted Assassinations.* London: John Murray.

Bouris, Dimitris. 2014. *The European Union and Occupied Palestinian Territories: State-Building without a State.* London: Routledge.

Bouris, Dimitris, and Irene Fernández-Molina. 2018. Contested States, Hybrid Diplomatic Practices, and the Everyday Quest for Recognition. *International Political Sociology* 12: 306–324.

Bull, Hedley. 1977. *The Anarchical Society: A Study of Order in World Politics.* London: Macmillan.

Charrett, Catherine. 2019. *The EU, Hamas and the 2006 Palestinian Elections: A Performance in Politics.* London: Routledge.

Coggins, Bridget. 2014. *Power Politics and State Formation in the Twentieth Century: The Dynamics of Recognition.* Cambridge: Cambridge University Press.

Cornago, Noe. 2018. Paradiplomacy and Protodiplomacy. In *Encyclopedia of Diplomacy*, ed. Gordon Martel, 1–8. Oxford: Blackwell-Wiley.

Council of the European Union. 2005. Council Joint Action 2005/797/CFSP of 14 November 2005 on the European Union Police Mission for the Palestinian Territories. L 300/65. Accessed December 10, 2021. https://eupolcopps.eu/uploads/1608725673624384742.pdf.

Dalby, Simon. 2008. Imperialism, Domination, Culture: The Continued Relevance of Critical Geopolitics. *Geopolitics* 13 (3): 413–436.

Document 4899. 2009. Meeting Minutes, Dr Saeb Erekat—Sen George Mitchell. October 21. Accessed December 11, 2021. ajtransparency.com/files/4899.pdf.

Duckacek, Ivo D. 1990. Perforated Sovereignties: Towards a Typology of New Actors in International Relations. In *Federalism and International Relations: The Role of Subnational Units*, ed. Hans J. Michelmann and Panayotis Soldatos, i–33. Oxford: Clarendon Press.

———. 2019. *The Territorial Dimension of Politics Within, Among and Across Nations*. London: Routledge.

Erekat, Saeb. 2012. Palestine 'Non-member State': The day After? The PLO: Department of Negotiations Affairs. Accessed November 30, 2021. https://info.wafa.ps/userfiles/server/pdf/Palestine_is_a_member_state_the_next_day.pdf.

EU Global Strategy (EUGS). 2016. A Global Strategy for the European Union's Foreign and Security Policy. European Union. Accessed November 22, 2021. https://europa.eu/globalstrategy/sites/globalstrategy/files/regions/files/eugs_review_web_0.pdf.

Euractive. 2012. EU Divided in UN Vote on Palestine's Status. November 30. Accessed November 19, 2021. https://www.euractiv.com/section/global-europe/news/eu-divided-in-un-vote-on-palestine-s-status/.

European Commission. 2013. Guidelines on the Eligibility of Israeli Entities and Their Activities in the Territories Occupied by Israel since June 1967 for Grants, Prizes and Financial Instruments Funded by the EU from 2014 Onwards. Accessed January 10, 2022. https://op.europa.eu/en/publication-detail/-/publication/044b0978-9f3f-4cdc-b0df-827d94af5c6c/language-en.

———. 2015. Interpretative Notice on Indication of Origin of Goods from the Territories Occupied by Israel since June 1967 (2015/C 375/05). Accessed November 5, 2021. https://www.europarl.europa.eu/meetdocs/2014_2019/documents/dpal/dv/4a_interpretativenoticeindicationorigin/4a_interpretativenoticeindicationoriginen.pdf.

European Community (EC). 1980. Venice Declaration. Accessed November 30, 2021. https://eeas.europa.eu/archives/docs/mepp/docs/venice_declaration_1980_en.pdf.

European Council. 1977. Statement on the Middle East. June 30. Accessed December 15, 2021. https://www.consilium.europa.eu/media/20785/london_june_1977__eng_.pdf

European Economic Community (EEC). 1997. Euro-Mediterranean Interim Association Agreement on Trade and Cooperation between the European Community, of the One Part, and the Palestine Liberation Organization (PLO) for the Benefit of the Palestinian Authority of the West Bank and the Gaza Strip, of the Other Part. *Official Journal of the European Communities* L187 (3): 3–126.

European External Action Service (EEAS). n.d. The Office of the European Union Representative (West Bank and Gaza Strip, UNRWA). Accessed November 30, 2021. https://eeas.europa.eu/delegations/palestine-occupied-palestinian-

territory-west-bank-and-gaza-strip/1886/about-eu-delegation-west-bank-and-gaza-strip-unrwa_en.
European Parliament. 2014. Resolution 2014/2964/RSP. December 17. Accessed November 30, 2021. http://www.europarl.europa.eu/sides/getDoc.do?pubRef=-//EP//TEXT+TA+P8-TA-2014-0103+0+DOC+XML+V0//EN.
———. n.d. DPAL: Delegation for Relations with Palestine. Delegations. Accessed November 22, 2021. https://www.europarl.europa.eu/delegations/en/dpal/about/history.
European Union (EU). 2012. Declaration by the High Representative on Behalf of the European Union on the Middle East Peace Process. Accessed November 25, 2021. https://www.consilium.europa.eu/uedocs/cms_Data/docs/pressdata/en/cfsp/133902.pdf.
Fabry, Mikulas. 2010. *Recognizing States: International Society and the Establishment of New States Since 1776*. Oxford: Oxford University Press.
Heikal, Mohammad Hassanein. 1996. *Illusions of Peace: Before and After Oslo*. Cairo: Dar Al-Shoroq.
Hocking, Brian. 1993. *Localizing Foreign Policy: Non-Central Governments and Multi-Layered Diplomacy*. New York: Macmillan.
Jerusalem Post. 2014. Liberman Calls Abbas "Diplomatic Terrorist Busy with Slandering Israel". September 26. Accessed November 21, 2021. https://www.jpost.com/israel-news/politics-and-diplomacy/liberman-calls-abbas-diplomatic-terrorist-busy-with-slandering-israel-376391.
Khalidi, Rashid. 2020. *The Hundred Years' War on Palestine: A History of Settler Colonial Conquest and Resistance*. London: Profile Books.
Kincaid, John. 2001. The State of U.S. Federalism, 2000–2001: Continuity in Crisis. *Publius: The Journal of Federalism* 31 (2): 1–69.
Kuus, Merje. 2014. *Geopolitics and Expertise: Knowledge and Authority in European Diplomacy*. Oxford: John Wiley & Sons.
Kuznetsov, Alexander S. 2015. *Theory and Practice of Paradiplomacy Subnational Governments in International Affairs*. London: Routledge.
Lidén, Anders. 2017. *Diplomati och Uppriktiga Samtal: I FN, Mellanöstern, Afrika och Finland*. Stockholm: Carlsson.
Masalha, Nur. 1992. *Expulsion of the Palestinians: The Concept of "Transfer" in Zionist Political Thought, 1882–1948*. Beirut: The Institute for Palestine Studies.
McConnell, Fiona. 2017. Liminal Geopolitics: The Subjectivity and Spatiality of Diplomacy at the Margins. *Transactions of the Institute of British Geographers* 42 (1): 139–152.
Merkley, Paul C. 1998. *The Politics of Christian Zionism 1891–1948*. London: Routledge.
Morris, Benni. 2004. *The Birth of the Palestinian Refugee Problem*, Revisited Ed. Cambridge: Cambridge University Press.

Müller, Patrick. 2017. The Revised European Neighbourhood Policy and the EU's Comprehensive Approach Towards the Israeli-Palestinian Conflict: Not so New, After All. In *The Revised European Neighbourhood Policy: Continuity and Change in EU Foreign Policy*, ed. Tobias Schumacher and Dimitris Bouris, 197–217. Basingstoke: Palgrave Macmillan.

Norweagian Government. 2011. Avtale mellom Norge og Den palestinske frigjøringsorganisasjon PLO. *Novdata*. Accessed November 30, 2021. https://lovdata.no/dokument/TRAKTATEN/traktat/2011-07-18-27.

Pace, Michelle, and Polly Pallister-Wilkins. 2018. EU–Hamas Actors in a State of Permanent Liminality. *Journal of International Relations and Development* 21 (1): 223–246.

Pace, Michelle, and Roberto Roccu. 2020. Imperial Pasts in the EU's Approach to the Mediterranean. *Interventions: International Journal of Postcolonial Studies* 22 (6): 671–685.

Palestinian Authority (PA). 2011. Palestine's Letter of Application for UN Membership/Declaration of President Abbas, SecGen note. Accessed December 28, 2021. https://www.un.org/unispal/document/auto-insert-184036/.

Palestinian Ministry of Foreign Affairs and Expatriates (PMFAE). n.d.-a. Tasks of the Ministry. Accessed November 28, 2021. http://www.mofa.pna.ps/ar-jo/الوزارة/مهامالوزارة.

———. n.d.-b. Vision and Message. Accessed November 28, 2021. http://www.mofa.pna.ps/ar-jo/الوزارة/.

———. 2019. We Continue Internationalising the Question of Palestine and the Search for a Peace Partner. September 17. Accessed November 29, 2021. http://www.mofa.pna.ps/en-us/mediaoffice/politicalstatement/pgrid/5918/pageid/3/artmid/5849/articleid/1511.

Palestinian National Authority (PNC). 1974. Twelfth Session. Cairo, September 1–8. Accessed December 2, 2021. https://info.wafa.ps/ar_page.aspx?id=3789.

Palestinian National Charter. 1968. Accessed April 5, 2022. https://yaf.ps/page-485-ar.html.

Pappé, Ilan. 2007. *The Ethnic Cleansing of Palestine*. Oxford: Oneworld.

———. 2012. Shtetl Colonialism: First and Last Impressions of Indigeneity by Colonised Colonisers. *Settler Colonial Studies* 2 (1): 39–58.

———. 2017. *The Biggest Prison on Earth: A History of the Occupied Territories*. London: Oneworld Publications.

Riksdag (Swedish Parliament). 2012. Avtal Mellan Sveriges Regering Och PLO, till Förmån För Palestinska Myndigheten. Accessed April 5, 2022. https://www.riksdagen.se/sv/dokument-lagar/dokument/proposition/avtal-mellan-sveriges-regering-och-plo-till_H00353.

Schneer, Jonathan. 2011. *The Balfour Declaration: The Origins of the Arab-Israeli Conflict*. New York: Random House.

Tartir, Alaa, and Filip Ejdus. 2018. Effective? Locally Owned? Beyond the Technocratic Perspective on the European Union Police Mission for the Palestinian Territories. *Contemporary Security Policy* 39 (1): 134–165.

Tuathail, Gearóid. 1996. *Critical Geopolitics: The Politics of Writing Global Space*. London: Routledge.

United Nations (UN). 1961. Vienna Convention on Diplomatic Relations 1961. Accessed December 10, 2021. https://legal.un.org/ilc/texts/instruments/english/conventions/9_1_1961.pdf.

———. 2012. General Assembly Votes Overwhelmingly to Accord Palestine "Non-Member Observer State" Status in United Nations. Accessed December 13, 2021. https://www.un.org/press/en/2012/ga11317.doc.htm.

Veracini, Lorenzo. 2006. *Israel and Settler Society*. London: Pluto Press.

Voltolini, Benedetta. 2016. *Lobbying in EU Foreign Policy-Making: The Case of the Israeli-Palestinian Conflict*. London: Routledge.

Wildeman, Jeremy. 2018. EU Development Aid in the Occupied Palestinian Territory, between Aid Effectiveness and World Bank Guidance. *Global Affairs* 4 (1): 115–128.

Wolfe, Patrick. 2006. Settler Colonialism and Elimination of the Native. *Journal of Genocide Research* 8 (4): 387–409.

Ynet. 2019. Israel versus the Prosecutor in the Hague: Anti-Semitism, Diplomatic Terrorism. December 22. Accessed December 10, 2021. https://www.ynet.co.il/articles/0,7340,L-5646604,00.html.

CHAPTER 9

Palestine and Russia

Raid M. H. Nairat and Ibrahim S. I. Rabaia

INTRODUCTION

The term "paradiplomacy" appeared empirically in the early 1980s, mainly in North America, in the renewed theory of federalism to analyze the international political practices of federal states (Aguirre, 1999).

The concept of paradiplomacy labels the international politics as politics of region. Noé Cornago (1999, 40) defines paradiplomacy as a "non-central government's involvement in international relations through establishment of permanent of ad-hoc contacts with foreign public or private entities, with aim to promote socioeconomic or cultural issues, as well as ant foreign dimension of their constitutional competences". While Cornago limited the political players of paradiplomacy to the non-central government, James McHugh (2015, 6) considered wider players in paradiplomacy by including sub-state actor that engage "informal representation with states, international organizations or other parties that are conventionally recognized under international law".

R. M. H. Nairat (✉)
Department of Political Science, An-Najah National University, Nablus, Palestine
e-mail: rnairat@najah.edu

I. S. I. Rabaia
The Palestinian Research Center, Ramallah, Palestine
e-mail: irabaia@birzeit.edu

© The Author(s), under exclusive license to Springer Nature Switzerland AG 2023
G. Gürbey et al. (eds.), *Between Diplomacy and Non-Diplomacy*,
https://doi.org/10.1007/978-3-031-09756-0_9

In this wide range of diversified political players of paradiplomacy, the practice can serve independence in the stateless nation building struggle for independence, and national identity. Also, the dynamic transformations in international relations and the deep globalization changed the tools and aims of diplomacy in general, and paradiplomacy in specific. For instance, transferring technology and investments became key aims for the regional diplomacy and led to a "new para-diplomacy" (Keating 1999).

The Palestinian-Soviet relations before 1991 focused on its political aim, which was preparing for independence, and utilized its political, social and cultural tools for this purpose. The conclusions say that such diplomacy was efficient as Moscow recognized the Palestinian independence in 1988, and supported the Palestinian struggle continuously before and after. This chapter starts with the Soviet era, and moves later to the Russian period; the main sectors of study are culture, official politics and the economic sector.

Defining Paradiplomacy in the Palestinian-Soviet Context

In dealing with the Palestinian case, diplomacy does not work as in the case of a fully sovereign state, the contemporary Palestinian representation started with the foundation of the PLO in 1964. But the Palestinian case has recorded its strong presence in international relations since 1948. In this context, there is no separation between the Palestinian issue and representation and Israel in any state diplomatic strategy in the Middle East. Moreover, until 1993, any strong ties with one of these parts meant weak or even no relations with the other part.

The Palestinian diplomacy after 1965 started as paradiplomacy, as it was seeking for recognition and acceptance as a non-state representative for the Palestinians. This major goal utilized the Arab diplomatic channels to get access to the major powers, mainly the Union of Soviet Socialist Republics (USSR) and China. Thus, the Palestinian representatives visited other countries as a member of the Arab delegations besides investing in the visits of the foreign delegations to the Arab capitals to conduct unofficial meetings.

The early period of the Palestinian diplomacy was between 1964 and 1973, where the Palestinian revolution was fascinated by the independent movements in Asia, Africa and Latin America. The main model was the

Algerian revolution, which was militarized and successful. The Palestinian diplomacy was led by a Palestinian senior diplomat, Ahmed Al-Shuqairi, the first leader of the PLO, who served in advanced diplomatic missions for several Arab states (Fayyad 1996).

The "soft" diplomacy of Al-Shuqairi was offset by the revolutionary diplomacy, which was created and led by the Palestinian resistance factions, mainly Fatah. Unlike the attempts of Al-Shuqairi to create diplomatic relations on regular state bases, Fatah worked on diplomatic ties with global resistance movements, the newly independent states and the global anti-colonialism and anti-imperialism platforms. The two visions competed until 1968;then the resistance factions dominated PLO and implemented the revolutionary diplomacy (Fayyad 1996).

The Palestinian diplomacy gained strength from the Arab defeat in the 1967 war and the Palestinian success in the Al-Karamah battle in 1968. Thus, the diplomacy at that point aimed to monopolize the Palestinian representation through the PLO and to get more friends independently, away from the Arab guardianship. For this purpose, also, the PLO worked intensively on providing the needed military assistance to the organization and its member factions (Fayyad 1996).

The diplomacy in that stage depended on revolutionary propaganda, which aimed to mobilize unofficial and official supporters to help achieve the revolutionary diplomatic goals. However, several political players were looking at the Palestinian goal of destroying Israel as nonrealistic and a barrier for the Palestinian diplomacy.

The mentioned stage was not institutionalized. The PLO leadership practiced their diplomatic work through special missions without creating official diplomatic channels and employing trained experts. The PLO worked at that period as a resistance movement with a non-state characteristic. The Palestinian diplomacy was at that point paradiplomatic but not sub-state diplomatic.

Paradiplomacy in the Palestinian case was not "parallel" diplomacy; it was not a different supportive track for diplomatic relations practiced by sub-players. Instead, both para- and official diplomacy worked on the same track as the goals and tools of the PLO served before 1973.

The Palestinian-Soviet Paradiplomacy

It was not easy for the PLO to establish its strong ties with the USSR, which was the first country to recognize Israel. However, this process started by the pressure of the Egyptian president Jamal Abdel Nasser, who visited Moscow in 1968 with a high-level Egyptian delegation that included Arafat.

The USSR supported founding a Jewish state and voted for the UNSC partition plan and the creation of two states, including an Arab state. It facilitated the Jewish immigration from Poland to Israel, and even supported the infant state with military equipment. Such support was reasonable for Moscow as it had no allies in the region; the major Arab countries were kingdoms dominated by the United Kingdom (UK), and Israel was the only possible accessible state for the USSR to the region.

The tension in the Arab-Soviet relations stayed till the end of Joseph Stalin's period in 1953, in parallel with the dramatic downfall of the Arab kingdoms to the benefit of revolutionary-military powers. The new Arab regimes, led by the Egyptian charismatic president Jamal Abdel Nasser, moved to the Soviet side and developed their relations with Moscow to be strategic. These developments in the Arab-Soviet relations were alongside with a decline in the Israeli-Soviet relation.

In 1956, Moscow criticized Tel Aviv by expressing its concerns about the Palestinian refugee issue; this was the first Soviet opinion in this case after long neglection. The USSR also called for consolidating the conflict with respecting the Palestinians' rights. Besides, the Palestinian issue was important source of legitimacy for the main presidents of the region, on the top of them Abdel Nasser and the Algerian president Ahmed Ben Bella; thus, the Soviet-Arab joint statements emphasized the Palestinian rights (Ankylesis 1985).

The USSR had no clear reaction on the foundation of the PLO in 1964. Al-Shuqairi tried to get Soviet support by meeting several Soviet ambassadors in the Arab countries. He tried to get recognition from Moscow and tried to open a representation office there, but the Soviet response was cold (Haidari 1990). In May 1966, the PLO president Ahmed Al-Shuqairi met the Soviet prime minister Alexei Kosygin in Cairo, in the first high-level Palestinian-Soviet meeting. However, this meeting did not bring any breakthrough in this relation.

Before 1966, the Soviet position on the Palestinian case was confused; on the one side it was developing its relations with the Arab republics, mainly Egypt, Syria and Algeria, while on the other side it was adherence to keep about its relations with Tel Aviv. In February 1966, the first secretary of the Soviet embassy in Tel Aviv, Evan Doyoyola, emphasized the defensive nature of the weapons that the USSR provided to its Arab partners. He also reminded the Israelis that his country sent weapons to Israel in 1948 and focused also on the Soviet role in creating Israel (Haidari 1990).

The 1967 Arab defeat and the Palestinian victory in the Al-Karamah battle in 1968 led President Abdel Nasser to adopt the militarized factions, which facilitated changing in the Soviet opinions of the PLO and these factions. Besides, Moscow had fears from the impact of the Chinese military and political support to the Palestinians on the Russian political presence in Middle East. Abdel Nasser led the breakthrough step in 1968 when Arafat joint the Egyptian delegation that visited Moscow; in this meeting the Soviet leadership supported Arafat with around $500,000 in military equipment (Fawzi 1988, 347).

Arafat invested in this visit to show the PLO opinions of Middle Eastern issues; he also emphasized the complementary roles between the Arab and the Palestinian resistance lines. Arafat positioned PLO in the anti-imperialism front, which was led by Moscow.

The Soviet Union became more involved in the Palestinian issue and continued to release its position about the events in the region. The Soviet letter to the Arab Summit in 1969, by Alexei Kosygin, said, "it is obvious that any regional consolidation in the Middle East should prevent the rights and interests of the Arab- Palestinian people', this was a new soviet speech, instead of the previous which was talking about the "rights of the Arab people in Palestine" (Abu Oun 1975).

Gradually, the Soviet Union started to deal positively with the Palestinian issue; in February 1970 Yasser Arafat had his second visit to Moscow; the Soviet television started also a special program to support the Palestinian resistance. The Soviet Afro-Asian Solidarity Committee was active in developing the Soviet support to the Palestinians by facilitating several high-level Palestinian visits to Moscow between 1970 and 1974 (Ankylesis 1985).

Also, the Soviet Ministry of Foreign Affairs supported the PLO in events in Jordan in September 1970. The ministry announced that it had contacted Nasser and called him to help solving the issue; the ministry also warned the United States (US) and the UK from any intervention in this issue and also warned Israel not to intervene in these events. The General

Secretary of the Communist Party Leonid Brezhnev also called Jordan to stop the conflict and clashes with the Palestinian factions (Abu Oun 1975).

In July 1970, Arafat met several high-level officials in the Soviet Ministry of Defense and succeeded in getting more Soviet weapons. After 1973, Moscow tried to develop its relations with the PLO to offset the decline in the Egyptian-Soviet relations. The USSR put pressure on Arafat during his visit to Moscow in November 1973 to create a government in exile and participate in the Geneva Peace Conference, which was not accepted from the Palestinian side (Abu Oun 1975).

Arafat's early visits to Moscow were not official as they were with invitations from the Soviet Afro-Asian Solidarity Committee. The first official visit was in July 1974; this visit also was concluded by establishing a permanent Palestinian diplomatic delegation in Moscow (Abu Oun 1975). However, it took around two years to open this office, which was not connected to the Soviet Ministry of Foreign Affairs, but it followed the Soviet Committee of Solidarity. This office was responsible for supporting the Palestinians with military equipment, mainly in the Lebanese civil war between 1975 and 1982.

The Soviet-Israeli Relations as a Determinant

In 1967, Moscow broke of its diplomatic relations with Tel Aviv due to the Six-Day war; however, the diplomats of both countries used to meet in several capitals. Israel tried to use all of its capacities to push the Soviet Union to facilitate the immigration of the Russian Jews, while the Soviet Union tried to keep this soft line in order to find any possible path for a role in settling the conflict in the region. Also, Moscow was keen to protect its properties in Israel and the occupied territories, including the properties of the Orthodox Church (Palestinian Affairs 1987).

In the 1980s, Moscow allowed the Eastern bloc countries to develop its relations with Israel; Tel Aviv opened a representation office in Poland and developed its bilateral economic relations with Hungary and Bulgaria. The Eastern European countries relaxed the restrictions on Israeli tourists. This situation was understood as a "distribution of roles" between Moscow and its allies (Palestinian Affairs 1987).

In 1987, Budapest hosted the annual meeting of the executive committee of the World Zionist Congress, with a wide range of participants from the Soviet Union republics and its allied countries. The chairman of the congress Edgar Bronfman announced in his speech his support for the

Soviet participation in any coming peace conference (Palestinian Affairs 1987).

In 1986, both countries renewed their diplomatic communication after a long negotiation in Helsinki; later, the Soviet minister of foreign affairs Eduard Shevardnadze and the Israeli minister Shimon Peres met at the United Nations (UN) headquarters in New York. In the following year both countries announced their agreement on diplomatic exchange. The Soviet focus in these meetings and the related negotiations was on the peace process with the Palestinians, while the Israeli focus was on the immigration of the Russian Jews (Khalil 1989).

THE FORMAL RELATIONS

The Palestinian revolutionary diplomacy declined in the 1970s as the PLO adopted the Ten Point Program, which was the first agreement to a gradual political solution and to the establishment of a Palestinian state on a part of Palestine as a first stage. In July 1977 Arafat met the General Secretary of the Communist Party Leonid Brezhnev, who emphasized the Soviet position of supporting a regional settlement that protects the Palestinian rights (Yasser Arafat Foundation 2015).

The Soviet position on the Palestinian issue changed from dealing with it as a refugee issue before 1974, to facing it as a political issue, with the PLO as a legitimate representative. This shift came after the Rabat Arab Summit, which legitimated the PLO as the only representative for the Palestinians (Dannreuther 2016, 70).

In an interview with Arafat, he said that his visit to Moscow in 1974 was successful. This visit was a positive turning point for Arafat in the Palestinian-Soviet relations, with progresses higher than anticipated. This visit was very important for Arafat as it was formal and with full diplomatic reception. Arafat invested this visit to enhance his ties with the Soviet Union through the public opinions, which had been reflected by the media and the meeting with the labor unions. Arafat repositioned the Soviet Union from being a seasonal supporter to be a major ally (Darwish 1974).

In 1974, the Soviet leadership officially called for an independent Palestinian state, with continuous developments in mutual relations. The Egyptian-Israeli peace agreement led to isolation of Cairo through a boycott by the other Arab states. Immediately after the agreement, the Arab League leaders met in Baghdad and agreed on refusing the Egypt's individual step. This political event strengthened the PLO-Soviet relations. Both sides met in Moscow in November 1978 after a request from Arafat. The meeting emphasized isolating Egypt and supporting the progressive forces in the Arab world and the USSR reflected full support for the PLO (Wilson Center 1978).

Earlier in 1975 and following to the visit of Arafat with a high-level Palestinian delegation to Moscow in April, the Soviet Union emphasized the importance of inviting the PLO to attend the Geneva Peace Conference as an independent party; the Soviet leadership shared this position with several Arab parties, such as Egypt. The Soviet position also put three determinants to the conference: the liberation of the occupied lands, the protection of the legitimate rights of the Palestinian people, the guarantee of the rights of each state. The Soviet Union took further steps by expressing the readiness to be the guarantor of the agreement (Sakhnini 1975).

Gradually, the Soviet Union was involved intensively in the Palestinian issue. In 1987, Moscow invested in its strong ideological ties with the leftist Palestinian factions to achieve Palestinian unity; this effort led to convene the 18th session of the Palestinian national congress in the following year. Also, Moscow supported the "pragmatic" transformations in the PLO politics, which was reflected in the outcomes of the mentioned congress, mainly by recognizing UN resolution 242 and 338 and condemning terrorism (Khalil 1989).

However, the Palestinian factions had overwhelming expectations in Moscow for decades; these expectations motivated the major leftist factions and several top leaders to call for expressing loyalty to Moscow instead of developing regular diplomatic ties. The former Palestinian ambassador in Moscow, Nabil Amro, warned against these expectations in one of the sections of the Palestinian congress, and he received harsh critiques on this from the participants. Amro built his conclusion on several occasions and discussions with Soviet journalists and politicians; one of them is the reporter of *Novosi* in Beirut, who said, "You have extremism in introducing the Soviet Union to your people, we support you and your issue, but this is not a holy alliance" (Amro 1995, 15–16).

This relation was influenced by the decline of the Soviet political power in the late 1980s; Israel invested in this situation to strengthen its ties with the Soviet leadership. The Soviet president Mikhail Gorbachev welcomed three Israeli ministers, who pledged to offer $200 million to Moscow municipality. While this period witnessed the largest wave of immigration from the Soviet Union to Israel (Amro 1995, 64).

The Palestinians on their side kept trying not to lose the Soviet's steady position on the peace in the region. Arafat emphasized this in his meetings with Soviet politicians, mainly the minister of foreign affairs Eduard Shevardnadze in Moscow and Cairo in 1989 (New York Times 1989). Shevardnadze adopted the Palestinian version in his speech in Cairo and said that any solution should protect the Palestinian national legitimate rights.

In January 1990, by the end of the Soviet era, the Ministry of Foreign Affairs in Moscow raised the Palestinian diplomatic representation to a full state representation. Later, the PLO and the Palestinian delegation in Madrid kept their cooperation with Moscow; the Palestinian delegation was the last Mediterranean diplomatic delegation to meet the last Soviet minister of foreign affairs before it collapsed in December 1991.

INFORMAL PLAYERS
AND THE PALESTINIAN-SOVIET PARADIPLOMACY

Moscow started developing informal ties with Palestinian political players; in 1965 the Soviet Union sent a delegation which represented several social-popular organizations to attend the first global Palestine seminar. The delegation was active in pushing several Latin American and European delegations to condemn Israel and the Zionist movement. The following years witnessed several progresses in the mutual relations through the labor unions.

The key Palestinian unions benefited deeply from this development; the main were the General Union of Students, Palestinian General Federation of Trade Unions, General Union of Palestinian Women and the General Union of Palestinian Writers and Journalists. These bodies benefited from the Soviet financial aid and technical trainings, but the most important was the Soviet political support in the international specialized unions (Abu Oun 1975).

Such paradiplomatic relations had been developed before formal political relations. For example, in March 1967, the Soviet Union held the key role in expelling Israel from the International Student Union, during its congress meeting in Mongolia (Amro 2021).

The Soviet Union had also a crucial role in developing unified positions for the communist parties globally; in June 1967, the leaders of the communist parties of the Warsaw Pact and Yugoslavia met in Moscow and decided to support the Arab people in the countries that lost the war against Israel; these parties decided to push their countries to boycott Israel, and this is what happened later (Abu Oun 1975).

One of the early and major Palestinian delegations visited Moscow in August 1968; these delegations included mainly units from the Palestinian revolution military factions and participated in the 9th World Festival of youth and Students, which was one of the major Soviet international events. The political statement of this festival focused on the solidarity with the Arab people: "We present out solidarity with the resistance of the Arab people, we call for immediate evacuation for the Israeli military forces from the occupied land, we support the resistance of the Palestinians to achieve their legitimate rights" (Abu Oun 1975).

In November 1972, the All-Union Leninist Young Communist League and the committee of the youth organization in the Soviet Union invited the PLO and the Palestinian General Federation of Trade Unions to the international meeting for the working youth. The final statement of this conference reflected support for the resistance of the Palestinian youth and people against Israel, Zionism and imperialism. This conference was an example for the Soviet role in offering platforms for the PLO to meet and establish relations with international semi-formal players (Alkatri 1973).

In 1980, the Palestinian politician and journalist, the managing editor of the leftist magazine *Al-Hadaf*, Bassam Abu Shareef, was awarded a special medal by the Soviet Union of Journalists (Al-Hadaf 1980).

CULTURE IN THE PALESTINIAN-SOVIET PARADIPLOMACY

In October 1972, three months after Arafat's visit to Moscow, the first Palestinian media delegation visited the Soviet Union. This delegation included four delegates of PLO media council, the managing editor and the deputy editor of the Palestinian media agency, and the key Palestinian leader Majed Abo Sharar, who was the president of this delegation. This delegation met the Soviet Journalists Union, *Pravda* newspaper journalists, and the Komsomol leaders (Abdulfatah 1973). This visit had its special meanings as it helped the Soviet key policy makers and media leaders to understand the map of the Palestinian media and its challenges. Also, this visit emphasized the Palestinian position of the Soviet Union, and it also reflected the harmony between the political leadership and the semi-formal PLO institution, like unions and NGOs supported by PLO (Abdulfatah 1973).

In November–December 1980, Moscow celebrated the Week of Solidarity with the Palestinian People in the Soviet Union. This was the first wide and diversified occasion to reflect the Soviet public solidarity with the Palestinian people. The week included several events such as exhibits for books, posters, culture, fine arts and heritage (Bader 1980).

The PLO and its semi-official bodies—the representatives of the Palestinian civil society that are attached to the PLO in their structures and functions—participated intensively in these activities, while the chair of the Soviet-Palestinian friendship association—the deputy minister of culture in the Soviet Union Yuri Barbash led the preparations of this event. Barbash emphasized in the opening ceremony the Soviet solidarity to the Palestinian resistance and the legitimate Palestinian rights; he also welcomed the Palestinian diplomatic progresses of getting the recognition from more than 100 countries (Bader 1980).

The PLO and its semi-formal cultural arm, the General Union of Palestinian Writers and Journalists (GUPWJ), worked intensively on developing the related ties. The GUPWJ and the Writers Union of the USSR built strategic partnerships, which reflected in three components: the increasing appearance of Palestinian writers and their production in the Soviet Union, the enhancing of the Palestinian position in the Afro-Asian writers' association, and the supporting of Palestinian writers by getting the Lotus prize.

In 1969, the world-renowned Palestinian poet Mahmoud Darwish won the Lotus prize; the Indian prime minister Indira Gandhi awarded Darwish the prize in the 4th Afro-Asian writers conference. Darwish said in his speech, "Zionism in practice depended on two slogans to reach its goals; occupying land and occupying the labor, by which it merged the two sides of oppression that is practices against the Arab humans in Israel, This prize is a bouquet of flower for the renewed foundation of my people" (Zasypkin 1987).

In 1979, the prize had been awarded to the Palestinian poet Abdul Kareem Al-Karmi "Abu Salma", who was earlier responsible for the Afro-Asian Solidarity in the PLO, and became the chair of the GUPWJ one year later. The Palestinians saw in this prize for Abu Salma proper response to awarding the Nobel Prize for Literature to the American-Jew Isaac Bashevis Singer in 1978 (Abu Shawer 1985).

The GUPWJ established and developed a strong tie with the Soviet cultural players, mainly the counterpart union. Abu Salma, the chair of the Palestinian union, and the secretary general Darwish invested in their positions to enhance these relations. The relations with the Soviet Union attracted several Palestinian figures in literature from inside Palestine and outside, including Khalid Abu Khalid, Emile Habibi, Yehia Yakhlof, Tawfik Ziad and Rashed Hussain. The Palestinian union worked with its Soviet partners on mutual events, including festivals, workshops, seminars and trainings. But most important was the role of the Soviet Union in supporting the Palestinian literature in the Afro-Asian Writers Association (Halim 2012).

The Afro-Asian Writers Association was established in 1958, in Tashkent, the capital of the Soviet republic of Uzbekistan. The Soviet Union facilitated the establishing of this union to reflect its anticolonialism front of literature, with around 200 of the top figures in literature from Asia and Africa. This association was the Soviet vehicle to access postcolonial literature (Djagalov 2017). The Soviet influence in the association was an advantage for the Palestinian literature; beside the prize, the Palestinian novelist Ghassan Kanafani and the poets Mahmoud Darwish and Samih Al-Qasim were key editors in the editorial boards of *Lotus Magazine*, the major publication of the association.

The Arabic version of the magazine was located in Beirut, where the headquarters of PLO had been, and moved to Tunisia in 1982 after the PLO moved there. The Soviet policy makers and associations in this domain facilitated appointing the Palestinian literature figures in the editorial board of the Arabic version. Also, the deputy editor was a guaranteed position for the Palestinians; the first was the Palestinian leftist poet Moen Bseiso, who became the chief editor and got the Lotus prize[1] later (Halim 2012).

The new phase of the Palestinian-Russian cultural relations started by 2016. The Palestinian poet Abdullah Issa is the engineer of this relation. Issa moved to the Soviet Union in 1989 to continue his studies there and he joined the Maxim Gorky Literature Institute. Issa worked in several Russian media and academic institutions. In 2004 the Russian government asked him for help in negotiations with the militants during a hosteling accident. Issa worked through his translation in bridging both cultures and societies (Sudani 2021).

In October 2021, Abdullah was awarded the Gold Eurasian Medal of Honor, from the "21st Century Eurasia World" forum which became the

---

[1] This prize was obstructed from 1986 to 2019, when the Chair of the GUPWJ led the effort to renew the prize with Palestinian fund.

Russian cultural arm and its diplomatic entrance in this sector. The General Secretary of the GUPWJ had been chosen to be the vice president of the union, after accepting Palestine as a full member in this union, to be the first Arab country of the 54 member states (Sudani 2021).

The GUPWJ has also signed an agreement with the Maxim Gorky Literature Institute. Sudani emphasized the importance of this agreement as it comes with this top institution. This agreement allows the GUPWJ to benefit from the capacities of the institution in several domains including training, education, translation and conducting events (Sudani 2021).

Nabil Amro, the Palestinian ambassador in the Soviet Union and Russia (1988–1993), agrees with the importance of culture and its public figures in developing the Palestinian-Soviet and Russian relations. During Amro's period in Moscow, the Palestinian-American academic Ibrahim abo Lughod visited Moscow with a large Palestinian delegation, including academics and intellectuals. This delegation had been received directly in the Kremlin, which is not usual in diplomatic relations. This event, for Amro, proved the importance of culture in the Soviet diplomacy (Amro 2021).

The Palestinian-Russian Paradiplomacy

From the second half of the twentieth until the beginning of the twenty-first century, several strategic changes occurred that affected the decline of paradiplomacy between Palestine and Russia. This period witnessed the collapse of the Soviet Union, and the absence of the Soviet global role, which affected the nature and policies of Russia toward the Middle East, mainly on the Palestinian level. This stage witnessed tremendous transformations which negatively affected paradiplomacy between the two sides.

The first transformation was the Oslo peace process and the foundation of the Palestinian Authority (PA), as the formation of the PA played an important role in weakening parallel diplomacy in general, not only toward Russia. The bulk of the Palestinian political effort has been focused on building the institutions of the PA, and preoccupation with issues of transition from revolution to state.

Also, the concentration of the leadership became formalized through the relationship with states, donors and financiers. In addition, there was a feeling in international circles that the Palestinian issue had been solved and what remained were issues related to negotiations on certain political issues.

Secondly, the weakness of the Palestinian leftist forces had negatively affected the bilateral relations. The weakness of the Palestinian leftist forces has led to the weakening of the Palestinian public diplomacy with the remaining leftist powers in the former Soviet Union in general, and the Russian in specific.

Thirdly, as mentioned before, the last days of the Soviet Union witnessed significant developments in the Russian-Israeli relations, especially after the massive immigration of Soviet Jews to Israel, which led to advancing the bilateral diplomatic, economic and social relations.

With the beginning of the second decade of the twenty-first century, a number of changes began in the Palestinian and Middle Eastern political scene, and this was accompanied by Russia's return to the international stage, which affected Russia's diplomacy toward the Middle East and the Palestinian cause. Whereas Russia considered that the North Atlantic Treaty Organization (NATO) strikes in Libya exceeded the resolution of the UN Security Council, and therefore it intervened militarily in Syria in order to not repeat the experience (Zasypkin 2017). Since this date, there has been a Russian-Middle Eastern policy different from the previous stages. According to Nikolai Koganov, Russia has been dealing with the Middle East as a commodity to barter its relations with the West, or to win concessions in its relations with the US (2017).

As for the Russian foreign policy in the Middle East after 2015, it has become based on achieving several clear goals, which are represented in three main set goals. The economic goals lie in Russia's benefiting from active economic relations in the region to compensate for the losses of the Western economic blockade on Russia. Russia's political goals are affected by the competition between Russia and the US, where the Russians say that their involvement in Syria and their participation in the Israeli-Palestinian negotiations are proof to the West that it cannot deal with these issues without them. The last set of goals are the security objectives (Koganov 2017).

The shift in Russian Middle Eastern policies was a direct reflection of Russia's stances and policies toward the Palestinian issue, and this emerged in the numerous and clear Russian stances toward the Palestinian central issues. These positions and policies have shown the possibility of betting on the Russian role in finding a balance with the unlimited American support for Israel. The most prominent of these positions are, firstly, Russia's position on the results of the Palestinian legislative elections and the Russian role in the Palestinian-Israeli negotiations. Secondly, Russia's position on the Palestinian-Palestinian reconciliation, and the Russian effort to resolve the Palestinian division. Thirdly, Russia's position on the US administration's proclaimed "Deal of the century", and the transfer of the US embassy to Jerusalem.

The transformations were not only on the Russian side, but also several factors and determinants emerged on the Palestinian scene that encouraged the revitalization of paradiplomacy toward the Russian Federation, and the most prominent of these issues are the failure of the Palestinian-Israeli negotiations, and the state of uncertainty in the Palestinian political project.

All these determinants, whether changes related to the Russian Federation Middle East strategy or new Palestinian political scene, which took shape after 2006 and the new Palestinian leadership diplomacy adopted in 2012, played a major role in revitalizing the parallel Palestinian diplomacy toward the Russian Federation.

Although the Palestinian-Russian paradiplomacy has its history, as mentioned, it cannot be denied that the new parallel diplomacy has a different character and form than the previous one. It is a mixture between semi-official diplomacy and non-official diplomacy, as it combines elements of the PA's efforts with civil society and societal forces efforts; it is also considered a mixture in its goals between semi-official political goals, and between cultural and societal goals.

Therefore, the Palestinian public diplomacy paths toward the Russian Federation will be examined through three main levels: The first is the parallel political diplomacy, the second is the economic aspect and the third is the cultural and academic aspect.

The Political Track

Understanding Palestinian paradiplomacy toward Russia leads us to focus on the developments that took place in the Russian politics toward the Palestinian cause and the Middle East-Russian policy. The Palestinians seek to develop their relations with Russia constantly, but due to many factors related to the Russian policies these relations are not as they should be. At the beginning of the twenty-first century the Russians activated their policies in the Middle East, so we witnessed an activation of the Palestinian-Russian paradiplomacy after this period.

Here we noticed that the PA needs another credible player to support them in the peace process negotiations, and for Hamas they seek international support to get legitimacy after the 2006 elections; as for the PA and Hamas, Russia played this role.

The Russian policy toward the Palestinian issue passed through two phases that affected Russia's policies and stances toward the Palestinian issue. The first that extended from 1991 to 2002 witnessed the absence of an active Russian role in the Palestinian issue, despite the continuation of Palestinian-Russian diplomatic relations, and the continuation of visits between the leaders of the two countries. However, this stage was characterized by several features, including Russia's absence from playing the role of balancing the Palestinian-Israeli relations as the Palestinian side had always demanded, and Russia was no longer an initiator of negotiations in the Palestinian-Israeli conflict. This stage culminated in Russia's absence from the Aqaba Conference (Nima 2017).

The Russian policy at this stage was more biased toward Israel than to the Palestinians, and the Israeli relations prevailed over relations with the Palestinians.

The second stage started after 2002 and continues until today, when Russia became a member of the Middle East Quartet. Despite this new and official role of Russia in the International Quartet, its role remained limited as it could not be an initiator in the conflict, and it remained occupying the third place after the US and France.

Russia's real role in the Palestinian-Israeli conflict began through parallel diplomacy with the beginning of 2005, when the Russian president Vladimir Putin surprised the world with his visit to Palestine in 2005. It was an attempt to restore Russia's role in the region; after this historical visit Russia continued its diplomacy on the Palestinian track but now in unique and distinguished steps when Russia used the Palestinian legislative elections in 2006 as a new opportunity to show the world that it has a different role toward international issues, so it invited the Hamas leadership to visit Moscow (Abi 2011).

Russia continued its parallel diplomacy with the Palestinians after the Palestinian legislative elections. The Russian position was explicit about the results of the elections, in contrast to the European and American positions. This role was strengthened after several meetings with Hamas leaders in Moscow and their reception at the headquarters of the Russian Foreign Ministry.

Also, this stage witnessed a clear change in the Russian foreign policy toward the Palestinian issue, at various levels, and Russia resumed providing tangible support to the Palestinians, whether in international institutions, or on economic, academic and cultural levels. This period witnessed three visits by the president of the Russian Federation to Palestine and the Palestinian president also made more than ten visits to Moscow.

Russian diplomacy has been active on two important levels. The first level is Palestinian-Palestinian relations, where Moscow hosted the various Palestinian parties over two days of talks with the aim of resolving the Palestinian-Palestinian division and strengthening the position of the Palestinian cause in the international arena (Aljazeera 2019). The second track was the Russian initiative to hold an international conference to solve the Palestinian cause and establishing a viable Palestinian state (Aljazeera 2005).

The Russian position culminated in Russia's opposition to the "Deal of the Century" presented by US president Donald Trump, as the Russian position was important because Russia is part of the International Quartet.

The Economic Track

The Palestinian-Russian economic relations were affected by a number of factors that reduced their ability to grow, most notably the nature of the Palestinian economy and its transformations under the PA, the volatile political situation, as well as the Protocol on economic relations between the Israeli government and the PLO, signed in 1994, and the Israeli economy's control of the Palestinian economy.

The Palestinian-Russian economic relations are regulated by a set of agreements that were signed between the two sides over many years, which are related to the development of economic relations between both countries. In 1998, an economic and commercial cooperation protocol was signed with the aim of exchanging information and encouraging investment. In 2014, both countries signed an agreement under the so-called "protocol for the first session of the first Palestinian working group meetings", and stipulated a customs exemption for Palestinian exports to Russia, an increase in the volume of trade exchange and cooperation in the fields of electric energy, oil and transportation (Aburaida 2020).

A remarkable growth in signing agreements was in the year 2016, which witnessed the signing of six Palestinian-Russian agreements during the visit of Russian president Dmitry Medvedev to Palestine. The first agreement stipulated the encouragement and protection of mutual investments.

As for the second agreement, it was a memorandum of understanding on the establishment and development of industrial zones and industrial technological zones; the third agreement related to the signing of a cooperation plan in the field of occupational safety and health, employment and vocational training for the years 2017 and 2018. The fourth is a joint statement on holding Palestinian Culture Days in Russia and Russian Culture Days in Palestine.

The fifth agreement included a memorandum of understanding on cooperation between the Palestinian General Authority for Industrial Estates and Industrial Free Zones, and the special economic zones of the Russian Federation, and the sixth agreement included cooperation between the chambers of commerce and industry in the two countries.

A joint cooperation protocol was also signed in 2017, which provided Russia's support for the accession of the State of Palestine to the World Trade Organization (WTO), as well as cooperation in the fields of industry, trade and services (Aburaida 2020).

The signing of these agreements was followed by several Palestinian and Russian economic activities and meetings between the various economic levels in both countries, in particular the meetings of the Palestinian-Russian Joint Committee for Trade and Economic Cooperation, which are held annually on a regular basis between both sides (WAFA 2019).

In addition, Palestine witnessed the visits of many economic delegations at the level of chambers of commerce, municipalities and health centers in order to develop and enhance cooperation between the two countries, especially during the corona pandemic (WAFA 2020). In terms of financial support of the PA, Russia has been supporting the Palestinian budget since 2006 with an amount of 40 million dollars annually (WAFA 2016). Russia also provides scholarships for Palestinian students to study in Russian universities at the rate of 200 scholarships annually (Asmar 2011), and Russia provides support for the PA security sector, when it supported the Palestinian Security Forces with fifty police tanks (AlArab 2010).

Despite the large number of agreements signed between the two countries, as well as the diversity in the levels of the relationship between the different government sectors, or at the level of chambers of commerce and municipalities, trade exchange is still modest and does not reach the hoped level, and this is not only due to a shortcoming in the relationship, but mostly due to objective circumstances that govern the PA in the first place.

Beside the cultural track, which was detailed earlier, Russia tried to increase its appearance in Palestine through culture. In 2017, the

Palestinian president Mahmoud Abbas and his Russian counterpart Vladimir Putin opened the "President Putin Palestinian Organization for Culture and Economy" in Bethlehem. This project was funded by the Russian presidency alongside the Russian Museum, the Russian school and the Russian cooperation organization. Also, Moscow is funding the rehabilitation project of the historical road of Church of the Nativity (RT Arabic 2017).

Conclusion

The Soviet Union was one of the major allies of the Palestinian revolution since 1965. This special relationship depended on the official diplomacy as well as the paradiplomacy. The Palestinian unions, organizations, factions and figures played a crucial role in creating and developing such relations.

The Palestinian revolution benefited from such diplomacy by advanced capacity building programs in military and civil society, equipment and developing new diplomatic relations with third parties. Thus, the Palestinian-Soviet paradiplomacy was the major way for the PLO to the Soviet allied block.

The collapse of the Soviet Union and the peace process led to decline in the bilateral relations on its official and para faces. One the other side, the Russian-Israeli relations became strong due to the huge immigration waves. However, the last 20 years have witnessed developments in the Palestinian-Russian relations, on its political, economic and cultural sectors, through official and non-official players.

References

Abdulfatah, Ziad. 1973. Palestinian Discussions in Moscow. *Palestinian Affairs* 18: 178–183.
Abi, Wisam Issa. 2011. *The Russian Stance towards Hamas: 2006–2010*. Beirut: Al-Zaytona center.
Abu Oun, Refat. 1975. The USSR and the Palestinian Revolution (1965–1975). *Palestinian Affairs* 41–42: 573–591.
Abu Shawer, Rashad. 1985. The Palestinian Olive tree Abu Salma. *Palestinian Affairs* 85: 198–199.
Aburaida, Luai. 2020. The Current and Future Palestinian-Russian Trade Relation. *An-Najah Journal for Research—B (Humanities)* 34 (2): 345–346.

Aguirre, Iñaki. 1999. Making Sense of Paradiplomacy? An Intertextual Enquiry About a Concept in Search of a Definition. *Regional & Federal Studies* 9 (1): 185–209.

Al-Arab. 2010. *Russia Sends 50 Military Tanks to the Palestinian Authority, and Israel Prevents Their Entry.* July 20. https://www.alarab.com/Article/316492. Accessed 17 Dec 2021.

Al-Hadaf. 1980. Bassam Abu Shareef Awarded a Soviet Journalism Medal. *Al-Hadaf Magazine* 11 (487): 17.

Aljazeera. 2005. *Putin Renews Call for Holding a Peace Conference in the Middle East.* April 29. https://www.aljazeera.net/news/arabic/2005/4/29/. Accessed 11 Dec 2021.

———. 2019. *The Palestinian Talks in Moscow. Lavrov Considers the "Deal of the Century" Destructive.* February 12. https://bit.ly/37mXrEV. Accessed 12 Dec 2021.

Alkatri, Younis. 1973. Media Letter From Western Europe: The International Meeting for the Working Youth. *Palestinian Affairs* 18: 170–174.

Amro, Nabil. 1995. *1000 Days in Moscow.* Cairo: Alshorooq.

———. 2021. Personal Interview. Ramallah, November 8.

Ankylesis, Cynthia. 1985. The USSR Position of the Palestinian Issue and PLO 1947–1982. *Palestinian Affairs* 148–149: 26–43.

Asmar, Amani. 2011. *Russian-Palestinian Relations After the Collapse of the Soviet Union and its Impact on the Peace Process.* Birzeit University.

Bader, Liana. 1980. The Week of Solidarity with the Palestinian People in the Soviet Union. *Palestinian Affairs* 98: 142–144.

Cornago, Noé. 1999. Diplomacy and Paradiplomacy in the Redefinition of International Security: Dimensions of Conflict and Co-Operation. *Regional & Federal Studies* 9 (1): 40–57.

Dannreuther, Roland. 2016. *The Soviet Union and the PLO.* Wiesbaden: Springer.

Darwish, Mahmoud. 1974. An Interview with Yasser Arafat About His Recent Discussion in Moscow, Warsaw and Berlin: A Turning Point in the Palestinian Work. *Palestinian Affairs* 37: 5–10.

Djagalov, Rossen. 2017. *The Afro-Asian Writers Association and Soviet Engagement with Africa.* https://www.aaihs.org/the-afro-asian-writers-association-and-soviet-engagement-with-africa/. Accessed 14 Dec 2021.

Fawzi, Mohammed. 1988. *The Three Years War (1967–1970).* Cairo: Alwihda Publishing.

Fayyad, Ali. 1996. The Palestinian Diplomatic Experience. *The Palestinian Studies* 27: 150–178.

Haidari, Nabil. 1990. The PLO and the Soviet Union (1964–1970). *Palestinian Affairs* 213–214: 41–75.

Halim, Hala. 2012. Lotus, the Afro-Asian Nexus, and Global South Comparatism. *Comparative Studies of South Asia, Africa and the Middle East* 32 (3): 563–583.

Keating, Michael. 1999. Regions and International Affairs: Motives, Opportunities and Strategies. *Regional & Federal Studies* 9 (1): 1–16.
Khalil, Awad. 1989. The Soviet Union and the International Conference. *Palestinian Affairs* 197: 75–94.
Koganov, Nikolai. 2017. *Arab-Russian relations today. Russia. Russia and the Arab World Conference*. Issam Fares Institute for Politics and International Affairs. https://bit.ly/34vupkX. Accessed 13 Dec 2021.
McHugh, James T. 2015. Paradiplomacy, protodiplomacy and the foreign policy aspirations of Quebec and other Canadian provinces. *Canadian Foreign Policy Journal*: 238–256. https://doi.org/10.1080/11926422.2015.1031261.
New York Times. 1989. Israeli Minister Meets Soviet Aide in Cairo This Week. February 20. https://www.nytimes.com/1989/02/20/world/israeli-minister-meets-soviet-aide-in-cairo-this-week.html. Accessed 18 Dec 2021.
Nima, Kazem. 2017. Russia and the Middle East after the Cold War: Opportunities and Challenges. *The Arab Center for Research and Policy Studies* 1: 73–75.
RT Arabic. 2017. Opening Putin Palestinian Organization. May 11. https://bit.ly/3qKWKMo. Accessed 14 Dec 2021.
Sakhnini, Issam. 1975. The Palestinian Resistance. *Palestinian Affairs* 46: 239–248.
Sudani, Murad. 2021. Personal Interview. Ramallah, December 16.
WAFA. 2016. *Dmitry Medvedev, Prime Minister of the Russian Federation*. Russia and Palestine are Moving Forward. October 11. http://www.wafa.ps/ar_page.aspx?id=ekz1Kea727572339615aekz1Ke. Accessed 20 Dec 2021.
———. 2020. Shtayeh Receives the Visiting Medical Delegation to Palestine. https://wafa.ps/Pages/Details/13636. November 29. Accessed 17 Dec 2021.
Wilson Center. 1978. *Notes on Yasser Arafat's Visit to Moscow in October 1978*. November 14. https://digitalarchive.wilsoncenter.org/document/114538.pdf?v=fee2b4b8308cac4a38a9fbc7e413bd78. Accessed 21 Dec 2021.
Yasser Arafat Foundation. 2015. *Arafat's Speech About His Visit to the USSR*. December 7. https://yaf.ps/page-573-ar.html. Accessed 21 Dec 2021.
Zasypkin, Alexander. 1987. The Israeli- Soviet Relations: The Israeli Understanding for the Soviet Directions. *Palestinian Affairs*, 172–173: 111–116.
———. 2017. *Opening Speech at the Russia and the Arab World Conference*. Issam Fares Institute for Politics and International Affairs. https://bit.ly/34vupkX. Accessed 13 Dec 2021.

CHAPTER 10

Kurdistan-Iraq and China

Sardar Aziz and Mohammed Shareef

HISTORICAL DIMENSION OF RELATIONS BETWEEN KRG AND CHINA

How the Kurds see their relationship with China is the subject matter of this chapter. The authors identify three phases in Kurdistan-China relations: mythical, ideological and overt interaction. These periods merge into each other and thus are not necessarily disconnected. When it comes to current perceptions and attitudes toward China, the aforementioned phases have influenced the making of attitude and imaginations toward China.

The chapter tries to answer how and why Kurdistan-Iraq wants to establish and develop paradiplomatic relations with China? How it is constructed, implemented and maintained? It tries to do these by gauging, political, economic, cultural and military interactions or its lack thereof.

In terms of research methodology our approach has been diverse. The chapter is divided into three parts: a phantasm era, an ideological era and

---

S. Aziz (✉)
Policy Analyst, Erbil, Kurdistan Region, Iraq
e-mail: aziz.sardar@gmail.com

M. Shareef
University of Kurdistan Hewlêr, Erbil, Kurdistan Region, Iraq
e-mail: Mohammed.Shareef@ukh.edu.krd

© The Author(s), under exclusive license to Springer Nature Switzerland AG 2023
G. Gürbey et al. (eds.), *Between Diplomacy and Non-Diplomacy*,
https://doi.org/10.1007/978-3-031-09756-0_10

201

an institutionalized economic era. To decipher the phantasm era, the researchers pinpointed China's name in folklore, religious and classical texts. The existence of this stage in Kurdistan-China relations makes China unique among other countries in the world with which the Kurds have relations. It could be argued, nevertheless, fantasy perceptions are not limited to the past. It is present in the contemporary era as well, albeit differently. The ideological era is a part of Maoist global history. Maoism entered the Kurdish political landscape due to a combination of domestic and global factors. To conceptualize this era, we rely on semi-structured interviews, memoirs and secondary literature. The ideological era in the relationship primarily focuses on Patriotic Union of Kurdistan (PUK)-China interaction, the first political party to relate to China and how those memories help shape the current relationship.

The last and main part of the chapter focuses on various aspects of the current relationship, whether economic, political and cultural. Main actors from the KRG have been interviewed in semi-structured interviews for this purpose. The news and events in the media have been used to build data on various aspects of the relationship. These all have been couched in a framework of a non-state (fragile) actor relating to an emerging powerhouse.

Kurdish impressions of China were long held before any tangible relations emerged. Though mythical in nature they are instrumental to our current understanding of the current relationship. The phantasm era, as the authors like to call it, pinpoints China's name in folklore, religious and classical texts. The existence of this stage in China-Kurdistan relations makes China unique among other countries in the world with which the Kurds have relations. It could be argued, nevertheless, fantasy perceptions are not limited to the past. It is present in the contemporary era as well, albeit differently.

This era predates any actual knowledge and information on China. As a tool, the authors see phantasm as a "pre-structural guiding pattern" (Stingl 2011), based on common notions and unexamined awareness. Our definition of "phantasm" follows closely from Ernst E. Boesch (2002, 119). It is therefore a myth, not even a theory or precise idea; it is an "unspecified 'mold' of receptivity and evaluation" (Boesch 2002, 119). We can paraphrase as such: what we call phantasms are the perceiving, transforming as well as anticipating images, bound up with the acting party. "Phantasms are, of course, over-determined" (Stingl 2011). They provide a way in which culture influences the way we think and evaluate, shape our action and interaction.

The sources we employ to construct Kurdish Chinese phantasm are folklore, religious expressions and poetry. The Chinese claim that the Kurdistan-China relationship dates back 2000 years. "Chinese people and the Kurdish people belong to the ancient peoples of the world. We have a long history of civilization and our exchanges began as early as 2000 years before, through the Silk Road," states Chinese Consul-General Ni Ruchi, in an interview with the main media outlet in the region (Ali 2021). This statement might be a diplomatic gesture with little or no historical accuracy. Yet still, the Kurds in Iraq, who were influenced by traditional Islamic literature and a worldview, acknowledged China and saw it as a hard to reach faraway place.

Iraq's former ambassador to China, Mohammed Sabir, interviewed on October 2, 2021, asserts that the perception is reciprocated as Iraq is seen by the Chinese as one of the five ancient civilizations.

An example of this would be the folklore verse below:

I divided the night by being vigilant/My endeavours became like a Chinese Farhad (Bakir 2021b; [translated from Kurdish by the authors]).
The verse refers to a popular love story in Kurdistan, Iran and Turkey, known as Shirin and Farhad. In addition to folklore, religion has generated phantasm in China. One common saying "Seek Knowledge, even unto China" (Islam in China 2007) is regarded as a saying "hadith" of Prophet Mohammed; it has greatly shaped the traditional Kurdish view on China.
Albeit the saying is considered "weak" (Islam in China 2007) (i.e., unsubstantiated) it is largely circulated amongst Muslim Kurds.

Another example (below):

You are wrong to say that China and 'Machin' are pleasant/We will not go, as what is more wonderful than collecting kisses here (Muddarris 1978, 345; [translated from Kurdish by the authors]).
It appears that Kurds did not see China as a united place in the ninetieth century. "Machin" originates from the Chinese word Mangi which is a derivative of the Chinese word "Manzi" which means Southern Barbarians (Haw 2014, 8). Nali, a prominent poet in southern

Kurdistan, compares China to her lover's hair style.[1] The Kurdish name for China phonetically is "cheen" which rhymes with the Kurdish word چین 'cheen' which means layer. Basically, a play around with homonyms. Essentially, it is worth noting that for the Kurds, China was historically a fascinating place, unique, unparalleled in that no other distant land has been acknowledged in its folklore or ancient literature.

The phantasm period for the Kurds lasted until Mao's revolution and arrival of Maoism as part of a global phenomenon (Lovell 2019). In the phantasm phase China is not observed as a political entity per se, but as a geographical location and culture. China is mentioned and used for its supposed characteristics. Throughout this period China was imagined as a mythical, faraway, cultured and beautiful place. This perception is unique to China. No other country or civilization occupies such a place within the Kurdish classic and folk literature and subsequently psyche. This particular position signifies that China influenced the region but remained an obscure place throughout history. The phantasmic images have set the foundation for a familiar and unfamiliar relation to China. China's rise is materializing this myth and representing it at the same time. This mythical era set the premise for the ideological phase that followed. In the ideological era, the emerging myth was made possible through China's new revolution and the charisma of Mao Zedong.

At present, China attempts through media outlets to build myths and narratives as a soft power tool. According to Barthes, "message can consist of modes of writing or of representations; not only written discourse, but also photography, cinema, reporting, sport, shows, publicity, all these can serve as a support to mythical speech" (Barthes 1972, 108). Through this myth, a system of communication is built in order to create favorite impressions and positive images. China's experience from abject poverty, only half a century ago, to eradicating starvation and numerous colossal infrastructure projects serves as material for propaganda and soft power in a country that still suffers from a lack of basic infrastructure in many places.

---

[1] Nali: Mallah Xidir Ehmed Şawaysî Mîkayalî. بیروک (رەنگ) رەسمی یەدەسمەد یوەسی لە|ئە یی گەیی کەیلیایلی ٨٥٦١). Nali was born in 1800 in Khaku-Khol, a village that belongs to Sharazur in Sulaimany, and died in 1856. He is considered to be one of the greatest Kurdish poets of the classical nineteenth-century period because of his contribution to the Sorani school of poetry and in making Sorani the literary language of southern Kurdistan.

In the mid-fifties and sixties of the twentieth century, Maoism became a global revolutionary theory. It attempted "to create an alternative vision of modernity, or a vision of alternative modernity, by way of transforming Marxism into a non-European, henceforth more universal, vision of modernity" (Kang 2015, 13).

In the early 1950s Kurds became aware of Maoism as an alternative to Soviet Maoism and European Marxism, as Mohammad Sabir, the former Iraqi Ambassador to China, told the authors during an interview (Sabir 2021). In essence, it was more befitting to the characteristics of the Kurdish liberation movement. In his profile to Jalal Talabani, the first Kurdish president of Iraq, the *New Yorker* journalist John L. Anderson writes, "Talabani was a Marxist, and then a Maoist, attracted by 'Mao's idea of popular war, of fighting in the mountains against dictatorship" (Anderson 2007). Talabani, a young revolutionary, traveled to China in 1955, as the head of an Iraqi socialist student delegation. Talabani's visit was the first ever Kurdish political encounter with China (Sabir 2021).

Jalal Talabani met with Zhou Enlai, the Chinese Prime Minister. He saw Mao Zedong, but only from a distance. This fascination, later on, in the 1960s developed into a convenient ideological connection. Maoism became a global ideology with its own features distinct from Soviet communism. In 1964, the Kurdish political landscape had fractured with the KDP split into two factions (Gunter 1996, 228). Mohammad Sabir (2019) regards the split as the main factor behind the Talabani faction's attraction toward Maoism. When the Kurdish resistance split, two poles emerged, inspired by the Cold War, 'progressive' and 'reactionary.' Since the KDP was criticized by the splinter faction as being feudal and reactionary, the splinter group (i.e., politburo wing) through these criticisms found themselves submerged in global politics. There was one problem, however. The Iraqi Communist Party (ICP) was on the progressive side already and the split faction did not wish to be associated with the ICP. These circumstances made Maoism the right choice.

The ideology reached Sulaymaniyah via an Iranian splinter group. In 1964, a dissident faction broke with the Tudeh Party's leadership exiled in Europe. Maoist in orientation they called themselves the Revolutionary Organization of the Tudeh Party of Iran (Matin-Asgari 2014). At that time Maoism had gained global appeal it was seen as the appropriate worldview for progressive movements around the world. As Arif Dirlik puts it, "Mao's thoughts (and the inspiration of the Chinese Revolution in general) was presented most conspicuously during the period of national liberation movements from the 1950s to the 1970s, movements that also produced a whole range of home-grown visions of revolutionary renovation across the breadth of Asia, Africa and Latin America" (Dirlik 2014, 234).

This fusion of socialism with nationalism was also part of the Kurdish leftish movement. Names like Toilers Group of Kurdistan and Kurdistan Socialist Party demonstrate clearly the hybridization of socialism and nationalism. The Kurdish leftist elites thought the two sides shared many features and similarities. For Kurds Mao's China was an agrarian society, similar in many ways to Kurdistan. Moreover, Maoism helped the newly established Kurdish leftist groups in Iraqi Kurdistan to reconcile communism and nationalism, as Mohammad Sabir (2021) during the interview stressed. "Mao Zedong's thinking was crucial because it achieved the 'sinification' of Marxism, and became therefore an irreplaceable tool of nationalism and patriotic performance" (Brown 2018, 198). This view is reiterated by Julia Lovell (Lovell 2019).

The Kurdish leftist intellectuals, the likes of Ibrahim Ahmed and Jalal Talabani, resembled in many ways the activists of the May 4, 1919, movement in Beijing (Ropp 1980). They were departing from their heritage but simultaneously were not at ease with western modernity. Kurdish Maoists were attracted by Mao's many phrases and slogans: "semi-feudal, semi-colonial," "every Communist must grasp the truth," "political power grows out of the barrel of a gun" (Mao 1938, 224).

Despite the self-acclaimed affiliation, Kurdish Maoism was short-lived; it did not develop a strong ideological tie with neither Maoism ideology nor China. China, despite advocating Maoism rhetorically, remained a nation state and pursued a nationalist foreign policy. Nor did it in any shape or form support the Kurdish liberation movement in southern (Iraqi) Kurdistan. This ideological tie serves as a pillar of today's multilayered relationship between Kurdistan and China. This is particularly true when addressing the China/Communist Party relationship with the Patriotic Union of Kurdistan. China's approach to Kurdish political parties, mainly PUK and KDP, is one of the particularities of the China-Kurdistan relationship. According to Azad Jundiany (former PUK politburo member), the PUK asked the Chinese officials in a visit to China to build relations with the KDP as well (Jundiany, October 2021). However, China's shift from an ideological foreign policy to a focus on pragmatism, economy and trade made relations between China and a political party like the KDP easier. In post-Mao China "it doesn't matter whether a cat is black or white, as long as it catches mice" as Deng Xiaoping famously said (Hasmath 2014, 6). The ideological period is merely a memory between the PUK and China. This memory is highlighted today as a part of a narrative, as every relationship needs a foundation.

Both fantasy and ideology create the necessary foundations that help deconstruct the current discourse and contribute toward appreciating the nature of the relationship. In remaking a fantasized image, reference is made to an idealized world through an ahistorical approach to the past and fantasized look into the future.

This descriptive and analytical narrative has a range of features which vary from context to context, but one common crucial element is the obstacle preventing the realization of all aspects of reality.

Current Relations, Interests and Motivations

The current Belt and Road Initiative (BRI) period is radically different from the past two periods. It emerges primarily after the toppling of Saddam Hussein's regime. Both Kurdistan and China are at a different stage. China is a rising global power, which has embraced a policy vision entitled "The Belt and Road Initiative." The initiative originates in China and according to the Chinese "belongs to the world" according to the office of the leading group for promoting the BRI (Office of the Leading Group for Promoting the Belt and Road Initiative 2019, 2).

In this process, the Middle East will become ever more strategic to China in many ways, with the KRI a major component. In the last decade China is becoming more and more visible in the region. Kurdistan's semi-autonomous status, having an independent policy in areas of energy, diplomacy, allows it, as many of its officials reiterated during interviews to develop relations with China on a par with what the region already has with other major international powers. KRG's attempt to build paradiplomacy with China has a number of particular features.

Diplomatic/Political Relationship

While China opened consulate in Erbil, in 2014, KRG has yet to open an office in Beijing. Opening or not opening the representation is an issue in question. This fact makes Kurdistan-China relations different from other KRG paradiplomacy.

For KRG paradiplomacy, the opening of consulates of the sending countries and receiving their representatives is significant in many ways. According to Article three of the Vienna Convention on Diplomatic Relations 1961, the functions of a diplomatic mission are multifaceted (United Nations 2005, 3).

The article clearly stipulates that having representatives in other countries establishes representation, protection of interests, negotiating on behalf of the government, ascertaining and promoting the emissary's home country (United Nations 2005, 3). For a KRG representation to open in China is an acknowledgment by a global power and permanent member of the United Nations Security Council (UNSC). It also upgrades the relationship to an institutional level. This is significant for the KRG as it signifies permanency and having a channel to access a great and emerging major world power.

The saga of opening the Chinese representation in the KRG and possibly a KRG office in Beijing is a tale that tells the story of China's diplomatic approach to a sub-entity like Kurdistan, and the latter's struggle to build and solidify this relationship. When China opened its consulate general it was the last country among the five permanent members of the UNSC to do so. The delay in opening is a sign of China's reservations and hesitation when it comes to the Kurdistan Region as a non-state actor. According to Falah Mustafa Bakir, former KRG head of Department of Foreign Relations, "we argued on the basis that all other members of the UN [United Nations] Security Council were already present in Kurdistan, except China" (Bakir, October 2021a). After this request they agreed to open the consulate.

According to our research, there are three different views on this. Firstly, according to the former Iraqi Ambassador Mohammad Sabir, after a request from the Kurdish side was made, China suggested to the former Iraqi president Jalal Talabani that the KRG open a commercial office instead, registered under a company name to operate as a political representative. (Sabir, October 2021). We take this approach as pragmatic: willing to have relationships without recognition. This shows how China's domestic policy, that is, one China policy, impacts and shapes the foreign policy. "Domestic politics is typically a crucial part of the explanation for states' foreign policies (Fearon 1998, 289–90). It was mostly due to China's sensitivity to Iraq's sovereignty. However, the Chinese consulate Ni Ruchi stated that "the reason for not opening a KRG office in Beijing is the lack of a request from the KRG" (Rudaw 2021). This statement appears to be more a diplomatic expression rather than the reality. As Sabir put it during the interview, "the consul is not accurate" (Sabir, October 2021). After seven years of the opening, the KRG has yet to open an office in Beijing.

The second view on this is "after the passing of the Iraqi new constitution in 2005, the new Iraqi constitution recognized the region of Kurdistan, along with its existing authorities, as a federal region" (Council of Representatives 2005, Article 117). This status of Kurdistan being a constitutional entity within Iraq was helpful for China to start with, as Falah Mustafa Bakir indicated in an interview with the authors (Bakir, October 2021a). As Shichor puts it, "one of the basic components of post-Mao China's policy, domestic and international, is opposition to separatism," "These rules also apply to the Kurds" (Shichor 2006). Through the constitutional recognition China overcame fears of Kurdish separatism. In spite of this, however, China did not hurry to take steps forward. Only a decade after the legal and constitutional confirmation, China opened its general consulate. This might reflect the assertion that China, unlike the United States (US) and other democratic powers, is a long-term thinker (Kissinger 2012, 133).

The third assertion is that the delay in opening the KRG office in Beijing is technical rather than anything else. Both Falah Mustafa Bakir, senior advisor to President Nechirvan Barzani and Safeen Dizayi, the KRG's head of Department of Foreign Relations, stressed that the Islamic State in Iraq and Syria (ISIS) war and austerity were among the main factors preventing the opening of a representation in Beijing. They also emphasized that the KRG is currently conducting a study to review the regions' representation offices abroad. (Dizayi, October 2021; Bakir, October 2021a). One outcome of that study is the need for having representatives in eastern and Asian countries. Safeen Dizayi said the opening of a KRG Representation in Beijing is strictly related to "costs associated with such a venture, especially so with the region's income in decline due to the pandemic and difficulties with Baghdad in gaining Kurdistan's share of the national budget" (Dizayi, October 2021).

In addition to this, Ni Ruchi, China's Consul General in the KRI during his interview with Rudaw (Ali 2021), stated that the Kurdistan Regional Government has plans to open a representation office in China, though he added the KRG officials have not officially requested the opening of an office in Beijing, and should this request be made China would be happy to accommodate it. In spite of all these, China built its relations with the main political parties PUK and KDP before official governmental relations, all our interviewees reiterated.

Looking for a Big Friend

The expression uttered by more than one interviewee was P-five. It signifies the powerful five permanent members of the UNSC. China is a member of the council. According to Council on Foreign Relations, "The UN Security Council is the premier global body for maintaining international peace and security" (Council on Foreign Relations 2021). As Dizayi put it during the interview: "Having a contact there, helps" (Dizayi, October 2021). China's first interaction with the Kurdish issue in Iraq through the UNSC was in April 1991 when the body passed Resolution 688 (United Nations Security Council 1991) to protect the Kurds from Saddam Hussein's regime. China expressed sympathy toward the Kurdish refugees, but it eventually abstained because it argued that the UNSC does not have the authority to interfere with domestic affairs of a sovereign state (People's Daily 1991). Despite its reservations, this shows that China was not against humanitarian intervention to aid the Kurds during their time in distress.

"China abstained from voting on Resolution 678, which authorized military action to enforce Resolution 660's demand. This abstention demonstrated Beijing's distinct reluctance to endorse the Security Council's authorization of the use of force by member states under Chapter VII" (Davis 2011, 222). China's abstention rather than veto is probably the most one can expect from China, for domestic, historic and international order reasons. This poses a question: Can China be KRG's friend?

Answering this question is not easy and might be at best rhetorical. China, similar to other powers, is a self-interest country, albeit with different methods and ethos. In this imbalanced relationship the two sides of the relation are extremely different in every possible way.

Areas of Cooperation

Both trade exchange and construction are the two main components of China's current outlook on to the world. Kurdistan is no different. One of the aspects of China's appeal is its ability and willingness to build infrastructure. KRG hopes through paradiplomacy to engage China in future construction projects in the region.

Historically there has been a correlation between infrastructures and international relations. This is more so in the case of China and the BRI. For Kurdistan a mega project like the BRI and the connectivity that potentially results from it are important, as the region suffers from being landlocked.

The BRI connects numerous countries on three large continents and thereby provides the potential for increased trade among those regions. The rhetoric is strong and special events are on the rise. Events are organized to forge trade ties between the Region's businesspeople and their Chinese counterparts. Areas such as construction, medical equipment, clothing and energy are given special attention. There are collaborations between the Chinese Consulate General in Erbil and various government agencies to this end, said Gaylan Haji Saed, on a K24 TV interview (August 31, 2021).

One project which clearly stands out is the construction of a mega-residential, tourism and sports project called Happy City. The project is predicted to create 8000 new jobs in the region at a cost of five billion US dollars (Basnews 2021). The project will be built in north-west of Irbil province. The implementation of such a mega project will make China a big player not only in Erbil but in the wider region. According to media sources, the project was a Chinese initiative. Chinese consulate's Facebook page confirms the project (Consulate General of China in Erbil 2020).

"Today, China's strategy in Iraqi Kurdistan follows an ambitious geopolitical goal: to scale up Big Asia's vector" (Malik 2021). This colossal geopolitical goal is potentially a double-edged sword for the KRI. On the one hand, it connects KRI to a bigger wider network; on the other, being within such a vast network might diminish the KRI's power.

LIMITATIONS OF COOPERATION

In its relation with China a non-state actor like Iraqi Kurdistan faces a number of hurdles. China is unwilling to recognize or to deal with KRG political elites as statesmen. The Kurdish political elites have been hosted in other world power capitals in the highest offices, for instance the White House (The White House 2015). These high diplomatic receptions have created a psychological feeling among the Kurdish political elite, to expect the same treatment from other big powers as well. According to the former Iraqi Ambassador to Beijing Kurdistan Region president, Masoud Barzani, cancelled his trip to Beijing when informed that he will not be received at the highest levels, Sabir told the authors during an interview (Sabir, October 2021). This incident clearly shows how China sets limits to KRG's ambitions. This was in tandem with China's refusal to allow the opening of an official KRG representation in Beijing at the time. This restricted diplomatic treatment has both domestic and international factors. China envisages itself as a unitary multi-ethnic state consisting of fifty-six different groups. According to Chinese law, minorities have the rights to territorial autonomy under the Regional Ethnic Autonomy (REA) regime, as well as to other preferential policies respecting financial, technical, social and cultural affairs. The REA regime allows minority groups to set up cultural affairs and autonomous agencies, through which they might exercise legislative, financial and cultural autonomous powers in areas where they live in concentrated communities (Linzhu 2015, 3–4). From this perspective China have no problem with similar rights and status for Kurds within Iraq. But China sees in Kurdistan independence ambition which makes Kurdistan in par with Taiwan and Hongkong. In the minds of Chinese Communist Party (CCP) leaders, Hong Kong, Macao and Taiwan are Chinese territories and must be reunited with the mainland (Chang 1992, 128). In addition to this the complex multinational and multi-state nature of the Kurdish issue makes China to limit its relationship to the KRG.

Another factor that contributes in limiting the Chinese relationship to the KRI is the formers attitude toward sovereignty. In the past "China had absolute sovereignty within its territory and Chinese leaders haunted by the power of emperor" (Coleman and Maogoto 2013, 254). This political memory and imagination contrasted with centuries of humiliation and instability. In the period between 1839 and 1949 China's government lost control over large portions of its territory at the hands of foreigners. This period is a key element of modern China's founding narrative (Wang 2012). This complex background and atypical Chinese relation to history is shaping today's China's view and grand narrative.

China adheres to five principles of peace, that is, "mutual respect for each other's territorial integrity and sovereignty," "mutual non-interference in each other's internal affairs," which are literary copied from Westphalian principles (Ministry of Foreign Affairs of the People's Republic of China 2014). "Traditional Westphalian notions of sovereignty not only describe the manner in which China operates on the international stage but also describe what is widely seen as the Chinese view of international affairs" (Panda 2014). These principles are seen by the KRG as threats to its survival. In alternative to these KRG as a non-state actor adheres to principles of Responsibility to Protect (R2P). This is clear in the UN Resolution 688/1991 (United Nations Security Council 1991).

The "overarching principle of Westphalian sovereignty is that sovereignty begins and ends with the state–no external actor or institution can undermine domestic structures. Under this principle, the Westphalian model also ascribes legal equality between states and bars states from intervening in the internal affairs of another state" (Panda 2014).

CHINA-IRAQ RELATIONSHIP

"China attaches great importance to developing relations with Iraq, and stands ready to promote their strategic partnership for greater development," said Chinese president Xi Jinping (China Daily 2021). China is becoming a big player in Iraq. Daniel J. Samet argued that "China, Not Iran, Is the Power to Watch in Iraq" (Samet 2019).

However, Mohammed Shareef argues that China has developed a form of dual diplomacy towards Iraq and Kurdistan, recognizing the Kurdistan Region's special status within the Iraqi state (Shareef 2016, 69). That being said, we see the more China is involved with the Iraqi central government, its relations with the KRI are dwarfed especially so potentially at times of crises. We argue that future Chinese engagements with the Iraqi central government will contribute in further consolidating the centralization of the Iraqi state. This might not be explicit. But for instance, the planned Chinese road and railway development in Iraq will consolidate central power authority over Arab Iraqi territory and the Kurdistan region alike.

There are other limitations to the KRI paradiplomacy toward China. The KRI as a substate entity without representation in China's capital will have little or no power to influence Chinese foreign policy decisions and decision makers, in time of crises. While China's foreign policy makers are changing, the "CCP's highest body—the opaque Politburo Standing Committee—retains the ultimate decision-making power" (Jakobson and Knox 2010, 8). For the KRI officials it is hard, if not impossible, to reach this small circle of decision makers, in a country where there is no free media, lobby and liberal division of powers.

CONCLUSIONS

This chapter attempted to deal with Kurdistan-China paradiplomatic relationships. The Kurdistan relationship with China went throughout a number of stages. The chapter divided the relationship into three stages: phantasy, ideological and contemporary post-ideological relationship. Despite these long historical links between China and Kurdistan the actual relationship is new. China opened its consulate after all the other members of the UNSC. From the historical trajectory and current relationship, it becomes clear that Kurdistan has little impact on the nature and direction of the relationship.

For China the relationship is part of the Middle East that is increasingly becoming an essential part of its One Belt One Road economic expansion program. One Belt One Road is China's bid for global advantage, both for its own economic interests and in competition with other great powers. Essentially China-KRG relationship is part of the pattern influence-without-entanglement relationship.

In essence this chapter defined the KRI-China relationship predominantly from the Kurdistan Region's perspective. The KRI officials made it clear through the interviews given to the authors that they see China as an important global player. It demonstrated that the Kurdish side is appreciative of the relationship but still unsatisfied with its nature. The relationship still lacks a political element which the Kurds see as vital to their existence, success, continuity and survival, which the Chinese cannot provide. To complicate matters furthermore, the relationship with China, though desired by the Kurdish political elite, is watered down due to the KRI's special relationship with the United States. The United States is weary of Chinese infringement on its sphere of influence, and subsequently the KRG is apprehensive about these American sensitivities. Despite fast development in areas of trade, energy and construction, the relationship, when compared with other big power relationships, suffers from a number of significant limitations.

References

Ali, Rebaz. 2021. Beijing's Envoy Praises Growing Ties Between Kurdistan and China. *Rudaw*, September 29. Accessed February 26, 2022. https://www.rudaw.net/english/interview/29092021.

Anderson, Jon L. 2007. Mr. Big. Where is Jalal Talabani taking Iraq? *The New Yorker*, February 5. Accessed August 12, 2021. https://www.newyorker.com/magazine/2007/02/05/mr-big.

Bakir, Falah Mustafa. 2021a. Interviewed on 5 October.

Bakir, Muhammed. 2021b. چۍن ها هندێدیتای کوردیا [*China in Kurdish literature*]. *Diplomatic Magazine*. Accessed March 5, 2022. https://diplomaticmagazine.net/opinion/3734.

Barthes, Ronald. 1972. *Mythologies*. New York: The Noonday Press.

Basnews. 2021. Foreign Investment in Erbil: Giant Project to Create 8,000 Jobs. August 12. Accessed November 5. https://www.basnews.com/en/babat/706760.

Boesch, Ernst E. 2002. The Myth of Lurking Chaos. In *Between Biology and Culture*, ed. Heidi Keller, Ype H. Poortinga, and Axel Schölmerich, 116–135. Cambridge: Cambridge University Press.

Brown, Kerry. 2018. *The Culture of Chinese Communism and the Secret Sources of Its Power.* Cambridge: Polity Press.

Chang, Parris H. 1992. China's Relations with Hong Kong and Taiwan. *The ANNALS of the American Academy of Political and Social Science* 519 (1): 127–139.

China Daily. 2021. Xi says China to Expand Cooperation with Iraq. August 18. Accessed April 4, 2022. https://www.chinadaily.com.cn/a/202108/18/WS611d0acaa310efa1bd669a5e.html.

Coleman, Andrew, and Jackson N. Maogoto. 2013. "Westphalian" meets "Eastphalian" sovereignty: China in a globalized world. *Asian Journal of International Law* 3 (2): 237–269.

Consulate General of China in Erbil. 2020. *Facebook*, October 27. Accessed February 26, 2022. https://www.facebook.com/ChineseconsulateErbil/posts/2713060395676494/.

Council of Representatives. 2005. Iraqi Constitution. Accessed February 26, 2022. https://iq.parliament.iq/en/wp-content/uploads/2022/01/Iraqi-Constitution.pdf.

Council on Foreign Relations. 2021. The UN Security Council. Accessed September 9 2021. https://www.cfr.org/backgrounder/un-security-council.

Davis, Jonathan E. 2011. From Ideology to Pragmatism: China's Position on Humanitarian Intervention in the Post-Cold War Era. *Vanderbilt Journal of Transnational Law* 44 (2): 217–284.

Dirlik, Arif. 2014. Mao Zedong Thought and the Third World/Global South. *International Journal of Postcolonial Studies* 16 (2): 233–256.

Dizayi, Safeen. 2021. Interviewed on 5 October.

Fearon, James. 1998. Domestic Politics, Foreign Policy, and Theories of International Relations. *Annual Review of Political Science* 1: 289–313.

Gunter, Michael M. 1996. The KDP-PUK Conflict in Northern Iraq. *Middle East Journal* 50 (2): 224–241.

Hasmath, Reza. 2014. White Cat, Black Cat or Good Cat: The Beijing Consensus as an Alternative Philosophy for Policy Deliberation? The Case of China. *University of Oxford Department of Social Policy and Intervention Barnett Papers in Social Research* 14 (2): 1–19.

Haw, Stephen G. 2014. The Persian Language in Yuan-Dynasty China: A Reappraisal. *East Asia History* 39: 5–32.

Islam in China. 2007. Seek Knowledge Even as Far as China. Accessed February 26, 2022. https://islaminchina.wordpress.com/2007/11/06/authenticity-of-seek-knowledge-even-as-far-as-china/.

Jakobson, Linda and Dean Knox. 2010. *New Foreign Policy Actors in China.* SIPRI Policy Paper No. 26. Accessed September 10, 2021. https://www.sipri.org/publications/2010/sipri-policy-papers/new-foreign-policy-actors-china.

Jundiany, Azad. 2021. Interviewed on 18 October.

K24 TV. 2021. سـەرچاوەی: نەخشەی ھەڵناوەندە نزیک لاسایی ھاوبە نزیندە نانگرزاد ناسەھەم ناناگرزاد سەرچاوە, Accessed January 10, 2022. https://www.youtube.com/watch?v=_SkcPWYKDYE.

Kang, Liu. 2015. Maoism: Revolutionary Globalism for the Third World Revisited. *Comparative Literature Studies* 52 (1): 12–28.

Kissinger, Henry. 2012. *On China.* New York: Penguin Random House.

Linzhu, Wang. 2015. The Identification of Minorities in China. *Asian-Pacific Law & Policy Journal* 16 (2): 1–21.

Lovell, Julia. 2019. *Maoism: A Global History.* London: Bodley Head.

Malik, Olga. 2021. What Is China's Endgame in Northern Iraq? *Politics Today,* March 16. Accessed January 15, 2022. https://politicstoday.org/china-northern-iraq-krg-economic-investments/.

Mao, Zedong. 1938. Problems of War and Strategy. Selected Works of Mao Tse-tung. Accessed August 5, 2021. https://www.marxists.org/reference/archive/mao/selected-works/volume-2/mswv2_12.htm.

Matin-Asgari, Afshin. 2014. Iranian Maoism: Searching for a Third World Revolutionary Model. *Middle East Research and Information Project* 270: 21–22.

Ministry of Foreign Affairs of the People's Republic of China. 2014. The Five Principles of Peaceful. Accessed April 3, 2022. https://www.fmprc.gov.cn/mfa_eng/wjdt_665385/zyjh_665391/201405/t20140528_678165.html.

Muddarris, Mala. 1978. *The Collection of Nali's Poetry.* Baghdad: Kurdish Academy Press.

Office of the Leading Group for Promoting the Belt and Road Initiative. 2019. *The Belt and Road Initiative: Progress, Contributions and Prospects.* Beijing: Foreign Languages Press.

Panda, Ankit. 2014. China's Westphalian Attachment. *The Diplomat,* May 22. Accessed November 7, 2021. https://thediplomat.com/2014/05/chinas-westphalian-attachment/.

People's Daily. 1991. Representative Explains China's Position on the Resolution of the Security Council on the Kurdish Issue in Iraq. April 7.

Ropp, Paul S. 1980. The May Fourth Movement. *Bulletin of Concerned Asian Scholars* 12 (2): 58–64.

Rudaw. 2021. Iraq-China Trade Reached $16 Billion in Six Months: Commercial Consul. August 31. Accessed February 3, 2022. https://www.rudaw.net/english/business/31082021.

Sabir, Mohammad. 2019. ەوھچین: لە دیدی تێۆڵامات٣/٤كەوە *China: Kurdish Diplomat View.* Sulymanya: Kurdistane New. [Kurdish Book].
———. 2021. Interviewed on 2 October.
Samet, Daniel J. 2019. China, Not Iran, Is the Power to Watch in Iraq. *The Diplomat*, October. Accessed January 12, 2022. https://thediplomat.com/2019/10/china-not-iran-is-the-power-to-watch-in-iraq/.
Shareef, Mohammed. 2016. China's Dual Diplomacy: Arab Iraq and the Kurdistan Region. In *Toward Well-Oiled Relations?* ed. Niv Horish, 125–147. London: Palgrave Macmillan.
Shichor, Yitzhak. 2006. China's Kurdish Policy. *China Brief*, January 3. Accessed December 11, 2021. https://jamestown.org/program/chinas-kurdish-policy/?fbclid=IwAR0Nf-YGnUUG_adT8tDCoZE2pH29mZrJO_oVhr8VDpp5K0c-e9zqHFvlbfY.
Stingl, Alexander. 2011. What is a Phantasm? Second Approach Towards Tackling this Travelling Concept. Accessed August 21, 2021. https://alexstingl.wordpress.com/2011/09/21/what-is-a-phantasm-second-approach-towards-tackling-this-travelling-concept/.
The White House. 2015. Iraqi Kurdistan Region President Masoud Barzani. Accessed February 3. 2022. https://obamawhitehouse.archives.gov/the-press-office/2015/05/05/readout-president-and-vice-presidents-meeting-iraqi-kurdistan-region-pre.
United Nation Security Council. 1991. Resolution 688 (1991)/adopted by the Security Council at its 2982nd meeting, on 5 April 1991. United Nations Digital Library. Accessed December 20, 2021. https://digitallibrary.un.org/record/110659?ln=en.
United Nations. 2005 (1961). Vienna Convention on Diplomatic Relations 1961. Accessed August 20, 2021. https://legal.un.org/ilc/texts/instruments/english/conventions/9_1_1961.pdf.
Wang, Zheng. 2012. *Never Forget National Humiliation: Historical Memory in Chinese Politics and Foreign Relations.* New York: Columbia University Press.

CHAPTER 11

Palestine and China

Guy Burton

How have the Palestinians used their contact with China to advance the establishment of a Palestinian state and the restoration of Palestinian rights? The chapter answers these questions by examining the relationship between different Palestinian representative entities and the People's Republic. It uses a descriptive historical account, identifying periods of convergence and divergence, the former associated with a common commitment towards greater militancy, the latter with the rise of diverse actors and interests. They include China's own expanding and deepening relationship with Israel, which comes at the expense of the Palestinian cause, as well as the existence of several Palestinian entities—the Palestine Liberation Organization (PLO), the Palestinian Authority (PA), the Fatah and Hamas political factions, and the Boycott, Divestment and Sanctions (BDS) movement—who have each engaged China with limited degrees of success.

The historical approach taken in this chapter is in line with much of the largely non-theoretical literature associated with diplomacy and paradiplomacy (Black 2012, 10–11; Jönsson 2012; Alvarez 2020; Schiavon 2019). In paradiplomacy, particularly, the absence of theory has prompted the

G. Burton (✉)
Brussels School of Governance, Brussels, Belgium
e-mail: shofmann@zedat.fu-berlin.de

© The Author(s), under exclusive license to Springer Nature Switzerland AG 2023
G. Gürbey et al. (eds.), *Between Diplomacy and Non-Diplomacy*, https://doi.org/10.1007/978-3-031-09756-0_11

219

subject to be studied through a wide range of lenses. Kusnetsov (2015) suggests at least 11 different dimensions, from constitutional or federal arrangements to national identity or the impact of regionalism, globalisation and the changes to the global political economy.

Although the Palestinians' international relations are seen through the lens of paradiplomacy, it is arguable that the framework does not provide an exact fit. While the quasi-state PA comes closest to the paradiplomatic model, the status of the land it operates on is contested. Moreover, it is territory that is internationally recognised as militarily occupied by Israel rather than being a constituent part of the Israeli state. This challenges one of paradiplomacy's precepts, that it entails parallel diplomacy by a sub-state unit that are part of a state on the basis of constitutional (federal) arrangements.

All the other Palestinian entities examined here also have no direct constitutional connection to the Israeli state. Indeed, the PLO, Fatah and Hamas were all formed independently from and against the Israeli state, even as their fortunes have been largely contingent and sometimes dependent upon it. Arguably then, the confrontational nature of the Palestinian experience towards Israel challenges another, perhaps implicit, assumption about paradiplomacy and its effectiveness: namely, that for it to be successful there must be a mutually positive relationship between the state and sub-state actors in question (Cornago 2018).

If paradiplomacy is problematic in the Palestinian case, is it more appropriate to call it protodiplomacy? Whereas paradiplomacy is diplomacy by sub-state units "in parallel" with states, protodiplomacy has a more nationalist and separatist edge. Using this perspective arguably suits the Palestinian goals and actions in the international arena and despite the scholarly discussion that exists regarding paradiplomacy and protodiplomacy; that is whether, the two entail entirely separate concepts (Paquin 2020) or are linked, paradiplomacy being a transitional process towards protodiplomacy (Kusnetsov 2015). While this chapter does not resolve this debate, the Palestinian experience does require attention to its wider international objectives: namely, the pursuit of a Palestinian state alongside the defence of Palestinian rights.

Palestinian Militancy and China

Palestinian contact with China began in the mid-1960s through the Fatah nationalist movement and the PLO. Eventually, this pluralism would disappear when Fatah took control of the PLO in the late 1960s.

The PLO was formed in 1964, nearly 20 years after Israel's establishment in historic Palestine. Until then and for some time after, Palestinian interests were mainly represented by self-appointed Arab nationalist leaders like Egypt's Gamal Nasser and the monarchs of Jordan. The pan-Arab linkage was also evident in the PLO's creation, having been formed under the auspices of the Arab League and closely watched by the Egyptian leadership (Behbehani 1981). Fatah was formed earlier, at the end of the 1950s by several young Palestinian exiles, including Yasser Arafat. Unlike the PLO and its control by other Arab leaders, Fatah promoted a more independent Palestinian line when it came to decision-making and armed struggle against Israel (Bröning 2011, 57).

Israel's military victory in the 1967 war led to a decline in pan-Arab nationalism and Arab leaders' control of the Palestinian question. Fatah gained most, its cadres eventually winning control over the PLO's internal committees and structure and becoming the largest internal party bloc by 1969. The change was recognised by the Arab states in 1974 when the Arab League passed a resolution that the PLO was the "sole and legitimate representative of the Palestinian people". That same year the PLO was also granted observer status at the United Nations (UN; PASSIA 2014; Arab League 1974).

Palestinian contact with China began early. In March 1964 Fatah sent a delegation to Beijing to establish political contacts. A year later, in March 1965 the PLO leader Ahmed Shukairy did the same. The Chinese extended diplomatic recognition and allowed the PLO to open an office. But Shukairy wanted more, in particular military assistance (Behbehani 1981; Israeli 1989).

The Palestinian appeal was well targeted. China had strong ties with Arab nationalist regimes like Nasser and the Baathists in Iraq and Syria and it opposed Israel which it saw as a Western proxy (Chen 2012; Shichor 1994). Initially, the Chinese were worried about the PLO's lack of a territorial base and the need to maintain good relations with Arab states to supply the arms. Nonetheless, it did so, calculating that the cost was relatively low (later estimates suggest China sent around $5 million in small arms between 1965 and 1970; Oppenheimer 2019) and because it helped Beijing undercut Soviet influence in the Arab world (Israeli 1989).

Fatah's relationship with China was positive in this period and despite other, more explicitly socialist groups like the Popular Front for the Liberation of Palestine or the Democratic Front for the Liberation of Palestine in the PLO. Fatah's majority status meant that Chinese leaders engaged primarily with its leaders than with its fellow ideologues (Harris 1994; Bröning 2011, 59).

In the PLO, the Chinese saw echoes of their own armed struggle against Japan and later the Nationalists. However, the reality of the Arab world was very different from East Asia. The PLO's autonomy presented problems for its hosts, first in Jordan and later in Lebanon. The PLO's cross-border attacks against Israel prompted reprisals. In addition, the PLO interfered in the two countries' domestic politics, threatening the existing authorities. In September 1970 Jordan's King Hussein forcibly removed the PLO from his country, leading to its relocation to Lebanon. There, the Palestinian struggle became intertwined with Lebanon's own internal splits and eventual civil war. Lebanon's weak state enabled the PLO to attack Israeli targets, but this led to a backlash: in 1982 Israel launched an invasion of southern Lebanon and, alongside its paramilitary proxies, pressured Fatah and PLO into exile once more, to Tunis.

The growing physical distance between the Palestinian leadership and historic Palestine made it harder for the PLO to carry out guerrilla attacks in the homeland. Instead, it turned to more urban-based terrorist tactics, including at the 1972 Olympic Games and aircraft hijackings in the 1970s and 1980s. But despite the widespread international attention, these actions did little to change their situation in relation to Palestine (Bröning 2011, 64–65).

These developments also influenced Palestinian relations with Beijing. The Palestinians' defeat in Jordan prompted a re-evaluation of Chinese support towards the Palestinians; Arafat was subjected to a lecture on "self-reliance" and the need for hard work if the Palestinians were to succeed during a visit to Beijing (Behbehani 1981). The Chinese were also confused by the fragmentation of Arab unity, both in relation to and surrounding the Palestinians. It became less clear what line they should take, as they also began to explore their own diplomatic outreach to states in the region.

For the Palestinians, Chinese coolness was not immediately problematic. As the PLO adjusted its strategy in the 1970s, it looked towards

Moscow as a sponsor and supplier (Reppert 1989; Harris 1994). This made sense, given the Soviets' status as one of two superpowers at the time and China's status as the junior communist power.

THE OSLO ACCORDS AND THE PALESTINIAN AUTHORITY

Despite the growing difference between the Palestinians and China in the 1970s and 1980, the two would eventually find common ground again. The 1973 war between Israel, Egypt and Syria and the Palestinian use of terrorism failed to shift Israel; increasingly, the Palestinian leadership concluded that Israel could not be militarily defeated. Arafat began looking for an alternative solution, leaving the door open to a negotiated settlement with Israel. That position was eventually formalised in the PLO's 1988 Algiers Declaration, when it announced that it was ready to end violence and pursue a two-state solution (PASSIA 2014).

China welcomed the Palestinian shift. During the 1980s, Beijing urged Washington to open talks with the PLO and pressed for an international conference to resolve the Palestinian-Israeli conflict. To that end, it even offered itself as a mediator on separate occasions, in 1984 and 1989 (Dillon 2004; Harris 1994).

While Chinese mediation was never tested at this time, an international conference did happen, following the end of the Cold War and the first Gulf War in 1991. Now the sole hegemonic power, the United States (US) pushed for Israel and the Arab states to meet each other at the Madrid conference. Although Israel opposed Palestinian participation, several of its leaders were able to do so as part of the Jordanian delegation. Initially China was not present, since it lacked formal diplomatic ties with Israel at the time (Shichor 1994). That situation changed, when China and Israel officially recognised each other in 1992 and enabled Beijing to sit in the subsequent multilateral talks that followed. The establishment of a full diplomatic relationship between China and Israel followed a more clandestine one that was based on Israeli arms sales to Beijing over the previous decade (Shichor 1998).

China's establishment of diplomatic relations with Israel was costly for the Palestinians, even if it did not seem so at the time. The previous absence of ties between China and Israel meant the Palestinians' position was more prominent and better represented in Beijing. After 1992, Palestinian influence was diluted, especially as the Sino-Israeli relationship took off.

A consequence of China's establishment of relations with Israel was its prioritisation of bilateral ties over the issue of the conflict. That effective delinking of the Palestinian-Israeli conflict from Chinese considerations was captured in several ways. One was Beijing's oversight of the asymmetry between Israel and Palestinian material resources and capacity—what the scholar and activist Jeff Halper (2008) calls Israel's "matrix of control" over Palestine and Palestinians. China's unwillingness or inability to engage with the disparity between Israel and the Palestinians has effectively undermined its rhetorical support of the Palestinians.

Another consequence of China's separation of conflict from bilateral relations is captured in the relative economic importance Beijing attaches to each. Israel is far more valuable. Sino-Israeli trade is nearly 35 times larger than China's trade with the Palestinians, having risen from $863 million in 2000 to $6.8 billion in 2010 and $11.9 billion in 2020; by contrast China's trade with the West Bank and Gaza grew from $89 million in 2000 to $181 million in 2010 and $344 million in 2020 (IMF n.d.). In terms of investment, Chinese investment in Israel is 40 times larger than its investment with the Palestinians: in 1998–2018 Chinese turnover in projects in Israel totalled $4.1 billion compared to $102 million in the West Bank and Gaza (National Bureau of Statistics of China various years).

China's blindness towards the conflict's dynamics was not unique. It was a common feature by many other states across the international community, especially in the wake of the Oslo accords which Israel and the PLO signed in September 1993. Indeed, despite the disparity between China's relations with Israel and the Palestinians, it was not felt at the time. Instead, the mood at the start of the 1990s was one of optimism. China—along with other states—became a strong backer of the accords, endorsing its principles of a Palestinian state and peace.

Although the Oslo accords did not mark the end of the conflict, it offered a promise that it might do so. It set out a process that was intended to run for five years, during which time all the difficult issues—for example, borders between Israel and a Palestinian state, land swaps, the status of refugees and Jerusalem—would be resolved.

A first consequence of Oslo was the creation of the Palestinian Authority. The PA was established in the West Bank and Gaza to provide the Palestinians with a limited and qualified form of self-government. It was conceived as transitional and would be succeeded by a full Palestinian state following a final peace settlement. The PA's principal purpose was to provide municipal administration in the most populated urban areas, but its jurisdiction was limited to less than 40 percent of the West Bank, leaving Israel with direct administrative and military control over the remaining two-thirds of occupied territory; further territory would only be handed over as the negotiations proceeded (United Nations: Office for the Coordination of Humanitarian Affairs 2010). The narrow remit of the PA also meant that it had no say over the status of Palestinian refugees outside of the West Bank or Gaza or in relation to the 20 percent of Israel's population who had Palestinian or Arab origins.

The PA's creation did not challenge the status of the PLO. Because the PLO had signed the Oslo accords and agreed to the PA's formation, the PA was "subordinate and dependent on the PLO" (PASSIA 2014). The PLO's scope was also broader than the PA's, including its representation of Palestinian refugees outside of historic Palestine as well. Additionally, the distinction between the PLO and PA was rendered moot by their overlapping membership: the new PA was soon staffed by the returning PLO leadership from exile, which meant that in practice Fatah's normalisation leaders dominated both entities; indeed, Arafat added the presidency of the PA to his existing status as the president of the PLO (PASSIA 2014; Bröning 2011, 65).

The closeness of the PLO, PA and Fatah in this period was reflected in the Palestinian relationship with China. So long as the leaderships between the three overlapped, then Beijing's contacts with the Palestinians were with the same individuals.

Fatah-Hamas Rivalry and China

Although the PA, PLO and Fatah were largely united at the outset of Oslo, the emergence of another Palestinian entity threatened that unity—and for a brief moment—Palestinian connections to Beijing. In December 1987, the Islamist political party Hamas was founded, the same month that the First Intifada (uprising) began. Both it and the uprising were helped by the relative absence of both Fatah and the PLO on the ground, following years of Israeli pressure. Hamas not only offered an alternative to Fatah that was religiously based, it was also opposed to the Oslo paradigm. Consequently, throughout the 1990s it stood apart from most other Palestinian groups, carrying out terrorist attacks which undermined the peace process (Mishal and Sela 2000; Bröning 2011, 19–20). Its actions were parallel to veto players on the Israeli side, including settler groups and their representatives such as Prime Minister Benjamin Netanyahu's first administration in 1996–1999 which was also opposed to Oslo.

Despite Hamas's contrary stance on Oslo, it was very much a minority one. Most Palestinians supported the peace process and diplomacy over armed struggle (Gil et al. 2020). Notwithstanding this, anti-Oslo groups like Hamas and those on the Israeli side were able to challenge and frustrate the elites and increase disillusion among the masses. That sentiment contributed to Oslo's collapse and the start of the Second Intifada in 2000. Arafat initially claimed ownership of the uprising, but he and the PLO leadership soon lost control over the insurgency and were outgunned by Israel. By 2005 Arafat was dead, the Palestinians defeated, and their Western backers demanded political renewal via fresh elections to the PA.

Hamas had refused to take part in the previous elections in 1996. But it did so in 2006 to "protect" the resistance and halt what it saw as Fatah's corruption in and of the PA (Bröning 2011). It surprised everyone, including itself, when it won the most seats. Yet even though the election was judged to be broadly free and fair, the PA's American and European backers rejected the result. They viewed Hamas as a terrorist organisation and imposed a financial boycott on the now Hamas-led PA. Strikes by PA employees and wider societal unrest prompted Hamas and Fatah to establish a short-lived national unity government in March 2007. Despite this, the two were unable to overcome their hostility towards each other and fighting soon broke out. The occupied territory was split in two, with Fatah in control of the West Bank and Hamas in Gaza. That situation has remained in place and despite occasional attempts at dialogue and national unity.

The political split in Palestine is unpopular with Palestinians and has led to a growing disillusion with both political parties and the peace process (Palestinian Center for Policy and Survey Research 2021). However, there are few means for Palestinians to challenge the two parties, both of whom have become more authoritarian and disconnected from society in the absence of elections since 2006.

Hamas's electoral rise complicated not only the Palestinian relationship with the West, but also the Chinese. Beijing had its own reservations regarding political Islam at home, especially among its Uyghur population in Xinjiang. Despite this, it tried to separate those reservations from the Palestinian context (Castets 2003; Burton 2016). Whereas Hamas was a proscribed terrorist organisation in the US, it was not in Beijing. Chinese leaders pointed out that since Hamas had won the election and had public support it should be engaged with.

Given this promising turn of events, the new Hamas government sent one of its leaders, Mahmoud al-Zahar, to participate in the China-Arab Cooperation Forum meeting in Beijing in his role as foreign minister (Zambelis 2009; Permanent Mission of the People's Republic of China to the UN 2006; Keinon 2006). But any further efforts to build relations between Hamas and China came to a halt when Israel lodged a complaint with the Chinese ambassador (Haaretz 2006). Although no statement was issued, the message was understood. Since then, Chinese contact with the Palestinian side has reverted to what it has usually been, by focusing primarily on its ties with Fatah officials in their roles as PA or PLO officials. That has remained even as Hamas has arguably become the principal Palestinian party involved in violent confrontation with Israel during the past decade and a half.

Contemporary Palestinian Strategies and China

The political split between Fatah and Hamas and the West Bank and Gaza has led to two contrary strategies. Hamas has pursued periodic bouts of fighting with Israel in and around Gaza as a form of resistance and bleed Israeli resources and morale. Fatah has adopted a more diplomatic route, trying to re-engage Israel in negotiations alongside an internationalisation strategy to establish a Palestinian state and rights.

Besides Fatah and Hamas, there is also a third, more civil society–led strategy being pursued by the Boycott, Divestment and Sanctions movement. The BDS was formed in 2005 from nearly 200 Palestinian organisations and groups. It represents Palestinians in the occupied territories, Palestinian citizens of Israel and the wider Palestinian diaspora, including refugees. It seeks to build ties with like-minded individuals and groups in other countries to lobby their governments and put pressure on them to take action against Israel's occupation and policies of discrimination and marginalisation.

With these three groups pursuing different ways to draw international attention and revulsion towards Israel's violation of Palestinian rights, how have they fared in relation to Beijing? To what extent have they advanced Palestinian interests with the Chinese leadership?

The short answer is relatively little. To date, none of the three strategies has substantially improved Palestinian interests generally or in how they are perceived by China. They have not challenged or transformed China's preference for an Oslo-style solution. In particular, Beijing has reiterated its support for a Palestinian state, to be achieved through negotiations with Israel—and despite the realities on the ground which has made that prospect ever more distant.

China's focus on dialogue is captured in several ways. One was its establishment of a special envoy in 2002, during the Second Intifada. The first, Wang Shijie, saw his role as maintaining contacts with various parties associated with regional conflicts there, especially that between Israel and the Palestinians. He and his successors based themselves in China rather than in the region. When they did travel, they tended to meet with state-level leaders in Israel, the Palestinian leadership and those in the neighbouring Arab countries (Zheng 2002).

Gering (2021) offers a critical take on China's special envoys. He argues that they have created a "false impression" of Chinese activity. In practice, the diplomats appointed to the position have been close to retirement age and their role has been more symbolic than substantive. Indeed, China's "declarative engagement" towards the conflict is also evident in its oft-stated expression of interest in joining the Middle East Quartet (i.e., the US, Russia, the UN and the European Union) without ever doing so.

The modest and limited nature of Chinese diplomatic engagement has been especially on show during the periods of Israel-Hamas violence, in 2008–2009, 2012, 2014 and 2021. In almost all instances, China made no attempt to publicly interact with Hamas and instead focused on its pre-established ties with the PA/PLO/Fatah. On only one occasion, in 2014, did it look like Beijing might change track and explore an alternate approach. Initially, and as on previous occasions, Chinese representatives shuttled back and forth between Israeli and PLO/PA leaderships as well as regional countries. But in addition to these meetings, China's then special envoy, Wu Sike, also made a trip to Doha, where he met with the Hamas leader, Khaled Meshal. However, Wu's message was not substantially different from that which he offered to other contacts during that summer; namely that China's wish was for a ceasefire and that Beijing was willing to interact with anyone who might be able to achieve it (Ministry of Foreign Affairs of the People's Republic of China 2014).

Since the end of fighting between Hamas and Israel in 2014, Hamas has not received the same level of attention from China. For example, in 2019 China's UN representative criticised Israel for its demolition of Palestinian properties and the use of violence. Then, when Hamas launched rocket attacks from Gaza and Israel retaliated by launching a two-week air campaign in May 2021, China condemned Israel's destruction of Palestinian property and focused its contacts with the Palestinians through the PA/Fatah leadership. In both cases, Beijing took no practical action.

Fatah, too, has struggled with the "China option". After negotiations with Israel all but stalled in the late 2000s, the PA leadership embarked on an "internationalisation" project in 2011. It hoped that by pushing for membership of international state-based organisations like the UN and International Criminal Court (ICC) that it would gain a means to demand redress against Israel through international law and from fellow states.

Unfortunately for the Palestinian leadership, China was not especially receptive to the move. It cautioned against the campaign for reasons of self-interest, in particular the message it might send to encourage separation by Taiwan or the Uyghurs in Xinjiang (Burton 2018a, 167).

Despite Chinese scepticism, some of the goals of the internationalisation campaign were achieved. In 2015 Palestine joined the ICC; six years later it was given notice that it had jurisdiction to rule on war crimes in the occupied territory. Whether a prosecution will take place and its judgement enforced, however, remains uncertain. Moreover, despite more than 120 states now recognising Palestine as a fellow state, there has been little, if any, substantive improvement in the Palestinians' international position vis-à-vis Israel and through any third-party pressure on Israel to do so.

Beijing's response to the internationalisation campaign was to reiterate its commitment to dialogue as the way forward between the Palestinians and Israel. In May 2013 the new Chinese President Xi Jinping presented a Four Point Plan for peace between Israel and the Palestinians. It drew heavily on established policy, including support for the Oslo process, negotiation between the two sides and the establishment of a Palestinian state alongside security for Israel (Huang 2013). However, Xi and the Chinese did little to push the plan forward and stood aside as another, American-led effort by the then Secretary of State John Kerry to pursue shuttle diplomacy was attempted—and failed—in 2013–2014.

Then, during Palestinian President Mahmoud Abbas's visit to Beijing in July 2017, Beijing relaunched the Four Point Plan. The new edition referenced what was becoming China's centrepiece foreign policy instrument: the Belt and Road Initiative (BRI) (Times of Israel 2017), which aimed to increase connectivity across the Eurasian landmass by bringing together Chinese capital and labour with partner governments to carry out large-scale infrastructure projects like new roads, airports, ports, railways and telecommunications (Garlick 2020).

Beijing also proposed to host a seminar for Israeli and Palestinian peace activists to find a way through the impasse (Ministry of Foreign Affairs of the People's Republic of China 2017). Later that year a Palestinian delegation led by Ahmed Majdalani, a PLO executive member and adviser to Abbas, travelled to Beijing to meet with an Israeli one, led by Hilik Bar, the deputy speaker of the Knesset.

Although the Palestinian leadership had long welcomed the principle of wider international participation in the peace process in order to weaken American influence and alignment with Israeli interests (Mearsheimer and Walt 2007, 47–48), the two-day workshop achieved little. The most that was possible between the two sides was to sign a non-binding declaration which largely reiterated a commitment to the peace process and a two-state solution (Eichner 2017). The Israelis also made it clear that while they welcomed China's involvement, they did not see it as a transformation of the peace process and that China should limit its role to being complementary (Bar 2017).

Beyond the Fatah and Hamas strategies, the BDS movement has pursued a more society-oriented strategy. However, its efforts at building transnational ties with like-minded individuals and groups to encourage bottom-up pressure on governments are tailored to more liberal political environments in which there is space for groups to organise and operate. As one of its founders, Omar Barghouti, has pointed out, much of the BDS's early efforts were in North America and Europe, because it was in in these countries that Palestinian solidarity campaigners have been strongest and where governments have historically had close relationships with Israel (Burton 2018b, 140).

By contrast, exchange between the BDS movement and China has been relatively limited. That is largely due to the lack of independent civil society in China with which it can build ties and persuade the government in Beijing to adopt a different course. In addition, the BDS is hampered by Beijing's claim and principle of non-interference in the internal affairs of other countries. To engage the BDS could therefore be seen as a challenge to China's prevailing formal ties with Palestinian institutions like the PA.

Perhaps because of this, the BDS has sought to claim credit for its strategy by pointing to developments where its fingerprints are not especially visible. One notable example was Beijing's request to its citizens and Israel that its migrant workers in Israel should not work in settlements in 2015.

The BDS movement reported this as a victory for its goals, but in their statements, Chinese officials made no reference to either economic or cultural boycotts; instead, the decision was made on "safety" grounds (Burton 2018b, 133).

Notwithstanding the BDS movement's efforts to claim credit for Chinese government decisions, its organisers concede that there is much work to be done in developing the movement's activities in relation to China (and other rising powers). Barghouti has pointed to the strong economic ties and self-interest that frames Sino-Israeli relations as a potential entry point for such contact (Burton 2018b, 140).

Conclusion

The chapter began by identifying some of the limitations and challenges associated with the concept of paradiplomacy in relation to the Palestinian case and experience. It also highlighted some of the distinction associated between it and protodiplomacy, with the latter suggested as a useful means for understanding Palestinian diplomatic efforts, given its efforts to achieve statehood.

While the Palestinians have tried to cultivate relations with other international actors to struggle for and realise a Palestinian state, the same cannot always be said of the Chinese—even if it did not begin that way. Initially the relationship was both close and strongly militant. China provided arms and ammunition to the PLO in its struggle against Israel. The closeness between the two sides was helped by Fatah's desire for greater Palestinian independence from Arab nationalist leaders to China's desire to undercut the Soviet influence, which at the time was placed in those same leaders.

From the early 1970s, however, that closeness began to abate as the PLO was driven further from the homeland. Increasingly, it pursued alternative strategies, including terrorism and outreach towards the Soviet Union as the more powerful partner in the communist world.

Notwithstanding the difference between the PLO and China during the 1970s and 1980s, the two found themselves broadly aligned once again by the end of that decade and as the Cold War was coming to an end. The PLO, led by the Fatah faction, reassessed the nature of its struggle with Israel and concluded it could not defeat it militarily. Instead, it accepted the principle of a two-state solution and negotiations with Israel to achieve it. That destination involved passage through Washington, especially following the Soviet Union's collapse and America's rise to become the sole hegemonic power regionally and globally—and which was reflected in its status as mediator of the Oslo accords, which the wider international community, including China, accepted.

The Oslo accords helped to create the PA. This new entity did not complicate the Palestinian relationship with China, owing to the overlap between the PA and the Fatah leadership during the former's first decade. But when the Islamist party Hamas, which had opposed Oslo, won the 2006 PA election, this presented China with a dilemma. Beijing acknowledged Hamas's status as the leading Palestinian party and engaged its leaders, despite animosity between it and Fatah. But ultimately it was protests from Israel which resolved the problem for the Chinese, making them step back.

The Fatah-Hamas rivalry eventually split the occupied territory from mid-2007. Since then, relations between the Palestinians and China reverted to what they have largely been since Oslo, where contact was dominated by the Fatah faction of the PLO/PA leadership. Indeed, that relationship has remained even as the PLO/PA has demonstrated little to no influence on the principal axis of conflict and violence between Palestinians and Israel, namely that by Hamas in and around Gaza. Yet even as this has happened, Chinese officials have been relatively reluctant to engage the Hamas leaders most affected.

Chinese wariness of engaging with other Palestinian actors is also evident in relation to civil society and the BDS movement. Unlike Fatah and Hamas, it has not sought contact with the Chinese government directly, and instead focused its efforts at building transnational links with like-minded groups and organisations. However, in the case of China this has been extremely limited, given the limited space for civil society there and the BDS movement's focus in the West to date. The relative lack of BDS interest in China has also been reciprocated, with Beijing making little effort to build ties as well.

Overall, whether it has been Fatah's changes in strategy from insurgency to diplomacy, Hamas's use of violence or BDS persuasion, China has offered relatively little to Palestinian interests in terms of advancing Palestinian rights or a Palestinian state. Despite the close ties between Fatah and China in the 1960s, Chinese assistance was never sufficient or decisive in relation to the Palestinians' armed struggle against Israel or in the growing confrontation with their Arab hosts.

Later, when the Oslo accords were signed, China enthusiastically supported them—and has continued to do so—even as it has exposed fundamental weaknesses and power asymmetry between the Palestinians and Israel. Meanwhile, Palestinians' hope for greater Chinese (and other) participation in the peace process as a way to counter Israeli inertia and American acquiescence has had little effect, even as China has become a more powerful global state in recent decades.

Viewed over time, Beijing's commitment to the Palestinian cause has been inverse to its own growing status as a global power. It has become less practical and more rhetorical, even as China's presence in the Middle East has grown from a modest one in the mid-1960s to a wider and deeper one in recent decades. Chinese support for the Palestinian cause must also be set against its growing diplomatic and economic ties with Israel and the declining salience of the Palestinian-Israeli conflict. Indeed, the Palestinian question has arguably lost its regional prominence as the economic and political weight of the Middle East and principal conflict zones and tension points have shifted eastward, towards the Gulf. It is there that China today has several more important partnerships than those historic ones with the Palestinians, including with Saudi Arabia, the UAE (United Arab Emirates) and Iran. That shift has not only diverted Chinese attention to the rivalries between the Arab Gulf states and Tehran, but also led to Beijing's enthusiastic welcome of Israel's normalisation following the signing of the so-called Abraham Accords between Israel, the UAE and Bahrain in 2020.

In short then, despite Chinese rhetorical sympathy for the Palestinian struggle for statehood and rights, its actions indicate an increasing divergence in their common interests. Today, China is more concerned with advancing its economic interests and ensuring regional stability in the Gulf. Consequently, it has shown itself less receptive to Palestinian efforts at diplomacy (Fatah and the PA), violence (Hamas) or economic and cultural boycotts (the BDS movement), or to use its own economic weight and influence to persuade Israel to make concessions. Indeed, looking ahead, it is hard to see that this state of affairs will change: Beijing will likely continue to declare its support for Palestinian statehood and both Chinese and Palestinian leaders will refer to their long and shared history of solidarity; but in practice neither these statements nor the historical legacy will lead to a change in Chinese behaviour or advance the Palestinians' prospects towards statehood. In that respect, China is little different from that of other states with whom Palestinian entities engage. However, what makes China different is its current status as a rising power, where it might arguably make more of a difference than it currently does.

References

Alvarez, Mariano. 2020. The Rise of Paradiplomacy in International Relations. E-International Relations. Accessed 14 September 2021. http://www.e-ir.info/2020/03/17/the-rise-of-paradiplomacy-in-international-relations/.
Arab League. 1974. Seventh Arab League Summit Conference: Resolution on Palestine. Accessed 31 January 2022. https://unispal.un.org/UNISPAL.NSF/0/63D9A930E2B428DF852572C0006D06B8.
Bar, Hilik. 2017. A Useful Wind from the East. *Jerusalem Post*, 17 December. Accessed 15 January 2018. http://www.jpost.com/Opinion/A-useful-wind-from-the-East-520341.
Behbehani, Hahim. 1981. *China's Foreign Policy in the Arab World, 1955–75: Three Case Studies*. London: Kegan Paul International.
Black, Jeremy. 2012. Diplomatic history: A new appraisal. In *Routledge Handbook of Diplomacy and Statecraft*, ed. B.J.C. McKercher, 3–14. Abingdon: Routledge.
Bröning, Michael. 2011. *The Politics of Change in Palestine: State Building and Non-Violent Resistance*. London: Pluto Press.
Burton, Guy. 2016. China and the Jihadi Threat. Middle East Institute. Accessed 28 September 2021. https://www.mei.edu/publications/china-and-jihadi-threat.
———. 2018a. How do Palestinians perceive China's rise? In *China's Presence in the Middle East: The Implications of the One Belt, One Road Initiative*, ed. Anoushiravan Ehteshami and Niv Horesh, 158–173. Abingdon: Routledge.
———. 2018b. *Rising Powers and the Arab-Israeli Conflict since 1947*. Lanham: Lexington.
Castets, Rémi. 2003. The Uyghurs in Xinjiang—The Malaise Grows. *China Perspectives* 49. Accessed 28 September 2021. https://journals.openedition.org/chinaperspectives/648.
Chen Yiyi. 2012. China's Relationship with Israel, Opportunities and Challenges: Perspectives from China. *Israel Studies* 17 (3): 1–21.
Cornago, Noé. 2018. Paradiplomacy and Protodiplomacy. In *Encyclopedia of Diplomacy*, ed. Gordon Martel. Oxford: Wiley.
Dillon, Michael. 2004. The Middle East and China. In *The Middle East's Relations with Asia and Russia*, ed. Hannah Carter and Anoushiravan Ehteshami, 42–60. London: Routledge Curzon.
Eichner, Itamar. 2017. Chinese-backed peace push embraces two-state solution. *Ynet*, 24 December. Accessed 28 September 2021. https://www.ynetnews.com/articles/0,7340,L-5061027,00.html.
Garlick, Jeremy. 2020. *The Impact of China's Belt and Road Initiative: From Asia to Europe*. Abingdon: Routledge.
Gering, Tuvia. 2021. Don't Interfere, Integrate: China Proposes (Yet Another) Middle East Peace Initiative. Jerusalem Institute for Strategy

and Security. Accessed 3 December 2021. https://jiss.org.il/en/gering-china-proposes-yet-another-middle-east-peace-initiative/.

Gil, Ines, Khalil Shikaki, and Rami Kukhun. 2020. Interview with Dr Khalil Shikaki: "A Majority of Palestinians Believe That the Two-State Solution Is No Longer Feasible Because of the Israeli Settlements." Les Clés du Moyen Orient, 28 May. Accessed 3 December 2021. https://www.lesclesdumoyenorient.com/Interview-with-Dr-Khalil-Shikaki-A-majority-of-Palestinians-believe-that-the.html.

Haaretz. 2006. Israel Protests China's Invitation to Hamas' Foreign Minister. 18 May. Accessed 28 September 2021. https://www.haaretz.com/1.4906601.

Halper, Jeff. 2008. *An Israeli in Palestine: Resisting Dispossession, Redeeming Israel*. London: Pluto Press.

Harris, Lillian Craig. 1994. Myth and Reality in China's Relationship with the Middle East. In *Chinese Foreign Policy: Theory and Practice*, ed. Thomas Robindon and David Shambaugh, 322–347. Oxford: Clarendon.

Huang, Cary. 2013. Xi Proposes Four-Point Plan to Resolve Palestinian Issue. *South China Morning Post*, 6 May. Accessed 28 September 2021. https://www.scmp.com/news/china/article/1231358/xi-proposes-four-point-plan-resolve-palestinian-issue.

IMF [International Monetary Fund]. n.d. Exports and Imports by Areas and Countries. Direction of Trade Statistics. Accessed 16 and 28 September 2021. https://data.imf.org.

Israeli, Raphael. 1989. The People's Republic of China and the PLO: From Honeymoon to Conjugal Routine. In *The International Relations of the Palestine Liberation Organization*, ed. Augustus Richard Norton and Martin Greenberg, 138–165. Carbondale and Edwardsville, IL: Southern Illinois University Press.

Jönsson, Christer. 2012. Theorising diplomacy. In *Routledge Handbook of Diplomacy and Statecraft*, ed. B.J.C. McKercher, 15–28. Abingdon: Routledge.

Keinon, Herb. 2006. Chinese Deny Forming Ties with Hamas. *Jerusalem Post*, 4 April. Accessed 28 September 2021. https://www.jpost.com/middle-east/chinese-deny-forming-ties-with-hamas.

Kusnetsov, Alexander. 2015. *Theory and Practice of Paradiplomacy: Subnational Governments in International Affairs*. Abingdon: Routledge.

Mearsheimer, John, and Stephen Walt. 2007. *The Israel Lobby and U.S. Foreign Policy*. New York: Farrar, Straus & Giroux.

Ministry of Foreign Affairs of the People's Republic of China. 2014. China's Special Envoy to the Middle East Issue Wu Sike Meets with Chief of Political Bureau of Islamic Resistance Movement (Hamas) Khaled Meshal of Palestine in Doha, Qatar. Accessed 28 September 2021. https://www.fmprc.gov.cn/mfa_eng/wjbxw/t1178876.shtml.

———. 2017. Special Envoy of the Chinese Government on Middle East Issue Gong Xiaosheng Holds Briefing for Media on Situation of Palestinian-Israeli Peace Symposium. Accessed 15 January 2018. http://www.fmprc.gov.cn/mfa_eng/wjbxw/t1522095.shtml.

Mishal, Shaul, and Avraham Sela. 2000. *The Palestinian Hamas: Vision, Violence, and Coexistence*. New York: Columbia University Press.

National Bureau of Statistics of China. Various year. *China Statistical Yearbook*. Beijing: China Statistics Press. Accessed 16 and 28 September 2021. http://www.stats.gov.cn/english/Statisticaldata/AnnualData/.

Oppenheimer, Shaina. 2019. Weapons and Ideology: Files Reveal How China Armed and Trained the Palestinians. *Haaretz*, 4 August. Accessed 28 September 2021. https://www.haaretz.com/israel-news/.premium.MAGAZINE-how-china-became-the-palestinians-biggest-ally-in-the-1960s-1.7619544.

Palestinian Center for Policy and Survey Research. 2021. Press Release: Public Opinion Poll No (81). Accessed 28 September 2021. https://www.pcpsr.org/en/node/854.

Paquin, Stéphane. 2020. Paradiplomacy. In *Global Diplomacy: An Introduction to Theory and Practice*, ed. Thierry Balzacq, Frédéric Charillon and Frédéric Ramel (trans: Snow, William), 49–61. Cham: Palgrave Macmillan.

PASSIA [Palestinian Academic Society for the Study of International Affairs]. 2014. PLO vs. PA. Accessed 28 September 2021. http://passia.org/publications/116.

Permanent Mission of the People's Republic of China to the UN. 2006. Foreign Ministry Spokesperson Liu Jianchao's Press Conference on 30 May 2006. Accessed 28 September 2021. https://www.fmprc.gov.cn/ce/ceun/eng/fyrth/t255751.htm.

Reppert, John. 1989. The Soviets and the PLO: The Convenience of Politics. In *The International Relations of the Palestine Liberation Organization*, ed. Augustus Richard Norton and Martin Greenberg, 109–137. Carbondale and Edwardsville, IL: Southern Illinois University Press.

Schiavon, Jorge. 2019. *Comparative Paradiplomacy*. Abingdon: Routledge.

Shichor, Yitzhak. 1994. Hide and Seek: Sino-Israeli Relations in Perspective. *Israel Affairs* 1 (2): 188–208.

———. 1998. Israel's Military Transfers to China and Taiwan. *Survival* 40 (1): 188–208.

Times of Israel. 2017. China Pushes Four-Point Israeli-Palestinian Peace Plan. 1 August. Accessed 28 September 2021. https://www.timesofisrael.com/china-pushes-four-point-israeli-palestinian-peace-plan/.

United Nations: Office for the Coordination of Humanitarian Affairs. 2010. Area C Humanitarian Response Plan Fact Sheet. Accessed 28 September 2021. https://www.ochaopt.org/sites/default/files/ocha_opt_area_c_humanitarian_response_plan_fact_sheet_2010_09_03_english.pdf.

Zambelis, Chris. 2009. China's Palestine Policy. Jamestown Foundation. Accessed 28 September 2021. https://jamestown.org/program/chinas-palestine-policy/.

Zheng, Guihong. 2002. China's First Special Envoy to the Middle East. *China. org.cn*, 8 November. Accessed 28 September 2021. http://www.china.org.cn/english/NM-e/48288.htm.

CHAPTER 12

Kurdistan-Iraq and Turkey

Arzu Yilmaz

INTRODUCTION

Turkey has relatively been the most difficult task on the KRG's foreign policy agenda. On the one hand, Turkey's obstinate anti-Kurdish stance for nearly a century, including denial of Kurdish identity at home and denial of any political status to Kurds abroad; on the other hand, Turkey's decisive role in both the survival of people, particularly in the 1990s, and the maintenance of economic and political interests after the 2000s, have put the KRG in a pickle. Nonetheless, relations between the KRG and Turkey have developed in a back-and-forth fashion and reached the level of "strategic partnership" at one point (Yeni Şafak 2012 [translated by the author]).

How did the KRG establish and develop relations with Turkey? What were the foreign policy objectives and motivations that shaped the relations between the KRG and Turkey? And what have the results been thus far?

The majority of analyses of the KRG-Turkey relationship have emphasized Turkey's security, economic, and political interests as the primary drivers of this relationship (Barkey 2009; Barkey 2010; Demir 2019; Park

A. Yilmaz (✉)
University of Kurdistan Hewlêr, Erbil, Kurdistan Region, Iraq
e-mail: arzu.yilmaz@ukh.edu.krd

© The Author(s), under exclusive license to Springer Nature Switzerland AG 2023
G. Gürbey et al. (eds.), *Between Diplomacy and Non-Diplomacy*,
https://doi.org/10.1007/978-3-031-09756-0_12

2014; Phillips 2007; Ustun and Dudden 2017). Turkey's interests in the Kurdistan Region of Iraq (KRI) from the 1990s to the late 2000s were primarily security-driven, since a developing Kurdish entity in Iraq would serve as a model for the country's own Kurds (Gunter 1997, 90). Thus, Turkey's objective for nearly two decades was to thwart the establishment of a Kurdish Autonomy in Iraq. Turkey posed a threat in this regard not just through diplomacy but also by military operations in the KRI, presumably, against the Kurdistan Workers' Party (PKK).

The first semi-official connections between Turkey and the two prominent Iraqi Kurdish parties, the Kurdistan Democratic Party (KDP) and the Patriotic Union of Kurdistan (PUK), arose during this era, largely in the context of Turkey's war against the PKK, which has been based in Iraq since 1984. Both the KDP and the PUK had no choice but to side by Turkey against the PKK. To begin, Turkey was on the ground of the KRI as a North Atlantic Treaty Organization (NATO) member and a United States (US) ally, the savior of the Kurds in the 1990s. On the other hand, the Ibrahim Khalil Gate, the border crossing with Turkey, served as a "lifeline" for Kurds enduring the impacts of embargo on Iraq (Gunter 1997, 79). Given Turkey's occasional military collaboration with the KDP, in particular, some studies also emphasized the importance of revenue from trade through Ibrahim Khalil Gate, as well as the military and political advantages acquired by the KDP over the PUK and the PKK (Černy 2018; McKiernan 2006; Romano 2008; Stansfield 2003).

Turkey, however, launched a new phase in the KRG-Turkey relationship in 2010 with the opening of the Turkish Consulate General in Erbil. From denial of the Kurds to recognition of a Kurdish entity called Kurdistan, a phrase that had been prohibited for decades, was undoubtedly a sea change for Turkey, while bilateral relations grew stronger in economic and political aspects. Similarly, studies focused mostly on Turkey's concerns rather than the KRG's. Turkey's "zero problems foreign policy" (Davutoglu 2010) was seen as the primary impetus for such a radical shift (Natali 2012). Besides, some scholars also argued that in order to become a "trading state" (Kirişçi 2009) or an "energy hub" (Erşen and Çelikpala 2019) and between the West and East, and/or to become the "successor state of the Ottoman Empire" (Öktem 2011) in the Middle East, Turkey recalibrated its stance toward the KRG. According to some experts, the shift in KRG-Turkey ties was also a result of the Justice and Development Party's (AKP) liberal approach to the Kurdish Question at home in accordance with the democratic progress on the path to European Union (EU) membership (Aydın-Düzgit et al. 2015)

In turn, the KRG's position was mostly regarded as part of a "win-win game" centered on shared economic interests and, to a lesser extent, shared political orientations in support of Western values (Barkey 2009; Barkey 2010; Park 2014; Phillips 2007). Meanwhile, the KRG's involvement as a mediator in the peace process between Turkey and the PKK's leadership cadres, including Abdullah Öcalan, lent new weight to the KRG's relations with Turkey. Finally, in 2013, Turkey and the Kurds as a whole posed as "strategic partners" on the eve of a new political setting in the Middle East (Mustafa and Aziz 2017).

As of today, the KRG-Turkey relations have encountered another wave of tensions, despite the fact that neither economic nor diplomatic contacts have broken down. Indeed, the deterioration of relations extends all the way back to 2014, when Turkey ignored the KRG's plea for assistance against the Islamic State of Iraq and Levant (ISIS) attacks (Ergan 2014). However, the Kurdistan Independence referendum held in 2017 marked a watershed moment. Turkey's vigorous opposition to the referendum was once again attributed to domestic security concerns regarding the Kurdish Question at home and the possibility of Kurdish autonomy in Syria (Park 2019). Following the failure of the peace process and the establishment of the Autonomous Administration of North East Syria (AANES) in 2016 with US backing, the KRI's independence referendum was the final straw that prompted Turkey's threat perceptions of a "Kurdish corridor" adjacent to its southern border with access to the Mediterranean (Günes and Lowe 2015). Since then, Turkey's devastating military operations have targeted not only the PKK in the KRI and its offshoot the Democratic Union Party (PYD) and the People's Defense Units (YPG) in Syria, but also all Kurdish political achievements, including the KRG (ANF News 2020).

Without a doubt, this literature has enriched our understanding of the KRG-Turkey relationship. Given the "asymmetric" nature of the relationship with regard to Turkey's military, political, and economic strength as a state vis-à-vis the KRG (Mustafa and Aziz 2017). However, it has largely attributed a dominant role to Turkey and failed to pay due attention to the KRG's foreign policy goals and motivations. To a significant extent, the KRG has been viewed as a passive participant in this relationship, mostly responding to Turkey's concerns and interests.

With a specific emphasis on this gap, I will argue in this chapter that, while the Kurds' survival in the 1990s and economic interests in the 2000s were main drivers of KRG-Turkey relations, what ultimately shaped the KRG's foreign policy were its political interests. To begin, the KRG, like other sub-states such as Quebec, Catalonia, Galicia, the Basque Country, and Wales (Keating 2000), has sought recognition as a nation rather than merely an entity. Given this, the KRG's objective has been first to appease Turkey's threat perceptions based on the specter of separatism; then, to ensure its degree of political recognition and status as a Kurdish entity in Iraq; and finally to carve out a larger political space for the KRG as a leading Kurdish authority in the Middle East.

Overall, the KRG's willingness, even enthusiasm, for collaborations with any conceivable partner has been the primary driver of the KRG's burgeoning diplomatic interactions. Nonetheless, until the early 1990s, the Kurds' restricted interactions with foreign parties were either "covert" or through third parties (Bengio 2012, 245). Moreover, after a century of Kurdish national struggle in the Middle East, the KRG's foundation in Iraq gave the Kurds with their first opportunity to speak on their own behalf on the world arena. In this context, cultivating diplomatic ties has also served to dispel misconceptions about Kurdish political activity as a source of conflict and instability, and to portray the KRG, in particular, as a source of regional peace and stability. And to this end, despite the hurdles, relations with Turkey have brought significant opportunities.

In the following sections, I will first discuss the parameters of KRG-Turkey relations with a particular focus on its impact on intra-Kurdish conflict in the 1990s. Then, I will trace the KRG's nation-building efforts after the US invasion of Iraq in 2003, which solidified its image as an international personality working for Kurdish common interests, as well as the ramifications for the KRG's relations with Turkey. Finally, I will explore how the KRG-Turkey relations developed within the context of the Kurdistan Independence referendum.

My arguments will primarily be based on literature, news, and media pronouncements. Given the difficulties of the inherent combination of formal and informal aspects in the KRG-Turkey relations, I have also conducted interviews with a number of diplomats, bureaucrats, politicians, and representatives of non-governmental organizations (NGOs) who have firsthand testimony of the KRG-Turkey relationship.

Appeasement Policy at the Expense of Intra-Kurdish Conflict

The deplorable conditions of life in the KRI in the 1990s resulted not just from United Nations (UN) Resolution 688's embargo on Iraq in 1991, but also from Baghdad's embargo on the KRI. As soon as the Iraqi soldiers retreated, Saddam Hussein, Iraq's president, suspended all public sector salaries in the KRI and prohibited any trade between the KRI and the rest of the country. Even traveling abroad was almost impossible while foreigners, especially relief workers, were unable to get to the KRI via Iraq due to a 10,000 United States dollar (USD) bounty on any foreigner's head (Gunter 1997).

As a result, Turkey was the only viable choice for the KRI's survival and connectivity with the rest of the world. Foreign humanitarian aid could only be transported through the Ibrahim Khalil gate on the Turkish border. More importantly, the Combined Task Force-Poised Hammer, constituted as part of Provide Comfort Operation II to deter Iraqi aggression against the Kurds, was based at İncirlik Airbase in Turkey on a six-month rotational basis with authorization from the Turkish National Assembly. Though authorizations were provided on a regular basis until the end of 1996, Turkey frequently blocked Ibrahim Khalil gate, even for humanitarian relief, because of growing domestic resistance to the deployment of troops at İncirlik Airbase and Silopi, a Turkish village adjacent to the Iraqi border. Given Turkey's preoccupation with the PKK's growing revolt for "Free and Independent Kurdistan" the overwhelming majority of Turks believed that the Combined Task Force-Poised Hammer and the US' ultimate purpose was to establish a Kurdish state (Oran 1998).

Thus, Turkey made no distinction between the PKK and the KDP or the PUK in light of such threat perceptions. Turkey's relationship with the KRG was, then, a necessity due to the wider national interests at stake in its collaboration with the US, the burgeoning superpower of the 1990s. On the other hand, Turkey believed that "the autonomous status of the [KRG] was temporary one that would eventually be replaced by Iraqi rule" (Bakir, January 2022). In either case, Turkey concentrated on increasing its military presence in the KRI in order to conduct cross-border operations against the PKK and to stymie the newly forming Kurdish entity.

Turgut Özal, Turkey's former President, was relatively an exception in this regard. According to one of the politicians Özal said that "[the US] comes from the other side of the ocean to save the Kurds; why don't we do the same but allow [the Kurds] to be used [by US]?" (Gürcanlı 2019 [translated by the author]). Having said that, Özal made an endeavor to establish cordial connections with the leaders of the KDP and PUK. He even convinced the PKK to proclaim a truce in 1993 with the assistance of PUK leader Jalal Talabani (Çandar 2012). All of those efforts, however, were futile when Özal died the next year. Since then, rather than the politicians, the Turkish military was in charge of Turkey's Kurdish policy, including the KRI.

Meanwhile, the KRG's primary priority was to maintain a stable relation with Turkey at the Ibrahim Khalil gate. As Turkey held the KRG responsible for any PKK activity, the Ibrahim Khalil gate was frequently shut down when the PKK attacked Turkish targets. Turkey's policy was, at best, a kind of intimidation, if not outright exploitation. In such circumstances, the KRG "wanted to demonstrate to Turkey that it is a friendly neighbor and it is not responsible from the actions of the PKK" (Bakir, January 2022). Hence, both the KDP and the PUK fought against the PKK in Turkey's ranks first in September 1992, and again 1996–1997.

The policy of appeasement, soon, triggered a KRI-wide intra-Kurdish armed conflict throughout the 1990s (Kurda 2015). The core causes of this conflict were largely regarded as a power struggle among mainly the KDP, the PUK, and the PKK, sparked by ideological disagreements and by a dispute over the allocation of border revenue. Given the agreements reached in 1983 between the KDP and the PKK and in 1988 between the PUK and the PKK, however, it was debatable whether each party's ideological orientations were the true source of the conflict. Yet, both agreements appeared to share a common goal of "unity of Kurds" against "all forms of imperialism." Even Turkey and Iraq were designated in the fourth clause of the 1983 agreement as "fascist regimes" against which the KDP and PKK would fight (Yıılmaz personal archive 1983; see also Imset 1988).

Though both agreements quickly became null and void soon, for instance, the KDP and the PKK continued to coexist in the border areas of Iran, Iraq, and Turkey triangle (Kurda 2015). And there were no clashes between them prior to Turkey's intervention in the KRI's political equilibrium. Following the initial KDP/PUK/Turkey joint operation against the PKK in 1992, however, the schism among Kurdish parties widened over time by allegations and aggressions.

Notwithstanding, Iran's role in escalating violence in the KRI was also critical. Until 1996, Iran supported each of those Kurdish parties occasionally in their conflict with one another. Similarly to Turkey, Iran's interest in the KRI was primarily driven by its security concerns over Iranian Kurdish organizations that were stationed in KRI camps since the Iranian Islamic Revolution. Iranian backing for the KDP and then the PUK was therefore conditional on regaining control over the Kurdistan Democratic Party-Iran (KDP-I) and Komala Party of Iranian Kurdistan (Komala) (Gunter 1997, 95–98). At the same time, Iran was also concerned by the US military presence near its borders, in alliance with its regional foe Turkey, and therefore destabilizing the KRI was in Iran's interest.

When the US implemented a dual containment policy against Iran and Iraq in mid-1990, however, the KRI's political balance was mostly restored. On the one hand, the KDP and Turkey, on the other, the PKK/PUK and Iran became closer. Meanwhile, Turkey's privileged status within the context of dual containment policy paved the way for establishment of the first Turkish military bases in the KRI towns such as Kani Masi, Begova, and Bamarni controlled by the KDP (Bengio 2012). Turkey was, then, not only a potential threat at the borderlines, but an adversary military force on the soil of KRI. Hence forth, the KDP's relation with Turkey evolved, including intelligence sharing and coordinated actions against not only the PKK but the civilians and refugees sympathetic with the PKK, such as those who fled Turkey in 1994 and settled in the Atrush Camp (Yılmaz 2016).

During this era, the KDP established an office in Turkey's capital city, Ankara, and cross-border trade expanded by illegal oil transit via trucks. However, relations between the KRG and Turkey did not reach to a political cooperation throughout the 1990s. On the contrary, for instance, Turkey established the Iraqi Turkmen Front as a political group in 1995 in Kirkuk with the purpose of inciting ethnic conflict in the KRI (Bengio 2012, 252).

In fact, there were no formal relations between the KRG and Turkey at all. Because the Kurdistan Parliament established following the May 1992 elections had never functioned properly. Additionally, the leaders of the KDP and the PUK that dominated the Kurdistan Parliament based on a 50/50 sharing policy chose to abstain from participating in the administration. Such a decision was made out of worry that the government would sabotage their international diplomatic relations (Kurda 2015). Thus, relations with Turkey were conducted on a daily basis through individual interactions with a focus on party interests whereas the KRI had already been divided into two administrations: one under the control of the KDP in Erbil and another under the control of the PUK in Sulaimaniyah. However, the fundamental premise that guided both leaders' actions and discourses regarding Turkey was ultimately "Turkey's geopolitical influence in the greater Middle East and its strong partnership with the US" (Bakir, January 2022). Whatever the case, Turkey could not help, in the end, to become a "reluctant builder of Iraqi Kurdistan" (Bengio 2012, 252).

NATION-BUILDING AT HOME AND ABROAD

By the new century, the KRI's fate shifted radically in response to the aftermath of the 9/11 attacks in the US. In this regard, the US invasion of Iraq in 2003 marked a watershed moment in the KRG's history. The KRG became a recognized federal body with significant economic and political rights, including foreign policy, once the newly written Iraqi Constitution was ratified in 2005. Additionally, Article 110 of the Iraqi Constitution stipulated that the KRG had authority over international treaties and debt policies independent of Baghdad, where prominent Kurdish politicians stepped in Baghdad to occupy critical governmental positions such as the Presidency and Foreign Ministry of the state of Iraq (Constitute Project 2005).

Kurdish awakening in the 1990s took the shape of nation-building under the auspices of the KRG in such conditions. The Kurdish Parliament chose Masoud Barzani, the leader of the KDP, as President of the KRG in its inaugural session in 2005, with the participation and cooperation of all Iraqi Kurdish parties. Kurdistan's flag replaced the Iraq's national flag in government facilities and international meetings attended by KRG representatives.

While the KRI was transforming into a solely Kurdish sphere in all aspects of life, Kurds from abroad were also engaging with the KRG through different ways and measures. Kurdish students applying to study at universities in the KRI received a monthly stipend funded by the KRG (Yılmaz 2016). Kurdish businessmen were privileged in construction bids. On the other hand, the KRI's burgeoning construction sector created employment prospects for Kurdish workers who faced political prejudice and economic disadvantage in surrounding countries (Kaya, January 2022).

The recruitment of non-Iraqi Kurds to the ranks of the KRG's armed force, the Peshmerga, was one of the most significant developments. For instance, several ex-PKK guerrillas joined the Peshmerga and became leaders of several special units. Similarly, some Kurdish refugees who escaped Turkey and Iran and stayed in completely isolated camps for decades in the KRI joined the Peshmerga or occupied positions in government institutions. By the way, pensions were provided to certain elderly Kurdish exiles who fought alongside the Peshmerga in the 1960s and 1970s. Until the late 2000s, the KRG's Interior Ministry even issued citizenship to Kurds from other countries, though it was only valid on the KRI territory (Yılmaz 2016).

Such a Kurdish unification in the KRI under the authority of the KRG was, in fact, based on a Kurdish political consensus reached by the KDP, the PUK, and the PKK in the late 1990s and early 2000s. First, the KDP and PUK signed a power-sharing agreement in 1998 in Washington, DC, under the auspices of the US. Then, following the capture of its leader Abdullah Öcalan, the PKK proclaimed a truce in 1999 and later joined the KDP-PUK consensus in 2002 as a Kurdish actor in the KRI territory. The crux of that consensus was to end the Kurdish-Kurdish armed conflict unconditionally and to refrain from interfering militarily or politically in the territories controlled by each side (Yılmaz 2016). On this premise, the newly formed KRG was acknowledged by all Kurds as a de-facto Kurdish state, though de jure it was a federal entity inside Iraq.

Two significant changes in this context fundamentally altered the nature of the KRG-Turkey relations. First, the KRG was no longer reliant on Turkey as the economic and military blockade of the KRI was over. Second, the strong ties between Turkey and the US deteriorated as the Turkish National Assembly refused to allow US soldiers to be stationed in Turkey prior to the Iraqi invasion in 2003. Since then, Turkey was almost isolated from the Iraqi theatre. More importantly, the US provided Peshmerga to fill the void left by Turkish military troops which provided the KRG to expand its control beyond the 36th parallel, including the oil-rich city of Kirkuk.

However, Kurdish dominance of Kirkuk, soon, triggered long-simmering Turkish nationalist stance against the KRG. The semi-official relations built in the 1990s were extinguished while the leaders of both the KDP and the PUK were demonized in Turkey (Milliyet 2008). Indeed, national sentiments on the KRG side were not dissimilar. During the negotiations with the US leading up to the 2003 intervention in Iraq, "Kurdish leadership [Masoud Barzani] did not want to risk the security of the KRI by allowing Turkish troops into its territory" (Bakir, January

2022). It is, for sure, debatable whether Barzani's opposition could change the US military plans for deployment of Turkish troops from the north of Iraq. Turkey, in the end, dropped itself from the military equation in Iraq. However, Barzani's stance toward Turkey was a clear indicator of an upcoming new chapter in the KRG-Turkey relations quite different from the 1990s.

Tensions between the KRG and Turkey reached a zenith on February 21, 2008, when Turkey began Operation Sun against the PKK bases in the KRI. Turkey's aim was ostensibly the PKK, which resumed war against Turkey in 2004. However, based on the discussions surrounding the Operation, Turkey's goal was not only the PKK, but also the KRG. Turkey was vehemently opposed to the KRG's rule of Kirkuk, claiming that "Kirkuk [was] a Turkish city" (Halıcı 2007 [translated by the author]. In response, Masoud Barzani declared, "If Turkey meddle[d] in the Kirkuk issue, [the KRG would] meddle in the Diyarbakır and other Kurdish cities in Turkey" (Sol Haber 2007 [translated by the author]). Such a statement was, on one hand, demonstrating the confidence that the KRG gained vis-à-vis Turkey and the breadth of its nation-building activities on the other. When Operation Sun began, thus, Turkey could not find the KRG on its side against the PKK. On the contrary, the KRG provided logistical and political support to the PKK (Yılmaz 2016).

In the meantime, a growing bottom-up demand derived mainly from Kurdish businessmen for closer economic ties between the KRG and Turkey fostered another type of cooperation among Kurds:

> Economic life in Diyarbakır came close to a halt in the mid-2000s. But on the KRI side there was a vibrant market, and [Kurdish businessmen in the KRI] were so eager to make trade with Turkey. However, even traveling between the two sides was almost impossible. [Kurdish businessmen in Turkey] were apprehensive about traveling to the KRI due to the political climate in Turkey. On the other hand, [people from the KRI] were not permitted to travel to Turkey. To tackle with such restrictions, [Diyarbakır Chamber of Commerce and Industry (DCCI)] applied to TOBB [Turkish Union of Chambers and Commodity Exchanges] twice in 2006 and 2007 for authorization to open a representative office in Erbil, but TOBB rejected. Finally, [DCCI] decided to establish a Bilateral Cooperation Development Center within the DCCI in 2007 to institutionalize the relations between the chambers in Diyarbakır, Erbil, Suleimania, and Duhok. (Kaya, January 2022)

Promptly after the establishment of the Bilateral Cooperation Development Center, the DCCI hosted over a hundred businessmen, mayors, and bureaucrats from the KRI at the Diyarbakır Trade Fair in 2007. The most noticeable development in that fair was that all Kurdish participants delivered their speeches on stage in Kurdish. Even the opening ceremony included a performance of the Kurdish national anthem. Such efforts resulted in signing protocols in 2008 between the chambers of commerce of Diyarbakır and Erbil, Sulaimaniyah, Duhok. Soon, trade with the KRI became the primary source of income for cities such as Diyarbakır, Mardin, and Şırnak. Encouraged with these interactions, businessmen from western Turkey also started to make trade with the KRI and, finally, Turkey became the KRI's largest importer at the beginning of 2010s.

However, what set the path for economic progress was, in fact, Operation Sun's failure. Yet, the military loss in the KRI first sparked ongoing political debates in Turkey over the military tutelage regime. Soon afterward, some Turkish generals (Rodrik 2011) were detained as part of the Balyoz and Ergenekon operations. Then the ruling party AKP, whose authority was curtailed and even threatened by General Staff of Turkish Armed Forces with a so-called e-memorandum in 2007, gained the ability to pursue its own political agenda in internal and foreign affairs (Koçak 2016). In both cases, the most remarkable step omitted was the "Kurdish Opening" (Deutsche Welle 2013).

"Ice-break" in the KRG-Turkey Relations

The informal meeting between the KRG and Turkish interlocutors at the Iraqi Presidency Residence in Baghdad on May 1, 2008, served as an "ice-break" in the KRG-Turkey relations. Talabani, Iraq's then-President, hosted the gathering. However, Nechirvan Barzani, the KRG's then–Prime Minister, attended the meeting on behalf of the Kurdish side. Murat Özçelik, Turkey's Special Envoy for Iraq, was leading the Turkish team at the meeting. Barzani told Özçelik that "[the KRG and Turkey] disagree on a number of issues. However, let's put those disagreements aside and concentrate on mutual interests" (Selcen, January 2022).

Given the booming economic relations between the KRG and Turkey after 2008, Barzani's emphasis on mutual interests was largely interpreted as economic interests. However, a closer examination of both parts' motivations, with the help interviews conducted for this chapter with Falah

Mustafa Bakir from the KRG and Aydin Selcen from Turkey, reveals that geopolitical considerations, rather than economic interests, made more sense.

The KRG was principally concerned with the volatility of Iraq's political equilibrium. On the one hand, rising sectarian conflict in Iraq and, on the other, Iran's support for Iraqi Prime Minister Nouri al-Maliki's anti-Kurdish stance were threatening Kurdish achievements. In addition, by the late 2000s, the KRG was disappointed in the sense that "Washington promised [the KRG] a lion's share of the changes that would take place in the new Iraq, but Washington and Baghdad neglected following through with this promise" (Bakir, January 2022). Therefore, reduced tensions, if possible, cordial relations with Turkey, would enhance the KRG's leverage vis-à-vis Bagdad and balance Iranian pressure on Erbil. At the same time, Turkey's accelerated EU accession process and its new foreign policy orientation in the Middle East as a soft power were providing an opportunity for the KRG to align with the West.

From Turkish perspective, it was obvious that the projections about the KRG's future that informed Turkey's policy in the 1990s were erroneous; in other words, the Kurdish rule in northern Iraq was not temporary but permanent. Furthermore, even though Turkey desired to reintroduce itself to the Iraqi theatre first by establishing relations with Bagdad, its interlocutors were necessarily Kurds serving as Iraq's President and/or Foreign Minister (Selcen, January 2022). Meanwhile, Turkish attempts to intervene the political equilibrium in Baghdad were futile, owing largely to Iran's already consolidated influence in Iraq. Therefore, for Turkey "Erbil [was] gateway to Basra" whereas for the KRG "Turkey was gateway to the West" (Turkish News 2009 [translated by the author]).

Overall, in fact, the US was the kingmaker of closer relations between the KRG and Turkey in the late 2000s. On the eve of the US troop withdrawal from Iraq, the US was about to reposition itself as an "off-shore balancer" in Iraqi affairs (Mearsheimer and Walt 2016). Enhanced by the Obama Administration's "leading from behind doctrine" (Krauthammer 2011), then, a rapprochement between the KRG and Turkey became critical in order to maintain stability in Iraq and balance Iran. To this end, the US even pressed the KRG for a reconciliation with Turkey as lately revealed on Wikileaks documents. Such a rapprochement would benefit both the KRG and Turkey, including their shared goal of "pacifying the PKK" (Barkey 2010). Reports entitled as "Disarming, Demobilizing, and Reintegrating the Kurdistan Workers Party" (Phillips 2007) referred to the KRG as an unavoidable component of resolving Turkey's Kurdish Question, while the PKK and Turkey were already at the negotiation table in Oslo, Norway, in 2008 (Çandar 2020).

Ultimately, the KRG and Turkey established a new chapter in their relations which soon paved the way for Turkey to exert more influence over all spheres of life in the KRG. Turkish construction companies reconstructed the cities and motorways, as well as Erbil Airport in the KRI. The streets were lined with Turkish-named shops selling Turkish-brand goods. Accordingly, a large number of young Kurds were learning Turkish through the most popular Turkish television series while the establishment of Turkish schools in the KRI, such as Işık and Bilkent, was the primary choice of parents. In addition, universities in the KRI began signing protocols of collaboration with Turkish universities one by one. Apart from student and faculty exchanges and sports activities, the most significant collaborative projects were language studies. Mardin Artuklu University and the University of Duhok together hosted a series of seminars to promote scholarly research on Kurdish language unification (Khalid, January 2022). Meanwhile, the first "Kurdish Conference" was held in Erbil in 2009 under the auspices of Turkey, bringing together academics, journalists, and intellectuals from Turkey and Kurdistan (Türköne 2009 [translated by the author]). The KRG, on the other hand, supported and hosted Kurdish transnational organizations such as the Kurdish Women Conference, the Kurdish Film Festival, and the Kurdish Doctors Conference which aimed to provide a common platform for different Kurdish groups to discuss their own issues, build their own networks, and establish their own mechanisms for intra-Kurdish dialogue (Khalid, January 2022).

Given this, seemingly, Turkification and Kurdification were developing concurrently in the KRI. While all the Kurds in the world were uniting in a transnational manner under the auspice of the KRG, the Kurds in the KRI were also integrating with Turkey in both cultural and social terms. By the early 2010s, the KRG and Turkey relationship had almost reached a degree of trans-border connectivity. Thus, the establishment of the Turkish Consulate-General in Erbil in 2010 was, in fact, a step taken to advance the ongoing ties rather than initiate first formal relations. According to Aydın Selcen, the first Turkish Consul-General in Erbil, indeed, Turkey didn't have a clear strategy for the KRG. Turkey's Foreign Ministry, for instance, didn't provide him with a road map in Erbil. Selcen, himself, decided to take actions such as inviting Masoud Barzani to a reception at the Turkish Consulate to commemorate the Turkish Republic's anniversary or planning a visit to Ankara for Masoud Barzani during his first three months in office. What guided to Selcen in those days were the statements made by Turkey's then–Prime Minister, Recep Tayyip Erdoğan, and a pro-AKP daily, *Yeni Şafak* (Selcen, January 2022).

Whatever the case, the significance of the KRG's role in Turkey's war against the PKK remained unchanged from a Turkish perspective. In contrast to the past, however, Turkey's expectation from the KRG was now not to combat the PKK, but to act as a mediator between the PKK and Turkey. Regardless of Turkey's expectation, in fact, such a role matched quite well with the KRG's post-2000 nationalist posture. Contributing to a peaceful resolution of Turkey's Kurdish Question would surely help the KRG in consolidating its status as the sole legitimate Kurdish authority. Additionally, by assuming this position, the KRG would also be able to carve out a larger political space for itself in the Middle East at a time when the region's status quo was about to change.

Kurdish-Turkish Strategic Partnership in the Middle East

Turkey's call for a new political order in the Middle East in the aftermath of the Arab Spring boosted the KRG-Turkey relationship. Turkey and the Kurds would work "under the banner of Islam" (Türkmen 2021) as their forefathers did in the sixteenth century, in a rapidly changing regional equilibrium. Such an aim was first raised publicly by PKK leader Abdullah Öcalan in 2013 within the context of a new round of peace discussions between the PKK and Turkey, called the "İmralı Process." However, it was the then-KRG President, Masoud Barzani, who first signaled an alliance of sorts by standing alongside the leaders of Turkey, Egypt, and Hamas during the 2012 AKP Congress, wherein he urged "[a]ll Kurds to support Erdoğan" (Gürcanlı 2012 [translated by the author]).

From a Turkish perspective, Erbil was no longer a gateway only to Baghdad, but to the Middle East as a whole. Turkey, repositioning itself as the Ottoman Empire's successor, sought to establish a Sunni axis in the region and the Kurds, who were predominantly Sunni and live on the Turkey-Middle East border, should essentially join with Turkey and make "Turkey bigger" (Can 2013 [translated by the author]).

From the KRG's perspective, first, Turkey's then–Prime Minister's announcement that the policy of Kurdish denial was over "was a momentous occasion and [the KRG] took it as a significant step toward healing Kurdish-Turkish relations." At the same time, "The US, the EU, and the international community [supported] Turkey as a democratic model in the Middle East" (Bakir, January 2022). It was uncertain if the region's status quo, including political borders, would endure, but Turkey's leadership role in the region was an apparent fact. In such conditions, as Nechirvan Barzani once stated, "For the independence of Kurdistan, support of an international power and, at least, one of the two neighboring countries was essential" (Selcen 2017 [translated by the author]), Following the KRG's rapprochement with Turkey, then, Turkey appeared to imply such a support when AKP's Deputy Chair, Hüseyin Çelik, remarked that "Kurds have the right to choose their own future" (Cumhuriyet 2014 [translated by the author]).

In this context, AANES served as a litmus test for both the KRG-Turkey alliance and Kurdish-Turkish collaboration in the Middle East. Indeed, Turkey has constantly refused any form of Kurdish autonomy in Syria. However, given the ongoing İmralı process and the international community's reluctance to launch a combined military campaign against the Assad regime, Turkey first pursued a variety of coercive measures. Allowing Jihadi forces that frequently attacked the PYD/YPG to enter Syria over the Turkish border was one of the measures in Turkey's toolkit. The other was to erode the power of the PYD/YPG by supporting the Kurdish National Council (ENKS), the umbrella organization of Syrian Kurdish parties which were struggling with the PYD/YPG's dominance in Syrian Kurdistan. At the same time, Turkey obstinately refused to allow the PYD/YPG to participate in the Geneva Talks but supported the ENKS's participation in both the Geneva Talks and the Syrian opposition meetings held in Turkey (Özkızılcık 2019).

In such circumstances, the KRG aimed "to deescalate the tensions and to help [AANES] to understand that Turkey [was] an important neighbor that [had] the support of the international community" (Hussain 2022). Despite its mediator role, in fact, he KRG was apparently in support of the ENKS, including its armed wing, Peshmerga Roj. The major problem was, however, the counterparts' stance vis-à-vis the Assad regime. The ENKS was aligned with Turkey to demolish the Assad regime, whereas the PYD/YPG was occasionally amenable to cooperation with the Assad regime due to its "third way" strategy (Yılmaz 2015).

Even though such tensions deepened and the relations between the PYD/YPG and ENKS and/or Turkey deteriorated in time, the KRG succeeded in gaining a strong foothold in Syrian Kurdistan by playing its role as a mediator. More importantly, the KRG soon consolidated its political influence even in Turkish Kurdistan. Masoud Barzani's appearance on the stage in Diyarbakir, the Kurdish city where Barzani vowed to intervene, was a watershed moment signifying the zenith of that power in 2013.

In accordance with such developments, oil exports from the KRG to Turkey increased to over 500,000 barrels per day in 2014, through a new pipeline connecting Kurdish oil reserves to the existing Kirkuk-Ceyhan pipeline (Park 2019). By this move, in particular, Turkey became an impetus on the way to independence of Kurdistan, since an economically free Erbil from Baghdad would seek independence sooner or later. Baghdad's decision to cut the KRG's budget in 2013 as a response to energy deals with Turkey ended up further alienating Erbil from Baghdad. Apart from the potential implications in terms of independence, what determined the KRG's energy policy was, in fact, its security concerns arising from the threats associated with the US ongoing withdrawal from Iraq and the increasing Iranian pressure. According to Masoud Barzani, "Energy agreements with international oil companies would enable the KRG to maintain security better than having a thousand tanks on the ground" (Yılmaz personal archive 2011). Thus, a strategic partnership with Turkey would guarantee the security of the KRG. To strengthen this collaboration, the KRG even "preferred to reach out to businessmen close to Turkey's leadership," rather than favoring Kurdish businessmen in the KRI's trade and construction sectors, as it had previously done (Kaya, January 2022).

Emergence of ISIS and Shifting Geopolitical Considerations

Turkey-KRG ties took a dramatic shift following the emergence of ISIS. In August 2014, ISIS launched an attack on Shingal, a KRG-controlled area on the Iraq-Syria border. When ISIS made a headed to Erbil, the KRG immediately called emergency assistance from Turkey. However, Turkey did not react to this call. Disappointed with Turkey's refusal, the KRG Chief of Staff said that "Turkey failed to keep its promise to protect the KRG in the event of any attack" (Ahmed 2014). However, deterioration in relations between the KRG and Turkey became apparent in September

2014, when ISIS stormed Kobane in Syria. Turkish President Recep Tayyip Erdogan's comment that "Kobane [was] about to fall to ISIS" (Deutsche Welle 2014) resonated as a green signal to ISIS, while Kurds in Iraq and Syria faced an existential threat.

In the end, neither Erbil nor Kobane fell under ISIS control as the US provided military assistance to the Kurds. Additionally, despite Turkey's concerns, the US also facilitated the passage of KRG military forces via Turkey to support YPG forces in Kobane and convened discussions in October 2014 to address the power imbalance between Kurdish political groups in Syria and Iraq by brokering the Duhok Agreement (Gümüştekin 2021). The Kurds and Turkey were obviously at odds in the Middle East. The Kurds' primary objective was to defeat ISIS, whereas Turkey was adamant about targeting the Assad regime but not ISIS. Such a divergence, soon, brought the US-Turkey relationship to a standstill. Even later in 2016–2017, when Turkey desired to join the anti-ISIS operations in Raqqa and Mosul, the US chose the Kurds as its strategic partner in the Middle East (Congressional Research Service 2016).

Turkey's political fallout, particularly following the emergence of ISIS, was disastrous. Its internal and foreign policy orientations were distant from being a "model country in the Middle East." Worse, by the ill-fated coup attempt on July 15, 2016, Turkey turned into an "illiberal democracy" siding by Russia against the West (Kirişçi and Sloat 2019). Meanwhile, the Kurds were once again referred to as Turkey's principal threat. Following the bombardment of PKK bases in the KRI in July 2015, which ended the İmralı process, harsh security measures took place first in Kurdish-populated cities, then in whole country. Thousands of members of the pro-Kurdish People's Democratic Party (HDP), including co-chairs and parliamentarians, have been imprisoned. In Kurdish cities, trustees appointed from Ankara replaced elected mayors (Curtis et al. 2021). Finally, the occupation of Afrin in 2018 and then Serakaniye/Gri-Spi in 2019 in Syrian Kurdistan demonstrated Turkey's escalating animosity toward Kurds beyond its borders.

Against this backdrop, however, the KRG-Turkey ties didn't break until the Kurdistan Independence referendum in September 2017. The KRG's path to independence had in fact gained more ground during the fight against ISIS. Given Nechirvan Barzani's comment on the conditions of Kurdistan Independence, the KRG appeared to be confident about the support of an international actor due to its strategic partnership with the US. On the other hand, course of developments on the ground was obviously in favor of the Kurds. In 2016, on the centennial of the Sykes-Picot Agreement, for example, Masoud Barzani stated that "I think that within themselves, [world leaders] have come to this conclusion that the era of Sykes-Picot is over. Whether they say it or not, accept it or not, the reality on the ground is that" (Chulov 2016). Yet nearly 200 kilometers of the Iraq-Syria border were under the control of Kurds on both sides. The AANES was ruling one-third of Syria, while the KRG was seizing full control of disputed areas in Iraq.

In such circumstances, the KRG was able to maintain its relations with Turkey, even in low profile, by focusing mostly on trade and energy cooperation. Meanwhile, deteriorating intra-Kurdish relations as a result of the shifting balance of power in Kurdistan were enabling the KRG to distance itself from the PKK and thus pursue a neutral stance in the PKK-Turkey conflict. With the declaration of the date for the vote on independence, however, Turkey's apathy, at best, to the KRG's progress abruptly morphed into open hostility. Turkey threatened the KRG with border closures, oil supply disruptions, and the use of force (Barut et al. 2017). Turkey, with the exception of a temporary deployment of Turkish troops at Ibrahim Khalil Gate and the suspension of flights to Erbil, took none of those measures. Since then, however, the feature of the KRG-Turkey relations that emerged in the aftermath of the Arab Spring shifted dramatically and the asymmetric nature of that relation became determinant once again, as it was in the 1990s.

Such a state of affair was, in fact, a consequence of the US position on the Kurdistan Independence referendum. Although Iraq was a failed state, the US adamantly opposed to Iraq's split. The US, in pursuit of territorial integrity of Iraq, first, turned a blind eye to militias supported by Iran taking control of disputed areas from Peshmerga, and then, to Turkish ground operations in the KRI balancing Iranian influence in Iraq. By Turkish operations, in particular, the US also got the opportunity to stymie the PKK's link with the AANES in Syria and to force the KRG to realign with Baghdad to survive merely as a federal entity in Iraq (Yılmaz 2021).

As of today, what the US urges in the Middle East is apparently a "favorable balance of power" (Yılmaz 2021), in which Turkey, the KRG, and the AANES preferably would align with its other allies in the region such as the Gulf States, Israel, and Egypt. It is doubtful, however, whether such a goal is achievable while the world is facing a geopolitical turmoil after the Ukrainian crisis in 2022. But what is clear for the KRG is that, rather than strategic partnerships, maintenance of a favorable balance of power in its relations with regional and international actors would be of its interest more.

Conclusion

The degree of political recognition that the KRG has gained so far as a federal entity in the field of foreign policy eclipses the efforts of many other sub-states on the world stage. In less than two decades, thirty countries, including the five permanent members of the United Nations Security Council (UNSC), opened official representations mostly as consulates general in Erbil. The KRG has fifteen representations in various countries. As of today, hardly a day passes in Erbil without a meeting between the representatives of the KRG and foreign countries. Such an outlook indicates that the KRG is an indispensable actor in the eyes of many, if not all, regional and international players in Iraq and the surrounding region.

In this context, the KRG-Turkey relations constitute a unique path given the back-and-forth fashion of its evolution. Up till now, for instance, the KRG could not open a representative office in Ankara because of Turkey's reservations. At the same time, however, Turkey could not ignore to initiate formal relations with the KRG by opening a consulate-general in Erbil. Furthermore, since the 1990s Turkey has sought for the KRG's support in its every step with regard to its Kurdish Question not only in Iraq but also in Turkey and Syria in the last decade as the KRG has, to a larger extent, affected its capability on Kurdish sphere. In this regard, it is fair to claim that what ultimately determined Turkey's policy toward the KRG was Turkey's security concerns rather than its economic interests. The economic cost of Turkey's stance against Kurdistan referendum is a clear sample to that end.

On the contrary, the KRG's approach to Turkey has basically been driven by its geopolitical considerations. Dependence on the US which has been supportive or, at worst, indifferent to Turkey's stance in the region, on one hand, and fear of Iranian dominance in the region which contradicts fundamentally with the KRG's foreign policy orientation in favor of Western values, on the other, have shaped such considerations. However, pursuance of independence either in the form of strategic partnership with Turkey under the banner of Islam or in the form of strategic partnership with the West against ISIS was a clear miscalculation, if not a maximalist posture. Despite such a failure, however, preserving the KRG's position in the region as an indispensable actor and a source of peace and stability has, undoubtedly, been a success on its foreign policy record.

Regardless of the past, the newly emerging geopolitical turmoil in the world requires a recalibration of not only foreign relations but domestic policies as well. "Foreign policy begins at home" argument of Richard Haass (2013), a veteran scholar in international relations, is valid today more than ever. Given that, the biggest challenge ahead that the KRG faces is first finding a balance between its national aspirations and interests considering the peace and stability at home. A search for finding balance in its relations with neighboring countries and international actors is another challenge of this new era. Therefore, dependence merely on the US in international arena or Turkey in the region would most probably cause more difficulties than before. To prevent this, then, conducting transactional relations instead of strategic partnerships would be more realistic and feasible for the KRG in future.

References

Ahmed, Hevidar. 2014. Senior Kurdistan Official: IS was at Erbil's Gates; Turkey Did Not Help. *Rudaw*, September 16. Accessed March 12, 2022. https://www.rudaw.net/english/interview/16092014.

ANF News. 2020. Türk devletinin saldırılarını kınadı. August 21. Accessed March 12, 2022. https://anfturkce.com/avrupa/edhem-barzani-tuerk-devletinin-saldirilarini-kinadi-144828.

Aydın-Düzgit, Senem, Daniela Huber, E. Meltem Müftüler-Baç, Fuat Keyman, Michael Schwarz, and Nathalie Tocci. 2015. *Global Turkey in Europe III: Democracy, Trade, and the Kurdish Question in Turkey-EU Relations*. Rome: Edizioni Nuova Cultura.

Bakir, Falah Mustafa. 2022. Interviewed on 13 January.

Barkey, Henri J. 2009. *Preventing Conflict Over Kurdistan*. Washington: Carnegie Endowment for International Peace.

———. 2010. *Turkey's New Engagement in Iraq: Embracing Iraqi Kurdistan*. United States Institute of Peace. https://carnegieendowment.org/files/USIP_SR_Turkey_Iraq.pdf.

Barut, Dirimcan, Dominic Evans, and Stephan Powell. 2017. Kurdish Independence Referendum: Turkish President Erdogan Says Kurds will Pay the Price. *Independent*, September 30. Accessed March 17, 2022. https://www.independent.co.uk/news/world/middle-east/kurd-independence-referendum-erdogan-pay-price-a7975666.html.

Bengio, Ofra. 2012. *The Kurds of Iraq: Building a State within a State*. Boulder: Lynne Rienner Publishers.
Can, Eyüp. 2013. Kürtler Türkiye'yi bölecek mi? *Radikal*, January 23. Accessed April 10, 2022. http://www.radikal.com.tr/yazarlar/eyup-can/kurtler-turkiyeyi-bolecek-mi-1118129/
Çandar, Cengiz. 2012. *Mezopotamya Ekspresi*. İstanbul: İletişim Yayınları.
———. 2020. *Turkey's Mission Impossible*. London: Lexington Books.
Černy, Hannes. 2018. *Iraqi Kurdistan, the PKK and International Relations: Theory and Ethnic Conflict*. London: Routledge.
Chulov, Martin. 2016. Iraqi Kurdistan President: Time Has Come to Redraw Middle East Boundaries. *The Guardian*, January 22. Accessed March 12, 2022. https://www.theguardian.com/world/2016/jan/22/kurdish-independence-closer-than-ever-says-massoud-barzani.
Congressional Research Service. 2016. Kurds in Iraq and Syria: U.S. Partners Against the Islamic State. Accessed April 10, 2022. https://crsreports.congress.gov/product/pdf/R/R44513/7.
Constitute Project. 2005. Iraq's Constitution of 2005. Accessed April 17, 2022. https://www.constituteproject.org/constitution/Iraq_2005.pdf?lang=en.
Cumhuriyet. 2014. Hüseyin Çelik'ten Bağımsız Kürdistan açıklaması. June 29. Accessed April 10, 2022. https://www.cumhuriyet.com.tr/haber/huseyin-celikten-bagimsiz-kurdistan-aciklamasi-88209.
Curtis, John, Nigel Walker, and Julie Gill. 2021. Kurdish Political Representation and Equality in Turkey. House of Commons Library. Accessed April 10, 2022. https://researchbriefings.files.parliament.uk/documents/CDP-2021-0172/CDP-2021-0172.pdf.
Davutoglu, Ahmet. 2010. Turkey's Zero Problems Foreign Policy. *Foreign Policy*, May 20. Accessed April 15, 2022. https://foreignpolicy.com/2010/05/20/turkeys-zero-problems-foreign-policy/.
Demir, Mustafa. 2019. *The Geopolitics of Turkey-Kurdistan Relations*. Lanham: Lexington Books.
Deutsche Welle. 2013. Turkey's Kurdish Opening. November 19. Accessed March 28, 2022. https://www.dw.com/en/turkeys-kurdish-opening/a-17239234.
———. 2014. Turkish President Says Kobane about to Fall to IS. October 7. Accessed March 12, 2022. https://www.dw.com/en/turkish-president-says-kobani-about-to-fall-to-is/a-17981034.
Ergan, Uğur. 2014. Türkiye'den yardım istedik, verilmedi. *Hürriyet*, August 29. Accessed March 10, 2022. https://www.hurriyet.com.tr/dunya/turkiye-den-yardim-istedik-verilmedi-27097749.
Erşen, Emre, and Mitat Çelikpala. 2019. Turkey and the Changing Energy Geopolitics of Eurasia. *Energy Policy* 128: 584–592.
Gümüştekin, Deniz. 2021. *Kurds Under Threat: The Role of Kurdish Transnational Networks During Peace and Conflict*. Lanham: Lexington Books.

Günes, Cengiz and, Robert Lowe. 2015. The Impact of Syrian War on Kurdish Politics Across the Middle East. The Royal Institute of International Affairs. Accessed April 15, 2022. https://syria.chathamhouse.org/assets/documents/20150723SyriaKurdsGunesLowe.pdf.

Gunter, Michael. 1997. *The Kurds and the Future of Turkey*. Houndmilles: Macmillian.

Gürcanlı, Zeynep. 2012. Barzani'ye Türkiye seninle gurur duyuyor sloganları. *Hürriyet*, October 1. Accessed April 9, 2022. https://www.hurriyet.com.tr/gundem/barzaniye-turkiye-seninle-gurur-duyuyor-slogani-21590650.

———. 2019. Cemil Çiçek Çekiç Güç sürecini anlattı: Özal Çekiç Güç'e onay vermedi. Sözcü. *Sözcü*, January 21. Accessed March 12, 2022. https://www.sozcu.com.tr/2019/gundem/cemil-cicek-cekic-guc-surecini-anlatti-ozal-cekic-guce-onay-vermedi-3206613.

Haass, Richard. 2013. *Foreign Policy begins at home: The Case for Putting America's House in Order*. New York: Basic Books.

Halıcı, Nihat. 2007. Kerkük krizi ihtimali kaygılandırıyor. *Deutsche Welle*, January 18. Accessed March 12, 2022. https://www.dw.com/tr/kerk%C3%BCk-krizi-ihtimalikayg%C4%B1land%C4%B1r%C4%B1yor/a-2519899.

Hussain, Shilan Fuad. 2022. A look into the Kurdistan Region's Foreign Policy: An Interview with Falah Mustafa. *K24*, February 10. Accessed April 10, 2022. https://www.kurdistan24.net/en/story/27212-A-look-into-the-Kurdistan-Region%27s-foreign-policy:-An-interview-with-Falah-Mustafa.

Imset, Ismet G. 1988. *PKK: The Deception of Terror (Countering Stability in Turkey) Part II*. Ankara: Briefing.

Kaya, Mehmet. 2022. Interviewed on 30 January.

Keating, Michael. 2000. Paradiplomacy and Regional Networking. Forum of Federations. Accessed April 15, 2022. http://www.forumfed.org/libdocs/ForRelCU01/924-FRCU0105-eu-keating.pdf.

Khalid, Asmat. 2022. Interviewed on 17 January.

Kirişçi, Kemal. 2009. The Transformation of Turkish Foreign Policy: The Rise of the Trading State. *New Perspectives on Turkey* 40: 29–56.

Kirişçi, Kemal, and Amanda Sloat. 2019. The Rise and fall of Liberal Democracy in Turkey. *Brookings*, February. Accessed April 15, 2022. https://www.brookings.edu/research/the-rise-and-fall-of-liberal-democracy-in-turkey-implications-for-the-west/.

Koçak, Cemil. 2016. *Darbeler Tarihi*. Istanbul: Timaş.

Krauthammer, Charles. 2011. The Obama Doctrine: Leading from Behind. *The Washington Post*, April 28. Accessed April 8, 2022. https://www.washingtonpost.com/opinions/the-obama-doctrine-leading-from-behind/2011/04/28/AFBCy18E_story.html.

Kurda, Karam. 2015. Bad Blood Between Brothers: The KDP, PUK, PKK conflict. *Independent Academia*. Accessed April 2, 2022. https://

www.academia.edu/34630684/Bad_Blood_Between_Brothers_The_ KDP_PUK_PKK_Conflict.
McKiernan, Kevin. 2006. *The Kurds: A People in Search of their Home Land*. New York: St Martin's Press.
Mearsheimer, John J., and Stephen M. Walt. 2016. The Case for Off-shore Balancing: A Superior U.S. Grand Strategy. *Foreign Affairs*, July/August. Accessed April 15, 2022. https://www.foreignaffairs.com/articles/united-states/2016-06-13/case-offshore-balancing.
Milliyet. 2008. Barzani'nin ajanları 13 askerin şehit olmasına neden olmuş. June 3. Accessed March 7, 2022. https://www.milliyet.com.tr/gundem/barzaninin-ajanlari-13-askerin-sehit-olamsina-neden-olmus-762366.
Mustafa, Sarah Salahaddin, and Mustafa Aziz. 2017. Turkey and the Iraqi Kurdistan Federal Region. In *Iraqi Kurdistan in Middle Eastern Politics*, ed. Alex Danilowich, 135–152. New York: Routledge.
Natali, Denise. 2012. The Limits of Turkey's Kurdish Efforts in Iraq. *Al-Monitor*, July 18. Accessed February 13, 2022. https://www.al-monitor.com/originals/2012/al-monitor/turkeys-tactics-in-iraq.html.
Öktem, Emre. 2011. Turkey: Successor or Continuing State of the Ottoman Empire? *Leiden Journal of International Law* 24 (3): 561–583.
Oran, Baskin. 1998. *Kalkık Horoz; Çekiç Güç ve Kürt Devleti*. Ankara: Bilgi Publications.
Özkızılcık, Ömer. 2019. Uniting the Syrian Opposition: The Components of the National Army and the Implications of the Unification. SETA Analysis. Accessed April 15, 2022. https://setav.org/en/assets/uploads/2019/10/A54En.pdf.
Park, Bill. 2014. Turkey-Kurdish Regional Government Relations After the U.S. Withdrawal from Iraq: Putting the Kurds on the Map? US Army War College Press. Accessed April 15, 2022. https://www.files.ethz.ch/isn/177967/pub1190.pdf.
———. 2019. Explaining Turkey's Reaction to the 2017 Independence Referendum in the KRG: Final Divorce or Relationship Reset? *Ethnopolitics* 18 (1): 46–60.
Phillips, David L. 2007. Disarming, Demobilizing and Reintegrating the Kurdistan Workers' Party. National Committee on American Foreign Policy. Accessed April 15, 2022. http://acikistihbarat.com/dosyalar/kurt-acilim-raporu-david-philips-15102007-english.pdf.
Rodrik, Dani. 2011. Ergenekon and Sledgehammer: Building or Undermining the Rule of Law? *Turkish Policy Quarterly* 10 (1): 99–109.
Romano, David. 2008. *The Kurdish Nationalist Movement: Opportunity, Mobilization and Identity*. Cambridge: Cambridge University Press.

Selcen, Aydın. 2017. Komşu Kürtlerin Bağımsızlığı. *Gazete duva R*, August 16. Accessed April 10, 2022. https://www.gazeteduvar.com.tr/yazarlar/2017/08/16/komsu-kurtlerin-bagimsizligi
———. 2022. Interviewed on 26 January.
Sol Haber. 2007. Barzani: Biz de Diyarbakır'a karışırız. April 8. Accessed March 12, 2022. https://arsiv.sol.org.tr/index.php?yazino=9692.
Stansfield, Gareth R.V. 2003. *Iraqi Kurdistan: Political Development and Emergent Democracy*. London: Routledge.
Turkish News. 2009. Erbil'de Başkonsolosluk açılacak. October 30. Accessed April 8, 2022. https://www.turkishnews.com/tr/content/2009/10/31/erbilde-baskonsolosluk-acilacak/.
Türkmen, Gülay. 2021. *Under the Banner of Islam: Turks, Kurds, and the Limits of Religious Unity*. London: Oxford University Press.
Türköne, Mümtaz'er. 2009. Kürt Konferansı. February 13. Accessed April 9, 2022. https://www.turkishnews.com/tr/content/2009/02/13/kurt-konferansi/.
Ustun, Kadir, and Lesley Dudden. 2017. *Turkey-KRG Relationship: Mutual Interests, Geopolitical Challenges*. Istanbul: Turkuvaz Haberleşme ve Yayıncılık A.Ş.
Yeni Şafak. 2012. Stratejik Ortağımız Türkiye'den daha çok işadamı gelsin. May 7. Accessed March 5, 2022. https://www.yenisafak.com/gundem/stratejik-ortagimiz-turkiyeden-daha-cok-isadami-gelsin-381828.
Yılmaz, Arzu. Personal Archive. 1983 PKK—PDK-I İttifak Protokolü, Damascus, 1983.
———. Personal archive. 2011. Masoud Barzani's speech at University of Duhok, Duhok, 9 October 2011.
———. 2015. Üçüncü Yol. *Birikim*, October 23. Accessed April 8, 2022. https://birikimdergisi.com/haftalik/7284/ucuncu-yol.
———. 2016. *Atruş'tan Maxmur'a*. Istanbul: İletişim Yayınları.
Yılmaz, A. 2021. What Will Happen to the Kurds if the US Withdraws from Syria and Iraq? *The Commentaries* 1 (1): 85–96. https://doi.org/10.33182/com.v1i1.2000.

CHAPTER 13

Kurdistan-Iraq and Iran

Nader Entessar

INTRODUCTION

The field of international relations has long been dominated by relations among sovereign nation-states. However, the emergence of substate actors as global has challenged the state-centric dimensions of inter-state relations. For a variety of reasons, in recent decades, a growing number of states have found it necessary to conduct diplomacy with non-state players, especially with substate actors that operate in the confines of an existing nation-state. These subnational players play an active role in international trade and political, social, and cultural relations with foreign governments at both the regional and global levels (Alvarez 2020; Kuznetsov 2020). These activities by subnational governments to promote their interests are referred to as "paradiplomacy." Some of these subnational governments have survived in the international system for decades and obtained many attributes of sovereign nation-states without formal recognition by other states. One of the best examples of an "unrecognized state" is the Kurdish region of Iraq that engages in extensive paradiplomacy with its neighbors as well as faraway governments in the

N. Entessar (✉)
University of South Alabama, Mobile, AL, USA
e-mail: nentessar@southalabama.edu

© The Author(s), under exclusive license to Springer Nature
Switzerland AG 2023
G. Gürbey et al. (eds.), *Between Diplomacy and Non-Diplomacy*,
https://doi.org/10.1007/978-3-031-09756-0_13

world (Caspersen 2012). The purpose of this chapter is to analyze the evolving relationship and paradiplomacy between the Islamic Republic of Iran and the Kurdish parastate in Iraq and its government, the KRG.

The main thesis of the chapter is that despite some initial reservations about the emergence of a self-governing autonomous government in Iraqi Kurdistan, Kurdistan Iraq has succeeded in convincing Iran to accept the permanency of the KRG. As a result, both the KRG and Iran have focused on commonalities of interests between them and have sought to develop a functioning framework for expansion of their socioeconomic and political relations. Notwithstanding the desire of both sides to develop amicable and long-lasting relations between themselves, a variety of regional and domestic factors have served as impediments to the blossoming of Erbil-Tehran relations.

The evolution of the KRG in the aftermath of Iraq's invasion of Kuwait and the ensuing 1990–1991 Gulf War presented new political and security challenges for Iran and Iraq. The emergence and evolution of the Kurdish self-governing entity following the Gulf War added another dimension to the regional security environment. The nascent Kurdish policies toward its Iranian neighbors were driven by the following considerations: (1) Keeping an open channel of communication with the Islamic Republic and providing support, albeit minimally and cautiously, to efforts to prevent the full restoration of the Ba'thi control over northern Iraq; (2) Identifying areas of common security interests with Iran, especially with respect to border security, and seeking to convince Iran to curtail its cross-border activities against the armed Iranian Kurdish groups in Iraqi Kurdistan; and (3) Preventing northern Iraq from turning into an anti-Iranian theater of operations (Vatanka 2014).

Between 1991 and 2003, officials in Kurdistan Iraq found it difficult, and at times impossible, to develop and sustain a consistent policy toward Iran. Although both sides maintained some relations with each other as reflected in cross-border movement of goods, the deep political fissure between Iran and Iraq made any meaningful relations between the two countries, even in the Kurdish-controlled northern Iraq, extremely difficult.

The United States (US) invasion of Iraq in 2003, which led to the overthrow of Saddam Hussein's regime and the subsequent establishment of a federal structure in Iraq, allowed the KRG to expand its sociopolitical and economic outreach to both the new Iraqi government and Iran. With the establishment of the Department of Foreign Relations in 2005, the KRG embarked upon an ambitious process of paradiplomacy to advance its interests (Abbas Zadeh and Kirmanji 2017). The opening of the Iranian consulate in Erbil and the KRG's representative office in Tehran is indicative of the KRG's commitments to use paradiplomacy to facilitate its formal interactions with Iran. Today, the KRG's representative office in Tehran serves as a de facto embassy. Moreover, in recent years, contacts between high-level officials of the KRG and the Islamic Republic of Iran have become routinized, and many top-level KRG officials and their Iranian counterparts have developed working relationship with each other; something that would have been cumbersome at the turn of the twenty-first century when Saddam Hussein was still in power in Iraq (Entessar 2010). Notwithstanding the improvement in KRG-Iran relations since 2013, there remain some contentious issues between the two sides as well as potential areas of cooperation between Erbil and Tehran.

The KRG and Iranian Kurdish Opposition Groups

One of the most enduring areas of friction between the KRG and Iran revolves around the status of the Iranian Kurdish opposition groups, which include the Kurdistan Democratic Party-Iran (KDP-I), Komala Party of Iranian Kurdistan (Komala), and the Kurdistan Free Life Party (PJAK), that operate from sanctuaries inside Iraqi Kurdistan (Entessar 2014; Hassaniyan 2021; Langanger 2015). Of course, the history of armed Iranian Kurdish opposition groups in Iraq dates back several decades. However, after the overthrow of the Ba'thi regime in Iraq, the Islamic Republic had hoped that political-military activities of the Iranian Kurdish opposition would be curtailed by the KRG. However, this proved to be wishful thinking as the KRG has neither been able nor willing to terminate cross-border operations inside Iran, especially by PJAK militants who seem to have supplanted both the KDP-I and Komala as the principal armed opposition groups against the Islamic Republic. Some elements in the Islamic Republic's security apparatus have long suspected that both the US and Israeli intelligence have co-opted Iranian Kurdish opposition groups in northern Iraq and have orchestrated armed attacks against targets inside Iran (Perry 2012). The KRG officials have repeatedly denied Iranian accusations of an Israeli presence in northern Iraq and Erbil's cooperation with Israel. Nonetheless, perception of Israeli security-intelligence activities on Iran's border regions with the KRG continues to remain a source of tension between Erbil and Tehran. In the same vein,

Iran has repeatedly warned the KRG that anti-Iran Israeli covert operations from Kurdistan Iraq and cross-border attacks from the KRG territories by Kurdistan-based Iranian Kurdish groups constitute Iran's red line. Consequently, Iran has launched missile and drone attacks against hostile targets inside Kurdistan Iraq to convey its resolve in confronting threats emanating from the KRG-held territories (Mehr News Agency 2021; Tasnim News Agency 2021a, b; Tehran Times 2021). That said, Israel's reliance on Kurdish oil has intensified. According to a report by the British daily *Financial Times*, Israel "has imported as much as three-quarters of its oil from Iraq's semi-autonomous Kurdish north in recent months, providing a vital source of funds to the cash-strapped region as it fights militants of the Islamic State of Iraq and the Levant (ISIS)" (Sheppard et al. 2015). The KRG has denied reports that it sells oil to Israel directly or indirectly. According to a senior Kurdish government advisor in Erbil: "We do not care where the oil goes once we have delivered it to the traders" (Sheppard et al. 2015). It is worth noting that the KRG has long viewed Israel as an asset to both counterbalance Iran's influence in Kurdistan Iraq and as a lever to advance Erbil's paradiplomacy.

In a similar vein, the Kurdish officials have at times accused Iran of turning a blind eye on operations by forces that have attacked Iraqi Kurdistan from the Iranian side of the border. In the months preceding the US invasion of Iraq, the Kurdish autonomous administration waged battle against a Sunni fundamentalist Kurdish group called Ansar al-Islam. This group operated from fortified positions on mountains along the Iranian border, and on occasion crossed into Iran for safety. During the early phase of the US attack on Iraqi targets in March 2003, the Iraqi Kurdish fighters, the Peshmerga, and US forces jointly launched an attack on Ansar al-Islam's strongholds and decimated much of its infrastructure. The original leader of Ansar al-Islam was Najmuddin Faraj Ahmad, an Iraqi Kurd commonly known as Mullah Krekar, who had entered Norway as a refugee in 1991. Krekar has steadfastly denied that he has ever been involved in any terrorist attacks against other Kurds.

However, the KRG has repeatedly asked Norway to extradite Mullah Krekar to Iraqi Kurdistan to stand trial. Although Norway revoked Mullah Krekar's refugee status in August 2002 when he traveled to Iraq, allegedly to direct terrorist activities, Krekar has not yet been extradited as requested by the KRG. In fact, on several occasions Krekar has successfully challenged the Norwegian government's attempts to incarcerate him despite court judgments against him. Even when Norway in February 2003 issued a deportation order for Mullah Krekar and ordered him extradited to Iraq, the order was not implemented because Norway, like many other European countries, does not extradite individuals to a country that practices capital punishment. Although the KRG issued a moratorium in 2008 on capital punishment, several individuals have indeed been executed since 2008 in Iraqi Kurdistan. In 2019, however, Mullah Krekar was rearrested in Oslo at the request of Italian authorities for leading a jihadist network. In July 2020, Mullah Krekar was extradited to Italy, where he is held at a prison in Milan.

In September 2002, Mullah Krekar entered Iran but was arrested by the Iranian authorities and sent to Holland, where he was arrested upon arrival in Amsterdam and was later sent to Norway. The porous Iran border with northern Iraq has allowed a variety of cross-border raids by the remnants of Ansar al-Islam into Iraqi Kurdish territory. Iran itself has been keenly aware of the danger of such raids and has undertaken several raids of its own into Iraqi territory in pursuit of Kurdish groups that use the Iranian territory for cross-border attacks. The Iranian raids have been a source of tension between the KRG and Iran. The extremist Salafi Kurdish fundamentalist threat has indeed been a source of concern for the Iranian government, especially considering the increasing presence of such groups in various Sunni mosques in the cities of Sanandaj and Sar-e Pol-e Zahab (Ghajar and Alavi 2017). Iran is unlikely to support Salafi Kurdish groups that are primarily anti-Shi'a and act as destabilizing forces inside Iran. In fact, the June 2017 terrorist attack in Tehran against two important targets, namely the majlis (parliament) and Ayatollah Khomeini's mausoleum complex, were carried out by extremist Salafi Kurdish individuals from Iran who were members of the so-called Islamic State (IS) operating in Iraq and Syria (Vatan-e Emrooz 2017). The ongoing Salafi Kurdish challenge to the KRG will act as destabilizing factor that may create a new angle for Iraqi Kurdistan's closer cooperation with Iran.

On the other hand, as stated earlier, both the US and Israel have lent support at various times to Kurdish elements that operate inside Iraqi Kurdistan and that have sought to destabilize Iran. As has been reported extensively by investigative journalist Seymour Hersh, both the US and Israel have conducted a proxy war inside Iranian Kurdistan through their support of PJAK and other Kurdish assets (Hersh 2004). The former PJAK leader Abdul Rahman Haj Ahmadi, who lives in exile in Germany, even traveled to Washington in July 2007 and met with some US officials. Although Washington has downplayed this event, Biyar Gabar, a PJAK commander from Sanandaj, was quoted in a *Newsweek* magazine report from the Iran-Iraq border as having said that Ahmadi's meeting in Washington was with "high level" officials and that they discussed "the future of Iran" (Newsweek Staff 2007). Likewise, Israel has always viewed its Kurdish card as an important asset in enhancing its strategic interests in the region. As noted by Scott Ritter, during the heyday of Israel's strategic relationship with Turkey, Ankara "would turn a blind eye toward Israel's support of Kurds in Iraq and Iran in exchange for Israel's assistance in clamping down on the Kurdish rebellion in Turkey" (2006, 21). In the final analysis, the challenge the KRG faces in its relations with Iran has placed Erbil between a rock and a hard place as Erbil seeks to balance its interests among regional and outside countries that have pursued their often-competing goals.

Economic Ties

Economic ties between the KRG and Iran are largely a function of Iran's economic relations with Iraq. It is important to note the KRG does not publish reliable statistics on the official volume of trade with Iran. Similarly, there are no reliable statistics on Iranian direct investments in Iraqi Kurdistan. Although Iran publishes trade statistics with foreign countries, the figures for Iraq are for the entire country and do not reflect separate statistics for northern Iraq. Another complicating factor in providing reliable statistics on KRG-Iran trade is that a significant amount of cross-border trade is in the form of informal or illicit trade. According to one estimate, the informal sector accounts for 70 percent of jobs in Iran's border regions (Abdollahi 2021). The case of Baneh, an Iranian Kurdish border town with a population of 90,000, has become the "hub of a multibillion-dollar illicit trade from Kurdistan Iraq in home appliances and electronics. Baneh's reputation as a cut-price shopping destination is known throughout Iran. Residents of big cities such as Tehran order goods for almost half the usual price or make the hours-long trek to the city, returning along rugged roads with television sets and air-conditioners strapped to the roofs of their cars" (Bozorgmehr 2014). Iran is the second largest (after Turkey) trading partner of the KRG, and its annual exports to the Iraqi Kurdistan have been estimated to be $4 billion (Ministry of Foreign Affairs, Islamic Republic of Iran 2021). However, Iran's Foreign Direct Investment (FDI) in Iraqi Kurdistan is minimal despite recent attempts by the Islamic Republic to facilitate private foreign investment in

Kurdistan Iraq and the establishment of a special economic zone in cities of Baneh and Marivan in the Iranian Kurdistan to encourage cross-border investment (Ministry of Foreign Affairs, Islamic Republic of Iran 2021).

A significant portion of economic activities between the two sides has been focused on the energy sector where Iran has long been active in providing a variety of energy needs to the Kurdistan region of Iraq. In 2014, Erbil and Tehran agreed to boost their energy ties when Iran agreed to build a major gas pipeline to Iraqi Kurdistan to fuel power stations with Iranian gas, and another pipeline to transport fuel to Iran from Iraqi Kurdistan. By late 2015, some 100 million cubic meters of gas had been injected to a new trans-national pipeline along the Kurdish border for use by both Kurdish towns and villages in Iran as well as for transport to Iraqi Kurdistan. Although the flow of natural gas from Iran to Kurdistan Iraq has experienced periodic interruptions, Iran has upgraded and improved its natural gas pipelines since 2019 and has planned to export up to eight million cubic meters of gas per day to Kurdistan Iraq (Financial Tribune 2019). The KRG, however, has been cautious about expanding cooperation with Iran in energy sectors due to the existing extensive American sanctions on Iran, and Erbil does not want to be penalized for violating Washington's sanctions regulations against Tehran.

Notwithstanding the aforementioned obstacles, Iran's Organization of Trade Expansion appears to have intensified its efforts to increase the volume of Iran-KRG trade by sponsoring trade expos and shopping areas (bazaars) along the Kurdish-Iranian border regions. One of the most noteworthy of these shopping areas is the Tamarchin bazaar, located within 15 kilometers of the city of Piranshahr in Iran and overlooking Haj Omran in Iraqi Kurdistan. The private sectors in Iran and Iraqi Kurdistan have also been increasing their leverage in the expanding commerce between the two sides. The chambers of commerce in the Iranian provinces of Tehran, Esfahan, Kermanshah, Elam, West Azerbaijan, and Kurdistan have been influential in the expansion of economic ties between Iraqi Kurdistan and Iran. The projected expansion of relations between Erbil and Tehran has spilled over into educational cooperation between the two sides. Iranian universities have conducted workshops and exhibitions in Erbil and other cities in Kurdistan Iraq to highlight and showcase the capabilities of Iranian universities to train Kurdish students and transmit their scientific and technical knowledge to Kurdish institutions of higher learning. Currently, there are an estimated 33 Iranian universities that have either branches or training centers in Kurdistan Iraq (Salahaddin University-Erbil 2018).

THE REGIONAL CHESS GAME AND ITS IMPLICATIONS FOR KRG-IRAN RELATIONS

The regional balance of power and strategic alliances changed dramatically in the aftermath of the US-led invasion of Iraq and the overthrow of Saddam Hussein's regime. The condition of the Kurds and the KRG's fortunes have been affected by the chess game involving Iran, Turkey and the US. As I have argued elsewhere, the Iraqi Kurds today are in the best position since the end of World War I to effect their own destiny (Entessar 2010, 67–105). However, the KRG's window of opportunity is narrowing as Iraq meanders through its civil conflict. Although US officials at various times have projected a confident image of "winning" the war in Iraq and establishing a functioning democracy in that country, Iraq remains a dysfunctional society. The invasion of Iraq has had unintended consequences beyond the country's geographic borders. As Peter Galbraith, a veteran observer of Iraqi Kurdistan argued, once Iraq was "broken up," the United States was unable to put the country back together again and stop the civil war (Galbraith 2006, 209). If this is the case today, then what options does the KRG have to safeguard its gains since 2003? For Galbraith, as well as some other analysts, "a fully independent Kurdistan appears to be a matter of when, not if. The younger generation of Kurdish leaders (those in their forties and younger) have no use for Iraq and will press for full independence as soon as the situation allows" (Galbraith 2006, 215). In fact, opinion polls have consistently shown that the overwhelming majority of the Iraqi Kurds favor independence from Iraq. Massoud Barzani, a denizen of Kurdish politics and former president of the KRG, as well as several other top-level Kurdish officials has on several occasions called for a referendum on Iraqi Kurdistan's independence (Iddon 2016; The Guardian 2014; Zaman 2015). The KRG's critics, however, have argued that the periodic calls for an independence referendum emanate from Barzani's own domestic legitimacy crisis, falling international oil prices, and the fulfillment of ending a traumatic relationship between Iraq's Kurds and the rest of Iraq. Advocating independence for the Kurds now serves as a convenient ploy to deflect domestic criticism over Barzani's indefinite rule and economic crisis, and allowing him to gain the support of his own base, as well as constituencies loyal to the KRG's other political parties, such as the Patriotic Union of Kurdistan. (Al-Marashi 2016)

Turkey and Iran, the two major regional players in Iraqi Kurdistan, as well as the US, do not favor the establishment of an independent Kurdistan. Each of these players has been playing its "Kurdish card" to affect the outcome of political developments in Kurdistan to suit its own geopolitical objectives. Despite a close alliance between the US and the KRG, Washington has taken measures to increase the power of Iraq's central government at the expense of the other political players in the country, including the KRG. The more confident the Iraqi government becomes, the less likely it is that it would compromise on constitutional issues that are important to the KRG. Moreover, several US analysts have argued that one of the major unintended consequences of the overthrow of Saddam Hussein's regime has been the enhanced power and strategic weight of Iran (Galbraith 2008, 167–180; Takeyh 2006, 177–187). In order to reduce the perceived power of Iran, these analysts argue, there should be limits to Iraq's devolution lest it becomes a weak and ultimately a failed state. It is beyond the scope of this chapter to deal with the broader US-Iran issues in Iraq. However, suffice it to say that if Washington and Tehran continue to fight their proxy war in Iraq, the KRG will inevitably become affected negatively by the outcome of the US-Iran chess game. When the US assassinated the Commander of Iranian Islamic Revolutionary Guard Corps (IRGC) Quds Force General Qassem Soleimani and Iraq's Deputy Commander of the anti-occupation militia Hashd al-Shaabi Abu Mahdi al-Muhandes in Baghdad on January 3, 2020, Iran and its allies retaliated against several American targets, including some in Kurdistan Iraq. For example, an operation in Erbil killed two high-ranking American and Israeli commanders: Lieutenant Colonel James C. Willis, 55, of Albuquerque and of the Red Horse Unit, is an American commander who was killed in an operation in Erbil, although according to a Pentagon report he died in a non-combat incident at Qatar's Al-Udeid base. This person was involved in the assassination operations of Soleimani and Abu Mahdi. Also (Israeli) Colonel Sharon Asman of the Nahal Brigade, said to have died of heart failure, was another person killed in Erbil. (The Cradle 2021) Tehran has repeatedly warned that activities that threaten Iran's security, including those by American and Israeli forces and personnel, will elicit commensurate retaliation inside Kurdistan Iraq (Nour News 2021).

Even during the early years of the US occupation of Iraq, the dangerous consequences of the US-Iran war of attrition in Kurdistan Iraq were evident when the US military raided the Iranian Liaison Office in Erbil on January 11, 2007. The ostensible goal of this raid was to capture two senior Iranian Revolutionary Guard (pasdar) officers, but there were no senior pasdar officers in the compound when the US forces arrived. Instead, they seized five mid-level diplomats. The Iranian detainees were then taken to a US prison in Iraq. The raid and the capture of Iranian officials embarrassed the KRG and put it in an uncomfortable diplomatic position. According to Hoshyar Zebari, the then Iraq's Kurdish Foreign Minister, the Iranians had been working in Erbil with the KRG's official permission, and that Iran's Erbil office had been in operation since 1992 carrying out routine consular activities, such as issuance of visas (Entessar 2010).

Furthermore, Iran had contended that the status of the office had changed to that of a consulate general, and that official diplomatic notes—note verbal—had already been exchanged between the governments involved. Therefore, the officials involved enjoyed diplomatic immunity under the Vienna Convention on Consular Relations. The then KRG President Massoud Barzani condemned the capture of Iranian officials and demanded their immediate release. In a tense confrontation, the KRG security forces also surrounded US military vehicles to prevent them from taking further military action.

In a similar direct challenge to the Kurdish authority, the US military forces raided the Sulaimani Palace, the city's best hotel, in September 2007 and took Mahmoud Farhady, the head of the visiting Iranian trade delegation, into custody. The Kurdish hosts who had invited the Iranians were outraged. Jalal Talabani, the then Iraq's Kurdish President, called the raid and capture of the Iranian trade delegate "illegal," while Sulaimaniyah governor Dana Majid, called it "kidnapping" (Watson 2007). These two incidents are illustrative of unpleasant repercussions of US-Iran conflict for the Kurds. As I indicated earlier, the KRG is caught between the proverbial rock and a hard place—it needs to be on the good side of both Washington and Tehran. As one KRG official stated, Iran is "like an angry big brother. It can reward you or punish you, depending on the mood" (Watson 2007).

Turkish regional geopolitics and Turkey-Iran relations have also had a lasting impact on developments in Kurdistan. Despite the complex, and at times acrimonious, relations between Iran and Turkey, the two sides have cooperated with each other more often than not in dealing with what is euphemistically called the Kurdish issue (Entessar 1996, 47–53; Olson 2004, 159–182, 2006, 15–33; Yildiz and Taysi 2007, 70–79). Although both Iran and Turkey have common interests in dealing with the Kurdish issue, Turkey has its own security concerns and ambitions in the greater Middle East. As such, Ankara has taken unilateral actions, including military incursions inside Iraqi Kurdistan, to safeguard its own security. Notwithstanding regular Turkish saber rattling and military incursions into Iraqi Kurdistan, the Turkish government and the KRG have taken steps to elevate and strengthen their relationship. Turkey-KRG energy cooperation began in earnest in November 2013 when the two sides signed a deal to export 45 billion barrels of oil from Iraqi Kurdistan via the Turkish port of Ceyhan (Serdaroglu 2015). Both the Iraqi government and Iran have opposed the KRG-Turkey energy deals as a challenge to Iraq's sovereignty and territorial integrity. Although the KRG sees its energy deals with Ankara as a way to enhance its economic independence, there are indeed inherent dangers involved in this relationship. As Denise Natali, an expert on Iraqi Kurdistan, has noted: Instead of Statehood or enhanced autonomy, however, the KRG has become more dependent on Turkey while remaining tied to Iraq. This dependency has deepened with the Islamic State (IS) threatening the region, territorial and resource disputes in Iraq remaining unresolved and Ankara and Baghdad pursuing a rapprochement. It leaves the KRG more deeply lodged between regional powers and enhances Turkey's control over Erbil's energy and political agendas. (Natali 2014)

David Romano, on the other hand, argues that recent events, including the expanding Ankara-Erbil energy cooperation and the rise of the IS, speak to "an enduring Ankara-Erbil relationship" and an emergent strategic alliance (Romano 2015, 90). Iran, on the other hand, has an interest in preventing the KRG from moving completely into the Turkish orbit. Kurdistan Iraq, therefore, is caught between the proverbial rock and a hard place and must engage in a delicate game of paradiplomacy between its two larger and more powerful neighbors.

Conclusion

The history of KRG-Iran ties and interactions has demonstrated that Erbil-Tehran relations remain fluid, and even unpredictable, in the near future. At times unforeseen developments, like the emergence of the IS that threatens the interests of both Erbil and Tehran, bring the two sides together in a marriage of convenience. When the IS forces had threatened the KRG, it was Iran that sent both military equipment and logistical support to Erbil and cooperated extensively with the KRG in military operations against their common enemy. The late General Qassem Soleimani, the commander of Iran's elite Quds Force, was welcomed by the KRG as a sign of strengthening relations between the KRG and Iran, and the KRG leaders expressed their appreciation to Soleimani for helping defeat the IS in Kurdistan Iraq (IFP Editorial Staff 2020; Malas 2014, A1 and A8). At the same time, the KRG's increasing alignment with Turkey and Ankara's strategic vision will work against Iran's interests in Iraq and the Persian Gulf region. On the other hand, increasing cross-border contacts between the Iraqi and Iranian Kurds and the emergence of transnational links between the two sides may result in the development of overlapping socioeconomic interests that could strengthen Iraqi Kurdistan's relations with Iran (Akbarzadeh et al. 2020, 2275–2278; King 2019, 52–55). In the final analysis, how Erbil and Tehran manage their competing and complimentary visions and goals will determine the contours of KRG-Iran relations in years to come.

References

Abbas Zadeh, Yoosef, and Sherko Kirmanji. 2017. The Para-Diplomacy of the Kurdish Region and the Kurdish Statehood Enterprise. *Middle East Journal* 71: 587–606.

Abdollahi, Mehdi. 2021. 70 Darsad-e Mashaghel-e Ostanhay-e Marzi Ghayr-e Rasmi Ast. *Farhikhtegan*. https://farhikhtegandaily.com/news/62867/. Accessed 2 Nov 2021.

Akbarzadeh, Shahram, Costas Laoutides, William Gourlay, and Zahid Shahab Ahmed. 2020. The Iranian Kurds' Transnational Links: Impacts on Mobilization and Political Ambitions. *Ethnic and Racial Studies* 43: 2275–2294.

Al-Marashi, Ibrahim. 2016. The Kurdish Referendum and Barzani's political survival. *Al Jazeera*, February 4. https://www.aljazeera.com/opinions/2016/2/4/the-kurdish-referendum-and-barzanis-political-survival. Accessed 4 Feb 2016.

Alvarez, Mariano. 2020. The Rise of Paradiplomacy in International Relations. *E-International Relations*, March 17. https://www.e-ir.info/2020/03/17/the-rise-of-paradiplomacy-in-international-relations/. Accessed 17 Mar 2020.

Bozorgmehr, Najmieh. 2014. Border Town in Iranian Kurdistan Booms Through Trade with Iraq. *Financial Times.* https://www.ft.com/content/5da88646-7a45-11e4-8958-00144feabdc0. Accessed 18 Dec 2014.

Caspersen, Nina. 2012. *Unrecognized States: The Struggle for Sovereignty in the Modern International System.* Cambridge: Polity Press.

Entessar, Nader. 1996. Kurdish Conflict in a Regional Perspective. In *Change and Continuity in the Middle East: Conflict Resolution and Prospects for Peace,* ed. M.E. Ahrari, 47–53. New York: St. Martin's Press.

———. 2010. *Kurdish Politics in the Middle East.* Lanham: Lexington Books.

———. 2014. The Kurds in Iran: The Quest for Identity. In *Kurdish Awakening: Nation Building in a Fragmented Homeland,* ed. Ofra Bengio, 233–251. Austin: University of Texas Press.

Financial Tribune. 2019. Iran Ready to Export Natural Gas to Iraqi Kurdistan. February 20. https://financialtribune.com/articles/energy/96788/iran-ready-to-export-natural-gas-to-iraqi-kurdistan. Accessed 20 Feb 2019.

Galbraith, Peter W. 2006. *The End of Iraq: How American Incompetence Created a War Without End.* New York: Simon and Schuster.

———. 2008. *Unintended Consequences: How the Iraq War Hurt America and Helped Its Enemies.* New York: Simon and Schuster.

Ghajar, Aida, and Shahed Alavi. 2017. How ISIS Infiltrated Iranian Kurdistan. *IranWire,* June https://iranwire.com/en/features/4660. Accessed 13 June 2017.

Hassaniyan, Allan. 2021. *Kurdish Politics in Iran: Crossborder Interactions and Mobilisation since 1947.* Cambridge: Cambridge University Press.

Hersh, Seymour M. 2004. Plan B. *The New Yorker,* June 20. https://www.newyorker.com/magazine/2004/06/28/plan-b-2. Accessed 20 June 2004.

Iddon, Paul. 2016. Barzani, Kurdish Independence and the End of Sykes-Picot. *Rudaw,* January 3. https://www.rudaw.net/english/opinion/03012016. Accessed 3 Jan 2016.

IFP Editorial Staff. 2020. Erbil Owes Existence to Gen. Soleimani, KRG Ex-President Tells Why. *Iran Front Page,* January 7. https://ifpnews.com/erbil-owes-existence-to-gen-soleimani-krg-ex-president-tells-why/. Accessed 7 Jan 2020.

King, Diane E. 2019. Borders as Ethnically Charged Sites: Iraqi Kurdistan Border Crossings, 1995–2006. *Urban Anthropology and Studies of Cultural Systems and World Economic Development* 48: 51–83.

Kuznetsov, Alexander. 2020. *Theory and Practice of Paradiplomacy: Subnational Governments in International Affairs.* New York: Rutledge.

Langanger, Simone. 2015. Kurdish Political Parties in Iran. In *The Kurds: History-Religion-Language-Politics,* ed. Wolfgang Taucher, Mathias Vogl, and Peter Webinger, 162–183. Vienna: Austrian Federal Ministry of Interior.

Malas, Nour. 2014. Iranians, U.S. Aid Kurdish Fighters. *Wall Street Journal.* August 14.

Mehr News Agency. 2021. IGRC attacks terrorist bases in Iraqi Kurdistan with drones. September 9. https://en.mehrnews.com/news/178435/IRGC-attacks-terrorist-bases-in-Iraq-Kurdistan-with-drones. Accessed 9 Sept 2021.

Ministry of Foreign Affairs, Islamic Republic of Iran. 2021. *Sulymaniyah Iraqi Kurdistan.* https://economic.mfa.ir/portal/newsview/648962. Accessed 23 Aug 2021.

Natali, Denise. 2014. Turkey's Kurdish Client State. *Al-Monitor,* November 14. https://www.al-monitor.com/originals/2014/11/turkey-krg-client-state.html. Accessed 14 Nov 2014.

Newsweek Staff. 2007. Trouble on the Iran-Iraq Border. *Newsweek,* September 12. https://www.newsweek.com/trouble-iran-iraq-border-100825. Accessed 12 Sept 2007.

Nour News. 2021. Daesh va Anche dar Eghlim-e Kurdistan-e Iraq Migozarad. https://nournews.ir/n/81740. Accessed 7 Dec 2021.

Olson, Robert. 2004. *Turkey-Iran Relations, 1979–2004: Revolution, Ideology, War, Coups and Geopolitics.* Costa Mesa: Mazda Publishers.

———. 2006. Relations among Turkey, Iraq, Kurdistan-Iraq, the Wider Middle East, and Iran. *Mediterranean Quarterly* 17: 15–33.

Perry, Mark. 2012. False Flag. *Foreign Policy,* January 13. https://foreignpolicy.com/2012/01/13/false-flag/. Accessed 13 Jan 2021.

Ritter, Scott. 2006. *Target Iran: The Truth About the White House's Plans for Regime Change.* New York: Nation Books.

Romano, David. 2015. Iraqi Kurdistan and Turkey: Temporary Marriage? *Middle East Policy* 22 (1): 89–101.

Salahaddin University-Erbil. 2018. Iranian Universities Exhibition in Kurdistan Region Is Underway. https://su.edu.krd/news/iranian-universities-exhibition-kurdistan-region-underway. Accessed 27 Dec 2018.

Serdaroglu, Ozan. 2015. The Turkish-Kurdish Energy Deal Could Pave Way for Iraq's Breakup. *Middle East Eye,* September 3. https://www.middleeasteye.net/opinion/turkish-kurdish-energy-deal-could-pave-way-iraqs-breakup. Accessed 3 Sept 2015.

Sheppard, David, John Reed, and Anjli Raval. 2015. Israel Turns to Kurds for Three-Quarters of Its Oil Supplies. *Financial Times.* https://www.ft.com/content/150f00cc-472c-11e5-af2f-4d6e0e5eda22. Accessed 23 Aug 2015.

Takeyh, Ray. 2006. *Hidden Iran: paradox and power in the Islamic Republic.* New York: Times Books.

Tasnim News Agency. 2021a. IRGC Warns of Harsh Strike on Terrorists in Northern Iraq. September 6. https://www.tasnimnews.com/en/news/2021/09/06/2567036/irgc-warns-of-harsh-strike-on-terrorists-in-northern-iraq. Accessed 6 Sept 2021.

———. 2021b. KRG-Based Terrorists Must Be Disarmed, Evicted from Iraq: Iranian Official. September 13. https://www.tasnimnews.com/en/news/2021/09/13/2570655/krg-based-terrorists-must-be-disarmed-evicted-from-iraq-iranian-official. Accessed 13 Sept 2021.

Tehran Times. 2021. Iraqi Kurdistan's Inaction Over Kurdish Militants Angers Iran. September 7. https://www.tehrantimes.com/news/464824/Iraqi-Kurdistans-inaction-over-Kurdish-militants-angers-Iran. Accessed 7 Sept 2021.

The Cradle. 2021. Exclusive: Resistance Axis Killed Two US and Israeli Operatives Involved in Soleimani/Muhandes Assassinations. September 20. https://thecradle.co/Article/news/2066. Accessed 20 Sept 2021.

The Guardian. 2014. Iraq: Kurdish President Proposes Independence Referendum. July 3. https://www.theguardian.com/world/2014/jul/03/iraq-kurdish-president-barzani-proposes-independence-referendum. Accessed 3 July 2014.

Vatan-e Emrooz. 2017. Ettehad-e Shoom dar Erbil. *Vatan-e Emrooz*, June 13.

Vatanka, Alex. 2014. Why Iran Fears an Independent Kurdistan. *The National Interest*, July 25. https://nationalinterest.org/feature/why-iran-fears-independent-kurdistan-10950. Accessed 25 July 2014.

Watson, Ivan. 2007. Tensions Mount Between Iraqi Kurdistan, Iran. *National Public Radio*, December 27. https://www.npr.org/templates/story/story.php?storyId=14781988. Accessed 27 Sept 2007.

Yildiz, Kerim, and Tanyel B. Taysi. 2007. *The Kurds in Iran: The Past, Present and Future.* London: Pluto Press.

Zaman, Amberin. 2015. Masrour Barzani: Kurdish Independence Would Help Defeat IS. *Al-Monitor*, July 1. https://www.al-monitor.com/originals/2015/07/turkey-iraq-syria-kurdish-independence-help-war-against-isis.html. Accessed 1 July 2015.

CHAPTER 14

Palestine and Iran

Seyed Ali Alavi

BACKGROUND

On February 17, 1979, the leader of the PLO, Yasser Arafat was the first foreign leader to visit Tehran post-revolution. During his visit Arafat made an emotional speech which emphasised two significant principles; first, the existence of a historical solidarity between anti-imperialist movements within the Global South; second, that Islam has become a vehicle of motivation for the emancipation of masses in the region (Alavi 2019, 48–50). Arafat's visit was a turning point in the politics of the region as it became the cornerstone of the PLO's relations with Iran. At this stage it is essential to provide a context on how the PLO devised its ties with the Iranian opposition groups during the pre-revolutionary era.

S. A. Alavi (✉)
School of Languages, Cultures and Linguistics, SOAS, University of London, London, UK
e-mail: sa137@soas.ac.uk

© The Author(s), under exclusive license to Springer Nature Switzerland AG 2023
G. Gürbey et al. (eds.), *Between Diplomacy and Non-Diplomacy*, https://doi.org/10.1007/978-3-031-09756-0_14

The Palestinian Cause: A Stimulus for the Iranian Anti-Shah Oppositions Throughout the 1960s–1970s

The connections between the PLO and the Iranian guerrilla movements date back to the 1960s and 1970s. Of the emerging Iranian leftist guerrilla groups, two groups surfaced as particularly organised: the *Sazmane Cherik-ha-ye Faday'an Khalq-e Iran* (The Guerrilla Freedom Fighters of the Iranian People), known as the Marxist *Faday'an*; and the *Sazman-e Mojahedin-e Khalq-e Iran* (The People's Mojahedin Organisation), generally referred to as the *Mojahedin* also known as MKO (Abrahamian 1980). In the early 1970s prominent members of *Faday'an* and the *Mojahedin-e Khalq* were routinely trained by the PLO in the Palestinian camps in Syria and Lebanon (Chehabi 2006, 185). Ties between the PLO and the MKO's leadership have consequently endured and to this day, both sides enjoy the political connections (Alavi 2019).

Iran's Pre-Revolutionary Islamists and the Palestinian Cause

Before investigating relations between pre-revolutionary Islamic figures and the question of Palestine, I intend to show how some of the Islamic revolutionaries interpreted and navigated the Palestinian cause within their discourse. Shortly after the establishment of the state of Israel in 1948, Ayatollah Kashani (a popular Shiite cleric) became one of the first clerics in the Muslim world to denounce the state of Israel and voice his support for the Palestinians (Alavi 2019). During the 1960s and 1970s, other prominent Shiite clerics, such as Ayatollah Taleqani and Ayatollah Mutahari, increasingly focused their attention on the Palestinian cause, voicing their support in both public and private meetings and raising religious taxes to help the Palestinian refugees in the Arab world. Ayatollah Mutahari particularly emphasised the moral obligations of the Shiite Muslims to provide aid to oppressed people of Palestine (Alavi 2019). In Iran it was not only the clerics that opposed the state of Israel. Non-clerical religious and revolutionary figures (including Ali Shariati and Jalal Al-e-Ahmad) strongly shared such revolutionary commitments. Ali Shariati is best known as an advocate of Third World movements in their battle against imperialism, arguing that Western imperialism and Zionism had formed a "united front" against Muslims (Alavi 2019). Attending a memorial service for Ali Shariati in the summer 1977, Yasser Arafat gave an emotional speech in Shariati's honour in Damascus (Chehabi 2006, 196).

A discussion of the roots and development of support for the Palestinian cause in Iran during the pre-revolutionary era is incomplete without mentioning Ayatollah Khomeini. Khomeini rose to prominence in 1963 when he publicly denounced the Shah's regime for its connections to Israel and the West. At the outset of his political career, Ayatollah Khomeini placed great importance on the Palestinian cause and conspicuously addressed the topic within his public pronouncements. For Ayatollah Khomeini, the Palestinian question transcends national borders, and is thus relevant to every individual Muslim. The pro-Palestinian ideas of Iranian-Islamic groups and prominent religious figures before the revolution manifest faith and religious ideologies that necessitate supporting the oppressed nation of Palestine and resisting against the Israeli occupation (Alavi 2019, 35).

PLO and Iran 1979–1998: From Revolutionary Brotherhood to Ideological Estrangement Given the serial wars that have occurred between Israel and the Arab states, the 1960s and 1970s were tragic and despondent decades for the Palestinian guerrillas. There have been four Arab-Israeli wars involving the surrounding states: in 1948 at the birth of Israel, in 1956 over the Suez Canal; in 1967, the so called Six-Day War; and in 1973, the so-called Yom Kippur War. In the first and third of these, Israel gained many territories from the Arab front (Chan 2017, 49–50). On the broader political level, the PLO suffered serious setbacks in 1978, principally through the conclusion of 1978 Camp David treaty between Egypt, Israel and the United States (U.S.). Against this background, the demise of the pro-Western regime of the Shah, perceived by the PLO as the citadel of America in the region, evoked a new dawn of hope for the Palestinians (Cobban 1984).

The victory of the Iranian revolution caused much rejoicing in Palestinian ranks, who had close links to the Iranian revolutionaries newly in power. The Palestinian guerrillas had long enjoyed a close relationship with revolutionary factions in Iran. The Palestinian controlled areas in and around the refugee camps in Lebanon blossomed with huge posters of the Iranian leader Ayatollah Khomeini, many adorned with the slogan "Today Iran, Tomorrow Palestine" (Cobban 1984, 104). During the first few years of the revolution, Iran's regional policy can be understood as particularly pro-PLO. This was most notable during the Israel-Palestinian conflict, as Iran adopted a tangible pro-PLO stance, based on the ideological outlook of the newly established leadership in Tehran. Shortly after the demise of the Pahlavi's dynasty, the revolutionary establishment embarked on a series of diplomatic initiatives to support likeminded movements within the Global South, simultaneously denouncing the state of Israel and "imperialism".

The goodwill between Arafat and Ayatollah Khomeini that was generated by these ideas, however, was largely undone by the events of the Hostage Crisis in 1979 and Iran-Iraq war in 1980. During his first visit (1979) Arafat had been greeted warmly by the revolutionaries in Iran as a national hero. He received the keys to the Israeli diplomatic mission in Tehran and symbolically, Iranian revolutionaries raised the Palestinian flag in the premises that still serve as the Palestinian embassy today, with PLO representatives. It was a significant achievement for the PLO leadership as it occurred at the time that Egypt had left the anti-Israeli campaign and signed the deal in Camp David (Alavi 2019).

The triumph of Islamic revolution became a source of inspiration for the PLO's leadership: if Ayatollah Khomeini could rise from obscurity and exile to conquer a seemingly invincible foe allied to and installed by the U.S., Arafat believed he could follow the same path. In a similar vein, simply handing the keys of the former Israeli embassy in Tehran to the PLO delegation gave a significant boost to Palestinian morale: "after more than two decades of struggle, this was the first piece of Israeli real estate Arafat had captured" (Alavi 2019, 51–52).

However, the optimism elicited by the developments in Iran did not last long for the leadership of the PLO. Two major consequent events profoundly impacted the relations between the Islamic Republic and the PLO's leadership. The first major crack occurred during the American Hostage Crisis in Tehran in November 1979. The Embassy's takeover triggered an international crisis that lasted for 444 days. At that critical moment for the White House, the PLO leadership communicated with U.S. officials expressing their desire to mediate between Tehran and Washington in order to help free the hostages. After obtaining endorsements from the White House, a three-man high-level PLO delegation arrived in Tehran to discuss the hostage crisis with Iranian officials. Despite the visit by senior PLO members to the U.S. Embassy in Tehran, they failed to convince the hostage-takers to allow them to enter the compound.

Almost as soon as the PLO's efforts at mediation begun, they backfired. Ayatollah Khomeini refused to receive the PLO's special delegate Abu-Walid, and the militant students denounced the PLO's mediation attempts (Ioannides 1989, 84). Arafat's mediation attempts not only infuriated the Iranians, they also caused dissonance within the PLO. Several PLO's internal bodies—including the Popular Front for the Liberation of Palestine (PFLP), the Sai'qa, the Democratic Front for the Liberation of Palestine (DFLP), and even Arafat's own Fatah—announced solidarity with Iran and backed the embassy's takeover (Alavi 2019, 61). Arafat appeared to the Iranians as acting on behalf of the American government against the interests of Ayatollah Khomeini, and ultimately a revolution that undermined U.S. and Israeli interests in the region.

After the failure of Arafat to secure the release of the American hostages, the PLO's leadership abandoned its pursuit of mediation. It is vital to understand the rationale behind Arafat's initiative. On the one hand, the PLO's leadership attempted to obtain credit from Washington and to improve its image among the Western powers. If successful, this would allow Arafat to play a role in future initiatives and negotiations orchestrated by the White House, such as the Camp David. The PLO's approach to the American hostage crisis demonstrated that its leadership underestimated the significance of religious and revolutionary ideologies as motivating factors in Iran's pro-Palestinian stance. Equally, the leadership of the Islamic revolution appeared unwilling to appreciate the reasoning behind Arafat's mediation attempts. In other words, regardless of the logic behind the PLO's mediation efforts, this episode created an ideological gap between the two sides (Alavi 2019, 62).

The second decisive event that underlined the ideological and strategic cracks between Arafat and the Islamic Republic was the Iran-Iraq war (1980–1988). In July 1979, Saddam Hussein gained full control of the Ba'ath party in Baghdad and executed pro-Syrian Ba'athists. Any hope the Palestinian leaders entertained for building an eastern front (Syria-Iraq-Jordan) against Israel were thereby dashed (Cobban 1984). In late September 1980, Hussein launched a full-scale military operation inside Iranian borders, invading Iranian towns and villages. The devastating war would last for eight years. These events significantly impacted the PLO's politburo. The Iraqi invasion of Iran caused new clashes between pro-Iraqi and pro-Iranian PLO factions in Beirut and therefore weakened the PLO's positions in Lebanon (Chehabi 2006; Cobban 1984). Almost immediately, Arafat identified the distressing impacts of the Iran-Iraq war on the 'anti-Israeli front', and the possible downgrading of the Palestinian cause to second place in the region. Subsequently, the leadership of the PLO rushed to mediate between the two sides. Shortly after the Iraqi invasion of Iranian border towns, Arafat visited Tehran and Baghdad several times and attempted to persuade both sides to agree on a ceasefire and to negotiate. However, Arafat's mediation efforts recoiled with the Islamic Republic's leadership losing even greater confidence in the intentions of Arafat.

The leadership of the PLO found itself facing a bitter choice between Tehran on the one hand, and Baghdad and its Arab conservative allies on the other. Yasser Arafat made a *volte-face* regarding the PLO's position towards the Iran-Iraq war. From a pro-revolutionary position, Arafat gradually moved towards a distinct pro-Saddam stance. The pro-Iraqi PLO leadership was looking for legitimacy with the majority of Arab conservative states and wanted to present itself as a reliable pan-Arab nationalist movement. Moreover, Arafat aimed to solidify his legitimacy within the PLO cadres as the "true" vanguard of the secular pan-Arab ideas. Finally, in April 1984, Arafat publicly stressed the PLO's support for Iraq in its "just" struggle to "defend" its land and sovereignty and achieve a "just peace" (Alavi 2019, 66). It is necessary to now consider two key factors in what happened: the roots of the PLO's shift from favouring Iran to favouring Iraq, and the reasons that the Islamic Republic rejected mediation efforts and the proposed 'ceasefire'. I suggest that ideology was pivotal in Iran's denunciation of mediation attempts. Equally, Arafat's pivot away from Iran towards Ba'athist Iraq had its roots in pan-Arabism. While Arafat was attempting to mediate between Iran and Iraq, he continued to maintain cordial relations with the leadership of the Mujahedin-e-Khalq Organization (MKO), the main anti-Khomeini opposition group (Chehabi 2006, 209), which further strained relationships with Tehran. We can thus interpret Arafat's diplomacies towards Iran against this conceptual landscape.

The Oslo Accord: A Divided Palestinian Front

A few months after the end of the Iran-Iraq war (1988), Arafat delivered a reconciliatory speech at the United Nations (UN) General assembly and at a press conference in Geneva, explicitly recognising Israel's right to exist and denouncing all forms of terrorism. Simultaneously the First Intifada (1987–1988) had been launched at the initiative of the Palestinians in West Bank and Gaza and not the leadership of the PLO. The PLO lost further credibility in the eyes of local Palestinians upon entering into negotiations with the U.S. in 1988. Finally, the PLO's diplomatic and financial position perceptibly weakened when Arafat embraced Saddam's invasion of Kuwait. His policy estranged the pro-Western Arab Sheikhdoms.

With the end of the Cold War and the following collapse of the Soviet Union, the PLO had no alternative source of support. Against this backdrop, Arafat actively displayed his interest in entering negotiations with Israel (Hassan 2011, 66). At the same time the 1991–1992 Persian Gulf war and the collapse of the Soviet bloc fundamentally altered the geopolitics of the Middle East as the U.S. emerged as the so-called sole superpower. This change encouraged Washington to try to reshape Middle Eastern politics through fostering better relations between the Arab states and Israel. The Arab states and PLO were required to go along with Washington's new unipolar system, to attend the Madrid conference in 1991 and to sign the Oslo Accord in 1993. Subsequently, the PLO altered its charter and dropped the objective of destroying the Jewish state (Hunter 2019, 59).

In contrast, the Islamic Republic of Iran strongly denounced the U.S.-led new world order and remained the core voice of anti-Israeli and anti-American campaigns in the region. The recognition of Israel by Arafat was a turning point in PLO's relations with Iran. According to Takeyh (2009, 173) Oslo hit Tehran like a thunderbolt. Iran's inflammatory attacks became even sharper as Ayatollah Khamenei castigated Arafat as "that puny ill-reputed blackguard" whose crime was greater than Anwar Saddat's acceptance of Camp David (Takeyh 2009, 174). The recognition of Israel by Arafat through the Oslo Accord plunged PLO's ties with Iran into a new ice age. This shift revealed the huge divergence between PLO and Iran in thought, aims and interests. Tehran thus turned towards the Palestinian Islamic Movements as organic allies against Israel. Nevertheless, Ramallah and Tehran did not sever their communications during the post–Oslo Accord era and the Palestinian embassy in Tehran remained as PLO's political office. In December 1997, Yasser Arafat was invited by the Islamic Republic to attend the eighth summit of the Organisation of Islamic Conference in Tehran. Arafat met with the Iranian president Khatami and delivered a speech at the conference. Asked whether ties with Iran were improving, Arafat told reporters, "We hope so, we hope there will be a new page between us and our brothers in Iran" (Fouad 1998).

The Rise of Palestinian Islamic Movements; Palestinian Islamic Jihad and Iran: A Quest for a Theological Chemistry

Neither the PLO nor the state of Israel had been able to prevent the rise of the Palestinian Islamic Movements. The emergence of the Palestinian Islamic Movements and their ideologies is a compelling subject, particularly given their role in the Palestinian political terrain since early the 1980s. In February 1979, the inspirational waves of the Islamic Revolution in Iran reached the shores of Gaza. Fathi al-Shiqaqi, a Palestinian activist living in exile in Egypt, was influenced by the idea of the Islamic Revolution in Iran. Frustrated with the failure of the Arab nationalist front during the Six-Day War in 1967 and the impassivity of the Muslim Brotherhood towards the Palestinian cause, Al-Shiqaqi authored a book praising Khomeini's ideology of political Islam (Alavi 2019).

Soon after publishing his book *Khomeini, the Islamic Solution and Alternatives* in 1979, Al-Shiqaqi was arrested in Egypt and expelled from the Muslim Brotherhood. Al-Shiqaqi was inspired not only by Khomeini's Islamic ideas but also by the Revolutionary resistance against its well-equipped adversaries (Alavi 2019, 95). In 1981, Al-Shiqaqi and his comrades established *Saraya al-Quds* (al-Quds brigade) which would become Islamic Jihad military wings. Subsequently the Palestinian Islamic Jihad (PIJ) emerged as a product of the Six-Day war and the Islamic Revolution in Iran. According to Skare (2021, 38) the centrality of Palestine and the struggle for its liberation holds a historical and Qur'anic dimension for PIJ's founding fathers. The Qur'anic dimension contains the religious aspects of the cause; we shall overview this now. Shortly after the triumph of the revolution, Ayatollah Khomeini declared the last Friday of Ramadan as *Yom al-Quds* (The day of Jerusalem), calling on all Muslims to demonstrate solidarity with Palestine (Alavi 2019). In other words, the leadership of the Revolution in Iran began the process of the "Islamisation" of the Palestinian cause, aiming to situate the question beyond its Arab-Israeli context. The PIJ founding fathers appreciated that despite the geographical distance, Khomeini treated the Palestinian cause as an internal problem (Alavi 2019, 94), especially during the Iran-Iraq war. Unlike the PLO that later sided with Saddam's Iraq, Al-Shiqaqi described the isolation of Iran as the "war against Islam" (Skare 2021, 41).

As Al-Shiqaqi and the other members of PIJ aspired to liberate Palestine, this support necessarily affected and inspired them, as the success of the revolution did (Skare 2021, 53). Against this backdrop, December 1987 stands out as a turning point in the Palestinian socio-political terrain. Palestinian frustration boiled into action and the first popular uprising known as Intifada erupted throughout the occupied lands following the killing of four PIJ members by the Israeli armed forces (Alavi 2019).

Following the outburst of the Intifada, Islamic Jihad's key figures were either jailed or involuntarily exiled to Lebanon in 1988. The expulsion of Islamic Jihad's leadership created a new momentum for its leadership to become closer with the Islamic Republic of Iran and Hezbollah. Hatina (2001, 41) argues that with the move to Lebanon and Syria, the ideological link of the Islamic Jihad to Iran as a revolutionary model was further translated into a close political and organisational tie. Soon after moving to Lebanon and Syria, PIJ opened its diplomatic office in Tehran. Since then, PIJ's delegates actively attend political events in Iran, particularly during the annual conferences in Tehran on Palestine.

According to Skare (2021, 107) the exile and subsequent alliances provided the possibility for PIJ militants to participate in the training camps of Hezbollah in Lebanon. This new opportunity and the corresponding coordination of Al-Shiqaqi manifested in close-knit alliances resulting in economic aid and weapons from Iran, sanctuary in Syria, and training camps provided by Hezbollah (Skare 2021, 109). In terms of alliance building and aid, PIJ managed to exploit the exile. After the assassination of al-Shiqaqi in October 1995, his successors, Ramadan Shallah and Ziad al-Nakhala, crafted their Iran policy with similar bravado.

Hamas and the Islamic Republic of Iran: A Strategic Enquiry

We turn now to Hamas and what might be called the "Islamisation" of the Palestinian governance. In examining the Palestinian movements, Skare (2021, 144–145) observes that several years before Hamas, the PIJ engaged with armed struggle against Israel and had created a social base in the Occupied Palestinian Territories. Inspired by the Islamic revolution in Iran, PIJ appropriated the discourse of resistance and imbued it with Islamic rather than nationalist or secularist values to distinguish it from other forms of resistance. One of the most important outcomes of this process of "Islamisation" was the formation of the Islamic Resistance Movement, known in Arabic as *Harakat al-Muqawama al-Islamiya*:

Hamas. The emergence of Islamic Palestinian factions further encouraged the Iranian leadership to deepen its pro-Palestinian stance. The Islamic Republic viewed Palestinian Islamic factions as closer ideologically than the PLO (Alavi 2019). Israel and Iran have been at loggerheads since the revolution in 1979. The Islamic Republic views the state of Israel as its ideological and strategic adversary and therefore welcomes Palestinian movements that reject the concept of the occupation. In 1992, Hamas published a pamphlet entitled the "Holiness of Palestine" which replicated Ayatollah Khomeini's contention that Palestine is holy to all Muslims (Seliktar and Rezaei 2020, 63). Hamas categorically refuses to recognise the state of Israel and established its military wing, *Ezza-din Qassam* Brigades, to launch military operations against the Israeli army throughout the occupied lands. This approach towards the Palestinian cause became the main source of intimacy between Iran and Hamas.

Since the First Intifada in 1987, Iran diverted its attention towards the Palestinian "rejectionist" movements. Tehran soon established political relations with Hamas, only to be followed by the Oslo Accords between the PLO and Israel in 1993. Despite the propaganda from the PLO favouring the Oslo Accords, most Palestinians were frustrated by the PLO's recognition of Israel's occupation and turned instead towards Hamas and Islamic Jihad. After 1993, Hamas continued its strong electoral showing—beating Fatah in al-Najah student elections in 1996 and again in 1997. In April 1998, Sheikh Ahmad Yassin, Hamas' spiritual leader made a state visit to the Islamic Republic of Iran and was warmly received by its leadership (Alavi 2019).

The year 2000 was a turning point in the regional history. After two decades—in compliance with United Nations Security Council (UNSC) Resolution 425—the Israeli army pulled its troops from south Lebanon and dismantled its militias. Some have attributed Israel's defeat in south Lebanon to Iranian and Syrian support for Hezbollah. According to Khatib and Matar (2014, 73), the liberation of southern Lebanon on May 25, 2000 was a watershed. It was the first time that Israeli troops had been expelled from Arab lands "at the hands of an Arab paramilitary group" since 1948, when the state of Israel was formed (Khatib and Matar 2014, 73). Hezbollah's victory emboldened its Palestinian allies of Hamas and PIJ to intensify their activities and further cement their ties with Iran. Shortly after Hezbollah's triumph in south Lebanon, Israeli provocations kindled a second Palestinian uprising throughout the occupied territories. On September 28, 2000, Ariel Sharon's unwelcome visit to *Haram al-Sharif*—Islam's third holiest site—under heavy security protection by Israeli armed force triggered the Second Intifada and unified the Palestinians as never before.

The peace negotiations proved to be less fruitful than many Palestinians hoped, as the Israeli government failed to comply with the commitments it made within the interim peace accords (such as withdrawing from the occupied territories and not expanding the settlements in the West Bank). Shortly after the Second Intifada began, Iran and Hezbollah exhibited solidarity with the *al-Aqsa* Intifada. Some wounded Palestinians were treated in hospitals in Iran and in April 2001, Ramadan Shallah, the leader of PIJ, visited Ayatollah Khamenei, who agreed to increase the organisation's funding by some 70 percent. Iranian financial support was not limited to the Palestinian Islamic movements, as some funding supported PLO affiliates. For instance, Iran funded the *Tala'e Al-Jayish al Shaabi Kataeb Al Awdah*, The Pioneers of the Popular Army-Return Brigade (Seliktar and Rezaei 2020, 71). In a message to President Khatami in June 2001, Yasser Arafat called on the Islamic Republic to come to the Palestinians' aid. In his message, Arafat stated, "We look to all the people of the Islamic world, foremost among them the Muslim Iranian people and their faithful leadership, to support, aid and assist Palestine" (Tehran Times 2001). Seliktar and Rezaei (2020, 72) claim that Arafat worked out an agreement with the Iranians and subsequently PLO's chief procurement officer, Adel Moughrabi, in October 2000, brought the *Katrina A*, a vessel which allegedly carried Iranian weapons for the Palestinian Authority (PA).

In August 2005 Israel withdrew its armed forces from Gaza. After 38 years, the occupation of Gaza had ended. Led by Hamas, the people of Gaza celebrated and attributed the victory to the defeat of Israel's superior military might. Tamimi (2009, 206–207) argues that the failure of repeated peace negotiations—whether the Oslo Accords, Bush's Road Map or Sharon's disengagement policy—vindicated Hamas' approach. On January 26, 2006 Hamas gained a landslide victory in Gaza's legislative elections. The 2006 elections became a rocky road for the PA. Rejecting the perceived corruption of the secular Fatah organisation, Palestinians gave Hamas a reverberating triumph. The outcome of the election was not what the White House was hoping for. Instead of acknowledging the outcomes and endorsing the Palestinian democratic process it had promoted, the Bush administration hurriedly called for an embargo on Hamas and stopped all funding to its government. Ostovar (2016, 170) is well founded when he argues that the vacuum created by its abandonment of financial support for the Hamas-led administration opened the way for Iran to step in. Sustained by a precipitous increase in oil prices, Iran was able to become the leading financial supporter of the Hamas-led government. Also, through its sponsorship of Hamas, Iran obtained another client able to influence the Israeli-Palestinian issue.

Palestinian Movements and Iran in Post–Arab Spring Era: Turbulent Moments

The political locus of Hamas altered according to the shifting opportunities in the regional political atmosphere. With the deviations that occurred at the regional level, characterised by the rise of the Muslim Brotherhood in Egypt and Tunisia, Hamas contemplated these conversions as a triumph and provision for its own status. Subsequently Hamas' political leadership changed its approach towards the "axis of resistance". It left Syria (which embraced, supported and trained its military wing) in order to join the Muslim Brotherhood alliance, represented by tripartite of Egypt, Turkey and Qatar, under pressure from the Global Muslim Brotherhood and the leadership of Hamas abroad (Salah 2017).

The Islamic Republic and its allies were caught off guard when Hamas moved its offices from Syria and endorsed the anti-Assad forces. Nevertheless, the Islamic Republic's authorities avoided any direct criticism of Hamas and maintained the channels of communication (Alavi 2019). This is understandable when we consider that the political leadership of Iran was aware of the central role that Hamas played in Gaza and its anti-Israeli policies, and maintained its commitment to the Palestinian cause. Nevertheless, during the early stages of the Arab Spring, Hamas prioritised its common theological ground with the international Muslim Brotherhood over its anti-Israeli stance with Iran, Syria and Hezbollah.

It soon became clear that Hamas lost its bet on the collapse of the Assad regime. Instead, in July 2013, Morsi's Muslim Brotherhood was toppled and replaced with a government dominated by the military. Hereafter, General Fatah al-Sisi, the new head of government in Cairo, pressurised Hamas by isolating it economically and politically to purge the country of the Muslim Brotherhood (Alavi 2019). Syria severed its ties with Hamas and Iran reduced its financial support. According to Salah (2017) Hamas faced a risky gorge; it could not return to the "axis of resistance" in the absence of trust that followed its attitude change on regional and internal levels. The internal leadership and the military wing were ashamed of the movement's political move, which let down those who had embraced it when everyone else had abandoned it (Salah 2017, 571). In October 2013, the deputy chief of Hamas Musa Abu-Marzouk stated that "Khaled Mesha'al was wrong to have raised the flag of the Syrian revolution on his historic return to Gaza at the end of last year" (Alavi 2019, 141). Subsequently, Iran refused to receive Khaled Mesha'al for his role in moving away from the "axis of resistance". Simultaneously the Hamas military wing, *Ezzadin al-Qassam* Brigade, and Iran maintained ties. Israel's wars on Gaza in 2012 and 2014 marked a turning point in Hamas' relations with Iran and created a reconciliatory environment for both sides.

In both November 2012 and July 2014, Gaza was heavily bombarded by the Israeli defence forces, and intensive military campaigns ensued. Israel's aim was to eliminate the Palestinian Islamic movement's firepower. Nonetheless, repairing relations with Hamas seemed imperative for Iran in order to guarantee the balance of power against Tel Aviv. Overall, after its support of the Syrian regime, the Islamic Republic estranged many Sunni Arabs that perceived Tehran regional policies as "belligerent sectarian-driven gestures". Rapprochement with Hamas could enhance Iran's regional status beyond the sectarian dichotomy within the Sunni world. Meanwhile Hamas faced some regional challenges that limited its relationship with Iran. On a number of occasions, the Egyptian government prevented Hamas officials from travelling to Iran through Cairo. Egypt desires to keep Gaza as its exclusive diplomatic file (Abu Amer 2018). Despite all these challenges, Hamas seemed determined to mend relations with its traditional ally, Iran.

In November 2012, as Iranian-manufactured rockets were fired out of Gaza, large billboards on three major road junctions in the Gaza Strip bore the message "Thank you Iran" in Arabic, English, Hebrew and Farsi. The posters also depicted the Iranian Fajr-5 rockets. It was the first time that there has been such public admission of Iran's role in the arming of the Islamic fighters in the territory (Alavi 2019, 139). Hamas sturdily confronted the Israeli military aggression and utilised all its tools to slow down the Israeli sophisticated war-machine. Over time, the idea that Hamas is still the major Palestinian power, capable and determined to resist against Israel, once again began to gain currency in Iran. The Palestinian resistance in Gaza received public support from various strata of the Iranian state, including the supreme leader, the Iranian Revolutionary

Guard Corps and the presidency. Both conservative and reformist factions within the Iranian parliament unanimously voiced their strong support for the people of Gaza (Alavi 2019).

On the other side of the Palestinian political domain, PIJ retained its stance within the "axis of resistance". Following the outbreak of the Syria crisis, PIJ's leadership declined to sever relations with Damascus and preserved its neutrality. In January 2012, Ramadan Abdullah Shallah and his entourage visited the Iranian supreme leader. During the meeting, Ayatollah Khamenei referred to the unfolding situation in Syria, stating: "Regarding Syria, if the developments are considered from a broad and comprehensive perspective, it becomes completely clear what plot America has designed for Syria and unfortunately certain countries inside and outside the region are cooperating with America in this plot" (Alavi 2019, 136). In fact, with the election of Shallah, PIJ began to terminate its contact with a number of non-state armed Islamic groups.

Skare (2021, 157) suggests that PIJ's policy of disconnecting with other jihadi movements in the region demonstrates that the movement became more rationally oriented as its formal connections were with its benefactors: Syria and Iran. In the words of Ramadan Shallah, PIJ adhered to a "principled pragmatism" in order to preserve the alliance of the movement in the Palestinian arena and the region (Skare 2021, 192). This is not to suggest that PIJ has little autonomy in formulating its policies and that it only follows its main benefactor, Iran. Conversely, in the case of Yemen, PIJ pursued an independent path from its traditional allies. As civil war broke out in Yemen, PIJ echoed its obstruction to intervene in the internal affairs of the region and refused to publicly support the Iranian backed Houthis. PIJ even attempted to diversify its fiscal networks beyond Iran, looking for alternative sources of financial support in Turkey and Algeria. This support, however, never exceeded what has been provided by Iran (Skare 2021, 195). Similarly, Hamas has been proactive in widening its regional networking beyond Iran since the beginning of the Arab Spring. In October 2012, Qatar's Emir became the first head of an Arab state to visit Gaza and since then Hamas enjoys close ties with Doha. In May 2021, Ismail Haniyeh thanked, during a visit he made to the Emir in Doha, Qatar and its people for their popular support for the Palestinian people (Hamas 2021). Commenting on Qatari Emir's donations to Gaza, Ismail Haniyeh stated, "We have received with high evaluation the decision of His Highness Sheikh Tamim bin Hamad al-Thani, the Emir of the state of Qatar, for offering $360 million in humanitarian aid to Gaza in 2021" (Qods International News Agency 2021).

Palestinian-Iranian ties during the Arab Spring era were not monopolised by the Palestinian Islamic Movements per se. Two years after the Syrian Crisis erupted, and despite historical and political disagreements, Mahmoud Abbas, the head of the PA met with the Iranian president on the sidelines of the Organization of Islamic Cooperation Summit in June 2013. Mahmoud Abbas publicly thanked President Ahmadinejad for Iran's support of the Palestinian bid for UN membership (Kais 2013). In an interview in 2014, PA's foreign minister Riyad al-Malki highlighted that the PA has normal relations with Iran and stated that "we have an embassy, and we have attended official meetings with Iranians outside the region" (Kuttab 2014). Having said that, the PA in West Bank anxiously navigates Iran's support towards its main political rival, Hamas. In a controversial gesture, Mahmoud Abbas met with the MKO's leader, Maryam Rajavi, in July 2016 in Paris. The Iranian government regards the MKO as a "terrorist organisation". The leadership of PLO aimed to send a signal of protest to Tehran in response to Iran's close relations with Hamas and PIJ. According to Houk (2016) between January 2014 and February 2016, Mahmoud Abbas sent three special envoys to Tehran, all tasked with trying to persuade Iran to stop its support for Hamas.

We now turn to the impacts of rivalry between Iran and Saudi Arabia in the region on the Palestinian political landscape, specifically on Palestinian relations with Iran. The main point to be made here is that the Palestinian factions are divided over the conflict between Iran and Saudi Arabia. This division has grown since the beginning of the Arab Spring era when the two regional powers became locked in a proxy battle for regional hegemony. In a meeting with the Saudi King Salman in November 2017, Mahmoud Abbas reiterated PA's support of Saudi Arabia against the Iranian-backed Houthis in Yemen and condemned the rocket attacks on Saudi soil. According to Abumaria (2017), Mahmoud Abbas was summoned to Riyadh in November 2017 as part of Saudi's leadership campaign to recruit Sunni Arab leaders to its side against Iran. Further, the Saudi leadership remained concerned over the prospect of the incorporation of Hamas into the Palestinian government and the ramifications of Hamas close relations with Iran. In October 2019, the Saudi Crown Prince Mohammed bin Salman and Mahmoud Abbas met in Riyadh and agreed to establish a joint Saudi-Palestinian economic committee. The PA's finance ministry records show that Saudi Arabia contributed

$132.8 million to the PA between January and August 2019 (Rasgon 2019). For the PA in West Bank, it is vital not to alienate Riyadh as its main regional benefactor and to maintain the balance of diplomatic relations within the region.

On the other side of the spectrum, Saudi Arabia has been increasingly pressurising Hamas. Saudi's leadership initiated an anti-Hamas campaign on its own territory. Since April 2019 dozens of Saudi citizens, Jordanians and Palestinians (including Hamas' representative in Saudi Arabia, Mohammed al-Khudari) have been arrested and accused of belonging to and supporting Hamas. According to Abu Amer (2019), since Hamas was formed in the 1980s, its leadership enjoyed good relations with Riyadh for years. Although Saudi authorities never directly funded Hamas, they allowed fundraising to take place on their territory. Nevertheless, Hamas and Saudi relations were outshined by the Egyptian military coup in 2013 which removed the Egyptian president Mohamed Morsi. Saudi support for the removal of the first democratically elected Egyptian president and Hamas' opposition strained their connection. Feeling increasingly isolated as a result of the Egyptian and Saudi pressure on Gaza, Hamas began to reach out to Iran. Azzam Tamimi (2021) argues that when King Salman ascended to the throne and his son, Mohammed bin Salman, became the kingdom's de facto ruler, things deteriorated for Hamas rapidly. It did not take long for Hamas to learn why: Mohammed bin Salman planned to make peace with Israel. Nevertheless, in hope that Iran-Saudi Arabia recent diplomacy will develop into more robust regional supports for the Palestinians, Hamas and PIJ call for "unity" between the regional rivals, Iran and Saudi Arabia. In a statement issued in May 2021, the Hamas spokesperson claimed, "We hope the talks [between Iran and Saudi Arabia] will succeed, and we expect that this would help stabilize Iran and the whole region, this for sure will help increasing solidarity with the Palestinians" (O'Connor 2021a).

ABRAHAM ACCORD, SHEIKH JARRAH INCIDENT AND THE WAR ON GAZA 2021: UNDERPINNING PALESTINIAN CONNECTIONS WITH IRAN

In January 2020, standing side by side with the Israeli Prime Minister, Donald Trump unveiled details of his vision for the Middle East peace. Trump's 181 pages of plan reversed decades of policy by refraining from endorsing the internationally backed two-state solution. It further recognised Jerusalem as Israel's capital, cut millions of dollars in aid to Palestinians and announced it no longer views Israeli settlements in occupied territory as "inconsistent with international law". Palestinian leaders were absent from the event, having pre-emptively rejected his proposal, citing flagrant bias (The Guardian 2020).

Subsequently the PA cut its ties with the Trump administration and Israel after rejecting the so-called Middle East peace plan. Mahmoud Abbas refused to discuss the plan with Trump by phone and asked for an emergency meeting with the Arab League. However, after Trump unveiled his plan, some Arab states including Bahrain and United Arab Emirates (UAE) appeared, despite historic support for the Palestinians, to prioritise close ties with the U.S. and a shared hostility towards Iran over traditional Arab alliances (France24 2020, 24). In response, Iranian foreign minister Javad Zarif contacted Mahmoud Abbas and Hamas leader Ismail Haniyeh to express opposition to the so-called U.S. deal of the century. He reiterated Iran's position backing the Palestinians, and its willingness to exert diplomatic and political effort to support them. As Abu Amer (2020) points out, Iran demonstrated great opposition to the U.S. deal. Before Zarif's contacts with Abbas and Haniyeh, Esmail Ghaani, who replaced Qassem Soleimani as chief of Iran's Quds Force, called Ismail Haniyeh and Ziad al-Nakhala, the leader of PIJ, to voice his rejection of the deal. Ghaani expressed Iran's readiness to work to thwart the deal. In contrast to some Arab regional powers that pursued silence, the Palestinian political elites received political support from Iran.

Like the creak of a sail-rig as a ship begins to turn, a sign of political rapprochement between some Arab states and Israel can prove decisive. A few months after announcing Trump's so-called deal of the century, the foreign ministers of Bahrain and UAE appeared on the Truman balcony of the White House besides Benjamin Netanyahu and Donald Trump, signing a general declaration of principles that the White House named the Abraham Accord in September 2020. The overriding detail of the accord was mainly about how the three states will normalise their ties at all levels including trade, political and cultural relations, tourism and security. The accord made negligible reference to the fate of the Palestinians. Even some advocates of the accord, like Jeremey Ben Ami, the president of J Street, stated that "It's not conflict resolution and it's not peace, this is a business deal. Israel's decades-old conflict with the Palestinians remains unaddressed with this agreement" (Crowley 2020). In fact, the accord is another step towards the formation of a de facto alliance between some conservative Gulf monarchies and Israel under the supervision of the Trump administration against their common rival, Shiite Iran. The Palestinians expressed their anger over the agreements by launching rockets into Israel from Gaza during the White House ceremony (Crowley 2020).

From my point view, the Abraham accord was a drama replete with Shakespearean twists that has unfolded in full public glare. For many Palestinians, the solidarity of the Arab states of Bahrain and UAE has loosened as national interests and rivalry with Iran come to the fore. The Palestinians caught flatfooted by the accord have criticised and condemned the agreement. Ahmad Majdalani, Social Affairs Minister of the PA, described the agreement as "a stab in the back of the Palestinian cause and the Palestinian people" (Aljazeera 2020a). In the besieged Gaza Strip, Hamas spokesman Hazem Qassem said Bahrain's decision to normalise relations with Israel "represents a grave harm to the Palestinian cause, and it supports the occupation" (Aljazeera 2020a).

Echoing Palestinian sentiments towards the Abraham accord, Iran's supreme leader Ayatollah Khamenei criticised the initiative and called it a "humiliation". He stated that "Muslim nations will never accept the humiliation of compromising with the Zionist regime" (Staff 2020). In his public speech, Ayatollah Khamenei stated that the UAE "betrayed the Islamic world and the Palestinians" by normalising ties with Israel (Aljazeera 2020b). The Palestinian factions in Gaza embraced Iran's political stance against the accord. In December 2020, Hamas and PIJ conducted their first joint military drill. On the eve of the exercise, a large portrait of Iranian military commander General Qassem Soleimani, who was assassinated in January 2020 in a U.S. attack in Baghdad, was erected along Gaza's main coastal road (al-Mughrabi 2020). More importantly, as Adib-Moghaddam (2021, 150–151) rightly argues, the Iranian pro-Palestinian position towards the UN resolution 242 on the right of return continues to be the default position of major Palestinian movements, including the PLO. Ayatollah Khamenei takes a more radical step by frequently calling for a referendum, after the return of Palestinian refugees, in an obvious attempt to tilt the demographics in favour of the Palestinians. Although under current conditions this approach is unlikely to harvest much support in the region, it morally appeals to the Palestinian streets.

May 2021 became a moment of reaping the whirlwind in East Jerusalem. The Israeli forces stormed Sheikh Jarrah, a tiny neighbourhood in East

Jerusalem, attempting to evict Palestinian families. According to Garbett (2021) Israeli Police vehicles, known as "skunk trucks", were spraying Palestinian homes and shops with putrid water. The water causes stomach pain and skin irritation. These forms of collective punishment aim to stop the growing movement to save Sheikh Jarrah and halt the dispossession of 27 Palestinian families of their homes there. Nevertheless, Palestinian anger swiftly spread to Gaza and resulted in an all-out war between the Israeli armed forces with Hamas and PIJ that lasted for 11 days.

While it was difficult to voice anti-Israeli opinion in the UAE when the Emirati embassy in Tel Aviv was tweeting congratulatory messages to Israel for its "independence" day (Harb 2021), in response to the war in Gaza, two non-Arab states of Iran and Turkey appeared more vocal against Israeli policies. The relative silence has been led by states that made peace with Israel in the last year of the Trump administration and are now standard bearers of the so-called Abraham Accords (Chulov 2021). While Turkish leaders called on Muslims to take a clear stance on Gaza (Reuters 2021a), Ayatollah Khamenei urged Muslim states to support the Palestinians financially and militarily (Reuters 2021b). Following the end of the Israeli war on Gaza, Ziad al-Nakhala and Ismail Haniyeh sent letters of appreciation to Ayatollah Khamenei. In his letter, al-Nakhala stated, "Your continuous, uninterrupted, clear support in all areas has played the greatest, most considerable role in the *Sayf* (Sword) of al-Quds Operation and its achievements" (Tehran Times 2021a).

Although much attention is given to the roots of wars in Gaza, far less is known about the impact of Palestinian-Iranian relations on the *modus operandi* of the conflicts. Iranian support of Gaza has enabled the Palestinian movements to enhance their military capabilities vis-à-vis the fully equipped Israel Defence Forces (IDF), despite having no regular army. Congratulating the authorities in Gaza, Iran's Revolutionary Guard issued a statement at the end of the war, underlining that "The intifada has gone from using stones to powerful, precise missiles" (Reuters 2021b). Referring to the barrage of rockets fired at Israel, Hamas representative in Iran, Khaled al-Qaddoumi, attributed the "Palestinians triumph to the support provided by Iran to the Palestinian resistance, including rocket technology" (Tehran Times 2021b). PIJ's military wing *Al-Quds* Brigade's spokesperson Abu Hamza thanked Iran and "forces of axis of resistance" in televised remarks and described them as "true supporters and patrons in strengthening the capabilities of the Palestinians in Gaza" (O'Connor 2021b).

While the Palestinian Islamic movements in Gaza face regional isolation, the Iranian government invited the leaderships of Hamas and PIJ to President Ebrahim Raisi's inauguration in August 2021. The seating arrangements of the Iranian presidential inauguration attracted global attention. During the ceremony, Iranian media showed the European Union (EU) representative, Enrique Mora, seated in the second row, behind the leaders of Hamas and PIJ who were positioned in the first row (Rasmussen 2021). Moreover, in October 2021, at the invitation of the Iranian leadership, both PIJ and Hamas delegates attended the 35th Islamic Unity Conference in Tehran and delivered a speech at the opening ceremony (Mehr News Agency 2021). Such diplomatic gestures by the Islamic Republic demonstrate the weight of Hamas and PIJ within Iran's political calculations and more importantly boost Hamas and PIJ's political confidence at the regional level.

Conclusion

In this chapter I have examined how Palestinian factions formulate their ties with the Islamic Republic of Iran. This examination suggests that Palestinian-Iranian relations have been determined by the character of their respective political specifications, ideologies, regional politics and most importantly, their stance on Israel. For the Palestinian movements, survival of their organisations and maintaining the Palestinian cause are the priorities. To this end, the Palestinian movements design their ties with regional and external powers. Intra-Arab politics and the kaleidoscopic pattern of partnerships in the region affect these ties. For the last four decades, the Palestinian Islamic movement's frustration with the Arab regional powers and their resentment towards the Israeli iron-fist policies translated into closer connections with Iran. For many of them, the Islamic Republic of Iran has proven to be a reliable "trench-partner", at least against Israeli hegemony. When assessing Palestinian relations with Iran, we also see that both Hamas and PIJ pursue foreign policies that are autonomous from Iran. Although Hamas and PIJ might be characterised as "junior partners" within Iran's "axis of resistance", both have demonstrated their political sovereignty from the Islamic Republic throughout the last decade, particularly during the Arab Spring era. On the one hand, PLO's leadership develops its relations with Iran within the framework of maintaining equilibrium of power against Israel. Despite ideological and political divergences, the PA in West Bank has maintained its diplomatic relations with Iran.

On the other hand, like all states, the Islamic Republic of Iran aims to expand its political and ideological hegemony throughout the region. By amplifying its pro-Palestinian rhetoric, the Islamic Republic attempts to extend its reach into the Arab world and the wider Sunni Muslim environment to sustain its position as the regional hegemon. Consequently, the Islamic Republic of Iran could not afford to lose Hamas and PIJ, and despite turbulent moments during the Arab spring era, Tehran maintained its connections with Hamas. The Palestinian movements in Gaza are not only Iran's close allies, but they are also fundamental to Iran's interests in the Levant. In fact, having close connections with Iran provided Hamas and PIJ with substantial leverage vis-à-vis Israel. It had been through Iran that the Palestinian movements in Gaza succeeded in elevating their military and financial capabilities under the Israeli siege.

Finally, the Palestinian factions proved that they are able to utilise their ties with Iran as a bargaining-chip in their interactions with the Arab states by tilting towards Iran when they are cold-shouldered by their Arab brethren. The evidence synthesised above shows that the nature of Palestine's relations with Iran is further fashioned by how the state of Israel approaches the Palestinian nation. The incessant Israeli policies against the Palestinians have brought them closer to Iran. The endless military operations in Gaza and the continuous occupation of the West Bank on the one hand, and Iran's strident anti-Israel posture and its uncompromising position on the Palestinian-Israeli conflict on the other, further concretised Palestinian-Iranian relations. Although the Israeli operations are often designed to put pressure on Hamas and PIJ, they further motivate them to consolidate their ties with Iran and its allies in the region.

REFERENCES

Abrahamian, Ervand. 1980. The Guerrilla Movement in Iran, 1963–1977. *Middle East Research and Information Project (MERIP)* 86: 149–174. https://doi.org/10.2307/3012295.

Abu Amer, Adnan. 2018. What Is Behind the Hamas-Iran Reproachment. *Aljazeera*, July 26. https://www.aljazeera.com/opinions/2018/7/26/what-is-behind-the-hamas-iran-rapprochement. Accessed 16 Sept 2021.

——. 2019. What is Behind the Saudi Campaign Against Hamas?. *Aljazeera*, September 23. https://www.aljazeera.com/opinions/2019/9/23/what-is-behind-the-saudi-campaign-against-hamas. Accessed 28 Sept 2021.

——. 2020. Iran FM Phones Abbas to Discuss US Peace Deal. *Al-Monitor*, February 12. https://www.al-monitor.com/originals/2020/02/palestine-iran-pa-contacts-abbas-zarif-haniyeh-hamas-fatah.html. Accessed 2 Oct 2021.

Abumaria, Dima. 2017. Why Abbas Was Secretly Summoned to Saudi Arabia. *Themedialine*, November 11. https://themedialine.org/news/featured/abbas-summoned-secretive-meeting-saudi-arabia/. Accessed 21 Aug 2021.

Adib-Moghaddam, Arshin. 2021. *What is Iran? Domestic Politics and International Relations*. Cambridge University Press.

Alavi, Seyed Ali. 2019. *Iran and Palestine, Past, Present, Future*. London: Routledge.

Aljazeera. 2020a. Stab in the Back: Palestinians Condemn Israel-Bahrain Deal. September 11. https://www.aljazeera.com/news/2020/9/11/stab-in-the-back-palestinians-condemn-israel-bahrain-deal. Accessed 18 Aug 2021.

——. 2020b. Iran's Khamenei Says UAE Betrayed Muslim World with Israel Deal. September 1. https://www.aljazeera.com/news/2020/9/1/irans-khamenei-says-uae-betrayed-muslim-world-with-israel-deal. Accessed 18 Aug 2021.

Al-Mughrabi, Nidal. 2020. Gaza Militants Fire Rockets Into the Sea in First Joint Exercise. *Reuters*, December 29. https://www.reuters.com/article/israel-palestinians-gaza-drill-int-idUSKBN2930TX. Accessed 18 Sept 2021.

Chan, Stephen. 2017. *Plural International Relations in a Divided World*. Cambridge: Polity Press.

Chehabi, Houshang. 2006. *Distant Relations: Iran and Lebanon in the Last 500 Years*. London: I.B.Tauris.

Chulov, Martin. 2021. Arab States Split for First Time on Refusal to Condemn Israel Over Gaza. *The Guardian*, May 17. https://www.theguardian.com/world/2021/may/17/arab-states-split-for-first-time-on-refusal-to-condemn-israel-over-gaza. Accessed 2 Oct 2021.

Cobban, Helena. 1984. *The Palestinian Liberation Organisation, People, Power and Politics*. Cambridge: Cambridge University Press.

Crowley, Michael. 2020. Israel, U.A.E. and Bahrain Sign Accords, With an Eager Trump Playing Host. *The New York Times*, September 15. https://www.nytimes.com/2020/09/15/us/politics/trump-israel-peace-emirates-bahrain.html. Accessed 18 Aug 2021.

Fouad, Alaa. 1998. The OIC Summit in Tehran: Herald of a New Beginning? *Insight Turkey* 12: 121–128.

France24. 2020. Palestinian Leader Mahmoud Abbas Suspends Relations with the US, Israel. February 1. https://www.france24.com/en/20200201-palestinian-leader-mahmoud-abbas-suspends-relations-with-the-us-israel. Accessed 27 May 2021.

Garbett, Lucy. 2021. I live in Sheikh Jarrah, for Palestinians This Is Not a Real Estate Dispute. *The Guardian*, May 17. https://www.theguardian.com/commentisfree/2021/may/17/palestinians-sheikh-jarrah-jerusalem-city-identity. Accessed 21 Aug.

Hamas. 2021. Haniyeh Thanks Qatari Emir for His Continuous Support for Palestine. https://hamas.ps/en/post/3431/Haniyeh-thanks-Qatari-Emir-for-his-continuous-support-for-Palestine. Accessed 2 Oct 2021.

Harb, Imad K. 2021. The Utter Failure of the Abraham Accords. *Aljazeera*, May 18. https://www.aljazeera.com/opinions/2021/5/18/the-utter-failure-of-the-abraham-accords. Accessed 19 July 2021.

Hassan, Shamir. 2011. Oslo Accords: The Genesis and Consequences for Palestine. *Social Scientist* 7 (8): 65–72.

Hatina, Meir. 2001. *Islam and Salvation in Palestine*. Tel Aviv: Tel Aviv University Press.

Houk, Marian. 2016. Why Abbas-MEK Meeting Made Ways of Everywhere But Palestine. *Al-Monitor*, August 8. https://www.al-monitor.com/originals/2016/08/meeting-abbas-iran-opposition-rajavi.html. Accessed 12 May 2021.

Hunter, Shirin. 2019. *Arab-Iranian Relations, Dynamics of Conflict and Accommodation*. London: Rowman & Littlefield.

Ioannides, Chris P. 1989. The PLO and the Islamic Revolution in Iran. In *The International Relations of the Palestine Liberation Organization*, ed. Augustus R. Norton and Martin Harry Greenberg, 74–106. Carbondale: Southern Illinois University Press.

Kais, Roi. 2013. Abbas Thanked Iran for Backing PA's UN Bid. *Ynetnews*, June 2. https://www.ynetnews.com/articles/0,7340,L-4341951,00.html. Accessed 11 May 2021.

Khatib, Lina, and Dina Matar. 2014. *The Hizbullah, Phenomenon, Politics and Communication*. London: Hurst & Company.

Kuttab, Daud. 2014. Palestinian Foreign Minister Open to Iran Visit. *Al-Monitor*, February 10. https://www.al-monitor.com/originals/2014/02/palestine-minister-riyad-malki-abbas-iran-hamas.html. Accessed 9 June 2021.

Mehr News Agency. 2021. 35th Islamic Unity Conference Kicks Off in Tehran. October 19. https://en.mehrnews.com/amp/179846/. Accessed 20 April 2021.

O'Connor, Tom. 2021a. Hamas Calls for Iran-Saudi Unity, Israel Issues Warning to Any Who Joins Its Foes. *Newsweek*, May 11. https://www.newsweek.com/hamas-calls-iran-saudi-unity-israel-issues-warning-any-who-join-its-foes-1590255?amp=1. Accessed 21 August 2021.

———. 2021b. Iran, Palestinian groups Praise Partnership Against Israel After Gaza War. *Newsweek*, May 21. https://www.newsweek.com/iran-palestinian-groups-praise-partnership-against-israel-after-gaza-war-1593791?amp=1. Accessed 21 Aug 2021.

Ostovar, Afshon. 2016. *Vanguard of The Imam; Religion, Politics, and Iran's Revolutionary Guards.* Oxford: Oxford University Press.

Qods International News Agency. 2021. Hamas Chief Thanks Qatari Emir for His $360m in Humanitarian Aid for Gaza. January 2. http://qodsna.com/en/351658/Hamas-chief-thanks-Qatari-Emir-for-his-$360m-in-humanitarian-aid-for-Gaza. Accessed 2 Sept 2021.

Rasgon, Adam. 2019. Abbas and Saudi Crown Prince Meet, Agree to Establish Economic Committee. *Times of Israel*, October 17. https://www.timesofisrael.com/abbas-and-saudi-crown-prince-meet-agree-to-establish-economic-committee/amp/. Accessed 2 Sept 2021.

Rasmussen, Sune Engel. 2021. Iran Swears in President Ebrahim Raisi as Unease Grows in West. *The Wall Street Journal*, August 5. https://www.wsj.com/articles/iran-to-swear-in-new-president-as-unease-grows-over-nuclear-deal-11628150225. Accessed 7 Oct 2021.

Reuters. 2021a. Turkey Calls on Muslims to Take Clear Stance Over Gaza. May 13. https://www.reuters.com/world/middle-east/turkey-calls-muslims-take-clear-stance-over-gaza-2021-05-13/. Accessed 2 June 2021.

———. 2021b. Iran Leader Urges Muslim States to Back Palestinians Militarily, Financially. May 21. https://www.reuters.com/world/middle-east/iran-leader-urges-muslim-states-back-palestinians-militarily-financially-2021-05-21/. Accessed 2 June 2021.

Salah, Aqel Mohammed Ahmed. 2017. The Hamas Movement and Its Political and Democratic Practice, 1992–2016. *Contemporary Arab Affairs* 4: 561–576. https://doi.org/10.1080/17550912.2017.1401739.

Seliktar, Ofra, and Farhad Rezaei. 2020. *Iran, Revolution, and Proxy Wars.* Palgrave Macmillan.

Skare, Erik. 2021. *A History of Palestinian Jihad; Faith, Awareness, and Revolution in the Middle East.* Cambridge: Cambridge University Press.

Staff, Toi. 2020. Iran's Khamenei: Muslim Nations Reject Humiliation of Compromise with Israel. *The Times of Israel*, October 21. https://www.timesofisrael.com/irans-khamenei-muslim-nations-reject-humiliation-of-compromise-with-israel/. Accessed 1 Sept 2021.

Takeyh, Ray. 2009. *Guardians of the Revolution: Iran and the World in the Age of Ayatollahs.* Oxford: Oxford University Press.

Tamimi, Azzam. 2009. *Hamas, Unwritten Chapters.* London: Hurst & Company.

———. 2021. Saudi Arabia: Crackdown on Hamas marks another costly misstep. *Al-Monitor*, August 1. https://www.middleeasteye.net/opinion/saudi-arabia-crackdown-hamas-marks-another-costly-misstep. Accessed 16 Sept 2021.

Tehran Times. 2001. Arafat Calls on Iran to Come to Palestinian's Aid. June 12. https://www.tehrantimes.com/news/65923/Arafat-Calls-On-Iran-to-Come-to-Palestinians-Aid. Accessed 21 Aug 2021.

———. 2021a. Ayatollah Khamenei Replies to Messages from Palestinian Resistance Leaders. May 24. https://www.tehrantimes.com/news/461292/Ayatollah-Khamenei-replies-to-messages-from-Palestinian-resistance. Accessed 21 July 2021.

———. 2021b. Hamas Ascribes Victory Against Israel to Iran's Support. May 26. https://www.tehrantimes.com/news/461359/Hamas-ascribes-victory-against-Israel-to-Iran-s-support. Accessed 21 July 2021.

The Guardian. 2020. Trump Unveils Middle East Peace Plan With No Palestinian Support. January 28. https://www.theguardian.com/world/2020/jan/28/donald-trump-middle-east-peace-plan-israel-netanyahu-palestinians. Accessed 21 May 2021.

CHAPTER 15

Conclusion

Gülistan Gürbey, Sabine Hofmann, and Ferhad Ibrahim Seyder

The individual contributions give explanations and causalities for a better understanding of Kurdistan-Iraq's and Palestine's paradiplomacy and paradiplomatic activities. Based on the key questions formulated in the introduction, now the findings can be summarized in order to (a) set out causes, capability, and capacities of Kurdistan-Iraq's and Palestine's paradiplomacy; (b) elaborate how and why Kurdistan-Iraq and Palestine develop and practice paradiplomacy; and (c) provide new insights into paradiplomatic contexts and practices beyond the state. Finally, the findings can be evaluated comparatively to answer the questions about the differences and similarities between the paradiplomacy of Kurdistan-Iraq and Palestine and the specific features of paradiplomatic activities in each of the two de facto states.

G. Gürbey (✉) • S. Hofmann
Department of Political and Social Sciences, Freie Universität Berlin, Berlin, Germany
e-mail: guerbey@zedat.fu-berlin.de; shofmann@zedat.fu-berlin.de

F. I. Seyder
University of Erfurt, Erfurt, Germany

© The Author(s), under exclusive license to Springer Nature Switzerland AG 2023
G. Gürbey et al. (eds.), *Between Diplomacy and Non-Diplomacy*, https://doi.org/10.1007/978-3-031-09756-0_15

The contributions not only illustrate similarities and differences between the paradiplomacy of Kurdistan-Iraq and Palestine. Above all, they show how both Kurdistan-Iraq and the Palestinian Authority (PA) were able to significantly expand and multiply their paradiplomatic activities over time.

The Kurdistan Regional Government (KRG) has achieved an overwhelming amount of progress and success in its international and regional engagement since its inception in 1992, due to the unique history of the region. The emergence and development of KRG's paradiplomacy is embedded in the historical context of modern state-building processes in the Middle East and the historical development of Kurdistan-Iraq since the end of the First World War. Above all, it is external, regional factors that exert a decisive influence and open windows of opportunities for the Kurds. These include two crucial regional political caesuras—the 1991 Gulf War and the 2003 Iraq War—both of which paved the way for a unique development in Kurdish history: The emergence of the de facto autonomous region created within the 1991–2003 no-fly zone and the constitutional recognition as a federal region of federal Iraq following the overthrow of Saddam Hussein and the establishment of federal Iraq in 2005. In the era de facto autonomy (1992–2003), the KRG set its paradiplomacy primarily on humanitarian, economic, and commercial relations. In the wake of the first parliamentary elections in de facto autonomy, the Ministry of Humanitarian Aid and Cooperation is established in 1992, through which the KRG achieves humanitarian aid from international organizations and states. This is the first milestone in Kurdish paradiplomacy, as international contacts are established and the KRG opens its first foreign missions.

Recognition as a constitutional federal region in 2005 triggers a golden era for the first time in Kurdistan-Iraq's history, marked above all only by a united Kurdish front in Baghdad and a rapidly flourishing development of the region. Thus, this upheaval is reflected in its own designation as "the other Iraq" and its accompanying public relations campaign. Most importantly, Kurdistan-Iraq, as a federal region, gains constitutional authority to conduct foreign relations for the first time. The Iraqi constitution itself protects the KRG's ability to conduct foreign relations and develop its paradiplomacy through its own legal framework. Thus, the Kurdish leadership is strategically using these powers that the new Iraqi constitution provides to the federal regions. For the first time in its history, the leadership established the Department of Foreign Relations (DFR) under Falah Mustafa Bakir in 2006 to institutionalize the region's foreign relations and overcome partisan politics. The DFR maintains relations with the international community; promotes trade, investment, and tourism; oversees the KRG's offices abroad; organizes visits of political and economic delegations to the Kurdistan Region of Iraq (KRI); coordinates with the Iraqi Ministry of Foreign Affairs; and promotes political, economic, cultural, and social relations with foreign states. In accordance with the Iraqi constitution, the KRG establishes offices abroad. It succeeds in establishing a network of KRG offices in selected states around the world to pursue political, economic, cultural, and social interests. KRG foreign offices serve as the main vehicle for Kurdish lobbying. They act as a bridge to the international community; attract foreign direct investment; promote Kurdish art, language, and culture; advocate for humanitarian aid; and promote the Kurdistan Region's reputation as a place of peace, coexistence, stability, and security in Iraq and the Middle East. As a result of these increasing institutionalization processes, the region manages to significantly increase as well as multiply its paradiplomatic activities within a short period of time. This is very evident in its numerous foreign missions, the foreign missions of other countries in the KRI, the frequent trips of international political actors to the KRI, the official visits of the KRG abroad, the numerous contacts with various states, international organizations, non-governmental organizations as well as in the participation in international conferences. Official international visits by the region's political actors also illustrate the success of the KRG's paradiplomacy. In 2010, paradiplomatic relations between the KRG and the international community are experiencing a peak. For example, President Masoud Barzani, ministers, and other high-ranking officials participate in more than 28 foreign visits, including official visits to the United States (US), Germany, France, Italy, Austria, Turkey, Saudi Arabia, Jordan, Lebanon, Egypt, etc. In many of these visits, President M. Barzani is received like a head of state. The importance of these visits is reflected in the diplomatic, economic, and cultural relations that have developed between the KRI and these states. The year 2014 is also particularly noteworthy because of the KRG's frontline military fight against the Islamic State (IS) and its ability to capitalize on this on the international stage. From 2014 to the September 2017 independence referendum, the KRG hosted nearly 200 high-level foreign visitors, including ministers, ambassadors, and political officials from nations and organizations in North America, Europe, Australia, Asia, and the Middle East. These developments reflect the progress and strength of the KRG's paradiplomacy.

The rise of the IS and the capture of Mosul in June 2014 trigger a security imperative that forces the Kurds to confront this existential threat, to manage the crisis and its far-reaching implications for the region, while also pursuing secessionist aspirations more vigorously than before in the face of this threat and in light of ongoing points of contention with Baghdad. Paradiplomatic activities are also increasingly shifting from the state-building process to crisis management. The war against the IS provides a golden opportunity for KRG to expand its foreign relations to include military cooperation and present itself as a reliable security partner to the West. The KRG's increased international visibility in the fight against IS strengthens Kurdish political actors in their desire to pressure the international community to mediate all outstanding disputes between the KRI and Baghdad, but also to hold the independence referendum in September 2017. The primary purpose is not to declare statehood directly, but to create leverage in negotiations with Baghdad on the outstanding constitutional and dispute issues and to use the results of the referendum as a negotiating tool to resolve disputes between Baghdad and Erbil. However, the referendum triggered harsh reactions from neighboring Turkey and Iran and the Baghdad central government, as well as rejection from the US, the European Union (EU), and the United Nations (UN). These setbacks not only increase the pressure on the Kurdish leadership, but also jeopardize its paradiplomatic achievements. As a result of this development, the KRG is forced to use all diplomatic means at its disposal to remedy the far-reaching consequences and, above all, to strike a balance with the central government, Turkey, and Iran.

Elementary instruments of the KRG's paradiplomacy are primarily communication and economic strategies. However, the use of social media and public diplomacy as new instruments of paradiplomacy is also becoming increasingly important in view of the digital communication possibilities. In particular, economic strategies are the most successful and pragmatic tool, as they result in foreign direct investments (FDI) and enable partnerships between the KRG and foreign states, companies, and organizations. The KRG's (para)diplomatic strategy to ensure economic stability is largely supported by the KRI's oil and gas industry. The KRG's economically attractive investment law enables the oil industry to develop diplomatic relations with numerous countries interested in investing in the KRI. In this regard, in order to attract further investment to the region, the KRG's core task is to ensure its stability. Due to its strong focus on investment opportunities in the public sector, private sector, education, and tourism, the KRG achieves a wide range of partnerships with various countries. These partnerships contribute significantly to the development of the region's infrastructure and the KRG's international visibility.

The essential core motive of Kurdistan-Iraq's paradiplomacy is to ensure the survival of the region and its inhabitants and to generate development, stability, and security. This is very closely related to the historical experience of decades of oppression and displacement, as well as the fact that the KRG is surrounded by anti-Kurdish neighbors. The fear of past atrocities, such as the Anfal genocide, or the chemical attacks on Halabja, shapes the collective memory and has a decisive influence on the KRG's paradiplomatic actions. By building good international relations and generating international support, the KRG aims to protect the next generations in the KRI from new atrocities. In the face of geographic encirclement, the KRG feels compelled to build trust with its anti-Kurdish neighbors through paradiplomacy to ensure the survival of the Kurdish people and the Kurdistan Region, to continue to maintain and foster relations with Baghdad to protect the Kurdish people's right to autonomy, representation, self-expression, security, identity, and culture without compromising the integrity of Iraq. This includes promoting a secure and stable environment for the KRI through paradiplomacy. For the KRG, a stable and peaceful environment is at once key to the success of all paradiplomatic activities and relationships as well as to achieving economic prosperity. Thus, paradiplomacy serves to escape the geopolitical constraints and uncertainties facing Kurdistan-Iraq, to mediate the historic (violent) conflict over self-determination, to build statehood capacity, and to advance state-building. The KRG uses paradiplomacy as a mechanism to promote its constitutional status, expand its regional autonomy, and assert and expand its de facto autonomy from the central government and gain maximum control over the region's economic resources, particularly oil and gas. The KRG is committed to expanding and multiplying its political, economic, and cultural ties and activities at the regional and international levels in order to develop alternative options to the central government and attract investment.

Obstacles that are elementary to Kurdistan-Iraq's paradiplomacy relate primarily to the internal structure of the political system, its difficult geographic location, and its limited maneuverability. The internal de facto political and territorial bifurcation into the Kurdistan Democratic Party (KDP) or Barzani bloc centered in Dohuk and Erbil provinces and the Patriotic Union of Kurdistan (PUK) or Talabani bloc centered in

Sulaymaniyah has negative consequences for Kurdish paradiplomacy and causes paradiplomacy fragility. On the one hand, this duality is a structural obstacle to the pursuit of unified paradiplomacy, and on the other hand, it affects the KRG's international standing and prevents unified representation at the international level. This is because it is not always clear who is authorized to represent the KRG at the international level, for example, whether it is the KDP or PUK external relations offices or the KRG external relations department. Overcoming this internal dual structure, however, is essential and a prerequisite for ensuring a paradiplomatic united front in the long term. While it is up to the Kurdish leadership to overcome this internal structural obstacle and thus strengthen its own paradiplomacy, the situation is different with regard to external structural factors, which also influence the KRG's paradiplomatic actions and over which, however, the Kurdish leadership has little influence. This relates to the difficult geopolitical situation due to the landlocked geography of Kurdistan-Iraq and the encirclement of anti-Kurdish neighbors traditionally focused on containing Kurdish autonomy and independence. This geopolitical location makes the Kurdish region particularly vulnerable as a buffer zone in the context of geopolitical rivalries and imponderables. At the same time, it increases the risk of strategic exploitation of the KRG by external actors. Due to these structural factors, the paradiplomatic and strategic maneuvering space for the KRG remains limited, which is further strengthened by the pressure and influence of the central government regarding Kurdish paradiplomacy and from the regional and international levels.

Overall, however, Kurdish paradiplomacy is characterized by a high degree of capability and performance. Despite the internal and external obstacles and the limited capacities of Kurdish paradiplomacy, as well as the structural asymmetry in its relations, the KRG manages to advance the process of institutionalization for paradiplomacy relatively quickly in a manageable period of time and to enter into diverse international relationships. Thus, the KRG successfully demonstrates a performance: Since 2005, it has been continuously expanding and multiplying its paradiplomatic activities at the regional and international levels, thus increasing its prestige and visibility in the international arena. It is expanding political, economic, and cultural relations with various states, including the important neighboring states of Turkey and Iran, the US, and Russia. Ultimately, the KRG succeeds in capitalizing on the fight against the IS and adds a military dimension to its paradiplomacy, positioning itself as a reliable security partner. Nevertheless, the setbacks caused by the independence referendum show how essential it is, above all, to overcome the structural duality internally in order to strengthen paradiplomacy, but also to reduce the region's vulnerability and generate more stability. This is one of the great challenges for Kurdish paradiplomacy, which depends primarily on the will and performance of the Kurdish elites.

In their quest for statehood, the Palestinians have achieved unique results in the diplomatic field and have proven themselves internationally as a political actor. Four developmental caesurae of paradiplomatic activity mark the dramatic process of evolution from the Palestine Liberation Organization (PLO) to the State of Palestine:

Firstly, in an unprecedented step, the UN decided in 1974 to recognize the PLO as a non-state actor and the sole legitimate representative of all Palestinians and to grant it observer status in the UN. Secondly, the PLO's Palestinian National Council declared the independence of the Palestinian people; the United Nations General Assembly (UNGA) recognized this decision in December 1988 and included "Palestine" as a member name. Thirdly, in 1994, the PA was established for the West Bank and Gaza Strip and the PLO leadership with Chairman Yasser Arafat returned from exile to the Palestinian territories. Fourthly, in November 2012, the UNGA admitted Palestine as a non-voting state with observer status. Since 10 September 2015, Palestine's flag has hung at the UN headquarters in New York. This marked the culmination of the Palestinians' paradiplomatic activities to date.

These results are an expression of the PLO's development in the balancing act between national liberation movement and state-building process. They are embedded in the settlement of the Israel-Palestine conflict and in regional and world political changes.

The PLO has undergone a dramatic transformation since its founding in 1964. In its striving for statehood, it developed from a military combat organization into the political and diplomatic representative of the Palestinians in the West Bank and Gaza Strip.

In the early phase of paradiplomatic activities, the PLO sought strategic partners and international support, both political and military and financial. In this period of the "Cold War," the PLO very quickly got caught up in the maelstrom of confrontation between the then great powers, the US and the Soviet Union, and their bloc policies, including the ones in the Middle East. The US showed less interest in the PLO than in the State of Israel. Consequently, the PLO intensified its international activities toward the Soviet Union, Eastern Europe, and China. In the 1970s and 1980s, it achieved regional and international paradiplomatic successes. It actively built relations of solidarity with Eastern European states and eventually attracted attention in Western Europe: In June 1980, the European Council officially recognized the PLO as the legitimate representative of the Palestinians.

After the declaration of Palestinian state independence in 1988 and the recognition of Resolutions 242 and 338, the PLO expanded its paradiplomatic activities worldwide and even the US now allowed contacts with the PLO. Following the international recognition, the PLO institutionalized its paradiplomatic activities. It established official representations abroad which elevated many Eastern European states to the rank of embassies. With the dissolution of the systemic East-West antagonism and in the wake of regional changes, a unique window of opportunity opened up for the practical implementation of the project of Palestinian statehood in the West Bank and Gaza Strip.

The PLO reaffirmed the diplomatic path in 1993. With the 1993 Declaration of Principles and the Oslo Accords came the "turning point"; from the declaration of statehood in exile, the PLO entered the de facto state-building process on the ground. In the wake of the Oslo Accords, the PA was established for the Gaza Strip and the West Bank. In addition to internal administration by the PA, the PLO expanded its paradiplomatic activities under President Yasser Arafat.

The first decade of the PA government was marked by a spirit of optimism and hope for an end to the Israeli occupation. With this confidence, the PA intensified and expanded its paradiplomatic activities, which was reflected in a visible greater international acceptance of the Palestinians. States opened their representative offices in Gaza and Ramallah, international organizations and civil society initiatives began operating and opening new offices, companies and private businessmen opened branches, Ramallah experienced a real estate boom, and Palestinians returned from the Diaspora. The PA was welcomed as a partner in international programs and accepted as a political actor. Thus, as early as 1997, the EC concluded a Euro-Mediterranean Interim Association Agreement with the PLO in favor of the PA for the West Bank and Gaza Strip. In the economic field, opportunities for Palestine's economic relations also opened in some areas in the region and worldwide. These steps contributed to a temporary political, social, and economic development process.

After the death of Yasser Arafat in 2004, Mahmoud Abbas was elected President of the PA and new hopes for progress and new paradiplomatic opportunities emerged. The joint initiatives of the Middle East Quartet of the EU, the US, UN, and Russia and the US-driven Annapolis Conference in 2007 strengthened the position of the Fatah-dominated PA and paradiplomatic activities against the backdrop of intra-Palestinian strife. Thus, the upgrading of Palestine in 2012 as a UN non-member observer state represents a victory for the Palestinian paradiplomatic initiative and in this regard also affirms the Palestinians' right to self-determination. The Israeli government, on the other hand, rejects the Palestinian state proclamation.

All actions of Palestinian paradiplomacy are directed toward the main political goal of the Palestinians: state sovereignty. Since its inception, Palestinian paradiplomacy has been concerned with achieving the creation of a viable Palestinian state based on United Nations Security Council (UNSC) resolutions.

In view of the stagnation in the conflict settlement, the Palestinians are intensifying their actions in the international arena. The purpose of the Palestinian paradiplomatic activities is to gain the greatest possible international recognition and support abroad for the implementation of Palestine's state existence. Underlying this is the important question of security, security in the narrow and in the broader concept, around state, collective, and personal security. Under the impact of the collective trauma and historical narrative of the Palestinians, the Nakba, the aim is to prevent renewed painful experiences of flight, displacement, wars, social and economic uprooting, and family suffering. The Palestinian government and the PLO are pushing to stop the Israeli land grab and expropriation of Palestinian land, as well as Israel's continued settlement policy in the occupied Palestinian territories. Another objective is to use paradiplomatic activity to reaffirm the Palestinians' political goal of statehood in the territories under the UN Resolutions 242 and 338 vis-à-vis neighboring states and the integrity of these states.

The impact of paradiplomatic activity is not only outward but also inward. With the expanded visible Palestinian representation, political identification with one's own state is also to be stimulated.

In view of Palestine's lack of resources and the conditions of regionalization and globalization, paradiplomatic activities must always be directed toward taking into account the interests of the local economy. One of the most important motives is to structurally and institutionally modernize Palestine's own economy and to create new jobs. The aim is to reduce the dependence of the Palestinian territories of the West Bank and Gaza Strip on aid payments from foreign donors and donor states.

Paradiplomatic activities were not clearly regulated even in the 2002 Palestinian Basic Law. Since 1974, the PLO has become the main actor in Palestine's international activities, granted state privileges even though it is not a state. The PLO remained responsible for this area, even though a dual structure of PA and PLO in institutional terms is the result. Following the UN decision in 2012 and the official presentation of Palestine at the UN headquarters in New York, PA President Mahmoud Abbas now officially introduced the title of Ministry of Foreign Affairs of the State of Palestine. Some PLO representative offices abroad changed their names and jurisdiction after 2012, thus also officially serving the Palestinian government in Ramallah and strengthening its paradiplomatic service.

In the broad spectrum of means in Palestinian paradiplomacy, the main tools are political communication and argumentation. In the meantime, 138 out of 193 UN members have recognized the PLO's request for recognition of the State of Palestine. Palestine has systematically expanded its paradiplomacy, is very active, and appears sovereign in the diplomatic arena. Palestine now maintains a total of 114 paradiplomatic missions worldwide, including in politically and economically leading states of the world, such as the US, China, Russia, Canada, Japan, and at important international organizations, such as the UN. The spectrum ranges from embassy to consulate and representative office, and all tasks customary in the diplomatic service are performed. In addition, diplomatic missions of foreign states operate in the Palestinian territories, such as 45 in Ramallah; some states even maintain consulates in East Jerusalem (such as France, Sweden, the United Kingdom [UK], and, until 2017, the US). The Palestinians' diplomatic engagement bore fruit and opened up new opportunities for membership in 200 important UN organizations. Having been a full member of United Nations Educational, Scientific and Cultural Organization (UNESCO) since 2011, Palestine joined the Rome Statute on the International Criminal Court and numerous UN conventions in 2015 and became a member of Interpol in 2017.

Palestine is now active in many more areas of practical paradiplomacy than in the first years of the PA's establishment. Global environmental and other problems increasingly challenge international cooperation and the joint engagement of actors beyond the constitutional nation-state. Palestine has expanded its paradiplomatic activities in many areas and has established special institutions for this purpose, such as the Palestinian International Cooperation Agency (PICA). The main purpose of this institution is to coordinate South-South cooperation and North-South cooperation, that is, above all cooperation with developing countries. Finally, it is intended to strengthen development policy as part of Palestinian foreign policy. Special focus is placed on supporting developing countries not only in, but also beyond, the Arab world.

Initiatives for the protection of water and the environment, sustainable energy production, education, health protection, etc. are areas of activity in which the Palestinians are visible and present and in which they represent their position beyond the political debate. These instruments expand the paradiplomatic scope for action and strengthen Palestine's national branding.

Above all, the diverse cooperation with the EU is characteristic of Palestinian paradiplomacy. For example, Palestine participates in university cooperation and exchange programs, such as the EU's Erasmus program, and is one of the founding participants in the Euro-Mediterranean Partnership launched by the current EU. Within the framework of this partnership, the EU initiates a wide range of programs at state and substate to local level, such as vocational training, trade promotion, and business promotion.

The PLO, as a legitimate actor for the PA and thus for Palestine, has meanwhile concluded important free trade and preferential agreements, for example with the EU, the European Free Trade Association states, the US, Canada, Russia, and the Mercosur group of states. With the motive of promoting the domestic economy, the PA invited to international Palestine Investment Conferences in 2008 and 2010 in Bethlehem and more than a thousand domestic and foreign entrepreneurs came to these representative events. This was an attempt to present Palestine as a competitive location in the regional environment and to attract foreign investors, for which the Law for the Encouragement of Investment in Palestine was also passed by the parliament.

In order to establish itself in the already entrenched state system and in the world economy, regional relations in the Middle East are an essential factor for Palestine in the process of globalization. In addition to political alliances, common interests are reflected in projects such as the establishment of cross-border industrial parks, links in infrastructure and energy, and joint environmental projects. In transnationally oriented areas, we find the implementation of projects that fall into different areas of paradiplomacy, from economic to trade, scientific, environmental, and cultural diplomacy to security and military diplomacy.

In this context, cultural diplomacy should be highlighted as an essential part of Palestinian paradiplomacy. Palestine uses the historical capital of the "Holy Land" and promotes sites of global significance in terms of religion and cultural history, such as Bethlehem and Hebron, which are now included in the list of significant UNESCO World Heritage Sites.

At the sub-state level, the Chambers are among the important and active actors in Palestinian public economic diplomacy. The Chambers, which have grown historically and are relatively manifest, are the main interlocutors for small and medium-sized entrepreneurs and businessmen on the ground. As their stakeholders, they have traditionally been active across local spaces and maintain relations especially with Chambers in surrounding Arab countries. Another area of Palestinian public economic diplomacy beyond the national border is the Palestinian International Chamber of Commerce, which represents the interests of the few, but economically strong, Palestinian capital enterprises.

Palestine has also been using modern instruments and means of paradiplomatic activities for a long time. Today, digital diplomacy in combination with public diplomacy has become indispensable, especially for expanding political communication and intensifying strategic network connections, as can be seen, for example, in the worldwide dynamics of the Boycott, Divestment, Sanctions (BDS) movement.

The main obstacles to Palestinian paradiplomacy are territorial separation, the de facto political-territorial division, and the internal divisions of the Palestinians into different political groups according to ideology, religion, and national goals. The competition between the main political groups Hamas and PLO and within them makes a united Palestinian front difficult. This also endangers a reliable, stable, coherent, and strong representation of interests. In addition, intra-regional conflicts and hegemonic and supremacist aspirations of Arab and Islamic states in the Middle East influence the internal Palestinian political settlement. However, the competition for Palestinian national representation also weakens the Palestinians in the dispute and conflict settlement with Israel and in the search for consensus with groups in Israel that advocate the Palestinians' right to self-determination.

Another obstacle is Palestine's high dependence on resources. Thus, Palestine's political system is only viable if the PA continuously receives financial resources from the donor states.

If we compare the paradiplomacy of Kurdistan-Iraq and PA, we can find a number of similarities, as well as differences. There are two parallelisms in particular that are fundamental to understanding paradiplomacy:

First, the emergence and development of paradiplomacy cannot be understood without the historical century-old violent conflict of the two areas embedded in the regional and international context and its far-reaching consequences. The long history of wars, violence, and external interventions also influenced the formation of paradiplomacy. Only with legal recognition and the legal foundation do true windows of opportunities open up for a differentiation of paradiplomacy. As a result of its constitutional recognition as a federal region in 2005, the Kurdistan Regional Government began to strategically use its legal powers to establish administrative bodies in charge of conducting paradiplomatic activities and relations and to steadily expand and multiply its paradiplomatic activities.

Second, the KRG's and PA's paradiplomacy is internally characterized by a structural parallelism. Both, Kurdistan-Iraq and the PA are internally de facto politically and territorially divided in two, where two decisive parties each hold monopoly and control, causing a duality with far-reaching consequences for politics and society. This duality also massively affects paradiplomacy. It prevents a unified paradiplomacy from emerging and thus weakens paradiplomacy as a whole. This in turn has negative consequences for prestige and credibility in the international arena. Without overcoming this dichotomy and duality, paradiplomacy as a whole remains fragile, while it depends primarily on the will and performance of the Kurdish and Palestinian elites to remove this internal structural obstacle and thus substantially strengthen paradiplomacy.

Nevertheless, historically there is a significant difference in terms of state recognition in the world of states and the mechanism for this. Thus, in 1974, the PLO was recognized as the sole and legitimate representative and agent of the Palestinian people and was granted all state privileges as an organization. This means that the PLO, as a non-state actor, legitimately represents the Palestinian people in all international organizations and counts as the main political actor of the Palestinians in their international relations. This is a unique phenomenon internationally to this day. Through their internationally recognized representative, the PLO, the Palestinians have taken both the constitutional and the declarative path to recognition of their statehood, and since November 2012 have been a non-voting observer state in the UN.

Key differences between the paradiplomacy of Kurdistan-Iraq and PA exist primarily in terms of core motives and tools. Due to its geographic location as a landlocked buffer zone and surrounded by anti-Kurdish neighbors, the KRG is exposed to increased geopolitical vulnerability and risk of strategic exploitation. It is therefore under increased pressure to manage and balance this precarious situation by differentiating its paradiplomatic activities. Coupled with this is the core motive, which is fed by the collective memory of experiences in the context of the long and bloody history of oppression and is therefore of existential importance: to ensure the survival of the region and its inhabitants and to prevent new atrocities and collective suffering. It is necessary to stabilize and expand autonomy, overcome dependencies on the Iraqi central government, and assert de facto autonomy vis-à-vis the Iraqi central government, gain maximum control over the region's economic resources, especially oil and gas. Above all, economic strategies are central tools of Kurdish paradiplomacy based on the resource of oil in order to establish and expand diverse partnerships in the international arena through investments, thereby also promoting international visibility. In addition, by using its military resource in the fight against IS, the KRG has managed to add a military dimension to its paradiplomacy and thus become a security partner.

In contrast to the KRG, the core motive of Palestinian paradiplomacy continues to be the political goal of drawing international legal attention to the ongoing occupation and of gaining support for ending the Israeli occupation of Palestinian territory. Paradiplomacy by de facto states under continued occupation, as in the case of Palestine, is a key difference from the KRG.

One of the most striking differences between the PA and PLO, on the one hand, and the KRG, on the other, emerges when one considers the material basis of the KRG and PA political systems. The Palestinian system has insufficient internal resources of its own. It is existentially dependent on external rent payments.

In conclusion, despite difficult conditions, both Kurdistan-Iraq and the PA have a high capability of establishing and developing bilateral and multilateral relations with state and non-state actors. In terms of the practical performance of their paradiplomatic activities, both governments have achieved notable political successes, for example, in terms of the specific justification and legitimization of their international activities. By expanding their paradiplomatic activities, both governments succeed in refuting their contested international capacity to act and present themselves as responsible actors capable of carrying out independent external activities and promoting their image in the international public sphere. However, paradiplomacy remains fragile as long as the structural dichotomy and duality are not eliminated internally, and the institutionalization process suffers. Therefore, it remains a constant challenge. Whether the Kurdish and Palestinian elites accept and overcome this challenge ultimately depends not on external factors such as regional events, but primarily on their own will. In contrast, elites have only limited influence on regional developments that have an impact on paradiplomatic capacities and performance.

BACK MATTER

'Kurds and Palestinians have never been fully integrated into the international society of sovereign states. Yet, they are well represented by entities that control territory, provide governance and secure popular legitimacy. This original and innovative volume, featuring scholars from the region, comparatively explains the growth, evolution and legal basis of Kurdistan-Iraq and Palestine's paradiplomatic cultural, economic and political engagements with sovereign states and other actors.'
　　—**Scott Pegg**, Professor, Department of Political Science, Indiana University Purdue University Indianapolis (IUPUI), Indianapolis, USA, and author of International Society and the De Facto State

'This book invites readers to a journey into the emerging field of paradiplomacy. It provides some valuable non-Western insights to all those interested in Kurdistan-Iraq and Palestine, and the way how these non-state entities claim to be heard and represented among the privileged few – i.e. internationally recognised states that form international society today.'
　　—**Eiki Berg**, Professor of International Relations, University of Tartu, Finland

'For over a century, the Kurdish and Palestinian national movements have struggled for self-determination, sovereignty, and statehood. This highly recommended volume examines the parallels and intersections of both movements. It is an essential resource for students and scholars attempting to understand the political and diplomatic obstacles that have prevented Palestinians and Kurds from achieving their goals.'

—**Osamah F. Khalil**, Associate Professor of History and Chair, International Relations Program, Syracuse University, New York, USA

The edited volume compares the involvement of Kurdistan-Iraq and Palestine (Palestinian Territory of the West Bank and Gaza Strip) in international relations from the viewpoint of their practical performance, capabilities, capacities and practical achievements. It highlights the similarities and differences and contributes to a better understanding of Kurdistan-Iraq's and Palestine's international affairs and paradiplomatic activities.

Gülistan Gürbey is Adjunct Professor of Political Science at Freie Universität Berlin, Germany.
Sabine Hofmann is Researcher and Associate Lecturer at Freie Universität Berlin, at Philipps Universität Marburg, and at Berlin School of Economics and Law, Germany.
Ferhad Ibrahim Seyder is Professor emeritus at Freie Universität Berlin, and Universität Erfurt, Germany.

Index[1]

A
Abbas, Mahmoud, 17, 54, 65–67, 108, 124–129, 197, 229, 230, 293, 295, 312, 314
Abraham Accord, 233, 294–298
Ahmadi, Abdul Rahman Haji, 267, 268
Algiers Declaration, 223
An-Nakba (the Catastrophe), 55, 114, 163, 164, 313
Ansar al-Islam, 266, 267
Arab League, 54, 56, 58, 59, 69, 81, 97, 114, 117, 185, 221, 295
Arab Spring, 37, 252, 256, 290, 292, 293, 298, 299
Arafat, Yasser, 17, 22, 54, 57, 58, 60, 61, 63–65, 69, 100, 102, 108, 115–118, 120, 121, 123, 124, 165, 171, 182–188, 221–223, 225, 226, 279, 280, 282–285, 289, 311, 312
Armed struggle, 15, 21, 53–54, 57, 58, 164, 221, 222, 226, 232, 287
Asymmetric, 241, 256
Autonomous Administration of North East Syria (AANES), 241, 253, 256
Autonomy, 10, 16, 31, 33, 36, 38–40, 60, 76, 77, 83, 86, 96, 114, 118, 119, 140–143, 151, 212, 222, 241, 253, 273, 292, 306, 309, 310, 318
Axis of resistance, 290–292, 298

B
Baathists, 221
Baghdad, 16, 38–44, 46, 47, 77n4, 83, 83n13, 86–88, 87n29, 142, 145, 147, 149, 150, 152, 185, 209, 243, 246, 249, 250, 252, 254, 256, 271, 273, 283, 284, 296, 306, 308, 309

---

[1] Note: Page numbers followed by 'n' refer to notes.

© The Author(s), under exclusive license to Springer Nature Switzerland AG 2023
G. Gürbey et al. (eds.), *Between Diplomacy and Non-Diplomacy*,
https://doi.org/10.1007/978-3-031-09756-0

Bakir, Falah Mustafa, 15, 16, 138, 140, 143, 149, 150, 208, 209, 243, 244, 246, 247, 249–250, 253, 306
Balfour Declaration, 163
Baneh, 268, 269
Bar, Hilik, 230
Barzani, Masoud, 40–46, 42n5, 80, 81, 85n24, 88, 148, 150, 211, 246–248, 251, 252, 254, 256, 270, 272, 307, 309
Barzani, Nechirvan, 78n6, 82n11, 149, 150, 209, 249, 253, 255
Barzanji, Shaikh Mahmud, 39, 40
Begin, Menachem, 118
Belt and Road Initiative (BRI), 207, 210, 211, 229
Boycott, Divestment and Sanctions (BDS) movement, 219, 227, 233, 316
Branding, 100, 109, 315
Budget, 56, 87, 87n30, 106, 123, 125, 196, 209, 254
Bush, George W., 124, 125, 289

C
Camp David, 59, 64, 123, 281–283, 285
Carter, Jimmy, 118
Celebrity diplomacy, 100, 102
Central Council, 55, 56
Central Intelligence Agency (CIA), 114–117
China, 6, 17, 18, 20, 21, 56, 57, 60, 79, 82, 180, 201–214, 219–233, 311, 314
City diplomacy, 100, 105
Clinton, Bill, 64, 122, 123
Common Security and Defense Policy (CSDP), 135, 136, 150
Conflict resolution, 93, 122, 295

Covid-19, 18n3, 106–107
Cross-border trade, 268
CSDP, *see* Common Security and Defense Policy
Cultural diplomacy, 104, 315, 316

D
Declaration of Independence, 61, 97, 103
Democracy, 81n10, 89, 100, 101, 108, 270
Democratic Front for the Liberation of Palestine (DFLP), 57, 68, 222, 283
Democratic Party of Iranian Kurdistan (KDP-I), 29, 38, 39, 41, 44, 78–80, 78n6, 81n10, 86, 88, 89, 152, 208, 209, 245, 264, 265, 306, 307
Democratic Union Party (PYD), 241, 253, 254
Deng Xiaoping, 207
Department of Foreign Relations (DFR), 29, 38, 39, 41, 44, 78–80, 78n6, 81n10, 86, 88, 89, 152, 208, 209, 264, 306, 307
Development, 2–4, 10–12, 14, 15, 18, 20, 22, 35, 38, 40, 77, 80, 82, 87n28, 89, 93, 95, 101, 103, 104, 106–108, 120, 138, 143, 152, 161, 167, 182, 185, 187, 192, 193, 195–197, 213, 214, 222, 230, 246, 249, 254, 255, 271–274, 281, 282, 292, 306–309, 311, 312, 315, 317, 319
DFR, *see* Democratic Party of Iranian Kurdistan (KDP-I)
Digital diplomacy, 109, 316
Diplomacy, 2–5, 15, 17, 19, 20, 33–35, 38, 45, 56–58, 62, 64,

INDEX 325

69, 77, 80n9, 82, 88, 93–95, 99,
100, 102, 104–106, 108, 109,
113, 115–118, 124, 136, 137,
139, 143, 157–165, 168–173,
180, 181, 185, 191–194, 197,
207, 213, 219, 220, 226, 229,
232, 233, 240, 263, 284, 294,
308, 315, 316
Diplomatic immunity, 170, 272
Diplomatic relations, 15, 19, 20, 22,
36, 82, 93, 94n1, 105, 139, 160,
165, 168, 172, 173, 181, 184,
191, 194, 197, 208, 223, 245,
294, 299, 308
Diyarbakır Chamber of Commerce
and Industry (DCCI), 248, 249
Dizayi, Safeen, 209, 210
Dohuk, 45, 309

E

Economic, 4, 7, 10, 11, 15, 18–21,
33, 36, 41, 42, 45, 77, 79–82,
88, 96, 101, 103–105, 107, 122,
124, 138, 141, 143–145,
147–152, 166–168, 171, 173,
180, 184, 192, 193, 195–197,
201, 202, 214, 224, 231, 233,
239–242, 246–250, 257, 264,
268–270, 273, 287, 293,
306–310, 312, 313, 315,
316, 318
Egypt, 15, 20, 54n1, 58, 61, 64, 68,
70, 79, 80, 103, 116, 118, 183,
185, 186, 223, 252, 256, 281,
282, 286, 290, 291, 307
Elections 2006, 194, 289
Erbil, 16, 40, 41, 43–47, 77n4, 86,
88, 143–145, 147, 149–151,
207, 211, 240, 246, 248–252,
254–257, 265, 266, 268, 269,
271–274, 308, 309

Euro-Arab Dialogue, 165, 166
Euro-Mediterranean Partnership
(EMP), 168, 315
European Commission issued
"guidelines," 170
European Community (EC), 19, 70,
165, 166, 312
Executive Committee, 55, 56, 184

F

Fatah, 57, 69, 115, 122, 125–128,
181, 219–222, 225–233, 283,
288, 289
Fateh, 114
Fateh (ḥarakat taḥrīr filasṭīn), *see* Fatah
Federal constitution, 34, 38
Federal government, 36, 38, 42, 44,
79, 83–87, 84n15, 85n23,
86n26, 87n28, 87n29, 87n30,
136, 145, 147n7, 148
Federalism, 3, 30, 32, 34, 45,
108, 179
First Intifada, 62, 225, 284, 288
Foreign policy, 2–5, 11, 12, 20, 21,
29–31, 32n3, 33, 34, 38, 39, 44,
83, 85, 101, 102, 105, 106, 109,
135, 136, 145, 148, 152, 167,
170, 192, 194, 206, 208, 213,
229, 239, 241, 242, 246, 250,
255, 257, 258, 298, 315
Four Point Plan, 229

G

Gaza, 15, 22, 53, 56, 58–63, 65–67,
69, 107, 117–120, 122,
124–127, 129, 158, 162, 164,
167, 224–227, 229, 232,
284, 286, 289–299,
311–313, 321
Gaza Strip, *see* Gaza

General Secretary of the Communist Party, 183, 185
General Union of Palestinian Writers and Journalists (GUPWJ), 187, 189, 190n1, 191
Geopolitical, 15, 19, 21, 22, 36, 46, 96, 145, 157, 158, 160, 162, 163, 165, 167, 168, 172, 173, 211, 246, 250, 256–258, 271, 309, 310, 318
Ghaani, Esmail, 295
Gulf states, 256

H
Haj Omran, 269
Halper, Jeff, 224
Hamas, 22, 61, 65, 68, 69, 120, 124–129, 148, 158, 162, 173, 193, 194, 219, 220, 225–228, 230, 232, 233, 252, 287–299, 316
Hamas (ḥarakat al-muqāwama al-islamiyya), see Hamas
Haniyeh, Ismail, 292, 295, 297
Happy City, 211
Hashd al-Shaabi, 271
Hezbollah, 287–290

I
ICC, see International Criminal Court
Ideology, 11, 14, 22, 68, 102, 205–207, 281, 283, 284, 286, 298, 316
Imperialism, 163, 188, 280, 282
Independence, 3, 7, 9, 15, 16, 18, 21, 30, 31, 36, 37, 39, 42–44, 46, 47, 63, 65, 67, 77, 80, 83, 88, 97, 103, 129, 148, 158–160, 162–164, 166, 180, 212, 231, 241, 253–257, 270, 273, 297, 307, 308, 310–312

India, 6, 34, 79, 82
Institutionalization/institutionalisation, 11, 15, 16, 42, 75–89, 93–109, 139, 149, 159, 160, 166, 169, 172, 307, 310, 319, 321
International Criminal Court (ICC), 67, 99, 126, 127, 171, 172, 229, 314
Internationalisation/internationalization, 11, 98, 100, 102, 105, 126, 127, 139, 160, 169–172, 227, 229
Internationalisation strategy, see Internationalisation/internationalization
International legitimacy, 97, 169
International Relations (IR), 1–5, 16, 17, 29, 30, 33, 36, 38, 64, 75, 76, 78–80, 78n6, 83, 93–97, 99, 101–104, 106, 108, 109, 136, 139, 161, 179, 180, 210, 220, 258, 263, 309, 317, 321
Intifada, 60–62, 119–121, 123, 124, 287, 289, 297
Iran, 17, 18, 21, 22, 32, 40, 43, 44, 47, 68, 79, 79n7, 80, 88, 138, 141, 203, 205, 233, 244, 245, 247, 250, 256, 263–274, 279–299, 308, 310
Iraq, 16, 21, 31–35, 32n3, 37, 39–41, 43–47, 63, 68, 69, 75–89, 121, 137–141, 143–145, 147n7, 149–151, 150n8, 203, 205, 208–210, 212, 213, 221, 240, 242–250, 254–257, 263–268, 270–274, 284, 306, 307, 309
Iraqi constitution, 16, 77, 78, 83, 85–87, 87n29, 89, 136, 147n7, 152, 209, 246, 306, 307
IRGC, see Islamic Revolutionary Guard Corps

IS, *see* Islamic State
ISIS, *see* Islamic State of Iraq and Syria
Islamic Revolutionary Guard Corps
  (IRGC), 271
Islamic State (IS), 16, 19, 42, 43, 46,
  145–148, 267, 273, 274, 307,
  308, 310, 316, 318
Islamic State of Iraq and Levant,
  241, 266
Islamic State of Iraq and Syria (ISIS),
  80, 82n12, 86n26, 87, 87n30,
  146–149, 151, 209, 254–257
Israel, 16, 18, 20–22, 43, 53, 55–70,
  58n2, 103, 107, 113–115,
  117–129, 162, 163, 165, 166,
  170, 171, 180–184, 186–189,
  192, 194, 219–233, 256,
  265–268, 280–289, 291,
  294–299, 311, 313, 316
Israeli settlements, 64, 66, 67, 118,
  123–125, 127, 169, 170, 295

J
Jerusalem, 14, 54, 54n1, 64, 66, 97,
  100, 128, 129, 193, 224,
  286, 295
Jewish immigration, 182
Jordan, 17, 18n3, 61, 61n3, 64, 69,
  79, 80, 97, 103, 106, 114, 115,
  119, 164, 183, 184, 221,
  222, 307
Jundiany, Azad, 206
Jurisdiction, 67, 85, 225, 229, 314

K
KDP, *see* Kurdistan Democratic Party
KDP-I, *see* Democratic Party of Iranian Kurdistan
Kermanshah, 269
Kerry, John, 127, 229

Khamenei, Ayatollah Ali, 285, 289,
  292, 296, 297
Khomeini, Ayatollah, 267, 281–283,
  286, 288
Kirkuk, 42, 43, 86n25, 147, 149, 245,
  247, 248
Kissinger, Henry, 58, 116–118,
  120, 209
Krekar, Mullah, 266, 267
KRG, *see* Kurdistan/Kurdish Regional Government
Kurdish National Council (ENKS),
  253, 254
Kurdistan, 16, 21, 22, 30, 40, 45, 46,
  75–89, 141, 144, 147, 149, 203,
  204, 204n1, 206–214, 240, 246,
  251, 253–257, 269–272
Kurdistan Democratic Party (KDP),
  15, 31, 34, 40–45, 77n3, 88n32,
  136, 139, 142, 143, 147, 148,
  150–152, 205, 206, 209, 240,
  243–247, 309, 310
Kurdistan Free Life Party (PJAK),
  265, 267
Kurdistan/Kurdish Regional
  Government (KRG), 9, 14, 32,
  40, 43, 45, 75, 77, 78, 136,
  201–207, 209, 239, 264,
  306, 317
Kurdistan Region of Iraq (IKR/KRI),
  9, 15, 19, 20, 32n3, 37–39, 41,
  42, 77n3, 77n4, 78–89, 78n6,
  80n9, 82n11, 82n12, 83n13,
  87n30, 88n31, 135–146, 142n4,
  147n7, 148–152, 207, 209,
  211–214, 240, 241,
  243–249, 251, 254–256,
  269, 307–309
Kurdistan Socialist Party, 206
Kurdistan Workers' Party (PKK), 142,
  240, 241, 243–245, 247, 248,
  251, 252, 255, 256

L

Lebanon, 69, 80, 116, 118–121, 164, 222, 280, 281, 283, 287, 288, 307
Legal framework, 15, 75–89, 93–109, 306
Liminal, liminality, 19, 157–159, 161, 162, 172
Lotus Prize, 189, 190

M

Mao Zedong, 204–206
Matrix of control, 224
Mesha'al, Khaled, 291
Meshal, Khaled, 228
Migration, 80n8, 150
Ministry of Foreign Affairs (MOFA), 17, 38, 64, 103–105, 107–109, 187, 212, 228, 230, 268, 269, 314
MOFA, see Ministry of Foreign Affairs
Motives, 11–16, 18, 42n5, 75–89, 93–109, 309, 313, 315, 318, 321
Al-Muhandes, Abu Mahdi, 271
Muslim Brotherhoods, 286, 290
Muslims, 280, 281, 286, 288, 296, 297

N

Nakba (Catastrophe), see An-Nakba (the Catastrophe)
Al-Nakhala, Ziad, 287, 295, 297
Nali, 203, 204n1
Narrative, 32, 44, 109, 165, 204, 207, 212, 313
Nasser, Gamal, 54, 54n1, 182, 183, 221
Nation, 7, 11, 12, 40, 94, 95, 99, 100, 105, 106, 108, 122, 157, 158, 162, 171, 206, 242, 281, 296, 307

Nation-building, 7, 11, 14, 21, 55, 87, 101, 102, 180, 242, 246–249
NATO, see North Atlantic Treaty Organization
Natural resources, 84, 145
Netanyahu, Benjamin, 122, 125, 127, 226, 295
Nixon, Richard, 116
No-fly zone, 33, 39, 140, 140n1, 140n3, 142, 306
Non-preferential treatment of settlement products, 170
Non-state actor, 1–4, 6, 8, 9, 15, 16, 82–83, 88, 99, 103, 105, 106, 108, 109, 151, 158, 208, 211, 212, 311, 317, 318
North Atlantic Treaty Organization (NATO), 135, 136, 192, 240

O

Obama Administration, 126, 128, 169, 250
Obama, Barack, 125
Obstacle, 15, 76, 82, 207, 269, 309, 310, 316, 317
Occupied Territories, 16, 59, 61, 67, 94, 118, 120, 184, 225–227, 229, 232, 288, 289, 295
OIC, see Organisation of Islamic Conference
Olmert, Ehud, 66
Operation Provide Comfort, 137, 140
Organisation of Islamic Conference (OIC), 285
Oslo Accord, 19, 22, 62, 69, 109, 113, 164, 166, 223–225, 232, 233, 284–285, 288, 289, 312
Oslo Agreement, 62–65, 68, 69
Ottoman Empire, 163, 240, 252

P

PA, *see* Palestinian Authority
Palestine, v, vi, 2–4, 8–10, 12–17, 19, 20, 22, 53–71, 79, 93–109, 113–130, 157–173, 179–197, 219–233, 279–299, 305, 306, 311–316, 318, 321
Palestine State, 53
Palestinian, 9, 53, 94, 113, 158, 180, 219, 280, 311
Palestinian Authority (PA), 9, 18n3, 20, 22, 63–65, 67–69, 122–130, 162, 164–172, 191, 193–196, 219, 220, 223–230, 232, 233, 289, 293–296, 299, 306, 311–318
Palestinian Culture Days, 196
Palestinian International Cooperation Agency (PICA), 104, 105, 108, 314
Palestinian Islamic Jihad (PIJ), 22, 286–289, 292–299
Palestinian-Israeli conflict, 57, 58, 61, 62, 167, 194, 223, 224, 233, 299
Palestinian National Authority (PNA), 16, 103, 104, 107–109
Palestine/Palestinian Liberation Organisation/Organization (PLO), 15, 53–63, 94, 113, 158, 180, 219, 279, 311
Palestine/Palestinian National Council (PNC), 55–59, 61, 97, 103, 120, 123, 164, 311
Paradiplomacy, vi, 2–20, 22, 29–47, 53–71, 75–89, 93–109, 135, 136, 139, 140, 147–152, 159–161, 165–168, 172, 179–184, 187–193, 197, 207, 208, 210, 213, 219, 220, 231, 263–266, 273, 305–311, 313–319, 321
Partition plan, 53, 54, 57, 58, 182

Patriotic Union of Kurdistan (PUK), 15, 31, 34, 40–44, 46, 77n3, 136, 139, 142, 143, 147–152, 202, 206, 207, 209, 240, 243–247, 271, 309, 310
Peace-building, 93
Peace conference, 62, 66, 116, 118, 121, 185
Peace process, 18, 65, 103, 108, 113, 114, 116, 118, 120, 121, 125–129, 167, 185, 191, 193, 197, 225, 226, 230, 233, 241
People's Defense Units (YPG), 241, 253–255
Permit system, 171
Peshmerga, 40, 41, 45, 82n12, 84, 86, 87, 87n30, 88n31, 147, 149, 246, 247, 256, 266
PFLP, *see* Popular Front for the Liberation of Palestine
Phantasm, 201–204
PICA, *see* Palestinian International Cooperation Agency
PIJ, *see* Palestinian Islamic Jihad
Piranshahr, 269
PJAK, *see* Kurdistan Free Life Party
PKK, *see* Kurdistan Workers' Party
PLO, *see* Palestine/Palestinian Liberation Organisation/Organization
PNA, *see* Palestinian National Authority
PNC, *see* Palestine/Palestinian National Council
Popular Front for the Liberation of Palestine (PFLP), 59, 68, 114, 222, 283
Practice, 2, 4–6, 12, 13, 16, 17, 30, 34, 47, 75, 76, 78, 83, 85, 87n29, 89, 93, 94, 97, 100, 101, 108, 157–161, 165, 169, 171–173, 179, 180, 189, 225, 228, 233, 267, 305, 321

330 INDEX

Protodiplomacy, 30–32, 36, 42–47, 158, 159, 161, 220, 231
Public diplomacy, 57, 88, 93, 102, 104–106, 192, 193, 308, 316
PUK, see Patriotic Union of Kurdistan

Q
Quartet on the Middle East, the, 167
Quds Force, 43, 274, 295

R
Reagan, Ronald, 119, 121
Recognition, 7–10, 16, 21, 22, 36, 37, 59, 60, 69, 70, 84n19, 85n24, 86, 96, 97, 99, 102, 117, 126, 159, 160, 162, 168–173, 180, 182, 189, 208, 209, 221, 240, 242, 257, 263, 285, 288, 306, 312–314, 317
Referendum, 9, 16, 21, 39, 42–44, 42n5, 46, 47, 80, 86, 86n25, 88, 147n7, 148, 149, 241, 242, 255–257, 270, 296, 307, 308, 311
Refugee Issue, 182, 185
Revolutionary diplomacy, 181, 185
Roadmap, 12, 167
Ruchi, Ni, 208, 209
Russian Foreign Ministry, 194
Russian-Israeli relations, 192, 197

S
Sabir, Mohammad, 203, 205, 206, 208, 209, 211
Saddam Hussein, 33, 40, 41, 62, 63, 76, 78, 121, 139–141, 140n1, 140n2, 144n5, 151, 207, 210, 243, 264, 265, 270, 271, 283, 285, 286, 306
Saudi Arabia, 68, 79, 80, 233, 293, 294, 307

Scotland, 35, 36
SDGs, see Sustainable Development Goals
Secession, 31, 37, 45–47, 162
Second Gulf War, 137, 140
Second Intifada, 65, 226, 228, 289
Security, 2, 16, 18, 45, 60, 63–65, 68, 76, 79, 81–83, 82n11, 84n18, 86, 86n26, 115–117, 122, 123, 127–129, 138, 152, 166–168, 192, 210, 229, 239, 241, 245, 247, 254, 255, 257, 264, 265, 271–273, 289, 295, 307–310, 313, 315, 318
Semi-formal players, 188
Settler-colonialism, 163
Shah, 40, 281
Shallah, Ramadan, 287, 289, 292
Shariati, Ali, 280, 281
Sharon, Ariel, 119, 124, 288, 289
Al-Shiqaqi, Fathi, 286, 287
Shukairy, Ahmed, 221
Shuqairi, Ahmed, 54, 54n1, 56, 57, 181, 182
Silk Road, 203
Soft power, 100, 103, 104, 109, 204, 250
Soleimani, Qassem, 43, 271, 274, 295, 296
Sovereignty, 3, 4, 7, 9, 10, 16, 34, 46, 60, 69, 85, 86, 97, 100, 109, 159, 161–163, 168, 172, 173, 208, 212, 273, 284, 298, 313
Soviet Afro-Asian Solidarity Committee, 183, 184
Soviet Union (USSR), 20, 22, 40, 56, 57, 60–62, 115–117, 121, 164, 180, 182–192, 197, 231, 232, 285, 311
State 194, 169
State building, 15, 40, 44–47, 99, 101, 102, 122, 167, 170, 306, 308, 309, 311, 312

INDEX 331

State recognition, 16, 97, 161, 317
Sub-state actor, 161, 179, 220
Sulaimani Palace, 272
Sulaimaniyah, 41, 44–47, 143, 145, 150, 246, 249
Suleimania, 248
Sumud, 163
Sunni, 252, 266, 267, 291
Sustainability, 95
Sustainable Development Goals (SDGs), 104
Syria, 32, 37, 58, 68, 69, 82n12, 116, 138, 146n6, 183, 192, 221, 223, 241, 253, 255–257, 267, 280, 287, 290, 292

T
Taiwan, 99, 212, 229
Talabani, Jalal, 40–42, 85n24, 139, 205, 206, 208, 244, 249, 272, 309
Theory, 5, 31n1, 93–95, 97, 122, 179, 202, 205, 219
Toilers Group of Kurdistan, 206
Trump, Donald, 99, 126, 128, 195, 294–297
Tudeh Party of Iran, 205
Tunis, 61, 120, 222
Turkey, 17, 18, 21, 32, 43, 44, 47, 79–82, 88, 88n32, 99, 138, 140–143, 140n3, 145, 147, 203, 239–258, 268, 270–274, 290, 292, 297, 307, 308, 310
Two-state solution, 57, 58, 66, 117, 125, 127–130, 168, 169, 223, 230, 231, 295

U
UN, *see* United Nations
UNGA, *see* United Nations General Assembly

United Kingdom (UK), 32, 36, 43, 65, 77, 79, 79n7, 80, 82, 99, 135, 137, 139–141, 140n3, 143, 170, 182, 183, 314
United Nations General Assembly (UNGA), 53, 59, 66, 67, 70, 98, 117, 311
United Nations Security Council (UNSC), 56, 98, 165, 182, 208, 210, 212, 214, 257, 288, 313
United Nations (UN), 17, 32, 37, 38, 43, 54–59, 61, 66, 67, 70, 76, 85n24, 93, 94, 97, 98, 104, 107, 125, 126, 128, 140n1, 160, 164, 165, 168, 169, 171, 172, 185, 208, 221, 227–229, 243, 284, 293, 308, 311, 313, 314, 317
United States (US), 17, 18, 18n3, 20, 21, 32, 34, 37, 41, 43, 46, 54, 56, 59, 61, 62, 64–67, 70, 77, 79–83, 79n7, 88n32, 99, 113–130, 140n1, 140n3, 141, 143, 145, 168, 169, 171, 172, 183, 192–195, 209, 211, 214, 223, 226, 228, 240–248, 250, 253–258, 264–267, 270–272, 281, 307, 308, 310–315
UNSC, *see* United Nations Security Council
UN Security Council Resolution 242, 56, 59, 60, 165, 166
US, *see* United States
USSR, *see* Soviet Union
Uyghurs, 226, 229

V
Vienna Convention, 82, 93, 94, 98n2, 160, 161, 208, 272
Visegrad group, 150

W

Wang Shijie, 228
Warsaw Pact, 164, 187
West Bank, 9, 15, 22, 53, 56, 58–67, 61n3, 69, 97, 107, 117–120, 124–126, 128, 158, 162, 164, 167, 169, 224–227, 284, 289, 293, 294, 299, 311–313, 321
Westphalia, 93
World Economic Forum, 149
Writers Union of the USSR, 189
Wu Sike, 228

X

Xi Jinping, 213, 229
Xinjiang, 226, 229

Z

Al-Zahar, Mahmoud, 227
Zarif, Javad, 295
Zebari, Hoshyar, 272
Zionism, 163, 165, 188, 189, 280

Printed in the United States
by Baker & Taylor Publisher Services